Henry Dunning Macleod

Elements of economics

Henry Dunning Macleod

Elements of economics

ISBN/EAN: 9783337278342

Printed in Europe, USA, Canada, Australia, Japan

Cover: Foto ©Suzi / pixelio.de

More available books at **www.hansebooks.com**

THE ELEMENTS

OF

ECONOMICS

BY

HENRY DUNNING MACLEOD, M.A.

OF TRINITY COLLEGE, CAMBRIDGE, AND THE INNER TEMPLE, BARRISTER-AT-LAW
SELECTED BY THE ROYAL COMMISSIONERS FOR THE DIGEST OF
THE LAW TO PREPARE THE DIGEST OF THE LAW OF
BILLS OF EXCHANGE, BANK NOTES, ETC.
HONORARY MEMBER OF THE JURIDICAL SOCIETY OF PALERMO

IN TWO VOLUMES

Vol. II — Part I

COMPLETING PURE ECONOMICS

NEW YORK
D. APPLETON AND COMPANY
1886

CONTENTS

OF

VOLUME II—PART I

BOOK II

PURE ECONOMICS—Continued

CHAPTER VII

ON THE RELATION BETWEEN VALUE AND QUANTITY OF LABOUR AND COST OF PRODUCTION

SECTION		PAGE
1.	Ricardo on Quantity of Labour and Cost of Production	3
2.	Examples to show the fallacy of the doctrine that Quantity of Labour or Cost of Production regulates Value	4
3.	The Expression Quantity of Labour is unintelligible	7
4.	Absurdity of the doctrine that all Values are Proportional to Quantities of Labour	7
5.	The same continued	9
6.	Error of the Doctrine that Cost of Production Regulates Value	10
7.	Cases in which Cost of Production appears to Regulate Value	13
8.	Malthus refutes Ricardo	15
9.	Scientific Principles of the Case	17
10.	Ricardo's doctrine violates the Law of Continuity	19
11.	Mill contradicts himself	19
12.	Cases to show the error of Ricardo's doctrine	21
13.	The Relation between Supply and Demand is the sole Regulator of Value	21
14.	Value is the Inducement to Production	24

SECTION		PAGE
15.	The Law acts on different Quantities in different Degrees	25
16.	Rules connecting Cost of Production and Value	26
17.	Fundamental error of Smith and Ricardo	26

CHAPTER VIII

ON PROFITS

1.	Definition of Profit	29
2.	Definition of Rate of Profit	30
3.	Error of Economists in their Definition of Rate of Profit	30
4.	Erroneous Doctrines deduced from the erroneous Definition of Rate of Profit	33
5.	Correction of these Erroneous Doctrines	34
6.	The same continued	35
7.	The same continued	36
8.	The same continued	36
9.	Examples of Trading Profits	37
10.	Traders must live by their Trades	39
11.	The same continued	40
12.	The same continued	41
13.	Disintegration of Trades	41
14.	An expression of Senior's inadequate	42
15.	Error of Smith on Agricultural Profits	42
16.	Error of the Doctrine that Rate of Profit is all	45
17.	Increase of Capital reduces Prices and Profits	45
18.	Mill attacks Smith	47
19.	Origin of schemes for Banks and Paper Money	51
20.	Smith right : his assailants wrong	52

SECTION II

UPON INTEREST AND DISCOUNT

21.	Of the Commerce in Debts	55
22.	Meaning of the Term Value of Money in the Commerce of Debts	55
23.	On the Prejudice against Interest	56
24.	Calvin first showed the error of the prejudice against Interest	60

Contents of Volume II—Part I

SECTION		PAGE
25.	The same continued	62
26.	Examples of Rate of Interest	62
27.	Circumstances which determine the Rate of Interest	64
28.	Differences in Rate of Interest dependent on different degrees of Security	65
29.	The same continued	65
30.	On the Effects of an Increase of Money on Prices and Interest	68
31.	Extracts from Hume	70
32.	Circumstances according to which increase of Money affects Prices and Interest	72
33.	The same continued	73
34.	Quotation from Hume	74
35.	Rates of Interest at different times	77

SECTION III

ON BANKING DISCOUNT

36.	Profits made by way of Interest and Discount	79
37.	To find the Amount of a given sum in any time at Simple Banking Discount	80
38.	Table showing the Difference of Profits at Interest and Discount	81
39.	To find in what Time a Sum of Money will Double itself at Simple Banking Discount	81
40.	Differences of Profits exemplified by figures	82
41.	To find the Amount of a given Sum in any time at Compound Banking Discount	84
42.	To find in what Time a Sum of Money will Double itself at Compound Discount	84
43.	Formulæ for calculating the Amount of any Sum for any time at Simple and Compound Interest and Discount	85
44.	To find the Difference in Profit at the end of the year between Discounting one Bill for £1,000 at 12 months: and discounting four Bills of £1,000 at 3 months in succession, at 5 per cent. Compound Discount	86

CHAPTER IX
ON RENT

SECTION		PAGE
1.	Definition of Rent	88
2.	On the Rent of Land	89
3.	On Ricardo's Theory of Rent	91
4.	Ricardo on Smith	92
5.	Difference between Anderson's and Ricardo's Theory of Rent	94
6.	Mill calls Ricardo's Theory of Rent the *pons asinorum* of Economics	96
7.	Carey's Theory of Rent	97
8.	Say, Chalmers, Thompson, Byles and ourselves condemn Ricardo's Theory of Rent	100
9.	Absurdity of Ricardo's Theory of Rent	101
10.	The Theory of Rent	102
11.	The same continued	104
12.	The same continued	105
13.	Payment of Rent does not influence the Price of Corn	105
14.	Error of Ricardo on Tithes	106
15.	Self-Contradiction of Ricardo on Rent	107
16.	Self-Contradiction of Mill on Rent	108
17.	The same continued	
18.	Difference between Anderson and Ricardo's Theory of Rent	110
19.	On the Rent of Shops	111
20.	Conclusion of the Ricardo Theory of Rent	113
21.	Smith on Rents in Shetland	114
22.	De Fontenay on Rent	115
23.	The same continued	116
24.	The same continued	117
25.	The same continued	118
26.	The same continued	121
27.	Rent an example of the General Equation of Economics	122
28.	Fallacy of Ricardo's Law of Value	123
29.	The same continued	124
30.	The Law of Value applied to Rents	125
31.	Malthus on Rent	126

CHAPTER X

ON LABOUR, OR IMMATERIAL WEALTH

SECTION		PAGE
1.	Personal Qualities are Wealth	130
2.	Definition of Labour	132
3.	Labour is a Commodity	133
4.	Labour may be Capital	134
5.	On Wages	135
6.	On the Wages Fund	136
7.	Error of the Common Doctrine	137
8.	Longe on the Wages Fund	139
9.	On Productive and Unproductive Labour	142
10.	Say condemns Smith's doctrine of Productive and Unproductive Labour	145
11.	Mill on Productive and Unproductive Labour	148
12.	The same continued	150
13.	The same continued	151
14.	On the Division of Labour	152
15.	Error of Smith	156
16.	Previous notices of	161
17.	Smith's Doctrines erroneous	173
18.	On the Rate of Wages and the Cost of Labour	177
19.	Error of Mill's four Fundamental Propositions respecting Capital	180
20.	The same continued	182
21.	Mill's Doctrine of Two Funds	188
22.	The same continued	189
23.	The same continued	190
24.	On Rate of Wages	190
25.	Ricardo on Natural Price of Labour	193
26.	Error of Ricardo	194
27.	Wages governed by Supply and Demand	195
28.	On Rate of Wages	196
29.	The same continued	197
30.	Say on	197
31.	Smith on Wages	198
32.	Error of Smith	199
33.	Smith's Rules reducible to Supply and Demand	200
34.	Smith's error regarding a lottery	200
35.	The same continued	201
36.	The same continued	201
37.	On the Workman's Share of the Price	202

SECTION		PAGE
38.	Two distinct kinds of Labour	204
39.	Brassey on	205
40.	On the *Droit-au-Travail*	206
41.	The same continued	207
42.	Working Men do not create Wealth	213

CHAPTER XI

ON RIGHTS OR INCORPOREAL WEALTH

1.	Rights are Wealth	216
2.	Varieties of Incorporeal Property	217
3.	Incorporeal Property of Two kinds	217
4.	On Rights of Obligation	218
5.	An Annuity is a Commodity	220
6.	Different kinds of Annuities	220
7.	On the Funds	223
8.	On Tithes	224
9.	History of Tithes	225
10.	Tithes in England	227
11.	The same continued	228
12.	Personal Tithes due by Law	229
13.	Commutation of Tithes	229
14.	Benefices and Advowsons	230
15.	Policies of Insurance	231
16.	On Rights of Expectation	231
17.	Shares in Commercial Companies	232
18.	Copyrights	233
19.	The same continued	234
20.	The same continued	236
21.	The same continued	237
22.	The same continued	238
23.	Patents	239
24.	The same continued	240
25.	The same continued	242
26.	Trade Secrets	242
27.	The Goodwill of a Business	242
28.	The Practice of a Professional Man	243
29.	Tolls and Ferries	244
30.	Shooting and Fishings	244
31.	Street Crossings	244
32.	General Conclusion	244

CHAPTER XII

ON THE FOREIGN EXCHANGES

SECTION		PAGE
1.	Nature of an 'Exchange'	246
2.	On the Nominal Exchange	247
3.	Effect of a Depreciated Coinage	247
4.	There can be no Par of Exchange between countries which use Different Metals as a standard	249
5.	If the Coinage is Depreciated to Determine whether the Exchange is Favourable—at Par or Adverse	249
6.	On Inconvertible Paper Money	251
7.	Lord King's Law of Paper Money	252
8.	On the Real or Commercial Exchange	255
9.	On Exchange with Four Parties	255
10.	The Time Par of Exchange	256
11.	On Foreign Exchange	257
12.	Effects of the Exchanges on London	258
13.	Exchange between London and Places from which it Receives the Variable Price	259
14.	Exchanges between London and Places to which it Gives the Variable Price	259
15.	On the Limits of the Variations of the Exchanges	260
16.	Effects of the Restoration of the Coinage on the Exchanges	261
17.	On Exchange Operations	262
18.	On the Real or Commercial Exchange	266
19.	The same continued	268
20.	The Balance of Trade	269
21.	The same continued	270
22.	On Foreign Trade	273
23.	The same continued	275
24.	The same continued	275
25.	The same continued	275
26.	Causes of the movements of Bullion	277
27.	The same continued	277
28.	The same continued	278
29.	The same continued	278
30.	The same continued	279
31.	The Balance of Trade	280
32.	On the Rate of Discount as Influencing the Exchanges	282
33.	On Foreign Loans, Securities and Remittances as affecting the Exchanges	284
34.	The French Indemnity	286

SECTION		PAGE
35.	The India Council Bills	292
36.	On Monetary and Political Convulsions as affecting the Exchanges	296
37.	On the Means of Correcting an Adverse Exchange	296

CHAPTER XIII

ON LAW'S THEORY OF PAPER MONEY

1.	On Lawism	299
2.	Definition of	299
3.	Other advocates of it	301
4.	Statement of Law's doctrine	303
5.	The same continued	304
6.	The same continued	304
7.	Difference between Chamberlain and Law	304
8.	Law's Theory	305
9.	The same continued	305
10.	The same continued	306
11.	The Essence of Lawism	307
12.	The same continued	308
13.	Law's Bank in France	308
14.	The Ayr Bank	309
15.	The French Assignats	309
16.	The same continued	311
17.	The Bank of Norway	313
18.	On Issuing Paper Money on Securities	315
19.	The only true foundation of Paper Currency	317

CHAPTER XIV

ON THE DEFINITION OF CURRENCY

1.	Legal meaning of the term Currency	318
2.	Decisions respecting	321
3.	Currency means Negotiability	324
4.	Difficulty respecting Currency as used as a technical term in Economics	325
5.	Lord Overstone's doctrine of Currency	328
6.	The same continued	330
7.	Examination of this doctrine	332

SECTION		PAGE
8.	The same continued	333
9.	The same continued	334
10.	The same continued	334
11.	The same continued	335

CHAPTER XV

ON THE ORGANISATION OF THE BANK OF ENGLAND

1.	Great complication of the Bank Act	338
2.	Principles intended to be enforced by the Bank Act	338
3.	Foundation and Constitution of the Bank of England	339
4.	Progress of the Bank	340
5.	Stoppage of the Bank in 1797	341
6.	Bank Notes at a discount in 1697	341
	Irish Bank Notes in 1804	342
7.	Bank Notes at a discount in 1809	342
	The Bullion Committee in 1811	343
	The Report rejected by Parliament	343
8.	Increased discount of Bank Notes	344
9.	The Act of 1819	345
10.	The Monetary Crisis of 1825	347
11.	Doctrines of the Bank in 1832	348
12.	Bank Charter Act of 1833	349
13.	Failure of the Bank's Rule of 1832	349
14.	Bank Act of 1844	351
15.	Organisation of the Bank under the Act of 1844	353
16.	Examination of the Fact whether the Organisation of the Bank agrees with the Theory of the Bank Act	354
17.	The same continued	355
18.	Examination whether the Mechanical Action of the Act conforms to the Intentions of its Framers	356
19.	Cause of the Failure of the Mechanical Action of the Act	357
20.	The Monetary Panic of 1847	358
21.	The Monetary Panic of 1857	359
22.	The Monetary Panic of 1866	360
23.	Cause of the Failure of the Bank Act of 1844	360
24.	On the Causes which compelled the Suspension of the Bank Act in 1847, 1857, and 1866	363
	Two Opposite Theories	363
25.	The Monetary Crisis of 1763	364
26.	The Monetary Crisis of 1772	364

SECTION		PAGE
27.	The Monetary Crisis of 1783	364
28.	The Monetary Crisis of 1793	365
29.	The Monetary Crisis of 1797	366
30.	The Monetary Crisis of 1825	368
31.	The Monetary Crisis of 1837	368
32.	The Monetary Crisis of 1847	368
33.	The Monetary Crisis of 1857	369
34.	The Monetary Crisis of 1866	369
35.	An Excessive Restriction of Credit Causes and Produces a Run for Gold	370
36.	Under the present System of Commercial Credit there must be some Source with the power of issuing Undoubted Credit to support solvent Commercial Houses in times of Monetary Panic	371
37.	Differences of Principle between the supporters of the Act of 1819 and those of the Act of 1844	372
38.	Examination of the Arguments alleged for maintaining the Bank Act	374
39.	Conclusion	375

BOOK II
PURE ECONOMICS
continued

CHAPTER VII

ON THE RELATION BETWEEN VALUE AND QUANTITY OF LABOUR AND COST OF PRODUCTION

1. It has been shown in the first part of this work that the ruin of a very large part of English Economics is owing to the undue prominence which is given to Labour as the Cause of, and as necessary to, Value. Smith begins by putting Labour in the forefront of his work as necessary to Value, for reasons which we explained in the first part of this work; although he has completely contradicted that doctrine in a subsequent part of it.

In Book I., ch. v., Smith has thrown the whole subject of Value into the utmost confusion by suddenly changing his notion of the Value of a thing from being the Quantity of Labour, or Commodities, it will purchase or exchange for, to the Quantity of Labour embodied as it were in its production. Hence the unfortunate and misleading expression, **Intrinsic Value**, has become firmly established in Economics: which is not only most manifestly self-contradictory, but it has greatly obscured the comprehension of the whole subject, and especially the Theory of Credit.

Ricardo perceived Smith's inconsistency, and censured him for it: but he has fallen into exactly the same contradiction himself; because he begins his work by defining the Value of a thing to be the thing it will exchange for: and as he goes on in his book he changes the idea of the Value of a thing to be the Quantity of Labour embodied in it.

From this unfortunate idea not only has the term **Intrinsic Value** become firmly established, but also the equally unfortunate idea of an **Invariable Standard of Value**. Smith and Ricardo imagined that if any commodity could always be produced with the same Quantity of Labour, it would be an Invariable Standard of Value.

Ricardo says—'If the Quantity of Labour realised in commodities regulate their exchangeable Value, every increase in the Quantity of Labour must augment the value of that commodity on which it is exercised, as every diminution must lower it.'

Ricardo calls the Quantity of Labour required to produce a commodity its **Absolute** Value : and says that if any commodity could always be produced with the same Quantity of Labour it would be an Invariable Standard of Value.

He says—'The Labour of a million of men in manufactures will always produce the same Value.'

Therefore, according to Ricardo, whether a commodity sells for £10, for £50, or for £100, it is of exactly the same Value!

Ricardo, however, constantly uses another expression as identical with **Quantity of Labour**, namely, **Cost of Production**.

It is, however, quite erroneous to use **Quantity of Labour** and **Cost of Production** as identical expressions : because nothing is more common than for wages to rise or fall, while Quantity of Labour remains exactly the same. Now Wages are certainly part of the Cost of Production : hence Cost of Production constantly varies, while Quantity of Labour remains exactly the same.

2. Even supposing, however, that Quantity of Labour and Cost of Production remained the same, it is quite easy to show by numerous examples that it is quite erroneous to say that they regulate Value.

1. It is quite common in a coal mine to have different strata of coal of different qualities. Some strata at the top may be of excellent quality : others lower down may be of very indifferent quality, mixed with shale and other rubbish : now the coals obtained from the inferior strata may require a greater amount of Labour or Cost to obtain them than the superior coals. But will they bring the same price in the market? Common sense and experience show that they will not. But that the better qualities of coal will sell for a higher price than the worse

qualities: no matter what the Cost of Production or Quantity of Labour may be.

2. Take the case of an orchard. The trees are of course cultivated with the same amount of Labour or Cost. Consequently each individual fruit must be the result of exactly the same Quantity of Labour or Cost of Production. Yet everyone knows that out of the very same orchard, and off the very same tree, fruit of very different qualities will be gathered. Will these different qualities of fruit bring the same price in the same market? Common sense and experience show that they will not: but that the superior qualities of fruit will bring a higher price than the inferior qualities, quite irrespective of Cost of Production or Quantity of Labour.

As an example of this, it is usual in the coffee plantations in the East Indies to separate the berries into three sizes: the larger, the middling, and the smaller: it is found that the value of the whole crop is much increased by this separation of the berries: while the three sizes sell for very different prices. Now as each heap is produced by exactly the same Quantity of Labour or Cost of Production, it is evident that it is a manifest fallacy to assert that Value is regulated by Quantity of Labour or Cost of Production.

3. Take the case of an ox or a sheep. Every part of these animals is the result of the same Cost of Production: and therefore every part of the same animal ought to bring the same price in the same market. But is this the fact? Common sense and experience show that they do not: but that different parts of the same animal bring very different prices.

4. It is quite common for a street of houses to be built in a new neighbourhood: and when first built they let for a moderate price: but as population and fashion increase in the neighbourhood, the rents of the houses, long after they are built, and are perhaps in a much inferior condition, will be much higher than they were when the houses were new.

5. All fruits of the earth are greatly affected by the qualities of the soil they are grown in. There are few which are more sensitive to the qualities of the soil and the influence of the weather than the vine. The slightest difference in the qualities of the soil, exposure to the sun or wind, produces the

most marked differences in the qualities of the wine, and on its price. It is impossible to select an example to show more clearly the fallacy of the doctrine that Cost of Production or Quantity of Labour regulates Value than the culture of the vine.

Ricardo was so entêté of the doctrine that all Value is due to human Labour, that he maintained that the sun and air and fine weather and moisture have no effect on the Value of the crops. He says—'But these natural agents, though they add greatly to *Value in use*, never add Exchangeable Value, of which M. Say is speaking, to a commodity. . . . But as they perform their work gratuitously, as nothing is paid for the use of air, of heat, and of water, the assistance which they afford us adds nothing to Value in Exchange.'

The glaring absurdity of this doctrine, so contrary to the plainest common sense, is sufficient to condemn the whole of Ricardo's system. In reply to this we may simply quote a paragraph from a daily paper of June 3, 1880 :—'The longed-for rains have come at last, and though the showers as yet have been gentle and rather local, the half inch of moisture which has refreshed the fields during the last seventy hours has been *worth at least a million sterling*. Every gallon of water which the thirsty soil has drunk up might be appraised at a tangible money value, for it has brought back life to the parched pastures.'

If Ricardo's doctrine were true, that sun, and air, and water have no effect on the value of the crops, it would equally follow that bad weather, storms, and other calamities would have no effect in diminishing their value.

In fact, if Ricardo's doctrine were true, the Value of the crop ought not to be more than the Labour expended upon ploughing and preparing the ground and sowing the corn : because human labour ends there : all the growth and increase is the agency of nature.

The direct consequence of Ricardo's doctrine that Labour is the cause of all value is that the growth of corn, and fruits, and of flocks and herds, is due to human labour, a consequence which was broadly asserted by some of his disciples.

The Expression **Quantity of Labour** *is unintelligible*

3. When Smith and Ricardo say that Value depends upon Quantity of Labour, the expression at first sight seems somewhat plausible, and has had many adherents : but the slightest reflection shows that it is absolutely unintelligible. For when things of different kinds are produced by different kinds of Labour, how is it possible to compare Quantities of different kinds of Labour?

Labour is the generic name for the exertion of **Thought** or Abilities of any sort : and there are of course as many different kinds of Labour as there are different species of Thought : and these are quite incommensurable with each other, and can by no possibility be compared with each other.

How can the Labour of a ploughman, a carpenter, or a bricklayer be compared with the Labour of a Newton, a Raphael, or a Shakespeare? How can we compare the 'Quantity of Labour' in the *Principia* with the 'Quantity of Labour' in the *San Sisto*, *Macbeth*, or the *Messiah*? How are we to compare the 'Quantity of Labour' in the *Comedy* of Dante with the 'Quantity of Labour' in one of Giotto's frescoes, or Ghiberti's doors of the Baptistery of Florence? How are we to compare the 'Quantity of Labour' in a Bethel conducting a great law case with the 'Quantity of Labour' in a surgical operation by Paget or Fergusson? How can we compare the Quantity of Labour in a watch with the Quantity of Labour in ploughing a field or steering a ship?

The fact is, that immediately we begin to endeavour to compare different kinds of Quantities of Labour together the attempt is so hopeless that it must be abandoned.

Absurdity of the Doctrine that all Values are Proportional to Quantities of Labour

4. The doctrine that Value is due to Quantity of Labour adopted by Ricardo, as applied only to certain commodities, was carried to an extreme by De Quincey, a fervent admirer of Ricardo's, in some dialogues on Political Economy.

One of the interlocutors asks if there is any one principle in Political Economy from which all the rest may be derived.

The other replies that there is : such a principle exists in the doctrine of Value; that the ground of the Value of all things lies in the Quantity of Labour which produces them. Here is that great principle which is the cornerstone of all tenable Political Economy : which granted or denied, all Political Economy stands or falls. . . . Mr. Ricardo's doctrine is that A and B are to each other in Value as the Quantity of Labour which produces A to the Quantity which produces B : or, to express it in the very shortest formula by substituting the term *base* as synonymous with *producing labour*: all things are to each other in Value as their bases are in Quantity.

'I affirm that when the labourer obtains a large quantity of corn, for instance, it is far from being any fair inference that wages are then at a high real value : that in all probability they are at a very low real value : and inversely I affirm that when wages are at their very highest real value, the labourer will obtain the very smallest quantity of corn. . . . But what is it that I assert? Why that there is no connection at all of any kind, direct or inverse, between the quantity commanded and the value commanding. . . . I should again be introducing the notion of a connection between the quantity obtained and the value obtaining, which it is the purpose of my whole argument to exterminate. For my thesis is that no such connection subsists between the two as warrants any inference that the real value is great, because the quantity it buys is great or small, because the quantity it buys is small : or reciprocally, that, because the real value is great or small, therefore the quantities bought shall be great or small.'

'Wages are at a high real value when it requires much labour to produce wages : and at a low real value when it requires little labour to produce wages : and it is perfectly consistent with high real value that the labourer should be almost starving : and perfectly consistent with low real value—that the labourer should be living in great ease and comfort. . . . Meantime I presume that in your use and in everybody's use of the word value, a high value ought to purchase a high value, and that it will be very absurd if it should not. But as to purchasing a great *Quantity*, that condition is surely not included in any man's idea of value.'

We have quoted this long extract in order to show the utter confusion in the word Value which Smith, Ricardo, and their followers have introduced into the science. The Value of a thing is any other thing it will purchase : and of course the greater the Quantity of that thing which it can purchase, the greater is its Value. But by considering the Value of a thing to be the Quantity of Labour bestowed in getting it, the absurd conclusion necessarily follows that the more labour is given and the smaller the result the more valuable the thing is. That is, according to De Quincey, a man's labour is much more valuable when he gets £10 in wages than when he gets £100 !

5. We will now show the absurd consequences of the doctrine that all Values are proportional to the Quantity of Labour bestowed on producing them.

It has been said that Macaulay received £20,000 for the copyright of his 'History of England.' Now 200 very fine oak trees would sell for £20,000 on the ground : also 1,000 cattle would sell for £20,000 : also 10,000 sheep would sell for the same. Therefore, according to this doctrine, the Quantity of Labour in Macaulay writing his History was equal to the Quantity of Labour in 200 oak trees growing : equal to the Quantity of Labour in 1,000 cattle growing : equal to the Quantity of Labour in 10,000 sheep growing !

A piece of ground on which a town is built sells for £10,000 : also a Bank Credit may be of the value of £10,000 : consequently the Quantity of Labour in the piece of ground is equal to the Quantity of Labour in the Bank Credit.

A girl's head of hair sold, as we have seen, for £5 : therefore the Quantity of Labour in the growth of the girl's hair is equal to the Quantity of Labour in about two and a half sheep.

Such are the doctrines of Political Economy which are still current in this country !

We have already seen that there is no labour at all in more than about 20 per cent. of things which have Value.

But all these perplexities and absurdities vanish at once when we clearly perceive that Demand is the sole cause of Value.

Error of the doctrine that **Cost of Production** *regulates* **Value**

6. It has already been shown that it is a profound error to suppose that Cost of Production regulates Value : and in practical Economics it often happens that Value regulates Cost of Production : *i.e.* Wages are regulated and adjusted by the Value of the commodity.

1. In the trial of W. Frend it is said—' But I believe it to be a notorious fact that, in proportion to the fluctuating Value of the manufactured commodity, the price of spinning a certain quantity of wool has varied in different degrees downwards from one shilling, which may be considered as the maximum.'

2. So it was said by a landowner in the East of England— 'Wages in the East of England during the present century— from 1800 to 1870—were always regulated by the price of wheat flour.'

3. So an Essex farmer says—' It is a very old custom in the East, South, and I believe in the West of England, to pay farm labourers in proportion to the current price of wheat. When wheat becomes dear the farmers, quite unsolicited, have been in the habit of raising the wages of their men, and *vice versâ.*'

4. So in the iron trade it has long been the custom to regulate wages by the price of iron : and in speaking of a conference to adjust differences between the Lanarkshire ironmasters and their men, a sliding scale was agreed to that when the price of iron was 60*s.* per ton the men should be paid 5*s.* per ton : and that a variation of 1*s.* per ton, either up or down, should mean a rise or fall of 1*d.* per ton in wages.

5. So it was said in a daily paper—' One of the most general movements in the coal trade is the adoption of the sliding scale method of determining wages by the price of the Product of the Labour. In nearly every one of the coal-producing districts there have been adoptions of this principle : in some cases at isolated collieries, and in others covering large associations. The principle is not new in the trade ; for it is well known that for two years before the strike in Durham last year, a sliding scale arrangement had been in force in that county, and in an allied industry—the iron trade—there had been an adoption of the principle for two periods under the auspices of the board of

arbitration for the manufacturing iron trade of the North of England. And in much earlier years it is stated that in the lead mining industry a somewhat similar method of determining wages was known. In the manufacturing iron trade there are special facilities for gathering these data, which are the best basis for such scales—figures showing the relationship between prices and wages for years. In one of the great centres of that trade the relationship has become in years so definite as to approach to the dignity of a rule : and the old standard of "shillings to pounds" is one well known. That is, for every pound in the price of certain classes of iron the puddler should receive for his part of the labour in producing that iron 1*s*. per ton. With this generally acceptable rule, it was easy to define a scale of advances suited to the special circumstances of the trade in a given district.'

6. So in the years 1872 and 1873 the price of coal rose enormously, to the dismay of every householder in the country. During this period also repeated rises took place in the wages of the colliers. The public are never very nice in observing the order of such events : and many persons thought that the long-prophesied failure of our coal supplies had come ; and that the increased price of coal was due to the increased cost of obtaining it. The complaints of the public were so loud that a Committee of the House of Commons was appointed to investigate the subject. They instituted a searching inquiry into the whole facts of the case, and they clearly showed that the enormous rise in the price of coal was due to the immense demand for iron : every ton of pig iron requiring three tons of coal ; and every ton of rolled iron requiring six tons of coal. The Committee said that they were satisfied that the prices of coal which prevailed several years before the present rise commenced were so low that they did not afford a reasonable profit to the owners of collieries in general, nor such remuneration as the workmen might, with regard to the hazardous nature of their labour, reasonably expect.'

The witnesses examined by the Committee were unanimous that it was the high price of coal that caused the workmen to demand higher wages, and not the reverse. Mr. Baker said—
'The iron trade has, generally speaking, owing to its large

consumption, ruled the price of coal and wages too.' Mr. Wardell said—' Wages have advanced in proportion to the price of coal.' Mr. Dickinson said that—' Coal has been selling at an unprecedentedly high price of late, and the consequence has been that wages have been similarly high.' Mr. Macdonald said—' In every case in Scotland the rise in the price of coal preceded the rise in the rate of wages. The workmen followed the employers' demand upon the public with a demand for an advance of wages. The advance of price was announced in the papers, and always preceded the demand of the men. In one case, where the men were satisfied that the rise in the price of coal was injurious to the manufacturing interests of the country, they agreed not to press their demand for wages if the employers would take off the last advance of price.' Mr. Halliday described the successive rises in the price of coal, which were followed by a rise in wages. He said that the custom from his youth upwards had been that the men should have a rise of 2*d*. for every 10*d*. rise in the price of coal: which custom had, however, not been strictly followed in the late rise. In 1869 wages were 3*s*. 6*d*. to 3*s*. 9*d*. a day. In 1871 they got an advance of 2*d*. per ton in consequence of the rise in coal. In November 1871 coal advanced 10*d*., and the men got 1*d*. In January 1872, coal rose 10*d*., and the men got 1*d*. In May coal rose another 10*d*., and the men got nothing. In June coal rose 1*s*. 3*d*., and the men got 2*d*. In July coal rose 2*s*. 6*d*., and the men got 3*d*. In September coal rose 5*s*., and the men got 3*d*. In December coal rose 3*s*. 4*d*., and the men got 2*d*.

The Report says—' It is clearly shown that the *real order of events has been the rise in the price of iron, the rise in the price of coal, and the rise in the rate of wages.* The increased payment per ton for labour employed in getting the coal cannot therefore be considered as the primary cause of the large increase in the price of coal: a rise in wages followed upon rather than preceded a rise in the price of coal.'

The same system has found favour among our antipodean fellow-citizens. It is said in the 'Times,' July 31, 1874—' In view of the difficulties that surround the labour question at home, I think it desirable to call attention to one mode of settling affairs of this sort adopted by the coal miners at Newcastle, to the north of Sydney. A demonstration signalising the settlement was held lately. The chairman of the miners' association took the opportunity to announce the terms of agreement accepted by the miners and managers, which were as follows—First, that the minimum rate of wages payable for hewing and all other work usually performed by miners at each of the above-mentioned collieries shall be the rates current thereat prior to July 23, 1872, when the selling price of second or best coal was 8*s.* per ton, and of small coal 3*s.* 6*d.* per ton. Second, that, subject to the above limit, the wages payable at each of the above collieries for hewing and all other work usually performed by the miners shall be *regulated by the price of coal, and rise and fall with it.* . . . On concluding the above, the chairman announced to coal buyers in Victoria, South Australia, New Zealand, Hong Kong, Batavia, and India that no hindrance in future would exist through strikes to the supply of ships: the commercial millennium of the port had arrived; strikes and lock-outs were a thing of the past. Various miners addressed the meeting in the same happy and reassuring strain.'

These instances are sufficient to prove the truth of the principle which we have been endeavouring to enforce, that it is just as often the Price of an article which governs its Cost of Production as the reverse.

Cases in which **Cost of Production** *appears to* **Regulate Value**

7. There are, however, undoubtedly some cases in which Value appears to follow, or to conform to, Cost of Production: and therefore hasty reasoners might say that Cost of Production **Regulates** Value.

But we have now to determine in a scientific point of view whether this is really so, or whether it is only *apparently* so—whether the same phenomena cannot be accounted for or explained by a much wider Theory. And if so, the general principles of Natural Philosophy compel us to adopt the General Theory and reject the Special one, which only accounts for *one* class of cases.

Ricardo says—' It is the Cost of Production which must

ultimately regulate the Price of Commodities, and *not*, as has been often said, the proportion between the Supply and the Demand: the proportion between Supply and Demand may indeed for a time affect the market Value of a Commodity, *until it is supplied in greater or less abundance*, according as the Demand may be increased or diminished; but this effect will only be of temporary duration. . . .

'The opinion that the Price of commodities depends solely on the proportion of Supply to Demand, or Demand to Supply, has become almost an axiom in Political Economy, and has been a source of much error in that science.'

He then quotes the doctrine of Say that Supply and Demand regulate Prices at all times, but that Cost of Production is a Limit below which they cannot remain any length of time, because Production would then be entirely stopped or diminished, and Lord Lauderdale's Law, which we have given in a previous chapter, and says—

'This is true of monopolised commodities, and indeed of the market Price of all other commodities *for a limited period*. If the Demand for hats should be doubled, the Price would immediately rise, but the rise would only be temporary: unless the Cost of Production of hats, or their natural price, were raised. If the natural Price of bread should fall 50 per cent. from some great discovery in the science of agriculture, the Demand would not greatly increase, neither would the Supply: for a commodity is not supplied merely because it can be produced, but because there is a **Demand** for it. Here, then, we have a case where the Supply and Demand have scarcely varied; or if they have increased, they have increased in the same proportion: and yet the price of bread will have fallen 50 per cent., at a time, too, when the Value of Money had continued invariable.

'Commodities which are monopolised either by an individual or by a company vary according to the law which Lord Lauderdale has laid down: *but they fall in proportion as sellers augment their Quantity*, and rise in proportion to the eagerness of the buyers to purchase them: their Price has no necessary connection with their natural Value. But the Prices of Commodities *which are subject to competition*, and whose Quantity may be increased in any moderate degree, will ultimately depend,

not *on the state of Demand and Supply*, but *on the increased or diminished Cost of their Production.*'

Mill agrees in this doctrine. He says that there is a Law *different* from Supply and Demand which regulates the permanent or average Values of the class of commodities we are considering. And, in agreement with Ricardo, he says—

'It is therefore strictly correct to say that the Value of things which can be increased in Quantity at pleasure does not depend (except accidentally and during the time necessary for Production to adjust itself) upon Demand and Supply: on the contrary, Demand and Supply depend upon it.'

'To recapitulate: Demand and Supply govern the Value of things which cannot be indefinitely increased: except that even for them, when produced by industry, there is a minimum Value determined by Cost of Production. But in all things which admit of indefinite multiplication, Demand and Supply only determine the perturbations of Value, during a period which cannot exceed the length of time necessary for altering the Supply.'

The student will observe Mill's reasoning. He says that the Value at any *particular* time is the result of Supply and Demand: the plain meaning of which is that the Value at *all* times is the result of Supply and Demand. And then he goes on to search for a Law *other* than Demand and Supply which regulates their permanent Value! That is to say, their permanent Value is regulated by a different Law from that which regulates it at *all* times!

8. Malthus, who was a good mathematician, naturally felt that Ricardo's method of reasoning was inadmissible. He says—

'It has been shown that no change can take place in the market prices of commodities, without some previous change in the relation of the Demand to the Supply; and the question is, whether the same position is true in reference to natural prices? This question must, of course, be determined by attending carefully to the nature of the change which an alteration in the Cost of Production occasions in the state of the

Demand and the Supply, and particularly to the specific and immediate cause by which the *change of Price* which takes place is effected.

'We all allow that when the Cost of Production diminishes a fall of Price is almost universally the consequence ; but what is it specifically which forces down the price of the commodity? It has been shown in the preceding section that it is an actual or contingent excess of Supply.

'We all allow that when the Cost of Production increases the prices of commodities rise. But what is it specifically which forces up the price? It has been shown that it is an actual or contingent failure of Supply. Remove these actual or contingent variations of the Supply ; that is, let the extent of the Supply remain exactly the same, without excess or failure, whether the Cost of Production rises or falls ; and there is *not the slightest ground for supposing that any Variation of Price would take place.*

'If, for instance, all the commodities which are produced in this country, whether agricultural or manufactured, could be produced during the next ten years without Labour, but could only be supplied exactly in the same quantities as they would be in the actual state of things; then, supposing the wills and means of the purchasers to remain the same, there cannot be a doubt that all prices would also remain the same. But if this be allowed, it follows that the relation of the Supply to the Demand is the dominant principle in determination of prices, whether market or natural, and that the Cost of Production can do nothing but in subordination to it, that is merely as it affects the ordinary relation which the Supply bears to the Demand.

'It is, however, not necessary to resort to imaginary cases in order to fortify this conclusion. Actual experience shows the principle in the clearest light.

'In the well-known instance noticed by Adam Smith, of the insufficient pay of curates, notwithstanding all the efforts of the legislature to raise it, a striking proof is afforded that the permanent price of an article is determined by the Demand and Supply, and not by the Cost of Production. The real cost of the education would in this case be more likely to be increased than diminished by the subscription of benefactors ; but a large part of it being paid by benefactors, and not by the individuals themselves, it does not regulate and limit the Supply; and this Supply, on account of such encouragement, becoming and continuing abundant, the price is naturally low, whatever may be the real cost of the education given.

'The effects of the poor-rates in lowering the wages of independent labour present another practical instance of the same kind. It is not probable that public money should be more economically managed than the income of individuals; consequently the cost of rearing a family cannot be supposed to be diminished by parish assistance; but a part of the expenses being borne by the public, and applied more largely to labourers with families than to single men, a fair and independent price of labour, adequate to the maintenance of a certain family, is no longer a necessary condition of a sufficient supply. As by means of parish rates so applied this Supply can be obtained without such wages, the real costs of supplying labour no longer regulate the ordinary wages of independent labour.

'In fact, in every kind of bounty upon production, the same effects must necessarily take place; and just in proportion that such bounties tend to lower prices, they show that prices depend upon the Supply compared with the Demand, and not upon the Cost of Production.'

9. Having now presented to our readers the opinions of these various writers, we shall endeavour to discover some principles which may decide the controversy which is at the basis of the whole theory of Economical Dynamics.

The doctrine, then, whose soundness we are going to investigate is this, that there are two classes of cases of value, in the first of which *Cost of Production regulates Value*, in the other the *Cost of Producing the last quantity raised regulates the Value of the whole*.

Now, before we investigate the truth of these laws, we shall lay down certain fundamental principles, drawn from the whole analogy of Physical Science:—

I. There cannot be more than One Grand General Theory of Value.

II. That if two, or more, Theories of Value will apparently account for any class of phenomena of Value, or Changes of Value, that Theory only is to be held as the true one which accounts for ALL the phenomena in the Science, and not that single class of phenomena only.

Hence it is quite clear that, if in any particular class of phenomena we have several theories which will apparently account for them, we have, in order to discover which is the true law, only to suppose a change in the relation of the quantities; and then that theory only which holds good for the altered relation of the quantities, and accounts for the change, is the true Law, and all others must be rejected.

This is in exact conformity with the 3rd Aphorism of the *Novum Organum*, Book I.—'Quod in *contemplatione* instar causæ est, id in *operatione* instar regulæ est.'—'That which in *Theory* is the *Cause*, in *Practice* is the *Rule*.'

The result derived from these principles is this, that the Law according to which Changes of Value take place, is the Law of Value at all particular times.

Now, as soon as these indubitable principles are laid down, the day is lost for Ricardo and his followers; because Ricardo himself admits that the law of *Supply and Demand* governs the market price of all commodities for a limited period. And Mill says that the Law of *Supply and Demand* only governs *perturbations* of value.

Now this concedes the whole question. Because the law which governs the Perturbations, or Changes, of Value, can be the only true law of Value in all particular cases.

There are several cases where 'Quantity of Labour' and 'Cost of Production' may be considered as equivalent, and the same argument will apply to show that neither *regulates* value. But take it as we may, either Quantity of Labour or money Cost of Production, we shall show that the doctrine that Cost of Production regulates Value is entirely false; because, if this doctrine be true, it must necessarily mean :—

1st. That all things which are produced by an equal Quantity of Labour, or an equal money Cost, must be equal in Value, independently of any other consideration.

2ndly. It must also mean that all changes in Value must be due to Changes in Cost of Production, and to nothing else.

3rdly. And if different things produced by equal Quantities of Labour must be equal in Value, still more rigorously, if possible, must it follow that all parts of the same thing, when once produced, must be equal in Value.

But we have already given a number of examples to show the entire fallacy of such a doctrine.

10. Ricardo says in the passage already quoted—'That if the Demand for hats should be doubled, the price would immediately rise; but that rise would only be temporary unless the Cost of Production of hats, or their natural price, were raised.' But if the hats rose from the increased Demand, why should they fall again without the Supply being increased? If they are to fall again, why should they have risen? If Cost of Production, Supply, and Demand remain exactly the same after they have risen, how can any Change in their Value take place? Ricardo has omitted to state, what he meant, no doubt, that upon the rise of prices from the increased Demand, a larger Supply would be produced, which would again reduce hats to their former Value. But the omission of this is the whole essence of the question. Because it was the increased Demand which raised them, and it would only be the increased Supply which would lower them. Thus showing that it is entirely through the operation of Demand and Supply that all changes in value take place.

Ricardo's doctrine that when prices are very high or very low they are governed by the Law of Demand and Supply, but that at some intermediate point they are governed by the Law of Cost of Production, is utterly contrary to the *Law of Continuity*, which says that *A Quantity cannot pass from one amount to another by any change of conditions without passing through all the intermediate magnitudes according to the intermediate conditions.* If, therefore, the Law of Demand and Supply be true at any one point in the range of prices, it must be true at *all* points.

11. Mill has on this, as in so many other cases, emitted doctrines which are contradictory. Thus he says—'For this reason, and from the erroneous notion that Value depends on the *proportion* between the Demand and the Supply, many persons suppose that this proportion must be altered whenever there is any Change in the Value of the commodity; that the Value cannot fall through a diminution of the Cost of Production, unless the Supply is permanently increased; nor rise, unless the Supply is permanently diminished. But this is not the fact.'

But afterwards he says—'It is simply the Law of Demand and Supply, which is acknowledged to be applicable to all commodities, and which in the case of money, as of most other things, is *controlled, but not set aside,* by the Law of Cost of Production, *since cost of production would have no effect on value, if it could have none on Supply.*'

So also, in speaking of another class of cases, he says— 'Since Cost of Production here fails us, we must revert to a law of Value *anterior* to Cost of Production, *and more fundamental,* the Law of Demand and Supply.'

Again, in speaking of the law governing International Values, he says—'We have seen that it is not their Cost of Production. . . . . We must accordingly, as we have done before in a similar embarrassment, fall back upon *an antecedent law,* that of Supply and Demand: and in this we shall again find the solution of our difficulty.'

Now these extracts exhibit the utterly unscientific character of Mill's system, which is contrary to the fundamental principles of Natural Philosophy. It is no more to be tolerated that different classes of Economic phenomena should be governed by different fundamental Laws of Value, than that different classes of Astronomical phenomena should be governed by fundamentally different theories; or that different classes of Optical phenomena should be explained on different theories of Light. When the analyst seeks for the Equation to a curve, he manifestly assumes that the Law which is true at any *one* point must be true at *all* points. For, if not, how can there be a *general* Equation to the curve? If different classes of Economical phenomena have different fundamental theories, how can there be any General Equation in Economics? How can it be a Physical Science? Now, as it is universally admitted to be a demonstrated truth that a great *many* cases of Value are governed by the Law of Demand and Supply, it follows that *all* cases *must* be so; and the distinctions which have been made are contrary to the principles of Inductive Philosophy, and must be swept away.

12. Wages are part of Cost of Production, and Smith says that high wages *cause* high prices; we have shown that this is a complete error; and that it is just as often that Wages, i.e. Cost of Production, are governed by the Value of the product as the reverse.

In a great number of cases it is impossible to say what the Cost of Production of any article is, and the very fact of a market being opened up for it is the very thing that confers Value on it. In the last century, eggs were at 1*d.* a dozen in the Highlands of Scotland, and salmon was so abundant that it had scarcely any saleable value at all, there being no communication with the Southern markets. When this communication was opened, eggs rose to 4*d.* or 6*d.* a dozen, and salmon acquired a Value of about 1*s.* a pound. That was because agents from the South came and bought up the produce; because eggs were, perhaps, 1*s.* 6*d.* a dozen in the London markets, and salmon was 2*s.* 6*d.* a pound. Now, eggs were not 1*s.* a dozen in London because they were 4*d.* a dozen in the Highlands, but people gave 4*d.* a dozen for them in the Highlands because they could get 1*s.* a dozen for them in London. What, then, becomes of the Ricardian rule, that Cost of Production *regulates* Value? In this case it was the Value of the eggs in the London market that regulated their Value in the Highlands, and not the reverse, and the same is obviously true of all other species of produce.

13. The universal law in Economics is, therefore, that THE RELATION BETWEEN DEMAND AND SUPPLY IS THE SOLE REGULATOR OF VALUE. This law, like the law of gravity, holds good in all cases whatever. It not only governs the Value of any article, but also governs the Value of every separate item of which that article is composed. All circumstances whatever that influence Value can be shown to do solely through their effect in altering the relation of Supply and Demand.

Price, then, is a perpetual struggle between the buyer and the seller, and the circumstances which compel one party to yield, are the only measure of Value at the time of the purchase. To say that the Cost of Production regulates price is only true in this sense, that no man would willingly sell any articles he has produced at a less price than that, together with something additional, by way of reward for his own labour, and he could not continue to do so for any length of time. But, having settled that in his own mind as the lowest limit, he always endeavours to get as much more as he can, without the smallest reference to the Cost of Production. On the other hand, the purchaser cares nothing for the Cost of Production; his only object is to buy as cheap as he can, and he takes no thought whether the seller is selling at a loss or not. The result of this will be that if the selling Value of any article falls below its Cost of Production for a length of time, it will cease to be produced. Every man endeavours to produce as cheap as he can, and to sell as dear as he can, and the two operations are quite independent of each other.

When we say that the Relation between Supply and Demand is the sole Regulator of Value, we mean to say that *a Change of Value depends solely upon a Change in that relation and upon nothing else.* No change in the Cost of Production will make any change in Value, unless it is also accompanied by a change in the relation of Demand and Supply, and it is only through and by means of causing such an alteration that a change in the Cost of Production is usually accompanied by a change in Value.

In order to illustrate this, let us take a few examples; let us take any article, such as stockings, and let us suppose that at any given time they bear a certain price in the market, no matter what, and that there is a certain demand for them at that price.

Let us suppose that, at a certain time before the introduction of machinery, a manufacturer employed 1,000 hands: let us also suppose that he at some time invents a piece of machinery by which he can produce the same quantity of stockings, but at the same expense as 50 men would be. Now, if he only produces the same Quantity as before, as he will of course take the best price he can get for them, the Demand remaining the same, it is quite evident that no alteration in price will ensue, and all the profit accruing from this diminution in the Cost of Production will go into the pocket of the producer; consequently, if he does not manufacture any additional quantity, no alteration in the market price will follow: everything will go on as before; the only difference will be that that particular manufacturer will make enormous profits, owing to his sagacity and skill in inventing this machinery. But if the materials for making the stockings can be supplied in unlimited quantities, the manufacturer will naturally wish to increase the Quantity he produces, and realise greater profits; but if he produce a greater quantity than before, that increased quantity will not be sold, unless offered at a diminished price, so as to increase the circle of buyers; but as the Cost of their Production has been diminished to him, he can afford to sell at a diminished price; and the more he wishes to sell, the more must the price be reduced. Now, it is quite evident that the increased quantity of this single manufacture thrown upon the market, and offered at a diminished price, will affect the prices of the whole quantity in the market, because everyone else must consent to sell at the same price to effect a sale at all. It is also clear that every single manufacturer must accommodate his price to the market price, and if he cannot produce at the market price he will have to cease producing: and as we may suppose that there are several degrees of skilfulness and economy among the various manufacturers, it is quite evident that at every successive diminution of the market price, those in succession will have to cease working who are least able to produce cheaply. Hence, it is quite clear that it is the market price which regulates the quantity of expense that can be afforded in producing, and that it is the quantity that can be produced at the least expense, compared to the whole quantity that can be sold, that regulates the market price.

Again, let us observe what is the result of a diminution of the cost of production, according to various circumstances. The Northern counties of Scotland export corn and cattle to the Southern markets. They were served by a Steam Company, which had a monopoly of the trade. The usual consequences of a monopoly followed. Those which concern us here, as a question of Economics, were, that the freights and fares were most extravagant, and all petitions for reduction were unheeded, as the Company thought there was no danger of opposition. However, the people of the North could stand it no longer, and they determined to provide steamboats of their own. The natural consequence immediately followed, freights and fares were reduced nearly one-half. Almost all the farmers subscribed for shares in the steamer, and many of them said that if they lost all the money sunk in the steamer, they would still be great gainers by the saving of freights. That is, the diminution in the Cost of Production (i.e., the expense of placing their produce in the Southern markets) went into their pockets. And why was this? Because the additional quantity of corn, &c., thrown by the Northern districts upon the Southern markets was a mere drop in the bucket compared to the demand of the Southern markets, and had no appreciable effect in lowering prices there: consequently, all the profits arising from the saving of freight, and the diminution of the Cost of Production, went into the pockets of the Northern farmers and landlords.

14. These considerations are sufficient to show the fallacy of the doctrine, that it is the Cost of Production which **Regulates** Price, or Value. On the contrary, it is generally the Value an article is expected to have, when produced, that causes it to be produced. The difference between the Cost of its Production and its Value is called the *profit*, and the course of a prudent man would be, first to calculate the Cost of Production of the article, then to consider what would be its probable Value when produced; and if the difference between the two, or the profit, is sufficient to make it worth his while to produce it, he will do so; if not, he should try to discover some more profitable operation. If the Value of the article when produced is only equal to, or less than, the Cost of Production, he must sell at a loss, and repeated operations of this nature will end by ruining him. The history of all commerce is but too full of examples of the Value of articles falling below the Cost of Production, and of mercantile enterprises which never pay their expenses. There is but one way by which a producer can govern price by the Cost of Production, and that is when he can obtain a command over the Supply, and limit it artificially, and not produce more than the public can be made to buy at a particular price. The Dutch acted upon this principle when they conquered the Spice Islands in the Eastern Archipelago. With contemptible selfishness, they cut down three-fourths of the spice-bearing trees, and so artificially enhanced the Value of the remainder. It is also said that there is but one mine in England which produces plumbago, or black lead for pencils, and this being in the hands of one proprietor, he carefully limits its annual produce to force up its price in the market.

15. It is necessary to observe that when we say that a change in price invariably depends upon a change in the relation of Supply and Demand, we by no means assert that the change in price is directly proportional to a change in that relation, so that, for instance, an addition of one-fourth of the quantity would produce a reduction of one-fourth in price. It is well known that this proportion does not hold ; and that a different proportion is found to obtain among different articles. Nor, though attempts have been made in some instances, such as corn, to discover the relation that exists between the two, does it appear that any satisfactory solution has been obtained. All that can be said is that it is a change in the one that produces a change in the other, without asserting that there is any fixed proportion between the two changes, because it may very well be, and we believe it to be the case, that that proportion follows no fixed law, but varies according to time and circumstances.

It is perfectly manifest that any diminution of the Cost of Production, through however large an extent of country it might cover, would have no effect whatever in altering the market price, until the extra quantity thrown upon the market bore an appreciable proportion to the previous supply. And if districts of country are excluded from markets, either by want of communication or by prohibitive laws, then, when there are markets opened to them, their produce will acquire an immensely increased value to what it had before. That is, the opening of the markets will immensely increase the Value of the produce in the country, and the increased quantity of produce thrown upon the market will tend to lower the Value of the produce in that market: and these two Values will approach to each other in the inverse proportion of the respective quantities: precisely as the space travelled through by each of the two bodies under the influence of gravity is in the inverse proportion of their masses. The establishment of steam navigation enormously increased the Value of produce in the north of Scotland; the repeal of the corn laws enormously increased the Value of produce in the Danubian principalities.

Rules connecting **Cost of Production** *and* **Value**

16. A consideration of the preceding examples will furnish us with the following Rules regarding the relation between Cost of Production and Value :—

1. No change in Cost of Production will cause a change in Value unless it is accompanied by a change in the relation of Supply and Demand.

2. A Diminution in the Cost of Production, when effected without an Increase of the Quantity produced, goes entirely to the benefit of the Producer.

3. A Diminution in the Cost of Production, in cases where the Quantity of the product can be Increased without limit, goes entirely to the benefit of the Consumer.

4. A Diminution in the Cost of Production, in cases where the Quantity can be Increased, but not without limit, goes partly to the benefit of the Producer and partly to the benefit of the Consumer: and the benefit is divided between the two in the inverse ratio of the extra Quantity added compared to the previously existing Supply.

Fundamental Error of Smith and Ricardo

17. The systems of Smith and Ricardo, although there may appear to be a difference between them, are nevertheless identical in their fundamental error. For they both look to the wrong person as conferring Value on a product. They both look to the Labour of the Producer as conferring Value: whereas it is unquestionably certain that the **Demand** of the Consumer is the sole origin and cause of Value. Smith says that it is the

Labour which the Producer bestows upon an article which gives it Value : whereas it is perfectly certain that things have not Value because Labour has been bestowed in producing them : but much Labour is bestowed in producing them because people desire to have them very much, and are willing to give a great price to possess them : and therefore they have great Value. But, as Condillac observed long ago, things have not great Value because much Cost of Production has been bestowed on them ; but great Cost of Production is bestowed on them because they have great Value when produced. Buyers do not give high prices because sellers have spent much money in producing : but sellers spend much in producing because they hope to find buyers who will give more.

It is quite true that the natural effects of competition will in many cases cause the price to approach very nearly to Cost of Production : and Ricardo's law will apparently be found to be true. But this is one of those cases which must be sedulously guarded against in science, viz. to give in a careless form of adherence to a form of expression which is radically erroneous because it appears to account for phenomena.

Formerly philosophers thought that the motion of projected bodies had a natural tendency to decay. They saw that the motion of a projected body always gradually diminished and finally ceased. It was quite easy to calculate results upon this principle. Given a certain velocity of projection, it was quite easy to calculate when the motion would cease upon the supposition that it naturally decayed. And the results would have agreed with the calculations. What could be more satisfactory? If, then, it is hastily assumed that because results may agree with calculations, the principles of these calculations are therefore necessarily true, these opinions might have held their ground. But it is well known that modern philosophers have entirely rejected the notion that motion has a natural tendency to decay. But they arrive at the same result by a different process of reasoning. They say that motion has no natural tendency to decay : but that in all the cases we see there are counteracting causes at work, such as the resistance of the air, friction, &c., which oppose it and finally destroy it. And they unanimously reject the former method of accounting for the results and adopt the latter. Hence we see that, though principles are manifestly erroneous which do not account for results, yet it does not necessarily follow that any principle which does account for results is therefore necessarily true: because it may in fact happen that several different principles may account for the result; and it requires judgment to decide which is the true one. Now the Ricardian principle of Value is just like the former of those of motion. It apparently accounts for results in some cases; and therefore it may impose upon an unwary thinker: but it wholly fails to do so in all others. But it is a dangerous and seducing error, utterly false in principle, and has been the cause of multitudes of calamities: and it is to be repudiated and rejected by all those who study Economics in the true spirit of science.

CHAPTER VIII

ON PROFITS

Section I

Definition *of* Profit

1. THE word **Profit** comes from the Latin *proficere*, to make progress. As the Chorus says in Marlowe's *Faustus*—

> So soon he **Profits** in divinity,

that is, makes progress.

The object and intent of every commercial operation is to make a profit. As George Herbert says—

> The merchant that gains not loses.

The expense of placing any object in the market is termed Cost of Production : and the hope and intention is that the Selling Price, or Value, should exceed the Cost of Production.

Profit is the Difference between the Cost of Production of any goods and their Price or Value.

This Difference may be in excess of the Cost of Production ; and then the Profit is positive, and is termed a **Gain** : but it may be in defect of the Cost of Production : and then the Profit is Negative, and is termed a **Loss**.

Profit is estimated by the Ratio between the Difference and the Cost of Production. Thus, if the Cost of Production be £100, and the Profit £10, it is termed a Profit of 10 per cent.

Profit is a general name for the difference between Cost of Production and Value, whether the matter traded with be Merchandise of any sort, or Money, or Credit.

We have shown in a preceding chapter that there are two grand divisions of commerce—the Commerce in Merchandise and the Commerce in Debts. Profits made in the Commerce of goods are termed **Profits** : Profits made in the Commerce of Money or Debts are termed **Interest** or **Discount**

Definition of **Rate** of **Profit**

2. When we speak of the Rate of anything it invariably means the Time in which it is done. If anyone speaks of the Rate at which a horse can gallop, or an athlete can run, or a ship can steam, it always refers to the Time in which the distance is accomplished. To say that a horse can gallop at the rate of 25 miles, or an athlete can run at the Rate of 14 miles, or that a ship can steam at the Rate of 15 knots, is evidently a defective form of expression, which conveys no definite meaning whatever. The Rate of speed in such cases is usually referred to the hour.

So in speaking of the Rate of Interest some time—usually the year—is always expressed. Thus the Rate of Interest is always so much per cent. and per *annum*.

Evidently, therefore, the term Rate of Profit must mean the amount of Profit made in some certain time, as the year. Hence, by analogy, and to compare Rate of Profit with Rate of Interest, we must speak of the Rate of Profit as being so much per cent. and per *annum*.

Error of Economists in their Definition of Rate of Profit

3. Economists, however, have committed an extraordinary oversight in their Definition of Rate of Profit: they entirely omit the element of Time: and define Rate of Profit to be merely the ratio of the Profit to the Capital.

Without giving any clear Definition of Rate of Profit, both Smith and Ricardo never perceived that a Profit made in a day is a different Rate of Profit than the same Profit made in a year!

But this error appears clearly in subsequent writers. Thus Macculloch says—

'The Rate of Profit is the proportion which the amount of Profit derived from an undertaking bears to the Capital employed in it.

'It is obvious that the Rate of Profit may be raised in three, but only in three ways.

'1. By industry becoming more productive.

'2. By a reduction in the rate of wages.

' 3. By a reduction in the amount of taxation. And it may be reduced by the opposite circumstances.
' 1. By industry becoming less productive.
' 2. By a rise in the rate of wages.
' 3. By a rise in the amount of taxation.
' Profits cannot be effected in any way not referable to one or other of these heads.'

So Malthus says—
'*Profit of Stock.*—When Stock is employed as Capital in the Production and Distribution of Wealth, its Profits consist of the Difference between the Value of the Capital advanced and the Value of the Commodity when sold or used.
'*The Rate of Profit.*—The percentage proportion which the Value of the Profits upon any Capital bears to the Value of such Capital.'
Again—' The Profits of Capital consist of the Difference between the Value of a Commodity produced and the Value of the advances necessary to produce it : and these advances consist of accumulations generally made up of wages, rent, taxes, interest, and profits.
' The Rate of Profits is the proportion which the difference between the Value of the Commodity produced and the Value of the advances necessary to produce it bears to the Value of the advances. When the Value of the product is great compared with the Value of the advances, the excess being considerable, the Rate of Profits will be high. When the Value of the product exceeds but little the Value of the advances, the difference being small, the Rate of Profits will be low.
' The varying Rates of Profit, therefore, obviously depend upon the causes which alter the proportion between the Value of the advances necessary to production and the Value of the product obtained.'

Lastly, Mill says—' The Profits of Stock are the surplus which remains to the Capitalist after replacing his Capital, and the Ratio which the surplus bears to the Capital itself is the Rate of Profit. . . .
' The Rate of Profit is the proportion which the Profit bears

to the Capital. . . . In short, if we compare the *price paid* for labour and tools with what that labour and those tools will produce, from this Ratio we may calculate the Rate of Profit. . . .

'Profits, then (meaning not gross profits, but the Rate of Profit), depend (not upon the price of labour, tools, and material, but) upon the Ratio between the price of labour, tools, and materials, and the produce of them. . . .

'The whole of the surplus, after replacing wages, is Profits. From this it seems to follow that the Ratio between the Wages of labour and the Produce of labour gives the Rate of Profit. And thus we arrive at Ricardo's principle that Profits depend on wages; rising as wages fall, and falling as wages rise. . . .

'This theory we conceive to be the basis of the true theory of Profits. . . . It is therefore strictly true that the Rate of Profit varies inversely as the Cost of Production of Wages. Profits cannot rise unless the Cost of Production of wages falls exactly as much; nor fall unless it rises.

'The variation, therefore, in the Rate of Profits and those in the Cost of Production of wages go hand in hand and are inseparable. Mr. Ricardo's principle that Profits cannot rise unless wages fall is strictly true.

'The only expression of the law of Profits which seems to be correct is, that they depend upon the Cost of the Production of wages. This must be received as the ultimate principle. . . .

'The Rate of Profits, therefore, tends to *fall* from the following causes :—

'1. An increase of Capital beyond population, producing increased competition for labour.

'2. An increase of Population, occasioning a demand for an increased quantity of food, which must be produced at a greater cost.'

'The Rate of Profits tends to *rise* from the following causes :—

'1. An increase of Population beyond Capital, producing increased competition for employment.

'2. Improvements producing increased cheapness of necessaries and other articles habitually consumed by the labourer.'

And he further says—' The Capitalist, then, may be assumed to make all the advances and receive all the produce. His

Profit consists of the excess of the produce above the advances: his Rate of Profit is the ratio which that excess bears to the amount advanced.

'It thus appears that the two elements on which and on which alone the gains of the Capitalist depend, are, first, the magnitude of the produce; in other words, the productive power of labour; and, secondly, the proportion of that produce obtained by the labourers themselves; the Ratio which the remuneration of the labourers bears to the amount they produce. These two things form the data for determining the gross amount divided as Profit among all the Capitalists of the country: but the Rate of Profit, the percentage on the Capital, &c. . . .

'We thus arrive at the conclusion of Ricardo and others, that the Rate of Profit depends upon wages: rising as wages fall, and falling as wages rise.

'The Cost of Labour, then, is, in the language of mathematics, a function of three variables: the efficiency of labour: the wages of labour (meaning thereby the real reward of the labourer); and the greater or less cost at which the articles composing that real reward can be produced or procured. It is plain that the cost of labour to the Capitalist must be influenced by each of these three circumstances, and *by no others*. These, therefore, are also the circumstances which determine the Rate of Profit: and *it cannot* be in any way affected except through one or other of them.'

Erroneous Doctrines deduced from the erroneous Definition of Rate of Profit

4. We have laid these long extracts before the student in order that he may see that what we said is true; that no Economist has seen that Time is a necessary element in the definition of Rate of Profit.

There is not a single Economist who has seen that a Profit of 5 per cent. made in a Day is a different Rate of Profit from a Profit of 5 per cent. made in a Week, a Month, or a Year!

It would be just as absurd to say that a sum of 5 per cent. paid as Interest is the same Rate of Interest whether it is paid for a loan of money for a day, a week, a month, or a year!

And this palpable arithmetical blunder has necessarily and logically led to consequences of the deepest practical importance. For Ricardo and his copyists assert that Profits can only be increased by a reduction of wages, and can only be reduced by an increase of wages.

Ricardo says that the Value of commodities is divided into two portions, one the Profits of Stock and the other the Wages of Labour: consequently he asserts that *nothing can affect profits but a rise in wages* . . . . profits depend on high or low wages.

From these doctrines they drew the necessary conclusion that the interests of Capitalists and Workmen were always antagonistic to each other: and that the gain of one must necessarily be the loss of the other.

It was this apparently hopeless doctrine of Ricardo's, along with a similar error regarding Rent: and the absurd doctrines of Malthus on Population, which are also founded on a palpable arithmetical error, which seemed to show that society must necessarily deteriorate with the increase of numbers, that led a caustic philosopher of the present day to nickname Political Economy the 'Dismal Science.'

Correction of these Erroneous Doctrines

5. But a very few sentences will dissipate these gloomy ideas: and a simple arithmetical calculation will show that Profits and Wages may very easily rise together: and that consequently there is no such necessary antagonism between Capitalists and Workmen as these Economists allege.

Suppose that the Capital advanced is £100, and the Profit is £20—

Then, if the Profit is made in a *Year*, the Rate of Profit is evidently 20 per cent. per *annum*.

If the Profit is made in a *Month*, the Rate of Profit is evidently 240 per cent. per *annum*.

If the Profit is made in a *Week*, the Rate of Profit is evidently 1,040 per cent. per *annum*.

If the Profit is made in a *Day*, the Rate of Profit is evidently 7,300 per cent. per *annum*.

These principles are so clear as to be beyond dispute: and we can test the doctrines of the writers we have quoted by them. They repeatedly assert that the Rate of Profit can by no possibility be increased except by a diminution of wages.

But the simplest arithmetical calculation shows that, supposing the Capital and the actual Profits to remain exactly the same, the Rate of Profit may be enormously increased by the accelerated rapidity with which Profits are made.

And similarly, if the Capital and the actual Profits remain the same, the Rate of Profit may be immensely diminished by a retardation of the periods in which they are made.

6. So also it is quite easy to show that Wages may be increased, and the actual Profit diminished, and yet the Rate of Profit greatly increased.

Suppose, as before, the Capital is £100, and the Profits £20, made in a year.

Suppose that the period of making the Profits is reduced to a month, then the Rate of Profit is 240 per cent. and per *annum*.

Suppose that, in consequence of making the greater rate of Profit, the capitalist advances Wages £5. Then Cost of Production is £105, and the Profit is £15 made in one month: or nearly 14·3 per cent. per month: which is Profit at the Rate of more than 167 per cent. per annum.

Suppose a still more accelerated sale, and that the trader makes the Profit in one day: then, as we have seen above, that is Profit at the Rate of 7,300 per cent. per annum.

Suppose that, in consequence of this greatly increased Rate of Profit, the trader raises wages so that Cost of Production amounts to £110. Then, with an outlay of £110, he makes a Profit of £10 in one day: being more than 9 per cent. per day: or at the Rate of more than 3,318 per cent. per *annum*.

Hence, while Price remains exactly the same, Wages may be considerably, and Rate of Profit may be enormously, increased by the simple acceleration of the periods of return.

These cases may, of course, be reversed. The Price may

remain the same, the Wages diminished, the actual Profits increased, and yet the Rate of Profit enormously diminished by the simple retardation of the periods of sale.

7. So also the Price may be reduced, and Wages increased, and therefore the actual Profit reduced both by an increase of Wages and reduction of Price, and yet the Rate of Profit greatly increased.

Suppose that in the last case the trader, in consequence of competition or for any other reason, reduces prices by £5; so that, as before, Wages come to £110: then actual Profits are £5: this would still be Profit at the rate of 4·545 per cent. per *day*: or more than 1,659 per cent. per *annum*.

Thus it is clearly proved that by the simple acceleration of the rapidity of sale Price may be reduced, Wages may be increased, actual Profit reduced, and yet the Rate of Profit increased: that is, the Capitalist, the Workman, and the Customer may all gain together: and of course, *è converso*, they may all lose together, by the reverse process of retarding the periods of return.

There may, therefore, very well be, and in most cases there is, a solidarity of interests between Customer, Capitalist, and Workman: and not a necessary antagonism, according to the doctrine of Ricardo and his copyists. The evident error of these writers arises from their having entirely omitted the most potent method of increasing the Rate of Profit, namely, accelerating the periods of return.

The current doctrine of Economists is that Rate of Profit varies directly as the excess of the Profit above the Cost of Production, whereas the true doctrine is—

Rate of Profit *varies* **Directly** *as the excess of the Profit above the Cost of Production, and* **Inversely** *as the* **Time** *in which it is made.*

8. Economists have adopted this manifest error from the usage of traders. When a banker charges his customer Interest or Discount on an advance, the Rate per cent. and per annum is agreed upon, and the customer pays a sum according to the *Time* of the advance. But when a trader buys goods from a wholesale dealer, he simply adds on to the goods a percentage on the wholesale price, and makes no difference whether he sells the next day, the next week, or the next month, and he erroneously calls that advance the Rate of Profit; thus throwing great obscurity and misconception over the whole subject. But certainly professed writers on Economics should have perceived this fallacy and have rectified it.

Examples of Trading Profits

9. To show how an apparently very moderate actual Profit is a high Rate of Profit, we may take a few examples.

A retail bookseller is entitled by the custom of trade to a reduction of 25 per cent. off the published price of the work. Many retail booksellers offer to obtain any book for their customers at a discount of 20 per cent. off the published price. Suppose the book is ordered one day and paid for the next. The customer is pleased at getting the book so cheap; and no one grudges the bookseller his apparently very modest profit of 5 per cent.

Let us now see what the Rate of Profit is. By such an operation he gains a Profit of 5 per cent. on three-fourths of the price of the book in one day, which is an actual Profit of 6·666 per cent. per *day*: which is at the rate of more than 2,433 per cent. and per annum. Traders complain when bankers charge 6 per cent. per annum: what would they say if a banker charged 6 per cent. per day?

A costermonger buys baskets of strawberries in Covent Garden Market at $2\frac{3}{4}d.$, and sells them the same afternoon at $3d.$: everyone would say that that is a very moderate Profit. Yet it is a Profit of one-eleventh part, or more than 9 per cent. per day: which is a Rate of Profit of more than 3,300 per cent. per annum.

Smith says—'Apothecaries' Profit is become a byeword denoting something uncommonly extravagant. This great apparent Profit, however, is frequently no more than the reasonable wages of labour. The skill of an apothecary is a much nicer and more delicate matter than that of any artificer whatever:

and the trust which is reposed in him is of much greater importance. He is the physician of the poor in all cases, and of the rich where the distress or the danger is not very great. His reward, therefore, ought to be suitable to his skill and his trust, and it arises generally from the price at which he sells his drugs. But the whole drugs which the best employed apothecary in a large market town will sell in a year may not perhaps cost him above thirty or forty pounds. Though he should sell them, therefore, for three or four hundred, or perhaps a thousand per cent. profit, this may be frequently no more than the reasonable wages of his labour, charged in the only way in which he can charge them, upon the price of his drugs. The greater part of the apparent profit is real wages, disguised in the garb of profit.

'In a small seaport town a little grocer will make forty or fifty per cent. upon a stock of a single hundred pounds, while a considerable wholesale merchant in the same place will scarce make eight or ten per cent. upon a stock of ten thousand. The trade of a grocer may be necessary for the convenience of the inhabitants, and the narrowness of the market may not admit the employment of a larger capital in the business. The man, however, must not only live by his trade, but live by it suitably to the qualifications which it requires. Besides possessing a little capital, he must be able to read, write, and account : and must be a tolerable judge, too, of perhaps fifty or sixty different sorts of goods, their prices, qualities, and the markets where they are to be had cheapest. He must have all the knowledge, in short, that is necessary for a great merchant, which nothing hinders him from becoming but the want of a sufficient capital. Thirty or forty pounds a year cannot be considered as too great a recompense for the labour of a person so accomplished. Deduct this from the seemingly great profits of his capital, and little more will remain, perhaps, than the ordinary profits of stock. The greater part of the apparent profit is, in this case too, real wages.'

What Smith says in the cases of the apothecary and the grocer is true to a certain extent, but not wholly so. The skill necessary to carry on a druggist's or a grocer's business is probably not more difficult to acquire than that required in many other trades. But they deal in immensely *smaller* sums. The druggist sells for a shilling what probably cost him a farthing. This apparently enormous profit is simply the necessary consequence of the exceedingly minute sums in which he deals. When a trader deals with large sums he can live on a profit of 5 per cent. per day, or less. But when the sums he deals in are pence and halfpence the profit must be enormous to enable him to live by his trade. Now people do not require medicine by pounds' worths, but by shillingworths or pennyworths, and hence this enormous profit is necessary to enable the trade to exist at all.

10. Persons who engage in trade must live by their trade : they must therefore necessarily charge their customers such prices as will in the long run enable them to support themselves out of the profits. Hence when transactions are very trifling in number and magnitude they must charge very high prices in order to enable them to live. It is this circumstance that compels small shopkeepers in rural districts to charge such high prices for their goods, to the great indignation of many well-meaning but unreflecting persons. It is not uncommon to hear such persons exclaim against what they call the extortionate charges of country shopkeepers, quite forgetting that if the traders cannot make a living out of their business they must give it up altogether, and the people be totally deprived of the convenience.

It has sometimes happened that gentlemen having plenty of other means to back them have established rival shops for the express purpose of beating down the prices of the country shopkeepers. The consequence has been that the traders who had nothing but their business to support them have been ruined, the gentleman in process of time either got tired of his whim, or for other reasons abandoned it, and the germ of a nascent trade in a district has been destroyed : a pregnant example of the Spanish proverb—' Hell is paved with good intentions.'

Laing mentions a striking instance of the mischievous consequences of irregular interference with trade. ' I was surprised on inquiring at the only bookseller's shop (in Drontheim) for a New Testament in the Norwegian tongue to find he kept none : I thought at first he had misunderstood me, but really found he did not keep any of late years. As he understood German, I asked him how, in a population of 12,000 people, the only bookseller kept no stock of Testaments and Bibles : he said that country booksellers did not find it answer, as the Bible Society in London had once sent out a stock which were sold much lower than the trade could afford, and it was only after the Society's Bibles were sold that they could get clear of what they had on hand : hence they could not venture to keep any now. It is plain if any benevolent society were to supply a parish with boots and shoes below prime cost until all the shoemakers in the parish had turned to other employments, the parish would soon be barefooted, and that they would do more harm than good unless they had funds to continue the supply for ever. This bookseller, a very respectable man, laid no stress upon the circumstance, but simply explained it as he might have answered any other inquiry about books : and a bookbinder whom I afterwards saw gave me the same reason. Men of the first capacity are connected with our societies for the distribution of the Scriptures, and it may well deserve their consideration whether such distribution may not in the long run do more harm than good. If the ordinary mode of supplying human wants, by affording a fair remuneration to those who bring an article to where it is wanted, be invaded, they may be interfering with and stopping up the natural channel by which society must in the long run be supplied with religious books.'

11. Hence we see that when transactions are few and paltry, prices and the profits upon each must be high ; and that a multiplication of transactions and an increase of their amount has a tendency to lower prices. Nowhere are rents so high as in the City of London : and nowhere are the prices of ordinary goods so moderate. In the City, goods are in many cases 25 per cent. cheaper than in the suburbs : and this is not entirely owing to competition, but it is the result of the great number and magnitude of their transactions. The profits upon each transaction are much less than a country shopkeeper receives : but it is found that a small profit upon a large and rapid circulation of commodities leads much faster to opulence than a large profit upon a slow and small circulation. Instead of the old idea of making as great a profit as possible upon each transaction, modern experience demonstrates that the true axiom of trade is *Small profits and quick returns.* Bacon saw clearly what has been far too much overlooked by writers on Political Economy, that the frequency of returns is of far more consequence than the magnitude of each case of profit. 'The proverb is true that light gains make heavy purses, for light gains come thick, whereas great come but now and then.'

12. As a familiar instance, we may take the fares of cabs in London and the provinces. Cabs are sixpence a mile in London, but much higher in all provincial towns. But the cost of maintaining cabs, feeding horses, rent of stables, &c., is much higher in London than in the provinces. And, therefore, according to the notion that Cost of Production regulates Value, the fares ought to be much higher. But the Demand for cabs is much greater in London than in the country.

13. It is because no single trade is sufficient to occupy a man's time or gain him a livelihood that dealers in country districts, and in the commencement of trade, are obliged to unite so many different kinds of business. At a small watering place in England we saw the prospectus of a tradesman who united thirty-six kinds of trade. As population and wealth increase there are more demands in each of these kinds of business, and the trader finds that he can gain a living by confining himself to a fewer number. At last everyone confines himself to a single business, being able to make a livelihood out of it. Employments gradually disintegrate. In time each person not only confines himself to a single trade, but even to one small department of it. Each department of a trade separates itself into a distinct employment. This is also the case in the sciences as soon as they attain a certain magnitude. In modern times not only do men devote themselves to a single science, but in many cases a single branch of that science is sufficient to employ a lifetime. This is that principle of the separation of employments which has long been observed by Economists, and which Smith calls the 'division of labour,' with which he has commenced his work, but which comes more naturally in a subsequent stage of the inquiry.

An Expression of Senior's Inadequate

14. Senior originated, as far as we are aware, an expression which is very inadequate. He said that Profits are the reward of Abstinence : meaning that all Capital is the result of saving.

This expression, which has been much used, is very inadequate : for Senior himself says that Economists are agreed that **whatever** gives a Profit is rightly termed Capital. Now Profits are made not only by employing the accumulated savings of the *Past*, but also the expected proceeds of the **Future**. A trader makes Profits in proportion to the extent of his Purchasing Power : and Smith acknowledges what every practical man of business knows, that a trader's Credit exceeds his stock or accumulation of the past many times. Mill acknowledges that a merchant's Purchasing Power is his Money, his Bank Notes, Bills and Cheques, and his **Credit**. The mechanism of the great system of Credit has been exhibited in preceding chapters : and it has been seen how enormously Credit exceeds Money in modern commerce.

Hence it clearly gives a most inadequate idea of Profits to say that they are only the reward of Abstinence ; they are to a very much greater degree the reward of **Foresight**.

Error of Smith on Agricultural Profits

15. The Physiocrates, as we have seen, maintained that Agricultural Labour only is **Productive** Labour, i.e. the only Labour which adds to the wealth of the country. Smith rebelled against this doctrine, and showed that the Labour of artisans and mercantile men is also Productive. But he was still so far under the influence of Physiocrate ideas, that he alleges that Agriculture is the most Productive, or Profitable, species of Labour.

He says—' No equal Capital puts into motion a greater quantity of Productive Labour than that of the farmer. . . . No equal quantity of Productive Labour employed in manufacture can ever occasion so great a reproduction. For them nature does nothing—man does all : and the reproduction must always be in proportion to the strength of the agents that occasion it. The Capital employed in agriculture, therefore, not only puts into motion a greater quantity of Productive Labour than an equal Capital employed in manufactures, but in proportion, too, to the quantity of Productive Labour that it employs, it adds a much greater value to the annual produce of the land and labour of the country, to the real wealth and revenue of its inhabitants. Of all the ways in which a capital can be employed, it is by far the most advantageous to the society. . . .

' It has been the principal cause of the rapid progress of our American colonies towards wealth and greatness, that almost their whole capitals have hitherto been employed in agriculture.

' It is thus that the same capital will in any country put into motion a greater or smaller quantity of Productive Labour, and add a greater or smaller value to the annual produce of its land and labour according to the different proportions in which it is employed in agriculture, manufactures, and wholesale trade.'

It is certainly extraordinary that Smith should make such assertions, which are most contrary to the plainest facts of history. Taking simply the increase of wealth, and omitting all moral and political considerations, is it the Agricultural or the Commercial States of the world which have attained the greatest amount of wealth? The single city of Venice carried on a war against the Empires of the East and the West at the same time. The small commercial republic of Holland conquered its independence from the Spanish monarchy, the most powerful state of the age.

The slightest appeal to experience shows the entire fallacy of Smith's assertion : and the explanation of it is very simple. The key to the whole question is to be found in the true meaning of Rate of Profit. It is not the quantity of money in a country which causes it to be wealthy ; but the rapidity of its circulation, which indicates the Rate of Increase or Progress. From the time of Colbert to the French Revolution the question whether the towns or the country contribute most to national opulence was keenly disputed, and as one side prevailed, it was favoured and encouraged, and the other neglected.

Now the velocity of circulation indicates the Rate of Progress : and, accordingly, whichever employment causes the Currency to circulate with the greatest rapidity, most augments national opulence. Now it is a well-known fact that of all species of industry, agriculture causes the most languid circulation of the Currency. By offering an extra stimulus of reward the Products of human industry can be multiplied and quickened to an extraordinary extent : but the process of nature is slow and cannot be accelerated at command. Different trading pursuits cause a brisker circulation of money, in different degrees : but all much faster than agriculture. A farmer turns over his Capital, as it is termed, only once a year : and perhaps in favourable times may make a Profit of 10 per cent. in the whole year. A tradesman puts a Profit of 10, 20, or 30 per cent. on the wholesale price of his goods, and may make that Profit in a day or a week. Even allowing for all improvements in agriculture, the income to be made by a farm soon reaches a definite fixed limit which cannot be exceeded. But a trader may increase his business without limit, according to the number of customers he can acquire. A purely agricultural country increases in opulence much slower than any other. Poland and Russia, which have few resources but agriculture, are the poorest and most barbarous in Europe. Great Britain and Holland, in which the smallest proportion of the inhabitants are engaged in raising food for the rest, are the wealthiest : and other countries very much in the inverse ratio of the persons engaged in agriculture compared to those engaged in other pursuits. The instances are not many in which persons have made large fortunes by agriculture, but there is scarcely a small country town in which some industrious and energetic individuals have not realised a competence by trading.

Hence, so far as mere increase of wealth goes, manufactures and commerce are immensely more productive than agriculture. Was it agriculture that made Holland the richest state in Europe? Was it agriculture that made Tyre, Sidon, Genoa, Venice, Florence, the Hans Towns, Nuremberg, Augsburg, and multitudes of other great and wealthy cities? For political stability, of course, the union of the three is most desirable. A commercial state may grow wealthy without agriculture ; but no agricultural state can become wealthy without manufactures and commerce. The resources of a purely agricultural state are soon exhausted. Was it agriculture, or was it her commerce and manufactures, which more contributed to make England, a small island with a scanty population, able to contend against all Europe in arms? If Smith had lived through the great revolutionary war he certainly would never have asserted that agriculture is more productive of wealth than manufactures and commerce.

Error of the doctrine that Rate of Profit in all employments of Capital is equal

16. It is sometimes supposed that Profits in all employments are equal. Thus Senior says—'It will be admitted that in the absence of disturbing causes the Rate of Profit in all employments of Capital is equal.' Even if it were admitted that there may be a tendency to equalise actual Profits, the difference of Time in which Profits are made completely destroys all equality in the Rate of Profit. If an active and pushing tradesman manages to effect sales with greater rapidity than his neighbours, he increases the Rate of Profit enormously. In fact, such a Person often begins by *lowering* his price in order to increase the rapidity of the sale of his goods.

But it is an egregious mistake to suppose that Profits are equal in all employments. The larger the Capital employed, the smaller is the Profit which the Capitalist can do with. If a man has a million of Capital he can manage to subsist on a profit of 5 per cent., which would bring him in £50,000 : but if he had a capital of only £100 it is not possible for him to exist and bring up a family on £5 a year.

Increase of Capital reduces Prices and Profits

17. Smith says—'The increase of Stock, which raises Wages, tends to lower [actual] Profit. When the stocks of so many rich merchants are turned into the same trade, their mutual competition naturally tends to lower its profit ; and when there is a like increase of stock in all the different trades carried on in the same society, the same competition must produce the same effects in them all. . . .

'It generally requires a greater stock to carry on any sort of trade in a great town than in a country village. The great stocks employed in every branch of trade, and the number of rich competitors, generally reduce the Rate of Profit in the former below what it is in the latter. But the Wages of Labour are generally higher in a great town than in a country village. In a thriving town the people who have great stocks to employ frequently cannot get the number of workmen they want, and therefore bid against one another, in order to get as many as they can, which raises the Wages of Labour, and lowers the Profits of Stock. In the remote parts of the country there is frequently not stock sufficient to employ all the people, who therefore bid against one another in order to get employment, which lowers the Wages of Labour, and raises the Profits of Stock.'

This account of Smith's is so perfectly true and so obvious to anyone who has practical knowledge of the subject, that it seems impossible that anyone could contest it. It is, however, vehemently denied by Ricardo and his copyists, McCulloch and Mill. But as we have shown that neither of these writers can even give a correct definition of the term Rate of Profit, it will be found that their criticisms are not worth very much.

Ricardo asserts that Profits depend on the quantity of Labour requisite to produce necessaries for the Labourer on that land or with that capital which yields no rent. McCulloch, copying Ricardo, says—'Profits are reduced in an advanced stage of society, because the quantity of produce is *diminished*, and because the Labourers get a larger share of this diminished quantity.

'The theory of Dr. Smith as to the circumstances which determine the Rate of Profit differs widely from the above. He seems to have had no idea of the fundamental principle of the decreasing productiveness of the capital successively applied to the soil, and not imagining that there was any natural cause why the produce obtained by the outlay of equal amounts of capital and labour should ever be diminished, he supposed that Profits were lowered through the *competition* of capitalists: that when capital increased, the undertakers of different businesses became anxious to encroach on each other : and that in order to attain their object they offered their produce at a lower price, and gave higher wages to their workmen.

'But though at first view this theory appears sufficiently plausible, it will not bear the least examination. *It is easy to see that competition cannot occasion a general fall of Profits.* All that competition can do, and all that it ever does, is to reduce the Profits obtained in different businesses and employments to the same common level, to prevent particular individuals realising greater or lesser profits than their neighbours. Further than this competition cannot go. . . .

'Hence it appears that that fall in the Rate of Profit that is invariably observed to take place as society advances is not owing to an increase of Capital ; or to the competition consequent upon that increase, but to an inability to supply Capital, (1) from a decrease in the fertility of the soils to which recourse must be had : or (2) from a rise of Wages : or (3) from an increase of taxation.'

18. Mill follows in the same strain—' The tendency of profits to fall as society advances, which has been brought to notice in the preceding chapter, was early recognised by writers on industry and commerce ; but the laws which govern profits not being then understood, the phenomenon was ascribed to a wrong cause. Adam Smith considered profits to be determined by what he called the competition of capital ; and concluded that when capital increased this competition must likewise increase, and profits must fall.' After quoting from Smith as above, Mill continues—' This passage would lead us to infer that in Adam Smith's opinion the manner in which the competition of capital lowers profits is by lowering price ; that being usually the mode in which an increased investment of capital in any particular trade lowers the profits of that trade. But if this was his meaning, he overlooked the circumstance that the fall of price, which, if confined to one commodity, really does lower the profits of the producer, ceases to have that effect as soon as it extends to all commodities ; because when all things have fallen, nothing has really fallen except nominally ; and even computed in money the expenses of every producer have diminished as much as his returns. Unless, indeed, labour be the one commodity which has not fallen in money price, when all other things have : if so, what has really taken place is a rise of wages : and it is that, and not a fall of prices, which has lowered the profits of capital. There is another thing which has escaped the notice of Adam Smith ; that the supposed universal fall of prices through increased competition of capitals is a thing which cannot take place. Prices are not determined by the competition of the sellers only, but also by that of the buyers ; by demand as well as supply. The demand which affects money prices consists of all the money in the hands of the community destined to be laid out in commodities ; and as long as the proportion of this to the commodities is not diminished there is no fall of general prices. Now, howsoever capital may increase and give rise to an increased production of commodities, a full share of the capital will be drawn to the business of producing or importing money, *and the quantity of money will be augmented in an equal ratio* with the quantity of commodities. For if this were not the case, and if money, therefore, were, as the theory supposes, perpetually acquiring increased purchasing power, those who produced or imported it would obtain constantly increasing profits ; and this could not happen without attracting labour and capital to that occupation from other employments. If a general fall of prices, and an increased value of money were really to occur, it could only be as a consequence of increased cost of production, and from the gradual exhaustion of the mines.

'It is not tenable, therefore, in theory, that the increase of capital produces, or tends to produce, a general decline of money prices. Neither is it true that any general decline of prices as capital increased has manifested itself in fact. The only things observed to fall in price with the progress of society are those in which there have been improvements in production greater than have taken place in the production of the precious metals, as, for example, all spun and woven fabrics. Other things, again, instead of falling, have risen in price, because their cost of production, compared with that of gold and silver, has increased. Among these are all kinds of food, comparison being made with a much earlier period of history. The doctrine, therefore, that competition of capital lowers profits by lowering prices is incorrect in fact as well as unsound in principle.

'But it is not certain that Adam Smith really held that doctrine; for his language on the subject is wavering and unsteady, denoting the absence of a definite and well-digested opinion. Occasionally he seems to think that the mode in which the competition of capital lowers profits is by raising wages. And when speaking of the rate of profit in new colonies he seems on the very verge of grasping the complete theory of the subject, " as the colony increases the profits of stock gradually diminish. When the most fertile and best situated lands have been all occupied less profit can be made by the cultivation of what is inferior both in soil and situation." Had Adam Smith meditated longer on the subject, and systematised his views of it by harmonising with each other the various glimpses which he caught of it from different points, he would have perceived that this last is the true cause of the fall of profits usually consequent upon increase of capital.' Mill also says Chalmers's ideas are 'more decidedly infected with the often-refuted notion that the competition of capital lowers general prices.'

On this subject Smith is undoubtedly in the right and his assailants in the wrong. Anyone who has the slightest knowledge of commerce would laugh at the notion that the competition of capital does not produce a fall of prices and profits. Any trader in the City of London would say that the competition is so strong that everyone is obliged to sell at the lowest price and the smallest profit.

The whole of this extraordinary doctrine is based upon Ricardo's fundamental fallacy that profits depend on the worst land in cultivation, or, as McCulloch says, profits are only reduced by diminishing production, i.e. quantity of produce detained.

To understand the question thoroughly, it will be necessary to refer to Ricardo's Theory of Rent, which is explained in the next chapter. Ricardo asserts that it is bringing inferior land into cultivation, and expending more labour on its production, which raises the price of corn, whereas, as Ricardo has himself elsewhere said, it is precisely the reverse, as we have shown, and that it is the increase of the price of corn which admits more value being employed in bringing inferior land into cultivation.

It is not *because* inferior land is brought into cultivation that profits are reduced : but manifestly precisely the reverse. It is only *when* general profits *have been* reduced that inferior lands are brought into cultivation ; or because the price of corn has risen so much that it will afford usual profits to bring it into cultivation.

Suppose, for example, that usual profits were 20 per cent. : and suppose that there was land which might be reclaimed and yield a profit of 5 per cent. on the average price of corn at any time.

Then, if in consequence of the increased demand for corn the price rose so high that the inferior land would yield a profit of 20 per cent., it would be cultivated.

Or suppose that the increased competition of capital reduces general average profits to 5 per cent., then the inferior land would be cultivated because it would yield usual profits.

No one would invest their money to produce 5 per cent. so long as they could invest it so as to produce 20 per cent. ; hence so long as capital produces higher profits no one would resort to land which would only yield 5 per cent. So if the usual rate of interest on money were 10 per cent. per annum, no one would borrow money at 10 per cent. to cultivate lands which would only yield a profit of 5 per cent.

But in the natural progress of society population and the demand for corn would raise its price, and so increase the profit of cultivating inferior land : and at the same time the increase of capital would reduce the usual rate of profit : so the profits to be made by cultivating inferior lands would *increase*, and general average profits would *decrease*, until they became equal : and then inferior lands would be cultivated because they would yield usual profits.

Hence the diminution of the general Rate of Profit greatly increases the value of all lands ; and a general rise of Profits and Interest would throw much land out of cultivation, or prevent a great quantity of land from being brought into cultivation; and greatly lower the value of all lands, as we shall show more fully in the next section.

Thus in this case, as in many others, Ricardo and his followers have simply inverted cause and effect. If Profit and Interest are very high, inferior lands are not cultivated, because it would not pay to do so: when Profits and Interest are low, inferior lands are cultivated, because it pays to do so. And manifestly it is not the reclaiming inferior lands which give a diminishing production that reduces profit; but the reduction of average general profits which enables inferior lands, which only yield a diminished production, to be cultivated.

Even supposing that it were true that bringing inferior lands into cultivation gave a diminished produce and profit, it is perfectly manifest that persons who had capital to lend would not advance it at a lower rate of profit for the purpose of reclaiming the land when they could get a higher rate from commerce. They would be actuated by no sentimental considerations in such matters. They will get the best profit they can. And the owners of the inferior land have no resource but to wait till the price of corn has risen high enough to make it profitable to improve them; or some means have been found of supplying cheap Capital.

19. It was precisely this circumstance that gave rise to the numerous schemes for founding banks and creating paper money which were so rife at the close of the 17th century. When men grew weary of burning and slaughtering each other for theological and political differences, they turned their energies to agriculture and commerce; and they rightly perceived that the very first requisite for the improvement of the land was cheap money, or capital. At that time the usual rate of interest for metallic money was 10 per cent. per annum. Of all species of industry, the profits from agriculture are the most moderate: and if agriculture would only give perhaps a profit of 6 per cent., it would have been manifestly impossible to borrow money at 10 per cent., which the additional demand would probably have raised still higher. Hence the numerous projects for founding banks for the express purpose of multiplying paper currency and reducing the rate of interest to 3 per cent. This was also the origin of the schemes for creating Paper Money on the basis of the land; of which John Law's was the most celebrated, and which he had the opportunity of carrying out on a great scale in France, and ended in the catastrophe of the Mississippi scheme, as is described in a future chapter. All these schemes sprang out of a real necessity of the times; and, although they were founded on a false theory, we must carefully refrain from considering them as mere fraudulent bubbles, as is so commonly done. The great system of banking in Scotland, whose mechanism and effects we have described in a former chapter, carries out their intention as far as it can be done with safety.

It is also a matter of the commonest observation that a long continued very low rate of interest is a very usual precursor of an outburst of speculative mania. High profits in particular businesses attract quantities of capital into these businesses; and, of course, often lead to great overtrading and catastrophes. But when the Rate of Interest remains for a long time at 1 or 2 per cent., persons' incomes are reduced so much that they become willing to adventure in enterprises to pay them a better profit. Hence, as is so often the case in Economics, the same effects are produced by opposite causes. Very high profits and very low profits are each the cause of a speculative mania. The most healthy condition is a medium rate of 4 or 5 per cent. When the rate is below that, every time it is lowered multitudes of new enterprises start into existence. At every raising of the rate, multitudes of new schemes are strangled in the birth. Now, it is not these new enterprises which lower the Rate of Profit; but it is the low Rate of Profit which is the greatest stimulant of new enterprises.

20. It is now manifest that those who have assailed Smith's doctrine proceed upon the plain fallacy of inverting cause and effect. But Mill's assertions are also self-contradictory, as is so often the case.

Mill says truly that prices are determined, not by the competition of the sellers only, but also by that of the buyers, by demand as well as by supply, which is most true. He says truly that prices are affected by the money in the hands of the

CH. VIII.   *Effects of Increase of Capital*   53

community to be laid out in commodities; and also that so long as the proportion of money to commodities remains the same, prices will not vary. Then he asserts that if commodities increase, the quantity of money imported, or produced, to buy commodities will increase in exactly an equal ratio, and therefore that no change in price *can* take place.

No doubt if this were true in fact, the consequence he states would follow. But notoriously it is not true in fact: and, as usual, he immediately proceeds to contradict himself. For he asserts that an increase of capital cannot produce a fall in prices, because if it did so money would be imported in an equal ratio to reap the profits to be made by buying these commodities very cheap; and then he says that this result only takes place in those commodities in which the improvements in production have taken place greater than in the production of the precious metals—such as spun and woven fabrics.

Now, as everyone knows, and he himself admits what cannot be denied, that an immense diminution in the price of these commodities *has* taken place, owing to the enormously increased quantity produced, what becomes of his previous doctrine that such a fall *cannot* occur, because money will always be imported to buy them in an *equal* ratio; and therefore their price *cannot* change?

Now it is an indisputable fact that an enormous mass of commodities have increased a great deal faster than money, and that their prices have immensely diminished in consequence of this increase: Mill, however, says that it is an often-refuted notion that the competition of capital lowers general prices.

But it unquestionably does so in all commodities which increase faster than money.

Now it is a mere accident that all commodities are not increased faster than money. All manufactured commodities are so: and if agricultural products have not hitherto been so, it is probably partly owing to the fact that they cannot be multiplied in such enormous quantities as manufactures, because, being far more bulky in proportion to their value, their cost of production—*i.e.* the cost of placing them in the market when they are offered for sale—cannot be reduced in the same proportion; and partly because the same skill and science have never hitherto been applied to increase the products of the earth as has been done in manufactures.

There is not the smallest doubt that by the application of skill and science the products of the soil could be increased to several times their present amount, and far beyond what is often supposed.

To give only one instance. Near Edinburgh there were some tracts of the sea-shore which were worth absolutely nothing. By the skilful application of the liquid sewage of the city these fields, which were originally nothing but pure sea sand, now yield *six* crops of hay in the year, and give a rent of £36 or £40 an acre. If this has been done at Edinburgh, why could it not be done in numerous other places?

When Mill says that the competition of Capital does not lower Profits by lowering prices, he seems to forget that the commodities produced are themselves Capital, as well as the money originally employed in producing them. The money was Capital because it was used for the purpose of profit. When the commodities were produced they were also equally capital, because they were intended to be exchanged away for profit.

If, then, a certain expenditure of money-capital produces (by means of skill and machinery) an enormously increased quantity of goods-capital, the immensely increased quantity of goods-capital can only be sold off by a very great reduction of price. Consequently the price and profits of each particular parcel are immensely reduced : but the profits upon the whole quantity are enormously increased ; and, of course, Mill contradicts himself in the very same chapter—'What would really be not merely difficult but impossible, would be to employ this Capital *without submitting to a rapid reduction of the Rate of Profit*'!!

Section II

Upon **Interest** *and* **Discount**

21. We have now to consider the Profits made in the other great branch of Commerce: the commerce in **Debts**.

We have already pointed out in the Chapter on Credit the ambiguity of the words, '**Loan**,' '**Lend**,' and '**Borrow**'; and that every Loan of Money is in reality a Sale, or an Exchange, in which the Property in the Money is ceded to the 'borrower': and that what the 'Lender' receives in Exchange for the Money is the Right to demand back an equal sum at a future time, with the agreed upon Profit.

This Right is the Property which is termed a **Credit** or a **Debt**; and it is a vendible Commodity, and may be sold, or exchanged, any number of times, like any material Chattel, until it is paid off and extinguished; and then it ceases to exist.

The Money is the Price of the Right of Action, or the Credit, or Debt; and the Right of Action is the Price of the Money.

All Commodities which are sold in the market are divided into certain Units for the convenience of sale. Coals are sold by the ton: wheat by the quarter: cloth by the yard: tea and sugar by the pound.

The Commodity termed Debt is also in a similar way divided into Units for the convenience of sale.

The **Unit** *of* **Debt** *is the* **Right** *to* **Demand** £100 *to be paid* **One Year hence.**

And all Profits are estimated with reference to this Unit.

22. The Money given to buy this Unit of Debt being termed the Price of the Debt, just as the Price of any material Chattel, the *Less* the Money given to buy the Debt, the *Greater* is the

Value of Money : and the *Greater* the sum given to buy the Debt, the *Less* is the Value of Money.

In the Commerce of Debts, however, it is usual to estimate the Value of Money in a somewhat different way.

In a Commercial Loan of Money the Profit may be made in two ways :—

1. The whole sum may be advanced, and the borrower agrees to repay the Principal sum, together with the agreed upon Profit, at the end of the agreed upon period : the Profit is then termed **Interest**.

2. The agreed upon Profit may be retained at the time of the advance and subtracted from the sum advanced : and then the entire Principal sum is repaid at the end of the period : in this case the Profit is termed **Discount**.

Thus if a person lends £100 for a year at 5 per cent. Interest, he gives the £100 to the borrower, and in exchange for it he receives the Right to demand £105 at the end of the year.

If he lends £100 at 5 per cent. Discount, the Profit is retained at the time of the advance : and the lender receives the Right to demand £100 at the end of the year.

As we shall show a little further on, there are two ways of making Profits by Discount.

On the **Prejudice** *against* **Interest** *or* **Usury**

23. At the present time it is not necessary to say very much respecting the extraordinary prejudice which prevailed for so many ages against Interest, or Usury on Money : a prejudice which has only died out very recently in this country : and still prevails in many foreign countries where Usury Laws still exist.

We may shortly explain, however, how the prejudice arose. If one plants corn in the ground, the corn increases in actual visible quantity, which is palpable to the senses : or if one has flocks or herds, they multiply and increase of themselves in the ordinary course of nature.

But if Money were sown in the ground it would not increase : nor are marriages celebrated between sovereigns giving rise to half-sovereigns. Consequently the idea took possession of men's minds that Money is in its own nature barren, and incapable of increase : and that it is a crime against nature to take Interest or Profit for the use of Money.

It was quite overlooked that Capital may increase by **Exchange**, as we have shown in a former chapter, as well as by increase of actual quantity.

The greatest minds therefore the world ever saw were enthralled with the extraordinary delusion that it was a great crime to take Interest for the use of Money. Aristotle considered the bounty of nature as the only true source of wealth, and had a strong aversion against trading. He observes that there are two uses of everything : its actual use, and exchange. The one he considers natural, and the other against nature. A shoemaker would, however, probably consider that the exchange of a shoe is quite as natural an operation as using it. Aristotle, however, looked with a very doubtful and jealous eye on all exchanges. And money being for the very purpose of facilitating exchanges was in its nature of a dubious origin : and when that purpose which is already dubious was changed into lending it at usury, the mischief was doubly aggravated ; and he pronounces the last mode of using it to be utterly detestable and abominable.

The Hebrew legislator and prophets strongly denounced Usury : but it is evident that they did not refer to interest on money advanced in the way of trade when its very purpose was to make profits : but to charitable loans to persons in necessitous circumstances.

Nevertheless, the Mosaic interdict of usury was adopted and confirmed in its broadest and most unqualified terms by the rulers of the Christian church. Money-lenders, never a very popular class anywhere, were laid under the Divine curse : the consequence of which was that in the sixth century the Jews had become the great money-lenders of Christendom. As the Jews had no hopes for the future, another sin, more or less, could not influence their destiny. While, therefore, usury was strictly forbidden to Christians, the Jews were not molested : and from that era we may date the strong bias of the children of Israel to this species of trading : which was further strengthened and aggravated by the treatment they subsequently received in every country in Europe.

When it was further discovered that the prince of the pagan philosophers concurred with the Divine legislator in condemning interest on the loan of money, it became a settled dogma, just as certain as the stability of the earth, that any Christian who lent out money at interest cut off from himself all hope of salvation. Usury was one of the deadly sins charged against the unfortunate Albigenses. Dante places the people of Cahors, a famous banking centre, as companions to those of the cities of the plain in the *Inferno*.

The irresistible temptation of Profit, however, induced many Christians to prefer seizing a present gain at the risk of a doubtful penalty. The active spirit of commerce demanded the use of Capital: and the instinctive sense of mankind rejected the absurdity that they who furnished the means and shared the risk of loss should not also share in the Profits: and numerous subterfuges were devised, so that while the name of usury was avoided, the thing might be done.

Nowhere were the inconvenience and absurdity of the wicked nature of interest more strongly felt than at the fountain of infallibility itself, the Papal Court: and nowhere was more ingenuity shown to circumvent its own dogmas. A Capital was collected for the purpose of lending to the poor for a certain time on pledges without interest. To forward these objects the Popes dispensed to those who contributed to them indulgences with liberal prodigality. Burdensome vows were allowed to be commuted into donations to lending-houses. A rich donation effaced the stain on the birth of wealthy libertines. But as these establishments required the services of a staff of officials, and as there could be no profits to pay them a salary, the Popes endeavoured to induce their servants to forego mundane necessaries and comforts in consideration of an unlimited supply of metatemporal blessings.

Such an organisation as this, however, could be of no long endurance. If it was a charitable thing to advance money for nothing to persons after they had become poor, it was far more prudent and sensible to lend them money at a moderate interest to help them to trade, and to prevent them from becoming poor. Rich persons found that Papal indulgences were but a poor return for hard cash: and as in the course of business the institution incurred some loss, they were obliged to borrow money at interest to pay their expenses. The Popes therefore determined to allow the lending-houses to receive interest for so much of their capital as was necessary to defray their expenses. When this breach was made, the next step was not long following. In order to attract a sufficient amount of Capital, those who advanced money were allowed to receive a moderate interest for its use, which was not entered on the balance sheet as 'Interest'—that would have been damnable—but was concealed under the euphemism of 'establishment charges.' The Papal bull allowed it to be given *pro indemnitate*.

However cunningly and speciously this 'artful dodge' was devised to do the thing they dare not name, the lynx-eyed divines soon saw through the trick, and a violent ferment immediately arose: and it was fiercely debated whether it was lawful to do evil—i.e. take interest—in order that good might come. When the tempest was at its height it was quelled by a folly of equal magnitude with itself. The Pope issued a bull declaring these holy mountains of piety—*sacri monti di pietà*—to be legal, and damning all who dared to doubt it. All scruples on the subject being silenced in so satisfactory a manner, other cities hastened to follow the example and establish lending-houses, and they became common throughout Italy in the fifteenth century. Notwithstanding, however, the Papal sanction they had received, many writers and preachers considered them to be criminal: and the dispute was revived with considerable warmth in the sixteenth century, until it was set at rest by Leo X., who, in the tenth sitting of the Council of the Lateran, issued a special bull declaring lending-houses to be legal and useful, and that all who dared to preach, dispute, or write against them should be excommunicated. He also justified them on the broad principle, which established the propriety of interest, that those who received the benefit should share the burden: *qui commodum sentit, onus quoque sentire debet.*

Notwithstanding the thunders of the Vatican, and the tempests which raged in the theological atmosphere regarding the sinful nature of interest, the practice flourished equally among the Christians as the Jews. The spiritual excommunications of the Church and the temporal punishments of princes were equally ineffectual to prevent men from following their natural instincts. Edward the Confessor had enacted that anyone convicted of usury should be stripped of all his possessions and be declared an outlaw, as he had heard the maxim at the French Court that usury is the root of every crime. Every country in Europe enacted similar penalties : and the frequency of the denunciation proves the extension of the practice. Notwithstanding all these terrible penalties the contest was vain, and several States were obliged to limit what they could not prevent. James I. of Arragon, in 1228, limited interest to 20 per cent. In the same year, at Verona, it was limited to 12½ : and at Modena, in 1270, to 20 per cent. An ordinance of Philip le Bel, in 1311, allows 20 per cent. after the first year of the loan. In 1336 Florence borrowed money to carry on the war against Mastino della Scala, and paid 15 per cent. Genoa paid 7 to 10 per cent. on its public debts. The Florentines opened money-lending houses in numerous places : their usual rate was 20 per cent. : and not unfrequently 30 or 40. At the present day the usual charge of the second class bill-brokers for discounting a tradesman's bill is a shilling in the pound for three months. This is discount at 20 per cent. : or interest at 25 per cent.

Smith says that in Bengal money is frequently lent at 40, 50, or 60 per cent., and the succeeding crop is mortgaged for the payment. The most ordinary banking charges at the present day are 12 per cent., and often higher : this is owing to the very undeveloped state of banking in that country: and this shows what a stimulus it would give to the industry and wealth of India to organise an extended and solid system of banking there.

24. Calvin was the first great man to demonstrate the fallacy of the popular notions of the wickedness of usury. Upon the question being formally submitted to his judgment, he said that it was nowhere forbidden in Scripture. The sense of the precept of Christ had been perverted. The law of Moses was political, and not to be stretched beyond what men and equity would bear. In various places the Hebrew word meant fraud in general, and could not be applied to usury. He said that the

Jewish laws and polity were adapted to the Jews only: and that modern society was totally different from that of the Jews. He treats the reasons of St. Ambrose and Chrysostom as of very slight weight, and then says—

'Money does not beget money! What does the sea? What does a house for the letting of which I receive a rent? Does money truly grow from the roof and walls? But the land also produces: and something is brought from the sea which afterwards produces [or draws forth] money: and the convenience of a house may be bought or exchanged for money. If, therefore, more profit can be made by trading than from the produce of any farm, is he who has let some barren farm to an agriculturist to be allowed to receive rent and profit, and another man not to be allowed to receive profit from money? And if anyone buys a farm with money, does not that money generate money every year? You would allow that the profit of the merchant comes from his diligence and industry. Who doubts that unemployed money is useless? Or that he who asks a loan from me does not intend to keep it idle when he has got it? Now, in truth, that profit does not arise from the money, but from the produce. I therefore conclude that we are not to judge of usury by any particular passage of Scripture, but only by the law of equity. This will be clearer by an example. Let us suppose some wealthy man with large possessions in farms and rents, but not much money. Suppose another man not so rich, nor of such large possessions as the first, but yet having more ready money. The latter being about to buy a farm with his own money, is asked for a loan by the wealthier man. He who makes a loan may stipulate for a rent for his money, and that the farm shall be mortgaged to him until the principal is repaid: but until it is repaid he will be content with the profit or usury. Why, then, shall the first contract without a mortgage, but only for the profit of the money, be condemned, when the much harsher one of the annual rent, with a mortgage of his farm, is approved? And what else is it than to treat God like a child when we judge of things by mere words, and not from the nature of the thing itself? as if virtue and crime could be perceived from the form of the words?'

No one can but admire the daring good sense of this argument in the mouth of a divine in defence of what was then considered one of the worst crimes men could be guilty of, and be amazed that such arguments made scarcely any impression, even in Protestant England, for upwards of 200 years.

25. Calvin put the whole subject on its true and common-sense footing. Money, it is true, does not of itself bear increase, but if it is employed in buying those things which do bear increase or profit, of course he who lends the money is entitled to a share of the increase. If a person employs his own money in agriculture or commerce he is entitled to any profit he can make by its use: and if, having no money of his own, he borrows it from someone else, what possible crime can it be to give that person a share of the Profits?

26. From the examples taken from so many countries, it would appear that about 20 per cent. is the fair average profit which must be paid for transactions in money which are perfectly safe.

These rates, however, only held where considerable sums were borrowed, and in *le haut commerce*. When sums are advanced to costermongers and persons who carry on the commerce of the streets, the rates are enormously higher. At Athens these persons paid $1\frac{1}{2}$ obolus a day for a drachma, i.e. 25 per cent. per day : or at the rate of 9,125 per cent. per annum.

Gerard Malynes says that a similar trade in London was carried on with money borrowed at the rate of 1*d.* per shilling per week, which is about 433 per cent. per annum.

Boisguillebert says that the small provision dealers of Paris thrive on money borrowed at the rate of 5 sous per week the crown ; or more than 400 per cent. per annum, because they sold perhaps 5 crowns' worth of merchandise per day, on which they gained one-half, or 50 per cent., which was at the rate of about 18,250 per cent. per annum : and if they could perform this operation five or six times a week, they could well afford to pay such interest to those who lent them the money.

Turgot cites the case of the same class of people in his day, who carried on their trade with money borrowed at 173 per cent. per annum, to show the absurdity of Usury Laws.

The most remarkable instance, however, is that cited by M. Gustave de Puynode from a speech of a member of the last Legislative Assembly of France. He said—'Every morning the small provision dealers received a 5-franc piece to buy the objects, which they resold with a profit of 3 or 4 francs. In the evening they repay the 5-franc piece and give 25 centimes in addition. They make no complaint of interest, which is yet at the rate of 1,800 per cent.' Nor had they any reason to do so, for by borrowing this 5-franc piece they made 3 francs profit, out of which they only paid ¼-franc for interest. If, therefore, the rate of interest was 1,800 per cent. per annum, the rate of profit, assuming the gain to be 3 francs a day, was at the rate of 21,600 per cent. per annum. And interest which is only one-twelfth part of the profit is not unreasonable. And yet by the law of France it is still punishable by law to take more than 6 per cent. per annum.

The progress of just legislation on this subject must always be remarkable as an instance of the extraordinary *vis inertiæ* of established law in this country where no great popular passion is brought to bear on it, even where no great interests are enlisted in defending it, and where abstract justice and good sense are not made a popular cry. In 1691 Locke published his 'Considerations of the Consequences of Lowering the Interest of Money,' in which he demonstrated the utter futility of Usury Laws. Smith showed less than his usual judgment in advocating their retention. But his doctrine called forth Bentham's 'Defence of Usury,' as splendid an example of an unanswerable argument as any in existence. It is said that Smith admitted that his opinions were mistaken: but they remained uncancelled in his work. The most eminent writers had pointed out, not only their utter futility to effect their purpose, but their highly mischievous effect in aggravating the very evil they were intended to prevent. The experience of several commercial crises had demonstrated that in consequence of the law attempting to prevent people paying more than 5 per cent. for the use of money, they often had to pay 50, 60, and 70 per cent. by the methods they were forced to adopt. In 1819 they were investigated by a Parliamentary Committee and condemned. Yet it was only in 1833 that the first breach was made in them by exempting bills which had not more than three months to run from their operation : and by temporary extensions and prolongations most other contracts were taken out of their operation : but it was not until 1854 that they were finally swept away from the Statute-book. Thus from their total demolition in argument till their total demolition in fact a space of not less than 161 years elapsed. Such was the period it required, even in this commercial country, to abolish laws equal in absurdity to those of witchcraft. The last trial for witchcraft in Great Britain took place in 1736 : the last case of Usury in our law books was in 1856.

Circumstances which determine the Rate of Interest

27. We have now to consider the circumstances which determine the Rate of Interest. As Interest is always a part of the Profit realised, it is clear that the first element which will determine its Rate is the expected Rate of Profit. The next is the proportion between the Capital and the Demand for it. If Capital be scarce, and those who want to borrow it numerous, they of course will give a greater proportion of the Profits to the Capitalist. But if the Capital be abundant and those who want to borrow it fewer, the Capitalist will have to be contented with a smaller share of the Profits, and Interest will be low.

These circumstances govern the Rate of Interest in ordinary times : but in times of great commercial difficulty, both general and particular sums are paid for the use of money very much higher than the usual rates. These, however, are exceptional cases : and are paid not out of the legitimate profits of business, but in some great exigency ; as for the use of sums for a short time to stave off the consequences which may ensue to a trader for not being able to meet his engagements. It is evident that Interest cannot for any length of time exceed Profits, any more than Cost of Production can continue to exceed Value. If it does so, the Supply of the commodities will be limited until the Value rises : so if Interest exceeds Profits production will be limited until the Profits are raised. Hence the most powerful method of curbing over-production is to raise the Rate of Discount so as to annihilate Profits.

28. In considering the Rate of Interest we have not admitted any idea of the danger of the security: the investment has been supposed perfectly safe: and it is only the sum paid for the use of money under a full sense of the security of the investment that should be strictly termed interest. But most investments are subject to more or less risk: and the sum received under the denomination of Interest or Discount must include two elements; one the actual hire of the money: and the other as a premium of insurance on the risk of loss: and just as the risk is greater the premium must be higher. It has already been seen in a preceding chapter that the Rent or Hire of an article comprises two elements; one the Interest on the Capital: the other to replace the deterioration or wear and tear of the article itself. Bad debts and losses in trade may be considered as the deterioration or wear and tear of Capital. And the sum paid for the use of money in particular employments must in a similar way include one element for the simple Profits, and the other sufficient to cover the usual risks and losses of that mode of investment. Hence the Rate of Interest or Discount will always rise in proportion to the risk of the security, and, therefore, there must always be in the same country, and at the same time, a different market Rate of Interest for every investment of a different degree of security: just as there is a different Rate of Rent or Hire for articles of a different degree of perishability: or different Rates of Insurance for buildings of different degrees of danger from fire. But these different rates will rise and fall together.

29. We may look at the question in another light. Lending out money at interest may be regarded as the purchase of an annuity, to last for a longer or a shorter period, according to the agreement of the parties. Hence, in purchasing such an annuity, the price of it has to be considered just in the same way as the price of anything else. Now, it is quite evident that the value of the annuity must, in a great measure, depend upon its certainty of being paid, or upon its security; and if there be one species of security more certain than another, it is quite clear that the former is a service of greater intensity than the latter, and must be paid for accordingly. Thus, we may say that a person who offers to take money at interest wants to sell an annuity to the lender of the money; and just in proportion as the security he can offer is good, so will he get a higher price for it; so that the interest of money paid by the borrower will be just in proportion to the risk run. Thus, money may be lent to merchants, to landowners, or to government. Now, merchants are always subject to unforeseen disasters, not only from their own speculations, which may turn out unfortunate, but they are usually so involved with others that they are always liable to suffer from the faults or misfortunes of others; consequently there is always some risk in lending them money. The owner of land is exempt from many of the risks a merchant is exposed to; he is not generally involved with others in his business, but his prosperity is based upon the land itself, and, as long as that is judiciously managed, it gives forth a sure increase, unless under the effects of some temporary dispensation of Providence. Consequently the security for the payment of an annuity based upon the increase of the earth is far greater than one which is liable to the casualties of commerce. A considerably higher price, therefore, will generally be given for an annuity whose security depends upon land than upon commerce; that is, a landowner can usually borrow on cheaper terms than a trader. The Government of this country, again, is considered to be more secure than either land or commerce; consequently, by the same rule, an annuity purchased from the Government should usually cost more than either of the two former ones. And this exactly corresponds with the fact; the interest obtained by investing money in the funds is usually lower than what is obtained either from mortgage on land or on mercantile security.

We may, therefore, consider that the price paid for the use of the money always includes these two elements, one of which is the fair earnings of the money itself, and the other is the insurance to cover the risk of the loan to the lender. Each of these varies at different times, according to the particular person to whom the money is lent, and the total effect will vary accordingly, and it is sometimes not easy to discriminate the effects due to each separate cause.

These, then, are the circumstances which determine the

relative market rates of interest on different species of security in any country at the same time. If the rates of interest be observed at any particular time, the difference arises solely from the difference in the estimated safety of the species of security. And it will also be found that if the rates in the same species of security vary, it is because there is more danger than usual in the particular security offered by an individual. Thus, in the species of security offered by Governments, which are usually called funds, the price of an annuity of £3 a year from the English Government is seldom much under £100; while no one would give more than £30 or £35 for a similar one from the dishonest and bankrupt Government of Spain. That is, the English Government can borrow money at little more than three per cent., while the Spanish Government can scarcely do so at nine. The same may be said in a greater or less degree of every one of the European Governments, and the prices of annuities to be paid by them vary exactly in proportion to the supposed honesty or capacity of each to fulfil its agreements. It is universally true that the value of the different kinds of annuities at the same time, and in the same market, will vary exactly in proportion to the estimated security of each. But this is by no means the case if the observation be made at different times, because the value of money itself changes from time to time, like that of any other commodity, and accordingly the price paid for its use will vary according to that value, so that the interest received from the most secure species of investment at one time may exceed that usually paid for the least secure species at another time, and this difference in value will be caused by an alteration in the relation of supply and demand, in accordance with the general principles that govern price. Thus, when commerce is stagnant, or there is a superabundance of money that cannot find employment, the competition for lending it increases, and the power of the borrower increases over each lender. On the other hand, when commerce is active there are more persons who wish to borrow, and, of course, the price will rise in proportion to the increase in the demand, and this will cause a rise in the market rate of all securities.

When this general change takes place in the market rate of interest, it by no means implies that the securities are more dangerous at one period than another, but only that money itself has risen in value, and the different species of securities will preserve the same relative differences as before.

A fall in the rate of interest is so far from proving the safety of the security that it will frequently be found to be worst, when interest has been much depressed below the usual rate. Because when that happens all sorts of wild schemes and speculations are set afloat, partly on account of the undue facility of obtaining capital, and partly because when Interest is so much depressed there are so many persons who live upon the interest of their money who become distressed by the diminution of their incomes that they are tempted to embark in all sorts of hazardous schemes which promise a better profit. All the great commercial crises of late years have been preceded by a continued and unusual depression in the Rate of Interest. On the other hand, when it rises much higher than usual, it puts a stop to a great deal of legitimate business, and so is injurious to the country. It is clearly then most for the public advantage that the interest of money should neither be so low as to tempt persons to embark in dangerous speculations, nor so high as to impede real and useful industry.

On the Effects of an Increase of Money on Prices and Interest

30. The term '**Value of Money**' has, as we have seen, two meanings in commerce, as it is applied to the purchase of Commodities or Debts. Changes in the Value of Money are produced by changes in the Supply and Demand of Money as well as by changes in the Supply and Demand of Commodities and of Credits or Debts. It might appear at first sight that a great increase in the quantity of Money which leads to a Diminution in its Value with respect to one of these Quantities would also necessarily lead to a Diminution in its Value with respect to the other. That is, that if Money fell to half its Value with respect to Commodities, it must also necessarily fall to half its Value with respect to Debts : i.e. the Rate of Interest should be reduced one-half.

Accordingly Smith says that several eminent writers have

maintained that the increase of the quantity of gold and silver in consequence of the discovery of the South American mines was the real cause of the lowering of the rate of interest through the greater part of Europe. Those metals, they say, having become of less value (i.e. of less purchasing power with respect to commodities) themselves, the use of any particular portion of them became of less value too, and consequently the price which should be paid for it. He says—'The following very short and plain argument, however, may serve to explain more distinctly the fallacy which seems to have misled those gentlemen. Before the discovery of the Spanish West Indies, ten per cent. seems to have been the common rate of interest through the greater part of Europe. It has since that time in different countries sunk to six, five, four, and three per cent. Let us suppose that in every particular country the value of silver has sunk precisely in the same proportion, and that in those countries, for example, where interest has been reduced from ten to five per cent. the same quantity of silver can now purchase just half the quantity of goods which it could have purchased before. This supposition will not, I believe, be found anywhere agreeable to the truth, but it is the most favourable to the opinion which we are going to examine, and even upon this supposition it is utterly impossible that the lowering of the value of silver could have the smallest tendency to lower the rate of interest. If a hundred pounds are in those countries now of no more value than fifty pounds were then, ten pounds must now be of no more value than five pounds were then. Whatever were the causes which lowered the value of the capital, the same must necessarily have lowered that of the interest, and exactly in the same proportion. The proportion between the value of the capital and that of the interest must have remained the same though the rate had never been altered. By altering the rate, on the contrary, the proportion between those two values is necessarily altered. If a hundred pounds are worth now no more than fifty were then, five pounds can be worth no more then two pounds ten shillings were then. By reducing the rate of interest, therefore, from ten to five per cent. we give for the use of a capital which is supposed to be equal to one-half of its former value, an interest which is equal to one-fourth only of the value of the former interest.' The fact is simply this, that the interest comprehends two elements, one part of the profits paid for the use of the money, the other as insurance for the risk of loss. Now, no diminution in the value of money with respect to commodities can make the slightest difference in respect to these two elements. Whatever the quantity of goods be, more or less, that £100 will purchase, the part of the profits paid for the use of the money will still be the proportion of the £100. Nor can any alteration in the value of money have the slightest effect in influencing the risk of the transaction. Whether the usual price of goods be £100 or £50, it can make no difference in the proportion of the profits agreed to be paid for the use of £100, nor in the risk, consequently it can have no influence whatever on the rate of interest. The evident proof of this is, that in America, where, of course, money has diminished in value with respect to commodities just as in the rest of the world, 10 per cent. is quite a common rate of discount for the best mercantile paper. In California, where bullion was almost a drug, during the six years ending 1856, interest varied from 1½ to 2 and 3 per cent. per month, or from 18 to 24 and 36 per cent. per annum.

31. Hume also observes the same thing—' Nothing is esteemed a more certain sign of the flourishing condition of any nation than the lowness of interest: and with reason, though I believe the cause is somewhat different from what is commonly apprehended. Lowness of interest is commonly ascribed to plenty of money. But money, however plenty, has no other effect, *if fixed*, than to raise the price of labour. Silver is more common than gold, and therefore you receive a greater quantity of it for the same commodities. But do you pay less interest for it? Interest in Batavia and Jamaica is at 10 *per cent.*, in Portugal at 6, though these places, as we may learn from the prices of everything, abound more in gold and silver than either London or Amsterdam.

' Were all the gold in England annihilated at once, and one and twenty shillings substituted in the place of every guinea, would money be more plentiful, or interest lower ? No surely : we should only use silver instead of gold. Were gold rendered as common as silver, and silver as common as copper, would money be more plentiful, or interest lower? We may assuredly give the same answer. Our shillings would then be yellow, and our halfpence white : and we should have no guineas. No other difference would ever be observed ; no alteration in commerce, manufactures, navigation, or interest; unless we imagine that the colour of the metal is of any consequence.

'Now, what is so visible in these greater variations of scarcity or abundance in the precious metals must hold in all inferior changes. If the multiplying of gold and silver fifteen times makes no difference, much less can the doubling or tripling them. All augmentation has no other effect than to heighten the price of labour and commodities : and even this variation is little more than that of a name. In the progress towards these changes, the augmentation may have some influence by exciting industry, but after the prices are settled, suitably to the new abundance of gold and silver, it has no manner of influence.

'An effect always holds proportion with its cause. Prices have risen near four times since the discovery of the Indies : and it is probable gold and silver have multiplied much more. *But interest has not fallen much above half.* The rate of interest therefore (!) is not derived from the quantity of the precious metals.

'Money having chiefly a fictitious value, the greater or less plenty of it is of no consequence, if we consider a nation within itself : and the quantity of specie, when once fixed, though ever so large, has no other effect than to oblige every one to tell out a greater number of those shining bits of metal for clothes, furniture, or equipage, without increasing any one convenience of life. If a man borrow money to build a house, he then carries home a greater load : because the stone, timber, lead, glass, &c., with the labour of the masons and carpenters, are represented by a greater quantity of gold and silver. But as these metals are considered chiefly as representations, there can no alteration arise from their bulk or quantity, their weight or colour, either upon their real value or their interest. The same interest, in all cases, bears the same proportion of the sum. And if you lent me so much labour and so many commodities, by receiving five *per cent.* you always receive proportional labour and commodities, however represented, whether by yellow or white coin, whether by a pound or an ounce. It is in vain, therefore, to look for the cause of the fall or rise of interest in the greater or less quantity of gold and silver which is fixed in any nation.

'High interest arises from *three* circumstances: a great demand for borrowing; little riches to supply that demand; and great profits arising from commerce: and the circumstances are a clear proof of the small advance of commerce and industry, not of the scarcity of gold and silver. Low interest, on the other hand, proceeds from the *three* opposite circumstances: a small demand for borrowing; great riches to supply that demand; and small profits arising from commerce: and these circumstances are all connected together, and proceed from the increase of industry and commerce, not of gold and silver.'

We see in the above extract that Hume is not consistent with himself. He first asserts that an increase of the quantity of money can have no effect on the rate of interest, and he then admits that the rate of interest had fallen one-half since the discoveries in America: and afterwards he expressly admits that the abundance of riches to supply the demand for borrowing lowers the rate of interest.

32. As, then, it is unquestionably certain that a diminution in the value of money, both with respect to Debts and Commodities, may be caused by an increase of money, it becomes a very important and a rather subtle question, to determine under what circumstances either or both of these results is produced.

It is evident that as an increase in the quantity of money is capable of acting on its Value, both with regard to Debts and Commodities, its first effects will be manifested in respect of that on which it first acts. Now, under the artificial system of the Currency produced by modern banking, the supplies of gold invariably find their way into banks in the first instance. And the business of banking, as we have seen, consists in buying Debts in a peculiar way. Now, the banks having an unusual quantity of money lodged with them, are of course eager to employ it profitably, and in order to do this they lower the Rate of Discount, i.e. they give a higher price for Debts. Now, though a bill of exchange in its proper sense always represents a past operation, yet they are brought for sale to bankers chiefly for the sake of funds to employ in a future operation. Now, leaving out of the question any part of the Rate of Discount which may be due to the risk, a high Rate of Discount is a proof and a sign of the activity of enterprise. And whenever the high Rate of Discount arises from the activity of enterprise, it may be laid down as a certainty that there is abundance of enterprise ready to start into existence, and which is only curbed by the High Rate of Discount. As soon as the Rate of Discount is lowered, this enterprise is called into existence, and new operations of all kinds are commenced; and as the increase of operations just corresponds to the increase of capital, no diminution in the Value of Money, with respect to Commodities, takes place, though it does with respect to Debts. An example of the truth of what we say occurred in the year 1844, when from various circumstances an unusual quantity of capital was accumulated in the hands of bankers, and the Rate of Discount fell to 2 per cent., but no increase in the prices of goods generally took place; that is, there was a great diminution in the Value of Money with respect to Debts, but no diminution in its Value with respect to Commodities.

33. But however enterprising the country may be, there is a limit to its enterprise, and as soon as that limit is reached, an increased quantity of money can lead to no fresh enterprise; the consequence of which is very manifest. The quantity of money being continually added generates no fresh enterprise, is forced into the previously existing Channel of Circulation, as it is called, and having no fresh work to do, it merely requires a greater quantity of money to do the same work that a less quantity did before. That is to say, a diminution in the Value of Money with respect to Commodities takes place. One hundred pounds perhaps will now only do the same work that fifty did before, a permanent alteration takes place in the exchangeable relations of bullion and commodities, *and the rate of interest will spring back to its former level.* Because, as we have already observed, the interest is always a definite portion of the profits. And the ratio of £5 to £100 must always be the same, whatever quantity of goods that £100 will purchase, be it much or little. We therefore obtain this fundamental law of the effect of the increase of the quantity of money :

That as long as the increase of the Quantity of Money affects the Value of Money with respect to Debts, it has no effect on its Value with respect to Commodities : and as soon as it begins to affect its Value with respect to Commodities it ceases to affect its Value with respect to Debts.

We have illustrated the first part of this proposition by a reference to the case of England in 1844 ; as a proof of the truth of the latter part of it we may take the cases of California and Australia, where the exchangeable relation of bullion and commodities were so very different from England, yet the rate of interest is very much higher.

34. Hume says—' Nor is the case different with regard to the *second* circumstance which we propose to consider, namely, the great or little riches to supply the demand. This effect also depends on the habits and ways of living of the people, not on the quantity of gold and silver. In order to have in any State a great number of lenders, it is not sufficient nor requisite that there be great abundance of the precious metals. It is only requisite that the property or command of that quantity, which is in the State, whether great or small, should be collected in particular hands, so as to form considerable sums, or compose a great moneyed interest. This begets a number of lenders, and sinks the rate of usury ; and this, I shall venture to affirm, depends not on the quantity of specie, but on particular manners and customs, which make the specie gather into separate sums or masses of considerable value.'

In this extract Hume has touched the right point. It depends on the *manner* in which money is used whether it produces a fall in the rate of interest or not. He himself in this essay quotes Garcilasso de la Vaga as saying that interest in Spain fell nearly a half immediately after the discovery of the West Indies.

The fact is that both these phenomena—a raising of the price of Commodities, and a raising of the price of Debts, i.e.

a lowering of the Rate of Interest, are examples of the great General Law of Economics. An increased quantity of money may be used in two distinct ways—either in the purchase of Commodities or in the purchase of Debts. If it is entirely used in the purchase of Commodities, and they are not increased in a similar ratio, the only effect can be a general rise of Prices ; and no change can take place in the Rate of Interest : but if the increased quantity of money be used in the purchase of Debts, for a similar reason the inevitable effect will be a raising of the price of Debts, i.e. a lowering of the Rate of Interest. But as commercial debts are usually created for the purpose of increasing the production of commodities, such a use of money does call an increased quantity of commodities into existence; and, consequently, no change in the value of money with respect to them need occur.

And, of course, if the increased quantity of money be used partly to purchase Commodities, and partly to purchase Debts, both effects will be produced ; the price both of Commodities and Debts will be raised ; neither, however, so much as if the increased quantity of money were used exclusively in either way. Therefore the Prices of Commodities will be raised *and* the Rate of Interest will be lowered. And this is exactly what did happen after the discovery of America. Hume and many other writers have observed that though the prices of all things rose greatly, they did not rise in proportion to the increased quantity of money. Smith and Hume also say that numerous writers observed that the Rate of Interest also fell very considerably. The reason of these two effects is perfectly plain. Part of the increased quantity of money was used to purchase Commodities directly, and part was used to purchase Debts ; and consequently the price of both was raised; that is, the Price of Commodities rose and the Rate of Interest fell.

The truth of these remarks is shown by the immense raising of the Price of Debts, i.e. lowering the Rate of Discount, the immensely increased production of commodities of all kinds, and the slight change which has taken place in the value of agricultural products effected by the institution of Banks. We have in a previous chapter fully exhibited the mechanism of banking ; and shown how utterly erroneous is the common opinion as to the effect of banking—that it is merely lending out money collected from the community: though even if it were confined to that, it would greatly reduce the Rate of Discount. But we have shown that all banking in this country consists in the *creation* of Credit, several times exceeding the quantity of money deposited. This increased quantity of Credit produces all the effects of an increased quantity of money in aiding in the production of Commodities, as well as in lowering the Rate of Discount. And it is precisely because these creations of Credit are mainly used to increase the quantity of commodities, that they have produced, comparatively speaking, so little effect on prices. It has been calculated that in the form of banking deposits alone in England Credit has been created to the amount of £800,000,000; and this produces exactly the same effects as so much Money.

Thus we see how bankers can exist with such very low profits. Ordinary traders often make profits at the rate of several thousand per cent. per annum, and no one complains: and the reason is that they deal with their own capital and on comparatively small amounts.

But a banker's own capital is but a very small part of what he trades with. He opens a shop for the purpose of buying other people's capital, either with a simple promise to pay, which costs nothing, or sometimes with a promise to pay a moderate interest. Having collected this basis of bullion, he then offers to buy commercial debts: and he also buys these with a simple promise to pay—his own Credit—which costs him nothing, but for which he charges exactly the same as if it were money. By this means he is enabled for all practical purposes to multiply the money in his keeping several times; and he is enabled to give a higher price for the Debts he buys. And when many bankers carry on the same kind of business simultaneously, they, of course, bid against one another, and this raises the price of debts, i.e. lowers the rate of discount, exactly as an equal quantity of money would do. This, then, shows how erroneous is the absolute doctrine that an increase of money cannot lower the rate of interest: and also when Mill says—'The rate of interest, then, depends essentially and permanently on the comparative amount of *real capital* offered and demanded in the way of loan'—such a doctrine is utterly unintelligible unless Credit be admitted to be Capital; because all banking loans are new creations of Credit, and it is this enormous creation of Credit which has brought the Rate of Discount so low in this country.

35. To appreciate more fully the great reduction in the rate of interest which the modern system of banking has effected, we have only to consider the usual rates which prevailed before the invention of the system, and which still prevail when transactions are in actual money.

At Athens, Solon, after his great measure of the Seisachtheia, with a sagacity which was 23 centuries in advance of the human race, abolished imprisonment for debt, and left interest absolutely free, and we find that it varied from 12 to 36 per cent. We may consider that 18 per cent. was about the medium rate, as in the only case in which it was fixed by law—in that of a husband who repudiated his wife, and refused to restore her dowry—it was fixed at that rate. Isæus says that Stratocles had lent out 40 minæ at interest at 9 oboli per mina per month, which is 18 per cent: and Timarchus borrowed at the same rate. Æschines Socraticus borrowed money at 36 per cent. from a banker to set up a perfumery shop, but finding it did not pay at that rate, obtained the sum from another person at 18 per cent. The Clazomenians, owing their troops 20 talents, paid them 4 talents as interest, or 20 per cent. At Corcyra, about 300 B.C., the State ordered some funds to be invested at the rate of 2 per cent. per month, or 24 per cent. per annum, on perfect security. Niebuhr says that 18 per cent. is the usual rate of interest in the Levant at the present day.

At Rome interest does not at first appear to have been regulated by law, but the debts of the common people having given rise to much discord and sedition, chiefly in consequence of the extreme severity of the law of debt, interest was limited by the Code of the XII. tables to *unciarium fœnus*. The meaning of this term has given rise to much difference of opinion among the learned, but Niebuhr and Walther agree that it means 10 per cent. per annum. All persons who took interest beyond this were obliged to restore it fourfold; a thief was obliged to return double what he had stolen. In 408 legal interest was reduced to one-half, and in 413 it was abolished altogether. And in 430, in consequence of a creditor having abused his rights, imprisonment for debt was abolished except by the sentence of a court.

Afterwards, but at what time does not distinctly appear, *centesimæ usuræ* was established as the legal rate. Niebuhr supposes this was a foreign rate first adopted by Sylla. *Centesimæ usuræ* was the same as *asses usuræ*, or 1 per cent. per month, or 12 per cent. per annum. And this continued to be the legal rate of interest up to Justinian, who reduced it one-half. Verres is said to have lent the public money on his own account to the *publicani* in Sicily at *binæ centesimæ*, or 24 per cent.; and Cicero says that the wealthy Romans lent money at 48 per cent. in the Greek provinces. Smith sneers at the virtuous Brutus for lending money at 48 per cent. in Cyprus.

Fufidius exacted *quinas usuras*, or 60 per cent., from his reprobate clients, and Juvenal speaks of a man who offered triple usury, or 36 per cent., but could find no one to lend him at that rate.

Section III

On Banking Discount

36. Profits made by the Loan of Money are made in two ways.

(1) By advancing the complete sum, and waiting till the end of the year for the Profit. This is termed **Interest**.

(2) By retaining the Profits at the time of the advance, and advancing the difference. This is termed **Discount**.

But there are two ways of making Profits by Discount.

1. According to the ordinary works on Algebra, the sum advanced should be such a sum as improved at the given interest should amount to the given sum at the end of the time.

The sum so advanced is called the Present Value of the given sum.

This species of Discount is used in certain branches of commerce: and it may be called **Algebraical Discount**.

But this species of Discount is never used in Banking.

2. In Banking the full sum charged as Profit is deducted, and the difference only is advanced: thus if a Banker discounts a Bill at 5 per cent.: he actually advances only £95, and receives £100 at the end of the year.

This species of Discount is evidently more profitable than Interest: because the Banker receives a profit of £5 on the advance of only £95 instead of £100.

So long as the rates are low there is not much difference: but as these increase, the difference increases at a very rapid ratio: as may easily be seen.

Thus, if a person lent £100 at 50 per cent. interest: he would advance £100, and at the end of the year receive £150, or his Profits would be 50 per cent.

If he discounted a Bill at 50 per cent., he would advance

only £50, and at the end of the year receive £100: i.e. he would make Profits at the rate of 100 per cent.

So discounting a Bill at 60 per cent. is Profits at 150 per cent.

It is somewhat strange that this kind of discount is entirely overlooked by Algebraists. We shall now trace the relation between Profits made by Interest and **Banking Discount**: as this kind of Discount may be termed.

To find the Amount of a given sum in any time at Simple Banking Discount

37. Let P = Principal sum in £
r = Rate of Interest on £1 for 1 year
D = Discount on P
n = Number of years
M = Amount of Principal and Discount
Then rP = Interest on P £ for 1 year
and P − rP = Sum actually advanced = P(1 − r)
Let r' = Profit by way of Banking Discount on each £ of sum actually advanced.

Then

$$\frac{r'}{r} = \frac{P}{P(1-r)}$$

$$\therefore r' = \frac{r}{1-r} : \text{also } r = \frac{r'}{1+r'}$$

Which is the relation which Banking Discount bears to Interest: and all Problems in Banking Discount may be solved by substituting $\frac{r}{1-r}$ for r in the Problems in Interest, both Simple and Compound.

$$\text{Now } D = r'P = P\frac{r}{1-r}$$

$$M = P + D$$

$$= P\left(1 + \frac{r}{1-r}\right)$$

In n years we have

$$D = P\frac{nr}{1-r} \quad . \quad . \quad . \quad (a)$$

and $M = P + D = P\left(1 + \dfrac{nr}{1-r}\right) \ldots (\beta)$

These two Equations will enable us to solve any question in the subject.

38. Adopting the Formulæ for calculating Interest and Discount, we have the following

Table showing the Profits per cent. and per annum at Interest and Discount.

Interest	Discount	Interest	Discount	Interest	Discount
1	1·010101	6	6·382968	20	25·
1½	1·522832	6½	6·951871	30	42·857142
2	2·040816	7	7·526881	40	66·666666
2½	2·564102	7½	8·108108	50	100·
3	3·092783	8	8·695652	60	150·
3½	3·626943	8½	9·311475	70	233·
4	4·166666	9	9·890109	80	400·
4½	4·701570	9½	10·496132	90	900·
5	5·263157	10	11·111111	100	Infinite
5½	5·820105	15	18·823529	—	---

A consideration of this table will show how Bankers' profits increase when discount becomes high; and also what discounting a bill at 50 and 60 per cent.—which we occasionally hear of in courts of law—means.

39. *To find in what time a sum of money will double itself at Simple Banking Discount*

The General Formula is—

$$M = P\left(1 + \dfrac{nr}{1-r}\right)$$

Let $M = 2P$

$$\therefore P = P\dfrac{nr}{1-r}$$

or $n = \dfrac{1-r}{r}$

Let $r = 5$ per cent. $= \tfrac{1}{20}$

$$\therefore n = \dfrac{1-\tfrac{1}{20}}{\tfrac{1}{20}} = 19 \text{ years.}$$

Hence a sum of money will double itself
    At 5 per cent. Simple Interest in 20 years
                       Discount in 19 ,,
Similarly the time for any other rate may be found.

40. The Difference in Profit in trading by Interest and Discount being connected by this relation, may be exhibited by either of the following figures.

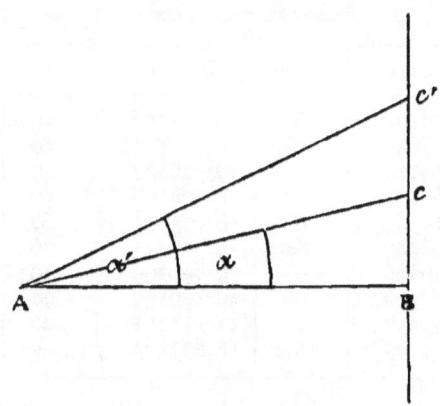

Let AB represent the given sum
Bc the amount of Interest
Bc' ,, ,, Discount.

Then
$$\frac{Bc}{AB} = r, \quad \frac{Bc'}{AB} = r'$$

$$\therefore r = \text{Tan } a \qquad r' = \text{Tan } a'$$
$$a = \text{Tan}^{-1} r \qquad a' = \text{Tan}^{-1} r'$$

$$\therefore a' = \text{Tan}^{-1} \frac{r}{1-r}$$

and
$$a = \text{Tan}^{-1} \frac{r'}{1+r'}$$

Hence, if either of the Quantities be given on the line Bc, a portion representing the other may be found.

On Banking Discount

Second method :—

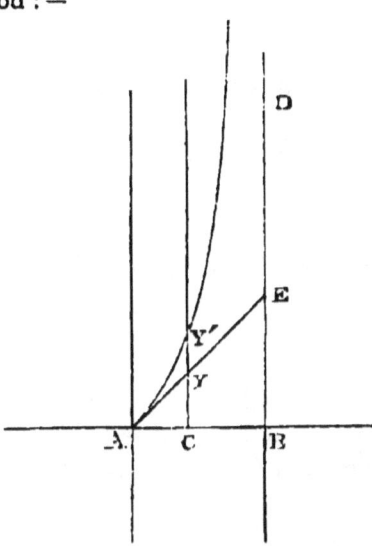

Let A be the origin
AB be any given sum, a
AC = amount of Profit = x
CY = y = Rate of Profit.

Then
$$\frac{x}{a} = r.$$

For Interest we have in all cases
$$y = x.$$

The Equation to a straight line passing through the origin at an angle of 45°.

For Banking Discount,
$$\frac{y'}{y} = \frac{r}{1-r}$$

$$\frac{y'}{y} = \frac{\frac{x}{a}}{1-\frac{x}{a}} = \frac{x}{a-x}$$

$$\therefore y' = \frac{yx}{a-x} = \frac{x^2}{a-x}$$

The Equation to a *Hyperbola*.

To find the Amount of a given sum in any time at Compound Banking Discount

41. Let R denote the amount of £1 with its Interest for one year.
$$= 1 + r$$

Let R' = amount of £1 with its Discount for one year.
$$= 1 + r' = 1 + \frac{r}{1-r} = \frac{1}{1-r}$$

Then PR' = amount of P in one year.
The amount of PR' in one year is PR'R' = PR'².
∴ PR'² = amount of P in *two* years at Comp. Discount
so PR'³ = amount „ *three* „ „ „
   .   .   .   .
and PR'ⁿ = „ „ n „ „ „

$$\therefore M = PR'^n = P\left(1 + r'\right)^n = P\left(1 + \frac{r}{1-r}\right)^n = P\left(\frac{1}{1-r}\right)^n$$

$$\therefore P = \frac{M}{R'^n}$$

$$n = \frac{\text{Log } M - \text{Log } P}{\text{Log } R'}$$

$$R' = \left(\frac{M}{P}\right)^{\frac{1}{n}}$$

The Profits gained in n years $= M - P$
$$= P\left\{R'^n - 1\right\}$$

To find in what time a sum of money will double itself at Compound Discount

42. We have $M = PR'^n$
Let $M = 2P$
            $\therefore 2 = R'^n$

$$\therefore n = \frac{\text{Log. } 2}{\text{Log. } R'}$$

$$= \frac{\text{Log. } 2}{\text{Log.}\left(1 + \dfrac{r}{1-r}\right)}$$

Let $r = 5$ per cent. per annum $= \frac{1}{20}$

$$\therefore n = \frac{\text{Log. } 2}{\text{Log.}\left(1 + \dfrac{\frac{1}{20}}{1-\frac{1}{20}}\right)}$$

$$= \frac{\text{Log. } 2}{\text{Log.}\left(1 + \dfrac{1}{19}\right)}$$

$$= \frac{\text{Log. } 2}{\text{Log. } 20 - \text{Log. } 19}$$

$$= \frac{\cdot 3010300}{1 \cdot 3010300 - 1 \cdot 2787536}$$

$$= 13 \cdot 51 \ldots \text{ years.}$$

Hence a sum of Money will double itself at 5 per cent. :—

At Simple Interest in 20 years
„ „ Discount 19 „
Compound Interest 14·206699 years
„ „ Discount 13·502550 „

43. The formulæ for the Amount of a sum in any given time at Simple Interest and Banking Discount : and Compound Interest and Banking Discount are :

$$\text{At Simple Interest} \quad M = P\left(1 + nr\right)$$

$$\text{Discount} \quad M = P\left(1 + \frac{nr}{1-r}\right)$$

$$\text{At Compound Interest} \quad M = P\left(1 + r\right)^n$$

$$\text{Discount} \quad M = P\left(1 + \frac{r}{1-r}\right)^n = \frac{P}{(1-r)^n}$$

These four formulæ will enable us to solve any Problems in the subject.

To find the difference in Profit at the end of the year between discounting one Bill for £1,000 at twelve months, and discounting four Bills of £1,000 at 3 months in succession at 5 per cent. compound discount

44.
$$M = PR' = P\left(1 + r'\right)$$
$$= P\left(1 + \frac{r}{1-r}\right)$$

Here $r = 5$ per cent. $= \frac{1}{20}$

$$\therefore M = P\left(1 + \frac{\frac{1}{20}}{1 - \frac{1}{20}}\right)$$
$$= P\left(1 + \frac{1}{19}\right)$$
$$= £1,000\left(1 + \cdot052631\right)$$
$$= £1052\cdot631.$$

For 4 Bills at 3 months we have—

$$M = P\left(1 + \frac{r'}{4}\right)^4$$
$$= P\left(1 + \tfrac{1}{4}\frac{r}{1-r}\right)^4$$
$$= P\left(1 + \tfrac{1}{4}\tfrac{1}{19}\right)^4 = P(1 + \tfrac{1}{76})^4$$
$$= P(1\cdot013157)^4$$
$$= £1,000\,(1\cdot05367 \ldots \text{ by Logs.})$$
$$= £1053\cdot67$$

To find the Profit on discounting at more frequent intervals than a year

45. Suppose the interval is 6 months, then $\dfrac{r'}{2}$ will be the discount of £1 for $\tfrac{1}{2}$ year.

At Compound Discount the amount of P in n years is $P\left(1 + \dfrac{r'}{2}\right)^{2n}$: because the amount is the same as if the number of years were $2n$ and the discount $\dfrac{r'}{2}$ on £1 for 1 year.

So for 4 months, or 3 intervals, the amount is

$$P\left(1+\dfrac{r'}{3}\right)^{3n}$$

For 3 months—

$$P\left(1+\dfrac{r'}{4}\right)^{4n}$$

CHAPTER IX

ON RENT

Definition of **Rent**

1. THE word **Rent** (*Reditus*) means any income or revenue from any source. It means an **Annuity,** or the Right to receive a series of payments.

Thus Chaucer, describing the well-to-do citizens of London, says—

> They had enough of Chattels and of **Rent**.

So in the *Monk's Tale*—

> And seyde—'King, God to thy fader sente
> Glorie and honour, regne, tresour, **Rente**.'

Also—

> When as he with his owen hand slew thee
> Succeeding in thy regne, and in thy **Rente**.

Sir David Lyndsay of the Mount says—

> Who fixed have their hearts and whole intents
> On sensual lust, on dignity and **Rents**.

Formerly it was also applied to the sums paid for the use of money as a permanent loan. Thus, when Charles II. shut up the Exchequer and confiscated the funds of the bankers in it, he promised them a yearly **Rent** of 6 per cent.

So in Boswell's Johnson it is said that a lady left Mrs. Williams an 'annual **Rent**.'

The use of the word Rent, however, as applied to the interest paid for a loan of money, has been discontinued in English. The only instance that we are aware of where it is used to denote persons who acquired Rights in return for a loan of Money are the **Renters** of Drury Lane and Covent Garden Theatres. They are persons who subscribed to rebuild the Theatres after they were burnt down, and received in exchange certain Rights of admission to the performances.

The word, however, is still used in this sense on the Continent. The Funds are there still called **Rentes**: a fundholder is called a **Rentier**. Turgot speaks of the *Intérêt Foncier* and the *Intérêt Rentier*, or the Landed Interest and the Moneyed Interest.

The word Rent, however, in English is now usually restricted to the Right to receive compensation for the use of lands, houses, pews, telegraph wires, mint dies, copyrights, patents, and other property held for a period of time.

On the **Rent** of **Land**

2. The subject of Rent has acquired an exaggerated notoriety in Economics from a controversy on the Rent of Land which arose from Smith's self-contradictions on Rent, which we have quoted in the preceding Book. In one set of passages Smith maintains that Rent is a Cause of Price, i.e. that it raises the price of corn to the Consumer: in another set he alleges that Rent is the effect of Price : i.e. that it comes out of Price, and therefore does not raise it.

The whole practical importance of the question is reduced to this—If the landlords were to forego their Rents, would corn be any the cheaper to the Consumer?

Smith's work was published in 1776, a few weeks before Hume died. The sagacious philosopher immediately detected Smith's error in alleging that the payment of Rent raised the price of corn, and wrote to tell him of it. In the following year Anderson, a practical farmer, who was also an extensive writer on agricultural subjects, and who invented the two-horse plough without wheels which has done so much for Scotch agriculture, wrote a pamphlet on the Corn Laws, for the purpose of advocating a sliding bounty. In this pamphlet he shows the fallacy of Smith's doctrine that the payment of Rent raises the price of corn. He shows that the price of corn depends entirely upon Supply and Demand : and that all variations in price are caused by changes in the relation of Supply and Demand. He shows that Rents entirely depend on the price of corn, and that any rise in the price would only temporarily benefit the farmer, but ultimately would go to the landlord.

'It is not, however, the Rent of the Land that determines the price of the produce, but it is the price of that produce which determines the Rent of the Land.'

He says that in every country there are a variety of soils, which may be supposed to proceed in regularly decreasing gradations of fertility : that the price of corn is regulated by the Supply and Demand : and that the price of corn indicates the worst soil upon which corn can be grown so as to pay its expenses. The possessors of the worst fields could only just afford to produce it at that price : but they could not afford any Rent. Those who possessed more fertile lands would have a profit above that ; and that profit would afford Rent.

Anderson then asks—If the landlords were from patriotism to lower or forego their Rents, would that reduce the price of corn? He shows that it would not : because the people require the produce of all the lands as before : and must pay the price necessary to induce the owner to cultivate them. The only consequence, therefore, of such a piece of Quixotism on the part of the landlords would be that the class of farmers would be enriched, without producing the smallest benefit to the consumers of grain.

Every one with the least practical knowledge of agriculture will see that Anderson's reasoning is quite correct. It is the price of corn which indicates the worst soil on which corn can be grown : and as the required price must be paid in order to enable corn to be produced in sufficient quantities to satisfy the demand, it can make no difference to the Consumer whether the Price goes entirely to the farmer or is divided between the landlord and the farmer.

Anderson's reasoning, therefore, is correct on the supposition that there are different degrees of fertility in the lands of the country. But it would appear from such reasoning that differences of fertility in the soil were the necessary condition of Rent being paid : and that if all the soil was of uniform fertility no such thing as Rent could be paid.

However, such a consequence as this is manifestly contrary

to common sense, and consequently there must be a flaw in the reasoning.

On Ricardo's Theory of Rent

3. Ricardo begins by defining Rent to be that portion of the produce of the earth which is paid to the landlord for the use of the *original and indestructible powers of the soil.*

This definition is purely arbitrary and futile: the earth has no *original and indestructible powers* in the sense Ricardo means. The only original and indestructible power that the land has is *extent*. There is scarcely any land whatever which is fit for cultivation without a very considerable expenditure of Labour and Capital: and the powers of the earth are so far from being indestructible that, except in a few favoured regions, they wear out very fast, and require a constant renewal of Labour and Capital to keep it in a fit state for cultivation.

He then says—'It is often, however, confounded with the Interest and Profit of Capital, and in popular language the term is applied to whatever is annually paid by a farmer to the landlord. If of two adjoining farms of the same extent, and of the same natural fertility, one had all the convenience of *farming buildings*, and, besides, was properly drained and manured, and advantageously divided by hedges, fences, and walls, while the other had none of these advantages, more remuneration would naturally be paid for the use of one than for the use of the other: yet in both cases this remuneration would be called Rent. But it is evident that a portion only of the money annually to be paid for the improved farm would be given for the original and indestructible powers of the soil: the other portion would be paid for the use of the Capital which had been employed in ameliorating the quality of the land, and in erecting such buildings as were necessary to secure and preserve the produce.'

With respect to this we may say that Rent is the word invariably applied to remuneration paid for the use of houses and buildings, and therefore nothing can be more proper than to include the sum paid for them in Rent. With respect to the other things which are necessary for the due cultivation of the farm, to deny the name of Rent to the remuneration paid for them is as frivolous as to say, speaking of a house, that the word Rent is to be restricted to the sum paid for the use of the bare walls, but that the remuneration paid for the painting, papering, fitting up, and all the decorations is to be called Interest for Capital.

4. Ricardo then says,—' Adam Smith sometimes speaks of Rent in the strict sense to which I am desirous of confining it, but more often in the popular sense in which the term is usually employed. He tells us that the demand for timber, and its consequent high price in the more southern countries of Europe, caused a Rent to be paid for forests in Norway which could before afford no Rent. It is not, however, evident that the person who paid what he calls Rent paid it in consideration of the valuable commodity which was then standing on the land, and that he actually repaid himself, with a profit, by the sale of the timber. If, indeed, after the timber was removed, any compensation were paid to the landlord for the use of the land, for the purpose of growing timber, or any other produce, with a view to future demand, such compensation might justly be called Rent, because it would be paid for the productive powers of the land; but in the case stated by Adam Smith, the compensation was paid for the liberty of removing and selling the timber, and not for the liberty of growing it.'

This objection of Ricardo's is manifestly of no weight, because Rent is in all such cases part of the profits of the produce of the soil, and the distinction made between the remuneration paid for the right of cutting that timber and the right of growing future timber is manifestly futile, because, though the sum paid for that single crop is limited, it is manifestly paid for the use of the productive powers of the earth, so far as regards that crop, just as much as the future produce of the productive powers of the earth.

Ricardo then goes on, ' He speaks also of the rent of coal mines and of stone quarries, to which the same observation applies—that the compensation given for the mine or quarry is paid for the value of the coal or stone, which can be removed from them, and has no connection with the original and indestructible powers of the land. This is a distinction of great importance in an inquiry concerning Rent and Profits, for it is found that the laws which regulate the progress of Rent are widely different from those which regulate the progress of Profits, and seldom operate in the same direction.'

The objection taken by Ricardo to Adam Smith has no force whatever. The fact is, that his own definition of Rent is purely arbitrary and futile. It is a matter of utter impossibility to distinguish the portion of the remuneration which is paid for the use of the *original and indestructible* powers of the soil, and the portion which is paid as interest of Capital expended upon it. To do that strictly, all the labour which has been expended upon bringing it from a state of nature must be called Capital expended upon it, and the remuneration paid for that must be subtracted from the Rent. And then what will remain for Rent? The fact is, that the separation of Rent and Profit, as proposed by Ricardo, is a thing that cannot be effected, and is nothing more than a play upon words.

Having thus proposed a definition of Rent which is highly incorrect, Ricardo then goes on to explain how Rent arises. He says that on the first settling of a country in which there is an abundance of rich and fertile land, a very small proportion of which is required to be cultivated for the support of the actual population, or indeed can be cultivated with the Capital which the population can command, there will be no Rent. For no one would pay for the use of land, when there was an abundant quantity not yet appropriated, and therefore at the disposal of whosoever might choose to cultivate it, any more than he would pay Rent for the use of air, and water, or any other of the gifts of nature, which exist in boundless quantities. It is only, then, because land is not unlimited in quantity, and uniform in quality, and because in the progress of population, *land of an inferior quality or less advantageously situated*, is called into cultivation, that Rent is ever paid for the use of it. 'When, in the progress of society, land of the second degree of fertility is taken into cultivation, Rent immediately commences on that of the first quality, and the amount of that Rent will depend on the difference of these two portions of land. When land of the third quality is taken into cultivation, Rent immediately commences on the second, and it is regulated as before by the difference of their productive powers. At the same time the Rent of the first quality will rise, for that must always be above the Rent of the second, by the difference between the produce which they yield, with a given quantity of Capital and Labour. With every step in the progress of population which shall oblige a country to have recourse to land of a worse quality to enable it to raise its supply of food, Rent on all the more fertile land will rise.'

Ricardo proceeds,—' Rent is always the difference between the produce obtained by the employment of two equal quantities of Capital and Labour.'—' Rent invariably proceeds from the employment of an *additional* quantity of Labour with a proportionally *less* return ;' and he then immediately proceeds to say, ' When land of an inferior quality is taken into cultivation, the exchangeable value of raw produce will rise, because more Labour is required to produce it.'

Ricardo's doctrine is,—'that corn which is produced by the greatest quantity of Labour is the regulator of the price of corn.' And, again—' The reason, then, why raw produce rises in comparative value, is because more *Labour is employed in the production of the last portion obtained*, and not because a Rent is paid to the landlord. The value of corn is regulated by the *quantity of Labour* bestowed on its production on that quality of land, or with that portion of capital, which pays no Rent. Corn is not high because a Rent is paid, but a Rent is paid because corn is high ; and it has been justly observed that no reduction would take place in the price of corn, although landlords should forego the whole of their Rent. Such a measure would only enable some farmers to live like gentlemen, but would not diminish the quantity of Labour necessary to raise raw produce on the least productive land in cultivation.'

5. It is often said Anderson was the originator of the Theory of Rent which Ricardo afterwards adopted and developed. But, on comparing the two theories, it will be seen that though they have one part in common, namely, considering that Rent arises from differences in the fertility of soils, yet they are fundamentally different. Anderson, as a practical farmer, makes the high price of corn to proceed exclusively from the great

Demand for it. This increased price causes it to be profitable to bring lands of decreasing fertility into cultivation, and consequently the lands which can produce corn at a cheaper rate can afford to pay a Rent. But Ricardo makes the whole price of corn to be regulated by the ' Quantity of Labour ' bestowed in obtaining the last quantity produced. Therefore, of course, all the corn produced at a cheaper rate can afford to pay a Rent. Now it so happens that the practical result of both theories is identical, and it is true. It is perfectly clear that the payment of Rent does not in any way influence the price of corn, and consequently if the landlords were to forego their Rents it would not make corn any the cheaper, but the Rents would go into the pockets of the farmers. But as a question of Science, the Theories are fundamentally distinct: for Anderson's theory makes the Value of corn to be governed solely by Demand and Supply; Ricardo's theory by 'Quantity of Labour,' or 'Cost of Production.'

In both theories, however, differences of the fertility of soils are made the necessary condition of Rent arising, which we shall show hereafter is an error.

All believers in Ricardo's theory of Rent make Rent to arise from the differences in the fertility of soils: thus McCulloch says—' The fundamental position laid down by Dr. Smith, that there are certain species of produce that always yield Rent, is contradicted by the widest and most comprehensive experience. Were such the case, Rents would always exist, whereas they are uniformly unknown in the earlier stages of society. The truth is that Rent is entirely a consequence of the *decreasing* productiveness of the soils successively brought under cultivation as society advances, or rather of the *decreasing* productiveness of the Capitals successively applied to them. It is never heard of in newly settled countries, such as New Holland, Illinois, or Indiana, nor in any country where none but the best of the good soils are cultivated. It only begins to appear when cultivation has been extended to *inferior* lands; and it increases according to the extent to which they are brought under tillage, and diminishes according as their culture is relinquished.' McCulloch has a long note at the end of his edition of Smith, but as it contains nothing different from Ricardo, it is superfluous to quote it. McCulloch's observation that Rent does not arise in new countries where there is abundance of fertile land would be easily answered if it were true, because Rent cannot arise until the relation of Landlord and Tenant is established ; Rent being the sum paid to a landlord for the use of land : and of course where there is abundance of land, every one would rather have land of his own than pay Rent to a landlord. And in the next place it is not true that Rent does not exist in these new settled countries; because the land in them belongs to the Government, and it is quite usual for the Government to demand a Rent for tracts of land. It is true, some colonies, for the sake of encouraging immigration, do give a certain amount of land free to desirable settlers : but McCulloch's assertion that Rent is *never* paid in new settled countries is wholly contrary to fact.

6. Mill goes so far as to call Ricardo's Theory of Rent the *pons asinorum* of Economics. He adopts Ricardo's division of the classes of commodities, and says—'The value, therefore, of an article is determined by the cost of that portion of the supply which is produced and brought to market at the greatest expense. This is the Law of Value of the third of the three classes into which all commodities are divided.' Again he says—'Rent, we again see, is the *difference* between the *unequal* returns to *different* parts of the capital employed on the soil.'—' Thus Rent is, as we have already seen, no cause of Value, but the price of the privilege which the *inequality* of the returns to different portions of agricultural produce confers on all except the least favoured portions.' Again—' Agricultural productions are not the only commodities which have several *different costs of production* at once, and which in *consequence* of that difference, and in *proportion* to it, afford a Rent.'

Thus Mill distinctly makes differences of Cost of Production the *necessary* condition of Rent arising. We shall see afterwards, however, that he is quite inconsistent with himself as to the regulating law of price, and that in some passages he leans to Ricardo, and in others to Anderson.

Carey's Theory *of* Rent

7. This Theory of Rent was vaunted as a most wonderful discovery soon after it was published. But it met with a stout antagonist in Carey, the American Economist. In his first works he dissented from the Theory, but he admitted men began by cultivating the best land first. Afterwards, however, he took up a new position altogether. He maintains that the first settlers in a country always begin by cultivating the inferior soils. He says that the best soils are always covered with immense trees that they cannot fell, or they are swamps that they cannot drain. These, he says, cannot be brought into cultivation till men and Capital increase. But there are always spots of an inferior degree of fertility, on the hill side for instance, where the thin soil has prevented the growth of trees and shrubs, which are always brought into cultivation first, because they afford the readiest return for Labour.

Carey then attacks the Ricardo Theory of Rent, and says,—' Nearly 40 years have elapsed since Mr. Ricardo communicated to the world his discovery of the nature and causes of Rent, and the law of its progress. The work by means of which it was first made known has since been the text work of that portion of the English community who style themselves, *par excellence*, political economists, and anything short of absolute faith in its contents is regarded as heresy, worthy of excommunication, or as evidence of an incapacity to comprehend them, worthy only of contempt. Nevertheless, imitating in this the action of the followers of Mahomet, in regard to the Koran, the professors, one and all, who have undertaken to teach this doctrine, insist upon construing it after their own fashion, and modifying it to suit their own views and the apparent necessities of the case ; the consequence of which is, that the inquirer is at a loss to determine what it is that he is required to believe. Having studied carefully the works of the most eminent of the recent writers on the subject, and having found no two of them to agree, he turns in despair to Mr. Ricardo himself, and there he finds in the celebrated chapter on Rent, contradictions that cannot be reconciled, and a series of complications such as never before, we believe, was found in the same number of lines. The more he studies, the more he is puzzled, and the less difficulty does he find in accounting for the variety of doctrines taught by men who profess to belong to the same school, and who all agree, if in little else, in regarding the new theory of Rent as the great discovery of the age. * * * * *

'At first sight, it looks to be exceedingly simple. Rent is said to be paid for land of the first quality, yielding one hundred quarters in return to a given quantity of labour, when it becomes necessary, with the increase of population, to cultivate land of the second quality, capable of yielding but 90 quarters in return to the same quantity of labour; and the amount of Rent then paid for No. I. is equal to the difference between their respective products. No proposition could be calculated to command more universal assent. Every man who hears it sees around him land that pays rent. He sees that that which yields forty bushels to the acre pays more rent than that which yields but thirty, and that the difference is nearly equal to the difference of product. He becomes at once a disciple of Mr. Ricardo, admitting that the reason why prices are paid for the use of land is that soils are different in their qualities, when he would *at the same moment, regard it as in the highest degree absurd, if any one were to undertake to prove that prices were paid for oxen because one ox is heavier than another; that rents are paid for houses because some will accommodate twenty persons and others only ten; or that all ships command freights because some ships differ from others in their capacity!*'

'It will be perceived that the whole system is based upon the assertion of the existence of a single fact, viz., that in the commencement of cultivation, when population is small, and land consequently abundant, the soils capable of yielding the largest return to any given quantity of labour alone are cultivated. The fact exists, or it does not. If it has no existence, the system falls to the ground. That it does not exist; that it never has existed in any country whatsoever; and that it is contrary to the nature of things that it should have existed, or can exist, we propose now to show.'

This, then, is the main purpose of his work. Carey, from a general survey of different countries, maintains that men always have, and necessarily must have, commenced cultivation on inferior soils, and when men and capital increased have then progressed to bring the best soils into cultivation. The reason for this general and sweeping conclusion is, as above indicated, because the best and most fertile lands are always covered with forest or swamp, and the inferior lands free from them. Hence settlers begin with those lands most easily attainable. The universality of this law Carey attempts to prove. This, then, is the basis of his theory of Rent, and as seen above it is in diametrical opposition to that of Ricardo. He also maintains that as men and capital increase, and better lands are brought into cultivation, Rents rise, and population becomes better off.

Carey maintains the necessary universality of this course, and he has taken a wide survey of the history of nations in different ages, in all countries of the world, to prove its truth.

Now Carey has undoubtedly so far succeeded as this. He has certainly completely overthrown the basis of Ricardo's Theory of Rent, which depends on the universality of men occupying the *best* land first. It is indubitably true that in a great many cases men do begin with the light middling soils first. And this is all that is required by the laws of Inductive Logic. But to assert as a necessary, invariable, and universal law, that men do and must in all cases begin by cultivating the inferior soils is preposterous. In multitudes of cases men did begin cultivation on the best soils. It has often been remarked what a keen eye for good land the monks had. In multitudes of cases the monasteries will be found placed in the centre of the richest and best lands.

Now if there are abundance of cases, as there undoubtedly are, in which men began by cultivating the best lands, that is fatal to the generality of Carey's theory, just as the instances which he has adduced of men beginning on the light middling lands are fatal to Ricardo's theory. Each of them has perilled his theory on the universality of a particular course of proceeding.

From every general theory all accidental and particular circumstances must be eliminated. The particular state of the case as asserted by Ricardo is sometimes true, and the particular state of the case as asserted by Carey is also sometimes true; and therefore it is clear that neither is true as a general theory. A true general theory must include them both.

8. Years ago, when we read Ricardo's Theory of Rent for the first time, we wrote—'Another most abundant source of error is, when two phenomena are related to each other, to mistake the cause for the effect. No more striking instance of this can be selected than the Theory of Rent propounded by Mr. Ricardo. In a few words, Mr. Ricardo's axiom is that the expense of raising corn on the worst land in cultivation will determine the average price of wheat, and afford and measure the rent of lands of a superior quality. . . . Notwithstanding these authorities, we have no hesitation whatever in saying that the Ricardo Theory of Rent is a mere delusion; and that it is fundamentally erroneous, inasmuch as it inverts the relation of cause and effect. From an intimate knowledge and observation of the action of prices in an agricultural district, and the views of farmers in taking farms, we have no hesitation in saying that it is *not* the cost of cultivating the worst lands which determines price, but the precise reverse, and *that it is the average value or price of corn which determines the worst quality, and most ill-situated land that can be cultivated with a profit, and also decides whether there can be any Rent for it*. . . . It is evident that this is no mere piece of vain logomachy, but is the very root of the matter; we have no hesitation in saying that Ricardo has inverted cause and effect, and that the whole Theory of Rent based upon this erroneous axiom is a delusion and a chimera, and that any course of action based upon so fallacious an axiom would infallibly lead to results precisely the reverse of what was intended and expected.'

This we wrote from our own practical knowledge of the subject. Since that work was published, we have found that J. B. Say has urged exactly the same objection against Ricardo's Theory of Rent. Say says—'We shall see further that it is the same false conception of the origin of value which is the basis of Ricardo's Theory of Rent. He pretends that it is the cost which is obliged to be made to cultivate the worst lands which makes a rent to be paid for the better ones, whereas it is the wants of society which gives rise to the demand for agricultural products, and raises the price of them sufficiently high for the farmer to make a profit to pay the owner of the land for the right of cultivating it.'

And this view, which is exactly the same as ours, he enforces further on.

So also Dr. Chalmers points out exactly the same fallacy. 'It is a signal error in a recent Theory of Rent that the difference of quality in soils is the efficient cause of it.... In affirming that it is the existence of this inferior land which originates the Rent, there is a total misapprehension of what may be termed the real Dynamics of the subject.' And he says—'The error of the Ricardo system of Political Economy on the subject of rent has been well characterised by Mr. T. Perronet Thompson as the fallacy of inversion. It confounds the effect with the cause. It is not because of the existence of inferior soils that the superior pay a rent, but it is because the superior pay a rent that the inferior are taken into occupation.'

Lastly, we may cite the opinion of the learned Judge, Mr. Justice Byles, who wrote to us—'I observe that in your economical writings you have assailed Ricardo's Theory of Rent. Fifty years ago I not only read Ricardo's book, but actually abridged it. Subsequent reflection and observation have convinced me that that theory is unsound, as, indeed, is most of his book.' We are happy to cite these testimonies, all agreeing with our judgment.

9. We have seen that Anderson and Ricardo, with his followers McCulloch and Mill, all make Rent to arise from *differences* in the returns to Capital, either from difference of fertility, situation, or differences of Capital applied to the same soil. And unless there were these differences of returns, it is manifest from the extracts given from these writers, that, according to their theory, there could be no such thing as Rent. Now, let us suppose some vast plains of illimitable extent on the earth's surface; all of uniform fertility; with markets thickly distributed over them so that their situation is uniform; and also equal amounts of Capital expended on the soil; such as the plains of Bengal, or Lombardy, or such as the plains of South America along the Amazons might be. Now, in such a country as this, could not there be such a thing as Rent? According to the doctrine of Ricardo, McCulloch, and Mill, there could not be such a thing as Rent in such a country! The very statement of such doctrine is enough to call forth the amazement and ridicule of any practical man of business.

The Theory *of* Rent

10. We have now to develope the Theory of Rent which is independent of *differences* of fertility, or *differences* of situation, or of *differences* of return to Capital.

First : What is the first thing necessary in order that Rent should arise?

It is that the relation of Landlord and Tenant should exist : Rent is the sum paid by one person to another for the use of land ; hence, unless the land is owned by one person and let to another, there can be no such thing as Rent.

Secondly : From what does the possibility of Rent being paid arise?

It arises from this, that a few persons, especially with the assistance of horses, cattle, and agricultural implements, can raise from the earth a very much larger amount of produce than is necessary for their own subsistence.

Thirdly : Let us consider when, or under what circumstances, Rent will arise.

Let us suppose that there is a large tract of country belonging to a landlord, either the State, or a private person, and comprising many different kinds of soil of varying fertility.

Now, suppose that any portion of this soil is parcelled out among families in such a way that each family has got only just exactly enough for its own subsistence. Those placed on the better lands will of course require a smaller amount of land than those placed on inferior lands.

Now, if the land were parcelled out in this way, it is manifest that these families could pay no Rent for the land, because they have no surplus produce to pay as Rent.

Again, let us suppose the same land parcelled out among a number of families, each with a very much larger portion of land in their possession than is necessary for their subsistence. Then, as each family would be able to maintain itself entirely on its own land, it is evident they could pay no Rent, as there would be nobody to purchase any produce they might raise above their own wants. (Supposing that they did not export it to foreign markets.)

Supposing, while the land is parcelled out in this way, a town springs up. Then, of course, the inhabitants of the town cannot raise food for themselves, and the tenants in the country would find it profitable to grow food to sell to the dwellers in the town.

Of course, when the town was very small the demand would be very small, and therefore the price low; and therefore it would only pay to bring in corn from the land nearest the town. But as the numbers in the town increased, the demand would increase: the price of the corn would increase: the Rent of the land nearest the town would increase: and then it would pay to bring corn from the second zone of land. As the town continued to increase, the demand would still more increase: the price would go higher still: the Rent in the first and second zones would increase: and then it would pay to bring the corn from the third zone, and so on.

It is also clear that if there were only *one* centre of population, the price of the corn arising from the demand would indicate the greatest cost that could be incurred in bringing the corn to market. And as this cost increased, there would be a zone from which it would just pay with ordinary profits to bring the corn to market, but which could pay no Rent.

Now Ricardo says that it is the cost of producing the corn from this outmost zone which *regulates* the price of all the corn sold in the market.

We say it is manifestly exactly the reverse. It is the price of the corn in the market which indicates the position of this zone.

Ricardo says—'When in the progress of society land of the second degree of fertility is taken into cultivation, Rent immediately commences on that of the first quality.'

We say it is exactly the reverse, and that it is—When Rent commences on land of the first degree, land of the second degree will be taken into cultivation.

Ricardo says—'When land of the third quality is taken into

cultivation, Rent immediately commences on the second. At the same time the Rent of the first quality will rise.'

We say it is exactly the reverse, and that it is—When in the progress of society the price of corn rises, the Rents on the first and second qualities will rise, and then the third quality will be taken into cultivation.

Ricardo says—'When land of an inferior quality is taken into cultivation, the exchangeable value of raw produce will rise, because more labour is required to produce it.'

We say that the sentence should have been written thus—'When the exchangeable value of raw produce rises, land of an inferior quality will be taken into cultivation, because more labour may be profitably employed to produce it.'

Ricardo says—'The value of corn is regulated by the Quantity of Labour bestowed on its production, or that quality of land, or with that portion of capital, which pays no Rent.'

We say it is exactly the reverse, and that—The value of corn indicates the worst quality of land upon which labour may be bestowed without paying Rent.

Ricardo says—'That corn which is produced by the greatest quantity of labour is the regulator of the price of corn.'

We say it is exactly the reverse, and—That the price of corn indicates the greatest cost which will be employed in producing corn.

11. Now we have supposed only one centre of town population: and under such circumstances Rents would no doubt progressively diminish till they vanished. But what need of supposing only one centre of town population? Let us suppose that there are any number of towns and markets spread all over the country. Then of course these numerous towns will tend to equalise Rents all over the country; and like as in Lombardy, we may suppose them so nearly equally spread over the country that differences of situation are practically annihilated. We may also suppose that equal portions of Capital have been applied to the land: so that the circumstances of an indefinite extent of country are absolutely equal. Now as long as the circumstances of the different parts of the country are different, Ricardo, McCulloch, and Mill allow that Rents may exist; but

as soon as the circumstances are absolutely equal all over the country—the possibility of there being such a thing as Rent ceases to exist!!

Now such is the logical conclusion of the Ricardo Theory of Rent! and we simply ask, can such a doctrine be received by any sane man?

We thus, by this means, eliminate differences of fertility, situation, or application of Capital, from the Theory of Rent.

12. What then are the circumstances under which Rent arises? They are these :—

1. That the land must belong to a landlord, and be let to a tenant.
2. That the tenant shall have in his possession a larger amount of land than is necessary for his own maintenance.
3. That the population in some parts of the country be collected in such dense masses that they cannot grow corn for their own subsistence on the land they occupy.
4. That the population in other parts of the country be scattered so widely that they cannot consume the produce of the soil, but they may sell some of it to the town population.

Under such circumstances the tenants in the country can give their landlords a share of the profits made by selling the corn to the townspeople, and that share is called Rent.

The Payment *of* Rent *does* Not *influence the* Price *of* Corn

13. Moreover the payment of Rent has no influence on the price of corn, because it is not part of the *Cost of Production*, but it is a *Share of the Profits*.

The proof of this will be an excellent example of the truth of the General Equation of Economics we established in a former chapter: It will also well exemplify a principle of great importance in the Theory of Taxation.

In many foreign towns an *octroi*, or custom house, is placed at the gates, at which duties are levied on all articles of food brought into the town.

Now suppose A keeps a farm outside the town, and brings his produce to the market. He is charged an *octroi* duty at the gates. This duty is part of the Cost of Production, i.e. of placing the produce in the market for sale. Hence he will add the duty to the price of the article, and the townsmen must pay it. Hence of course a tax on the product will raise its price.

Now if A is the possessor of the farm by himself, he will reap all the profits made by it. If he has a partner B, the same quantity of produce is brought into the market: but A and B will share the profits between them. A, no doubt, will have a less profit than if he was sole owner of the farm. But it is quite evident that because A has a partner B, and must share the profits with him, that can have no effect on the price of the produce. For this reason—the same *Quantity* is raised from the farm and offered in the market, and there is the same **Demand** for it. Hence it is clear that *a tax on the product raises the price of the product, but a share of the profits will not.*

Now suppose A and B are landlord and tenant. Then the produce is raised and brought to market; and the tenant pays the landlord a stipulated share of the profits. That cannot have any effect on the price of the produce, because it neither alters the Demand nor the Supply. Hence the price of corn cannot be affected whether a single person produces it, or whether two do so in partnership. That is to say, it has no effect on the price of corn whether one person produces it, or whether two produce in partnership. Hence in strict accordance with the theories of Anderson and Ricardo, it is perfectly proved that if the landlords were to forego their Rents, it would have no effect on the price of corn: but the price would simply go into the pockets of the farmers.

Error *of Ricardo on* **Tithes**

14. It is very strange that Ricardo, who agreed that Rent does not influence the price of corn, maintains that Tithes do. He says,—' Tithes are a tax on the gross produce of the land, and like taxes on raw produce, fall wholly on the consumer.' Now it is quite manifest that Tithes are a share of the produce, just as Rent is. If a farmer has to pay Tithes as well as Rent, it is quite clear that the produce of the farm is divided into three parts instead of two. But still the same Supply is brought to market, and there is the same Demand for it. Therefore its Price cannot be altered. The produce is shared between the

Landlord, the Tenant, and the Parson, but that can have no effect on Price. Therefore the distinction made by Ricardo between Rent and Tithes is entirely erroneous. The distinction between a Tax on the Produce and a Share of the Produce, or the Profits, will be found to be of the greatest importance hereafter in the Theory of Taxation.

Self-Contradiction of Ricardo on Rent

15. The slightest consideration will show that Rent and Tithes stand exactly on the same footing, and are exactly of the same nature. Rent is the share of the Produce which is given to the Landlord : Tithes are the share of the Produce which is given to the Parson. The whole Produce is divided into three parts : but as this Division of the Produce neither alters the Quantity brought into the market, that is, the Supply, nor the Demand, it is evident that neither of them alters Price. They in no way add to the Price of the Produce : nor would the Produce be any the cheaper if Rent and Tithes were abolished. The only thing would be that the whole Profits would go to one person instead of to three.

Ricardo, however, considers Tithes to be a tax on the gross produce of the land, and, like taxes on the raw produce, fall wholly on the Consumer : and he says they raise the Price of the Produce.

Ricardo's doctrine on Tithes therefore is quite contradictory to his doctrine on Rent. But he equally contradicts himself on Rent. For he says—

'Rent, then, it appears, always *falls on the Consumer*, and never on the Farmer.'

'The farmer, then, although he pays no part of his landlord's Rent, that being always regulated by the Price of the Produce, and *invariably falling on the Consumer*.'

'It must be admitted, then, that M. Sismondi and Mr. Buchanan, for both their opinions are substantially the same, were correct when they considered Rent as a Value purely nominal, and as forming no addition to the national wealth, but merely as a transfer of Value, advantageous only to the landlords, and *proportionably injurious to the consumer*.'

Now, when Ricardo in these passages says that Rent '*falls*

on the Consumer,' and is '*injurious* to the Consumer,' what can he mean except that the payment of Rent raises the Price of the produce to the Consumer? Thus he exactly contradicts his previous Theory. Thus he is shown to be in plain contradiction to himself on the only part of his Theory which is of any practical utility.

Self-Contradiction of Mill on Rent

16. The absurdities and self-contradictions of the Ricardo Theory of Rent are strikingly exhibited in Mill.

He says—'Agricultural productions are not the only commodities *which have several different Costs of Production at once, and which in consequence of that difference, and in proportion to it, afford a Rent.* Mines are also an instance. Almost all kinds of raw material extracted from the interior of the earth —metals, coals, precious stones, &c.—are obtained from mines differing considerably in fertility; that is, yielding very different quantities of the product to the same quantity of Labour and Capital.'

Now let us observe the necessary consequences of such doctrines. If the rent of mines arises solely from *differences* in the fertility of mines, and is only paid in consequence of that *difference*, it manifestly follows that if all the mines were of *equal* fertility there could be no such thing as Rent, a doctrine too absurd to require a moment's refutation. It would manifestly be just as absurd to say that Rent is paid for houses because houses are of different sizes: and that if all the houses in a great city, like London or Paris, were of the same size there could not be any such thing as Rent: or that Freights are paid for ships because ships are of different sizes: and that if all ships were of the same size, there could be no such thing as freights: or that wages or salaries are paid to men because men differ in capacity: and that if all men were of equal capacity there could be no such thing as wages or salary: and so on in innumerable similar cases: in short, if the Ricardo-Mill theory be true, prices are only paid for anything because things differ in quality or degree.

If the Ricardo-Mill Theory be true, that Rent only arises from *differences* of fertility between different Lands, Mines, or

Houses, it would follow that if there were only a single piece of Land, or Mine, or House, no Rent could be paid for it! Nor is this by any means an imaginary case. There is but one mine of Plumbago in England, and according to the doctrine of Ricardo and Mill no Rent can be paid for it: a doctrine at which the owner of the mine would doubtless smile. Nor could any Rent be paid for the quarries of Paros, Carara, or Pentelicus: a doctrine so manifestly absurd as to require no refutation.

17. But, in fact, Mill himself has entirely overthrown this Theory of Rent.

He says—'Whatever be the causes, it is a fact that mines of different degrees of richness are in operation; and since the Value of the produce must be proportional to the Cost of Production at the worst mine (fertility and situation taken together), it is more than proportional to that of the best. *All mines superior in produce to the worst actually worked will yield, therefore, a Rent equal to the excess. They may yield more, and the worst mine may itself yield a Rent.*'

So also he says—'If the whole land of a country were required for cultivation, *all* of it might yield a Rent.'

Now if this be true, as it undoubtedly is, what becomes of the doctrine that Lands, and Mines, and all other things only yield a Rent in consequence of their being of *different* degrees of fertility: and that Rent is the excess of the more fertile mines or lands above the least fertile one?

If *all* Lands and Mines can pay Rent, how can Rent be 'the *difference* between the *unequal* returns to different parts of the Capital employed on the soil': or the 'price of the privilege which the inequality of the returns to *different* portions of agricultural produce confers on all *except the least favoured portion?*'

Thus in one place he defines Rent to be the excess of the returns of all portions above the worst: thereby expressly excluding the worst portion from the capacity of paying Rent: and then he says in other places that *all* portions, even the worst, may pay Rent! Can anything be more contradictory or absurd?

It is obvious from these passages of Mill that he perceives that the Value of the produce is due to the *Intensity of Demand* and the *Limitation of the Supply*; and that the difference of degrees of fertility in the mines is a mere accident. If *all* Lands and Mines yield a Rent, how can it be *essential* to Rent that they should differ in fertility? As M. H. Passy truly observes, this is to take the circumstances which make a difference in the **Rate** of Rent for the **Cause** which produces Rent. In all these cases differences of fertility are the mere **Accident** of Rent, and not its **Essence**. It needs no ghost to tell us that Lands and Mines which possess superior advantages of fertility and situation will pay a higher Rent than inferior ones.

The capability of Rent being paid for a farm purely depends upon the question whether the Value of the produce of the farm leaves sufficient Profits after defraying the Cost of Production, farmer's necessary profits, &c., to pay Rent. The capacity of a Farm to pay Rent depends purely on its own particular circumstances, and has nothing to do with the consideration whether other farms are more or less fertile than itself. And the Value of the produce depends purely on the Intensity of Demand and the Limitation of the Supply of the produce in the market : and the whole question is thus brought under the dominion of the General Equation of Economics.

18. It has already been shown that Anderson's Theory of Rent is radically different from Ricardo's : though they are often thought to be the same. Anderson makes the Value of corn to spring from the Demand, and he shows that it is the Price of Corn which indicates the worst land which can be brought into cultivation.

Ricardo makes the increase of Price to proceed from the increased Labour in obtaining the corn : and it is quite clear that Ricardo's doctrine is, that bringing worse lands into cultivation must precede, and is the cause of, the increase of Price : and this is the sense which both his opponents, Say, Chalmers, Thompson, and ourselves, as well as his admirer, McCulloch, attribute to him.

But Mill, in accordance with Anderson, says—'The higher the market value of produce, the lower are the soils to which cultivation can descend, consistently with affording to the Capital employed the ordinary Rate of Profit.

Now this is no doubt true; but it is diametrically the reverse of Ricardo's Theory of Rent, which Mill declares to be the *pons asinorum* of Economics.

The only case in which Ricardo's Theory would have a semblance of truth would be this, where a country had a regularly decreasing gradation of lands, stretching out to an unlimited distance: then in such a case the Rent which might be paid for the superior farms would be *indicated* by the difference in the Value of their produce and the Value of the produce of the last quantity of land in cultivation. But then it is a pure *accident* that there should be such an unlimited series. For the Ricardo Theory to be true it would necessarily require that there should actually be such a series.

On the Rent of Shops

19. We thus see that the doctrine first positively announced by Anderson, and adopted by all Economists since, that Rent does not influence the price of agricultural products, such as corn, is true. Such a product is brought into a common market which no single producer can influence, and therefore he must conform himself to its conditions. A certain general price is necessary to attract a certain supply; and the differences in the cost of production of each particular parcel can have no influence on its price. The supply will be produced so long as its value affords the cost of labour and ordinary profits. No one created the land itself, and therefore remuneration for the use of it is not part of the necessary cost of production: and if any particular parcel of its produce will not afford both ordinary profits and Rent, Rent, of course, will vanish first. The producers of corn are far too numerous to combine to limit the supply. For a considerable time it was attempted to limit the supply of foreign corn by prohibitive or protective legislation, but all such laws have been for ever rendered impossible in this country; and consequently corn will come in from foreign countries so long as the value of it here will yield the ordinary profits of trade.

But where the producers are fewer in number the case is different. The owners of mines of different sorts are comparatively few, and they can without any great difficulty come to an agreement to limit the supply. It has been alleged that the owners of coal mines have on several occasions agreed to limit the supply in order to maintain it at a certain level in order to preserve their rents; though the same rule would evidently apply to minerals as to corn, if the producers were too numerous to combine. Minerals of all sorts are the free gift of nature, and not the creation of man, and therefore a remuneration for them is not a part of the necessary cost of production: and if there were no arbitrary limitation of supply they would continue to be produced so long as the producers obtained ordinary profits.

But the case is different with shops. In these Rent does undoubtedly enter into price, because in such cases it is part of the necessary cost of production. No man created the land or the minerals; but shops are not the gift of nature. They are created by the expenditure of capital, which is part of the necessary cost of production, and it must be replaced in the price of the articles. Moreover, each shop is a little market in itself, over which the producer has complete command, only controlled by other producers who are all in a similar position. A retail shopkeeper buys his goods at a certain price from the wholesale dealer, and he has a certain price to pay for rent; or if he built the shop himself he must have laid out a certain capital on it, and must have a certain interest on that expenditure. He must also provide for his own maintenance. He expects to have a certain amount of custom; he therefore fixes such a price upon his articles as he estimates will provide for all these things. If he cannot obtain these returns he must give up his business. All his competitors are in exactly the same condition, and thus the producers have the command of the market. The prices which each may fix are only controlled by what he thinks his customers will give, and his fellow-competitors will enforce as well as himself. None of these competitors, however, can afford to sell below that amount any more than he can. Consequently, in such cases rent is a part of the necessary cost of production, as being only the interest on capital expended : and production must cease unless such interest is afforded : and therefore in such cases it necessarily and justly forms a part of price.

It is easily seen that this is true by any one who considers the difference between the prices of fish, fruit, and vegetables as sold in shops where the shop is the fixed capital, and the same articles sold by costermongers in the street, whose only fixed capital is a barrow.

Conclusion of the Ricardo Theory of Rent

20. Although we have arrived at exactly the same practical result as Ricardo, yet this is no immaterial dispute about words; it is not mere logomachy ; but it is a fundamental difference of principle between two distinct systems of Economics. Ricardo has plainly inverted cause and effect. His views and principles are as entirely fallacious as if he had composed a treatise on heat, and laid it down as a fundamental principle that it is the rise of the mercury in the thermometer that regulates the heat of the atmosphere, or that the rise of the mercury in the barometer *causes* fine weather. And those who admire Ricardo's principles ought in consistency to maintain the two latter propositions. The schoolboy who screwed up his Barometer to 'Set fair,' to ensure fine weather for his holiday, was a true disciple of Ricardo.

It is so extremely important to understand the nature of the fallacy which runs through the whole of the Ricardian system, that we may give another illustration. It is well known that the cultivation of certain agricultural products, and the climate they can flourish in, are intimately connected. At certain points the cultivation of maize, the vine, olives, the palm, ceases, and it is possible to ascertain by experience the average temperature of the country in which these things occur. Now, reasoning exactly as Ricardo does, we ought to say that the boundaries of the cultivation of these products *regulate* the climate of that place ; when it is manifestly the reverse, it is the climate that *regulates* their production. The cultivation of a certain vegetable may *indicate* the climate, but it does not *regulate* it, any more than the speed of the paddle-wheels regulates the motion of the engines. The whole of Ricardo's palpable fallacy is based upon a misconception of the meaning of *to regulate*.

Or again, there is a certain kind of letter-weight which indicates the weight of the letter by raising a series of weights in succession; now it is quite clear that it is not the last weight raised which *regulates* the weight of the letter; but the weight of the letter which regulates which is the last weight which will be raised.

Exactly in the same way, it is not the cost of raising corn on the worst land which *regulates* the Price of corn : but it is the Price of corn which regulates the cost which can be afforded for it : and which indicates the worst land which can be cultivated : and the Price of corn is exclusively governed by the great Law of Supply and Demand.

We have now shown the entire fallacy of the Ricardo Theory of Rent : and brought the class of commodities it relates to under the dominion of the General Equation of Economics. That the Ricardo theory should be true was contrary to the whole analogy of Physical Science. But the Principle of the Continuity of Science is completely vindicated, and there is seen the beautiful conformity between the Principles of Natural Philosophy and Reality, and a great triumph for the prophetic genius of Bacon.

Smith on Rents in Shetland

21. Smith notices the high rent paid for land in some parts of Shetland—'The sea in the neighbourhood of Shetland is more than commonly abundant in fish, which make a great part of the subsistence of their inhabitants. But in order to profit by the produce of the water they must have a habitation upon the land. The rent of the land is in proportion, not to what the farmer can make by the land, but to what he can make both by the land and the water. It is partly paid in sea-fish ; and one of the very few instances in which rent makes a part of the price of that commodity is to be found in that country.'

It is quite clear that it is exactly the reverse, and that rents in Shetland are paid out of the bountiful supply of fish. It is surprising that Smith did not see that fishermen everywhere else must have a dwelling on land, as well as in Shetland, for which they must pay rent. And rent must bear the same relation to price everywhere else as it does in Shetland. Why should rent form a part of the price of fish in Shetland and not elsewhere? How is it possible that the Laws of Value can be fundamentally different in Shetland to all the rest of the world? This is just one of those examples which has brought the Science of Economics into such disrepute, because Economists, from want of a scientific education, make the whole subject a mass of contradictions and peculiarities, without any great fundamental principles. But the fault is evidently not in the subject, but in the manner of treating it.

A dwelling near the sea is necessary for the fishermen. The sea is part of their domain out of which they make their profits ; and it is the abundance of the fish which enables them to pay a high rent for the land. And the rent no more enters into the price of the fish than the rent of corn-land enters into the price of corn.

Rent in this case, as in all other cases of trading rents, arises out of the competition for a position by means of which profits may be made.

De Fontenay on Rent

22. A French writer, M. de Fontenay, has seen this truth very clearly. He says—' It may be as well to say something here of one of the most striking instances of the advantages of position. I mean the high price paid for buying or hiring spaces in a great city. Some Economists have thought they see in that the rent of land : they have let themselves be duped by a word, as Montaigne would say. To think that it is really for a piece of land that one pays in Paris two or three hundred francs the metre, is as if one were to think that in buying the number of a hackney coach it is for three yellow numbers that he pays six to eight thousand francs—and that when a notary sells his practice, it is a double knob of gilt copper, twenty paper cases or so, five or six shabby tables, and a bad earthenware stove, that he sells for 500,000 francs. The space of ground, like the number, the practice, is only a representative sign of the acquired rights, a title to advantages and profits which may be discounted. What one pays for in the price of the space of ground is a share in the enjoyment of innumerable improvements of an advanced civilisation: it is an immense opportunity to exert oneself and to shine, to know and to be known. It is a powerful agglomeration of rich consumers if one is a producer; of producers and products of all kinds if one is more especially a consumer. It is a multitude of free enjoyments, the pavement, the *trottoirs*, gas, water, *fêtes*, theatres, palaces, walks, museums, shops, libraries, marts of all kinds of wealth, material and intellectual. The inhabitant of Paris who gives up to a stranger his share in these advantages has the perfect right to sell them to him at a good price. For it is he, or they whose right he represents, the citizens of a great city, who have gradually made it what it is. It is they who by their labours, their sacrifices, their struggles of every kind, by their gold or by their blood, have acquired and paid for these rights, this security, this progress, this public luxury, these works of general utility, these refinements of civilisation, this immense development of intellectual and material life.'

23. And De Fontenay most justly says in other parts of the same work—' Wherever there is a revenue you perceive capital' —' The theory of revenue must be the same for all classes of human production.

' Unfortunately this simple and sensible idea has been falsified by the spirit of system. Ask an Economist who knows the masters by heart what revenue is; and he will answer: that industrial revenues, the net profits of the forge, of manufactures, of banking and commerce, &c., are the profits of *capital*; but that the income from land—the net profit of the farm or the vineyard—is quite another thing; that that is the price of a monopoly, a payment for the productive powers of the earth, a continued increase of the price of products, of interests opposed to the general interest; in short, of fundamental laws and essential phenomena so radically different to the laws and phenomena of production generally that it has been necessary to make a separate division in the Science, and an entirely exceptional theory for the income from land; or, as it is called, the rent of land.

'We propose here to abolish these false distinctions, incompatible with the character of harmony and simplicity which the laws of Economics ought to have, and to prove that there is one, and only one, law of Value, Income, and Capital under all its forms.'

24. Again—'It is known that Economists who have attributed one part of the value of products to the action of natural agents have confined the application of their theory to a single class of phenomena—that of the appropriation and cultivation of the soil.

' It is not surprising that the human mind thus proceeds by particular cases. It is quite natural that the analysis of production should begin by the first of human products.

'Of all the instruments of labour, in fact, the most indispensable, the most universally and the earliest employed, and consequently the most obvious, is unquestionably that most complicated instrument called *the earth*. Divided in its extent, varying in its powers, and its aptitudes so rigorously limited, so unequally divided among nations, families, and persons, that the possession or the desire for a greater part has in all ages been the principal object of wars and human discord, the earth everywhere, and at all times, has presented the phenomenon of profit under its most visible—and I will say also its most obnoxious—form; because from the earliest antiquity entire castes have lived upon the rent of land, freed from all labour by this excess of the labour of their fellow-men. Not only is agricultural labour the most ancient and the most important of all, but among many people it has been, and still is among some, the only industry properly speaking. Not only is landed property the most visible form of capital, but it has long been, and still is in backward countries, the only capital—including, of course, landed capital, cattle capital, and slave capital, which are attached to it. The elevation of other branches of human industry to the rank of property is a fact so recent in the history of the world, that it is quite natural that the property and income of land have been studied, regulated by legislators, discussed by philosophers and statesmen, long before any other form of property and income.

'When Economic Science was founded, it was therefore to agriculture and extractive production that it first gave its attention. When it entered upon a wrong path in attributing production and value to nature, all the errors and dangers of this system fell exclusively with all their weight on the property in land. It is somewhat strange, but if this error had been generalised it would perhaps have been less fatal and less tenacious : applied only to a particular case, as it has been, it has placed property in land in an exceptional and truly proscribed position. . . .

'That truly is an unpleasant position for the possessors of the soil, and it seems difficult from such premises to draw conclusions favourable to property in land. In fact, it is somewhat badly treated by this school. It is, according to J. B. Say, the least reputable of all property—in fact, it has for its origin conquest, a purely conventional right—it is a tolerated monopoly—a legal fiction, according to J. Garnier—a restriction on the laws of God, according to Scrope—a usurped privilege, according to J. B. Say—its useful purpose is limited, according to Senior, to stretching out its hand to receive the offerings of the community—the class of proprietors' profits at the expense of the others, according to Buchanan—its interests are constantly opposed to those of the rest of society, according to Ricardo—&c., &c. As for the rent of land, it seems that the *delenda Carthago* has been pronounced against it : one of the wittiest disciples of Ricardo calls it the product of a series of outrages against property from the earliest antiquity : many Economists flatter themselves that they can make it disappear by means of Free Trade :—Ricardo, Mill, &c., to make sure of this, have proposed to confiscate it legally by taxation : one of our official Economists has even written, we are coming to the time when all proprietors will be forced to cultivate or to sell, if they wish to have a revenue.'

25. Again—'I certainly need not remark how nearly the passages I have just quoted approach the most aggressive eccentricities of Socialism. The difference here between the mortal enemy of property and its pretended defenders is, that *they* treat it as a parasite, a usurper, and a mendicant, while he bluntly calls it robbery—that M. Proudhon wishes to make all revenue disappear, and the others only suppress *rent*, which is, in their definition, only a part of revenue.

'Undoubtedly, then, this doctrine openly attacks property in land. Will the abolition stop there? The Economists of this school have thought that in limiting the application of their principle to one case they could say to logic—You shall not go further than we do. But logic laughs at their impotent authority; and it is easy to see that all property, both movable and immovable, is brought into question by the same attack.

'Since, then, in fact, it is necessary to distinguish two independent agents in production, man and nature, two associates of whom one appropriates the wages of the other; instead of recognising only one agent, one voluntary and responsible active power—man; and an instrument inert, passive, indifferent to the good or evil of the result, and consequently unpaid—nature. Immediately that the merit and the value of the work is attributed to the means of action, and not to the actual cause—to the force which obeys, and not to the will which commands—to unconscious matter, and not to the intelligence which foresees and directs; this principle, good or bad, must be followed out to the end. We must see in all classes of production that which emanates from the thinking producer, and that which is the work of the unintelligent producer—in short, we must distinguish in the collective result the share of man and the share of the natural agent. For it is not in agriculture only that these natural agents appear: they most clearly act everywhere along with man, because everywhere man can only act by means of them, and everywhere they act in the same way. Human industry employs as aids light and heat, wind and waterfalls, the properties of imponderable fluids, mechanical and chemical action, innumerable combinations, in short, laws, movements, affinities, and throughout the infinite variety of physical phenomena, the forces of nature present themselves with the same Economical characters as in agriculture. They are indispensable to production; they cannot be utilised without being appropriated; they are limited in their use and extent; unequal in power, &c. The profit of the manufacturer, like that of the agriculturist, results from their assistance, and is proportional to the extent and energy of their action. For if one manufacturer produces more, that is, at less cost than his neighbours—all personal qualities being the same—it is always because there they employ a man whom they must pay, he employs a natural agent, whom he does not pay. And since this economy in the cost of production only benefits him, as he, of course, sells exactly at the same price as his competitors with inferior processes, it is clear that he intercepts and appropriates the wages of his inanimate worker, and this interception exactly constitutes his superior profit.

'Hence in manufactures the differences of power among the agents employed are enormous, and so are the differences of profit which result from them.

'In the transport of merchandise, for instance, what a shocking inequality of power between the shoulders of a porter, horses and waggons, and a railroad! In spinning what manual skill can turn the spindles or the wheel with the speed of mechanism? Be honest then—in manufactures, perhaps even more than in agriculture, it is the instrument which causes production. If, therefore, you attribute the power of the instrument to nature, the share which nature can claim in these profits is greater than in any others; and the greater profits of manufactures and commerce ought to be called *rent*, and the monopoly of *natural agents*, just as much as the moderate profits of 3 or 4 per cent. in agriculture. In short, in every kind of production you have the same mechanism, the same combination of the action of men with the action of nature, the same differences in the rate of profit, the same influence of the instrument and capital over the result. More than that, you have the same form in the division of the profit, you have the sale, the loan, and the lease; the proprietor and the farmer, the capitalist and the worker, he who furnishes the instrument and he who uses it; he who produces and he who only " stretches out his hand to receive profit." Either it must be clearly said that one has two weights and two measures; that one is determined to find quite right in one case what is abominable in another, or we must apply strictly to the profits of manufactures the severe analysis applied to the profits from land; we must extend to profits and interest (which only proceeds from them) and to capital this accusation of monopoly, of usurpation, of parasitism, which we have just seen so clearly expressed against rent and property in the soil.

'Thus we see all property, movable and immovable, destroyed, struck with the same charge of original injustice, and all reduced for protection to some article in the Code. It is not only as is now proposed that all rent must be confiscated by taxation : it is profits from manufactures and interest which must be attacked by a radical reform.'

26. Again—' But, simple as it is, this way of looking at *produit-net*, profit, revenue, and their consequences, must necessarily escape all those who, like Ricardo, Rossi, Sismondi, Proudhon, &c., define Value as the " quantity of Labour," and measure it by cost of production.

'In fact, profit is precisely the excess of selling value, or actual value, above the cost of production or theoretical value. They then consider it as an anomaly, a robbery, an iniquity. Hence these distortions and contradictions into which they have all more or less fallen. Ricardo himself has fallen into it headlong with a curiously blind simplicity. The *produit-net* has, as is well known, three principal manifestations, rent of land, profits of manufactures, and interest of capital. Ricardo, in *rent*, explains it by monopoly and the price of natural agents ; in *profits* by a deduction by the employer from the wages of labour; in *interest*, he never suspected that it is the same problem ; he admits interest as indisputable—educated and brought up on the London Exchange, from 3 to 5 per cent. was probably for Ricardo an article of faith. Proudhon, a much stronger and more daring logician, did not deceive himself as to the identity of the three words, *rent, profit,* and *interest* ; he has quite correctly placed them in the same class as *produit-net*—a service or product sold above its cost of production. And since, according to him, Ricardo, Rossi, Sismondi, &c., the cost of production is the theoretical measure of value, and is the just value, naturally all *produit-net* appeared to him an iniquitous deduction, and he says that *rent, profit,* and *interest* are robbery—and I do not know how to reply to Proudhon, if you admit that Value is defined by the quantity of material labour, and measured in each particular case by the cost of production.'

Now, without finding it necessary to agree with all that M. de Fontenay has said in his remarkable volume on Rent, he has at least pointed out the fundamental fallacy of breaking up Economic phenomena into separate classes and finding a separate law of value for each : and he has shown most irrefragably that rent, profit, and interest all proceed from the same cause—the excess of the Value above the cost of production, which can only be effected by the Intensity of the Demand and the Limitation of the Supply.

They all stand or fall together, and if the State has the right to confiscate the one, it has the right to confiscate the others ; and we earnestly commend M. de Fontenay's volume to the attention of those who believe in Mill's scheme of confiscating the rent of land.

27. The Rent of land is an excellent example of the general Equation of Economics. Rent is the money paid by the farmer to the landlord for the use of the land. The first indispensable condition of rent arising is, that one person is the owner of more land than he can conveniently cultivate himself. A landlord is a capitalist whose capital consists of land ; and, like all other capitalists, he either trades with it himself or lets part of it out to others to trade with, and of course he is entitled to receive interest for the use of his capital like any other capitalist. The difference between a landlord who cultivates his own land and a farmer, is just the difference between the man who trades with his own or on borrowed capital. A man who has a large amount of capital in land is in a very different position to one who has his capital in money, because no single man can trade with any very large amount in land. It is very rarely a man farms more than a thousand acres of land, but many a merchant trades with half a million of money. Now, unless a man can trade with his land himself, or get some one else to do so, it is of no value to him ; but if the merchant cannot trade profitably with half a milion of money, it will still be useful to him—he can always get some interest for its use, however small. It is, therefore, a positive necessity to a man who possesses a large estate to let part of it out to farmers. No misfortune to a large landed proprietor could be worse than to have a considerable extent of his estate thrown upon his hands at once. Now, this circumstance increases the power of the person who wants to borrow the capital over the one who wants to lend it; it is a greater service done to a landlord to take a farm than it is to a tenant to let it to him. In this case, like as in other loans of capital, we must consider the farmer as the purchaser of the service; but when the capital to be borrowed is land, the power of the purchaser over the seller is much greater than when it is money. Hence, we must expect that the price of it should necessarily be lower; and this is what we actually find to be the case. The rent of land, or the money paid for the use of that species of capital, is much less than in the safest mercantile operation. There are, no doubt, other causes which also tend to produce a similar effect, operating simultaneously to increase the difference: but the cause we first assigned is a true cause of a certain amount of that effect, though not of the whole of it. The rent of land rarely exceeds $2\frac{1}{2}$ to 3 per cent. of the value of the land, and is often less than that.

28. During the great revolutionary war, a succession of bad harvests, joined to other causes, produced an enormous rise in the price of corn, so that in 1812 it reached the price of 130s. a quarter. Owing to this extraordinary rise of price, an immense quantity of inferior land was taken into cultivation at an extravagant cost, because the farmers expected that high prices would be permanent. Now, let us suppose that the old lands in cultivation had produced no more than they had done during the years of scarcity, what would have been the necessary consequence of this additional quantity of corn added to the market? As the quantity of land taken into cultivation could only be increased gradually, the first quantity added to the existing supply would not have added much to it. The proportion between the increment and the existing supply would not have been great, consequently it would only lower prices a little, and would leave a large profit to the producer. But the more land that was brought into cultivation, the more would the quantity of corn brought to market be, and the more would prices be lowered. And this might go on until the constantly increasing quantities of corn lowered the price so much, that it would only just leave a profit, and further production would cease. And it is perfectly evident that it would always be the market price which would indicate how great an expense could be afforded as cost of production. Hence, we see that it was the increased price of corn that called inferior land into cultivation, and it was the increased quantity of corn produced that lowered the market price, until the cost of production and the market price might possibly meet. But whether they did so or not would entirely depend upon the quantity produced.

So, in the Highlands of Scotland, the rent of a sheep-farm depends upon the price of wool and sheep, and not the reverse. A Highland farmer would smile if he were told that the rent he paid raised the price of wool and sheep ; when he knew well enough that the rent he could afford to pay depended upon the price of the produce.

Hence, also, we see the utter fallacy of Ricardo's rule, that it is the cost of production under the most unfavourable circumstances that regulates price. The truth is that it is the exact reverse. The price regulates the greatest cost of production that can be afforded, or the most unfavourable circumstances under which production can take place.

29. From these observations we gather that the farmer is just in the same position as the manufacturer ; neither of them can command the price he pleases for the articles he has to sell ; consequently they must each consider what will be the probable value of it when sold, and then they must devote the whole of their skill and energy in diminishing the cost of production. In order to do this each of them calls in the aid of science ; the manufacturer in the mechanical form of machinery, the farmer in the chemical form of manures and draining, and every other means that science or skill can suggest to develop the productive powers of the earth. Neither of them can fix absolutely what the cost of production is, until every improvement in science has been adopted, and every resource exhausted. It is undoubtedly true that the cost of production and the value of the produce must have a relation to each other, but the question which is to govern the other is the whole difference between protection and free trade. Under the former system, the cost of production might be as extravagant and wasteful as possible; the land might be undrained and badly cultivated, and the object was to secure by law a price which should under all circumstances cover every conceivable piece of waste and bad management, which was, with somewhat of a *mauvaise plaisanterie*, called the *natural* price of corn. While the one system held out a direct reward for every species of mismanagement and ignorance, and stinted production, the other, on the contrary, encourages skill and energy, and stimulates production, and so confers upon the community at large the blessings of as great abundance and cheapness as circumstances permit.

30. Our formula at once explains a fact which is well known to every one who has a practical acquaintance with the management of estates, that it is far more advantageous for a landlord to have his estate divided into farms of moderate size than very large ones, because so many more persons have a moderate than a large quantity of capital, and consequently so many more are able to compete for a moderate-sized farm than a large one. The landlord being the seller of the service, his power over each competitor increases according to their number, and he can demand a higher price for it. But if a farm is very large, so few can compete for it, that the landlord's power over each diminishes, and he will usually be obliged to let it low. The same remark holds good in houses, and for the same reason; houses of a moderate size let much better than those of a large one.

Malthus on Rent

31. The fundamental objection to Smith's work is its total want of uniformity of principle. Each class of cases is explained by different principles, which is manifestly contrary to the fundamental nature of Natural Philosophy.

Colonel Perronet Thompson, who was a good mathematician, published a pamphlet entitled '*The True Theory of Rent in opposition to Mr. Ricardo and others*,' in which he maintained that the simple cause of rent is everywhere the same as that which gives rise to the rent of the vineyard which produces Tokay. That this must be true is manifest to any one who has the slightest notion of a Physical Science. But it is very surprising that Malthus, who was also a good mathematician, should dispute this. He says—' First: That the price of Tokay is not a necessary price, the same quantity would be produced although the price were considerably lower.

'Secondly: That neither the purchasers of Tokay, nor the cultivators of it, live upon the produce.

'Thirdly: That there is no limit to the price of Tokay but the tastes and fortunes of a few opulent individuals.

'How, then, can it possibly be said with truth that the simple cause of Rent is everywhere the same as that which gives rise to the rent of the vineyard which produces Tokay; and how entirely inapplicable is a reference to Tokay as an illustration of the true theory of Rent?'

It is amazing that so able a man as Malthus should bring so flimsy an objection against the manifest truth of Thompson's doctrine. Malthus's knowledge of mathematics should have shown him that it could by no possibility be anything else than true.

He says that neither the purchasers nor the cultivators of Tokay live exclusively upon the produce. But neither do the producers nor the purchasers of any other article whatever live exclusively upon it. The cultivators and purchasers of corn do not live exclusively upon corn. The purchasers and cultivators of kelp do not live upon kelp. The producers and purchasers of stones from quarries do not live upon the stones. The producers and purchasers of shoes, cloth, or any other manufactures, do not live upon cloth or shoes. The growers and purchasers of cattle do not live exclusively on meat; and so on, of all other products; no person can live upon any single product. The producers and purchasers of all these things do not live upon them *directly*, but upon them *indirectly*, i.e. upon their **Value**, that is upon the various things which they can get in exchange for them.

The cultivators of corn must have meat and clothing and many other things besides bread, which they obtain by exchanging a certain portion of their corn for these things; and the surplus Value of the corn which remains beyond that maintenance is what gives Profit and Rent.

So it is with shoes or any other product. Persons do not live upon them directly; but indirectly, by obtaining what they want in exchange for them, and the surplus value which remains after providing for their maintenance is profit.

It is manifestly precisely the same with Tokay. The producers of it must exchange away a certain portion of it to provide for their maintenance; and its surplus value above that gives Profit and Rent.

Now it is manifest that the whole Value of the product is due to the Intensity of Demand and the Limitation of Supply: and the greater the Demand and the greater the Limitation of Supply is, the greater will be the Value, the greater the surplus, and the greater the Profit and Rent.

Hence it is precisely the same principle in all products whatever; in Tokay, in corn, in kelp, in quarries, in cattle, in shoes, in manufactures of all sorts; it is the ratio of Demand and Supply alone which determines Value; and the greater the Demand and the less the Supply, the greater will be the surplus above cost. It is in all cases only a difference of degree, and not a difference of principle.

If the supply were greatly increased the Value might so much diminish, that not only there might be no profit at all, but not even sufficient to defray the cost, and then production must cease. Formerly the preparation of kelp was protected by very high duties on barilla and salt. In consequence of this great quantities of kelp were manufactured in the Western Islands and Highlands of Scotland, and brought great revenues to the proprietors. The kelp-shores of one island, North Uist, let for 7,000*l.* a year ; and about 20,000 tons were made in Scotland, which sold for about 20*l.* a ton. After the war the duties on barilla and salt were repealed. Barilla was so much cheaper and of such superior quality, that the Value of kelp immediately diminished ; at last it ceased to be produced, and most of the unfortunate proprietors, whose incomes came principally from kelp, were totally ruined. Now, the cost and the qualities of the kelp remained exactly the same as before ; but its Value was diminished by the greater cheapness and superior qualities of barilla. And since then barilla itself has, in its turn, been almost entirely superseded by the superior quality and cheapness of artificial soda.

The very same principle appears from Ricardo's theory of Rent. The actual quantity of corn necessary to support the producers remains exactly the same whatever its Value may be. But as the corn, at whatever cost produced, sells for the same price in the same market, the portion of it produced with the least cost leaves the greatest margin between Cost and Value, out of which all Profit and Rent comes ; and this excess of Value is entirely due to the Intensity of the Demand and the Limitation of the Supply.

Thus the same principle governs all cases whatever, in strict accordance with the principles of Natural Philosophy : and the Value of every product, invariably and at all times, depends exclusively upon Demand and Supply.

From this it follows that if all landlords were swept away the consumers would receive no benefit. The products of the earth would not be sold the least cheaper. There would be exactly the same Demand and exactly the same Supply, and therefore the Value would remain the same. It can make no manner of difference to the consumer whether the whole profits go to the farmer alone, or whether they are divided between landlord and farmer.

It is precisely the same with a capitalist and a trader or manufacturer. These latter almost invariably carry on their trade by means of money borrowed at interest. But the interest is not a cause of price, but must come out of Profits. If the trader traded on his own money, he and others would endeavour to limit the supply so that the Value of the product would afford an interest for the capital ; and whether he takes that interest himself, or divides it with a capitalist, can make no difference to the consumer.

Thus we see that Nature alone gives quantities and qualities, but man alone gives Value ; and whether Agriculture, Commerce, and Labour are productive, i.e. produce a Profit, or not, depends upon exactly the same principle, that is, whether the Intensity of the Demand and the Limitation of the Supply of the product or the labour are so great that their **Value** exceeds the Cost of Production, or the maintenance of the Labourers.

CHAPTER X

ON LABOUR, OR IMMATERIAL WEALTH

Personal Qualities *are* **Wealth**

1. IT has been seen in the preceding book that the author of the 'Eryxias' in ancient times demonstrated that Personal Qualities are Wealth: because persons can gain an income by their use as well as by exchanging gold and silver.

And in this all modern Economists agree. Smith expressly enumerates the natural and acquired abilities of persons as Fixed Capital, and part of the wealth of society. This is still more clearly enforced by Say, who classes the Abilities and Industry of the people as Productive.

Senior has enforced the same doctrine in an eloquent passage—' If the question whether **Personal Qualities** are **Wealth** had been proposed in classical times, it would have appeared too clear for discussion. [We have already seen that the question was decided in the affirmative in ancient times.] In Athens everyone would have replied that they, in fact, constituted the whole value of an ἔμψυχον ὄργανον. The only differences in this respect between a freeman and a slave are, first, that the freeman sells himself, and only for a period, and to a certain extent: the slave may be sold by others and absolutely: and, secondly, that the **Personal Qualities** of the slave are a portion of the Wealth of his master: those of the freeman, so far as they can be made the subject of exchange, are a part of his own Wealth. They perish, indeed, by his death, and may be impaired or destroyed by disease, or rendered **Valueless** by any changes in the customs of the country which shall destroy the **Demand** for his services: but, subject to these contingencies, they are **Wealth**, and Wealth of the most valuable kind. The amount of revenue derived from their exercise in England far exceeds the rental of all the lands in Great Britain.'

So again—' Even in our present state of civilisation, which, high as it appears by comparison, is far short of what may be easily conceived, or even of what may be confidently expected,· the **Intellectual** and **Moral Capital** of Great Britain far exceeds all her Material Capital, not only in importance, but even in productiveness. The families that receive mere Wages probably do not form a fourth of the community, and the comparatively large amount of the Wages even of these is principally owing to the Capital and skill with which their efforts are assisted and directed by the more educated members of the society. Those who receive mere Rent, even using that word in its largest sense, are still fewer: and the amount of Rent, like that of Wages, principally depends on the knowledge by which the gifts of nature are directed and employed. The bulk of the national revenue is Profit: and of that Profit the portion which is mere interest on Material Capital probably does not amount to one-third. The rest is the result of **Personal Capital**, or, in other words, of education.'

'It is not on the accidents of the soil or climate, or the existing accumulation of the material instruments of production, but on the quantity and diffusion of this **Immaterial Capital**, that the Wealth of a country depends. The climate, the soil, and the situation of Ireland have been described as superior, and are certainly not much inferior, to our own. Her poverty has been attributed to the want of Material Capital; but were Ireland now to exchange her native population for seven millions of our English north countrymen, they would quickly create the Capital that is wanted. And were England north of Trent to be peopled exclusively by a million of families from the west of Ireland, Lancashire and Yorkshire would still more rapidly resemble Connaught. Ireland is physically poor because she is morally and intellectually poor. And while she continues uneducated, while the ignorance and violence of her population render persons and property insecure, and prevent the accumulation and prohibit the introduction of Capital, legislative measures intended solely and directly to relieve her poverty may not indeed be ineffectual, for they may aggravate the disease the symptoms of which they are meant to palliate, but undoubtedly will be productive of no permanent benefit. **Knowledge** *has been called Power—it is far more certainly* **Wealth**. Asia Minor, Syria, Egypt, and the northern coast of Africa were once among the richest, and are now amongst the most miserable countries in the world, simply because they have fallen into the hands of a people without a sufficiency of the **Immaterial** sources of Wealth to keep up the material ones.'

So Mill says—' The Skill and the Energy and Perseverance of the artisans of a country are reckoned part of its Wealth,' and of course the Abilities of all other classes as well.

Definition *of* Labour

2. Any exertion of the Energies of the Mind, however manifested, whether by the tongue, the hand, or in any other way, is termed **Labour**.

However apparently simple work may be, it must be directed by **Thought.** All **Labour** is in reality **Thought** or **Knowledge**, accompanied more or less by muscular exertion: and the sedentary scientific student, the lawyer, the clergyman, the author, the professor, the painter, the cabinet minister, the banker, the merchant, are as truly **Labourers** and **Working Men** as any ploughman, or carpenter, or mason.

Each of the great sciences—Geometry, Astronomy, Optics, Chemistry, Medicine, Law, Engineering, Economics—is as truly the product of **Labour** as the Pyramids, or an ironclad, or a railway: and, indeed, there is no Labour so exhausting to the tissues of the brain as mental abstraction on scientific or philosophical subjects. Each of the great sciences and professions is in reality a great Estate, which supplies utilities to mankind, which are wanted, **Demanded**, and paid for, just as the land produces corn and cattle and other things which minister to the material wants of the body.

Labour, indeed, is often divided into muscular and nervous: and in common parlance it is more frequently applied to the exertion of the body than of the mind. And the term **Labourers** or **Working men** is often considered to include only those who work with their hands, as ploughmen, masons, carpenters, and other artisans.

Nothing can be more unfortunate, however, than making distinctions in kind where none exist in reality, and marking off certain portions of the community as **Working Classes**: and supposing that they are governed by peculiar laws different from those relating to other classes. The Lord Chancellor, the Archbishop of Canterbury, all the Judges and Bishops, Lawyers and Clergy, Physicians and Surgeons, Authors, Professors, men of science, bankers, merchants, &c., are all members of the noble brotherhood of **Labourers** or **Working men**.

Corin, in *As You Like It*, says truly—

> Sir, I am a true Labourer: I earn my bread.

Labour *is a* **Commodity** *or* **Wealth**

3. An exertion of the mind cannot be seen, nor handled, nor transferred from one person to another: but yet its *Value may be measured in Money*. In exchange for so much money a person may transfer to another the Right to demand so much service or exertion of mental energies, powers, or capacity. Consequently, as we have observed already, that **Res** is *anything* which can be the subject of a Right, jurists have pointed out that **Labour**, or human exertions, are included in the term **Res**.

All modern Economists agree with the author of the 'Eryxias' that Labour is a commodity and the subject of Property like any material chattel.

Thus Smith says—'The Property which every man has in his own Labour, as it is the original foundation of all other Property, so it is the most sacred and inviolable. The Patrimony of the poor man lies in the strength and dexterity of his hands.'

So De Quincey says—'The Estate of a serving man is in his Capacity to serve.'

So Huskisson—'As the Labour which is the Property of the workman.'

So Carlyle—'The poor man also has Property—his Labour.'

Labour, therefore, is a **Commodity** which is the subject of sale or exchange like any other Commodity. Ricardo, who does not give any definition of Wealth, says—'Labour which, like all other things which are purchased and sold . . . the natural Price of all Commodities, excepting raw produce and Labour.'

Dr. Stirling says truly—'Trade regards Labour itself simply as a subject of traffic and exchange ; a thing to be bought and sold in the market—a **Commodity**—one, indeed, of primary importance, compared with which all others dwindle into insignificance : but still a **Commodity** which varies in quantity and fluctuates in price: and the Value of which consequently is governed by the very same laws which regulate the Value of those Commodities which are the products of Labour. A day's or a year's Labour has its Price, just as an ounce of silver, or a bushel of corn, has its Price.'

'Labour, it cannot be too often repeated, is nothing but a subject of Sale and Merchandise, a Commodity liable to variations of Quantity, and consequent fluctuations of Price.'

Labour, therefore, being simply a Commodity, there is a market for it like for anything else. There is a Labour Market, just as there is a Corn Market, or a Meat Market, a Poultry Market, a Fish Market, or Fruit Market.

Labour *may be* **Capital**

4. Labour then, being simply a Commodity, may like any other Commodity be used in two different ways. First, for the Labourer's own enjoyment : and secondly, for the purpose of Profit : the Labourer may make an Income by the exercise of his Labour : and therefore he may use **Labour** as **Capital**.

If a person digs in his own garden for his own amusement : or if he gives lectures to his friends, or plays or sings in private society : such Labour is not used as Capital ; and does not enter into Economics.

But if he sells his Labour directly in any capacity, such as an artisan, a ploughman, or in any professional capacity, such as an engineer, a physician, an advocate, an actor, or performer of any sort, and earns an income by so doing, then such **Labour** is **Capital** to him.

Or if he bestows his Labour on any product which he intends

to sell and make an income or profit by: then such Labour is equally Capital.

Thus an author who writes books for sale or profit, uses his Labour as Capital: a man who cultivates his own land, and sells the produce, uses his Labour as Capital.

Thus Huskisson said—'that he had always maintained that **Labour** is the poor man's **Capital**.'

Mr. Cardwell said to his constituents—'**Labour** is the poor man's **Capital**.'

A writer in a daily paper said—'The only **Capital** they possess is their **Labour**; which they must bring into the market to supply their daily wants.'

The *Economist* spoke of the Irish farmers—'who have no **Capital** but their **Labour**.'

So another writer said—'In an agricultural society in the backward condition of Ireland is not the **Real Capital** of a country the **Labour** of its people?

On Wages

5. When the Labourer sells his **Labour** directly, the reward or Price he gets for it is called in old homely Saxon—**Wages**. The Labourer is said to be the *servant* of the hirer, whatever be the nature of the Labour, or the rank of the Labourer. A Servant is a person who sells his personal services. Thus the Cabinet ministers are said to be the Queen's confidential servants.

Modern refinement, however, in many cases disdains the homely old name of Wages: and it is now usually confined to the sums paid for manual labour, or domestic service. Labourers who consider themselves of a higher sort affect other names for their rewards. Officers in the services speak of their Pay: professional men of their *Fees*: employés of all sorts of their *Salaries*. But all these names merely denote the reward for Labour: and all who receive them are **Labourers**, whatever their rank, or the nature of their Labour may be.

As Wages is the sum given in exchange for Labour, of course the higher Wages are the greater is the Value of Labour: and the Value of Labour diminishes as the amount of the reward diminishes.

The **Wages Fund**

6. We have now to consider the Fund which supplies Wages: and we shall see in this case a striking example of the importance of a clear definition of Fundamental terms.

It is said that Wages come out of Capital. But what is Capital?

Mill lays down two fundamental propositions regarding Capital—

1. That Industry is limited by Capital.
2. That all Capital is the result of saving.

Many writers suppose there is some definite Fund set apart for the maintenance of Labour which they call the **Labour Fund**, or the **Wages Fund:** which they suppose regulates Wages.

Thus Senior says that the proximate cause which decides the Rate of Wages 'is the extent of the **Fund** [what Fund?] for the maintenance of Labourers compared with the number of Labourers to be maintained.'

So Jones, who confines Wealth to material objects only, says that Wages depend on the amount of Wealth devoted to maintaining Labourers.

'The amount of Wealth devoted to the maintenance of Labour constitutes the **Labour Fund** of the world: and the amount so devoted in any country constitutes the **Labour Fund** of that country.

'The third division of the **Labour Fund** consists of what is properly termed Capital; that is of the stored up results of past Labour used with a view to Profit.'

Mill says—'There is unfortunately no mode of expressing by one familiar term, the aggregate of what may be called the **Wages Fund** of a country.' And many other writers have spoken of this Wages Fund.

But what is this Wages Fund?

All these writers assert that the Wages Fund consists of Capital which they assert is the accumulation of the savings of the **past.** They allege that it is only increased Capital that can lead to the increased employment of Labour: and that increased Capital can only arise from the increased savings of the *past*.

7. But is this the fact? Is the Wages Fund confined to material Money the fruit of *past* savings? and are Wages paid in nothing but specie? Everyone who has the slightest knowledge of business, knows that such an idea is utterly erroneous, and that an enormous mass of Wages is paid in **Credit**.

Let the student refer back to the account of Cash Credits in Scotland given in a previous chapter, and he will at once see how utterly fallacious it is to say that the Wages Fund consists only of specie the accumulation of the past.

It is shown there that immense tracts of country have been reclaimed from the barren wilderness: that all public, canals, roads, railroads, docks, harbours, have been created by means of the £1 Notes issued by the Banks.

Now, if these things had been done by means of sovereigns, they would undoubtedly have been Capital, the accumulation of the *past*. The sovereigns would have been advanced as Wages, and they would have come back again out of the profits reaped by the execution of these works.

But there were no sovereigns in the country to execute these works: and if the country had had to wait until sovereigns had been accumulated from the savings of the past, it would have had to wait for an indefinite time for the execution of these works.

But the Banks, seeing this state of matters, advanced the necessary sums in their own £1 Notes: Wages are paid in these £1 Notes: and they have been part of the Wages Fund, exactly as if they had been money. The Banks gained exactly the same Profit by advancing them as if they were actual money: the proprietors and farmers have gained the same profits by reclaiming the lands and executing these public works by the use of these £1 Notes, as if they were money. And when the lands have been reclaimed and the works executed, the advances made by the Banks were paid off just in the same way as the original sovereigns expended in executing them would have been replaced. These £1 Notes then have produced exactly the same results to the community as if they had been actual money. They have been **Capital** exactly in the same sense and in the same way that an equal amount of Money would have been Capital. But were they the result of past saving? Evidently not: they were the **Present Value** of the *future* Profits.

What becomes then of the doctrine that the Wages Fund consists exclusively of the accumulation of *past* Labour? or that Capital is restricted to the savings of *past* Labour? What becomes of Mill's fundamental proposition that—*Industry is limited by Capital?* unless Credit is admitted to be Capital? What becomes of his fundamental proposition that—**All** *Capital is the result of saving?*

Hence we see that not only is the accumulation of *past* Profits brought into the Wages Fund: but also the anticipation of *Future* Profits.

As we have often said—*Every future Profit has a* **Present Value**—and that Present Value may be brought into the Wages Fund, and made Capital of, exactly in the same way as the accumulation of the past.

But exactly the same process goes on in every branch of industry, manufacturing and commercial. The anticipated proceeds of the Future are Capitalised and brought into the Wages Fund: and conduce to production exactly in the same way as so much Money.

And this doctrine is fully admitted by Mill. 'Wealth,' he says, 'is *anything* which has Purchasing Power.' 'Credit,' he says over and over again, 'is Purchasing Power:' therefore, by his own admission, Credit is Wealth. Again, he says that 'Bank Notes, Bills of Exchange, and Cheques circulate as Money and perform **all** the functions of Money.' Now all these documents are simply Rights to future payments and are **Credit.** And as Mill admits that they perform **all** the functions of Money, they of course may be used as Capital equally as Money, and form part of the Wages Fund.

The student will now see why we took such pains to exhibit Mill's self-contradictions on the subject of Credit. Mill says that Wages depend on the Ratio of Population to Capital. But what is Capital? Mill sneers at the imbecility of those who say that Credit is Capital, yet the very same Mill says—

'When Paper Currency, i.e. Credit is supplied as in our country by bankers and banking companies, the amount is almost wholly turned into **Productive Capital** . . . . . a banker's profession being that of a money lender [which it is not], his issue of Notes is a simple extension of his ordinary occupation. He lends the amount to farmers, manufacturers, and dealers who employ it in their several businesses. So employed it yields, like any other **Capital**, Wages of Labour and Profits of Stock . . . The **Capital** in the long run becomes entirely **Wages**, and when replaced by the sale of the Produce, becomes Wages again : thus affording a perpetual **Fund** for the maintenance of **Productive Labour**, and increasing the annual produce of the country by all that can be produced through the means of a **Capital** of that Value.'

And he says—' An effect of this latter character naturally attends upon some extensions of **Credit**, especially when taking place in the form of Bank Notes, or other instruments of exchange. The additional Bank Notes are in ordinary course first issued to producers or dealers to be employed as **Capital**.'

It is the same Mill who sneers at the confused notions of those who say that Credit is Capital—' Credit has a great, but not as many people seem to suppose a magical, power : it cannot make something out of nothing. *How often is an extension of Credit talked of as equivalent to a Creation of Capital : or as if Credit actually were Capital!*

The student will observe these flagrant and almost incredible self-contradictions : and he will also bear in mind that Mill says that to create Credit in excess of specie is robbery : and that no increase of Money can be of any use to a country !

8. The complete fallacy of the doctrine that the Wages Fund is limited to existing specie has also been observed by Mr. Longe—' The theory that the Wages of Labourers is limited by the amount of Capital which their employers have at their disposal prior to the sale, and independent of the Price of their goods, is very favourable to the doctrine somewhat in vogue among master manufacturers, that the Labourer has no right to look to the market price of the goods he makes, or assists in making, as a measure of the sums which his employers would be able to pay in Wages. Of late years, however, the workman in most of these trades have become too powerful and too intelligent to be hoodwinked in this way, and employers have found it necessary to impress on their workmen that *it is not their means, but the Purchasers' Demand, which limits the amount which they can afford to pay as Wages.* In the late dispute in the iron trade, when the employers taught an unruly and high-paid class of workmen the wholesome lesson that employers can combine as well as Labourers, the more intelligent workmen discussed the question on the proper ground, viz. with reference to the Purchasers' Demand for the finished goods, and their power of supplying themselves elsewhere if the English supply was too dear: and it being the general opinion that the works could not be kept going unless the Price of iron was reduced, the whole body of ironworkers, with the exception of the North Staffordshire men, agreed to submit to the proposed reduction of of Wages.'

Sir Rupert Kettle, County Court Judge of Worcestershire, a gentleman of great experience and success in adjusting disputes between masters and men, makes some pertinent remarks on the Wages Fund—' In the old-established relation between master and men, the experience of many years had fixed the price at which it was safe for the employer to guarantee full work : and for the journeyman to accept a certainty rather than incur the risk of independent trading. By tacit consent, founded on long experience, there was a rate from which in good times wages would rise, and in bad times fall. In the shoe trade variations in wages were very small. The journeyman knew well the selling price of the article he made, and what the material cost, and he could easily work the simple arithmetic which would tell him his Wages Fund. Both parties knew that if the proportions of Profit and Wages were not fairly adjusted, the workman could, by the exercise of a little thrift and self-denial, emancipate himself from the position of a journeyman. There was no trouble about adjusting Demand and Supply : they were convertible terms with Production and Consumption, and these two were near neighbours, so that the work of the hands easily balanced the wants of the feet.

'Now let us look at the factory operative and the mill-owner meeting to make a bargain. First as to the normal rate of wages. That will depend upon how you constitute the Wages Fund. The most fruitful source of disagreement between Masters and Men at present is the uncertainty as to what portion of the exchangeable Value of the joint product of Labour and Capital—that is of Price—should go into the Wages Fund. There is a complete unity of interest between Masters and Men throughout the whole course of Production and Exchange—their interest is that the combined action of Capital and Labour shall produce as much as possible, and that the Product should exchange for as high a Price as possible. Immediately the commodity is converted into Price their interests diverge : the employer's interest then is that a large portion of Price should be reserved for the Profit Fund—the workman's interest is that a large portion should go into the Wages Fund.'

'After making certain payments such as replacement of material, maintenance of plant, ordinary interest on Capital, premium to cover risk, and that disputable item, cost of management, the balance of Price then in the hands of the Master is what should be divided between the Wages Fund and the Profit Fund. The crux of the problem is what portion of this balance should be paid to each.'

And again—' Price is the Fund out of which both Profit and Wages are paid. This Fund comes into the hands of the master for distribution.'

The doctrine that the Wages Fund is existing specie is now utterly exploded. The **Price** of the Product is the **Fund** out of which both Profits and Wages come. The real question is, to determine how that Fund may be most equitably divided.

And how is this Price obtained before it has been actually realised? By means of Banking Credits. This is the precise use and function of Banks which issue Notes. It is to issue Notes which are the Present Value of the future Product in anticipation of the Price paid by the Consumer.

And thus we see the gigantic importance of a solid Banking system to the Labouring Classes. It multiplies the Wages Fund a hundredfold : and provides continuous employment for them so long as there is a prospect of a demand for their products.

On **Productive** *and* **Unproductive Labour**

9. We must now say something on a subject of much dispute, viz. **Productive** and **Unproductive Labour.**

The Physiocrates, who first spoke of Productive and Unproductive Labour, defined Productive Labour to be Labour which left a Profit after defraying the Cost of Production : and Unproductive Labour to be Labour which left no Profit after defraying the Cost of Production.

They alleged that Agricultural Labour is the only kind of Productive Labour? or which leaves a Profit after defraying the Cost of Production and augments the Wealth of the State.

They alleged that the Labour of artisans and the commercial classes leaves no Profit over after defraying the Cost of Production, and that it adds nothing to the Wealth of the Nation : consequently they called it **Sterile** or **Unproductive.**

We are not concerned here with the truth or the contrary of this doctrine : but only with the definition of Productive and Unproductive Labour.

As this is the true definition of Productive Labour, and the one in accordance with common usage, we have adopted it without remark in Chapter I., on the Fundamental Concepts of Economics.

The designation of Sterile or Unproductive Labourers to so many and powerful classes of society naturally raised a great clamour against them, as if they had meant it as an insult. The Physiocrates justly replied that they did not mean the term in a disparaging or humiliating sense, but purely as a matter of scientific classification. They acknowledged that the Labour of these classes was useful, and indeed indispensable and honourable ; but they did not term it Productive in a scientific sense. Their answer was just from their point of view, but it was obviously erroneous.

One of the great objects of Smith's work was to demonstrate the error of the Physiocrate doctrine, and to prove that the Labour of Artisans and men of commerce is Productive, and enriches a nation. This, of course, is obviously true : but, unfortunately, Smith quite changed the original meaning of the word Productive : and this has led to great confusion.

He says that there is one kind of Labour which adds to the value of the subject upon which it is bestowed : and another which does not. As the former produces a Value, he calls it Productive : and as the latter does not, he calls it Unproductive. Smith then enlarges the meaning of Productive to include manufacturing and commercial Labour as well as agricultural. But there he stops : and he bans all other Labour as Unproductive ; or, in his own words, endeavours to degrade it by the humiliating appellation of barren or Unproductive.

He says that the Labour of a menial servant adds to the Value of nothing. Manufacturers, it is true, advance the Wages of their workmen ; but this advance is restored to them in the Value of the Product. The Labour of menial servants has its Value, and deserves its reward as well as the Labour of artisans : but the Labour of the artisan fixes and realises itself in some vendible commodity, which lasts for some time at least after the Labour is past. It is, as it were, a certain quantity of Labour stocked and stored up to be employed if necessary upon some other occasion. That subject, or what is the same thing, the Price of that subject, can afterwards, if necessary, put into motion a quantity of Labour equal to that which had originally produced it. The Labour of the menial servant, on the contrary, does not fix or realise itself in any particular subject or vendible commodity. His services generally perish in the very instant of their performance ; and seldom leave any trace of Value behind them for which an equal quantity of service could afterwards be procured.

Now, according to Smith, the cook at an hotel is a Productive Labourer : she prepares, dresses, and cooks the various articles of food eaten by the guests. Her labour adds to their Value, and is charged for in the bill : it is fixed and realised in a vendible commodity, which lasts for some time after that Labour is passed : and her Labour tends to the Profit of the Landlord : her Wages are all repaid to him in his customers' bills.

But the cook in a gentleman's family, who performs exactly the same functions, is a menial servant, and therefore, according to Smith, she is an Unproductive Labourer. Where is the sense of such a distinction? By Smith's own doctrine, the various articles of food are more valuable after she has dressed and prepared them for the table than before. Her Labour is fixed and realised in material commodities which last after that Labour is passed. When these two persons perform exactly the same functions, and are equally paid for their services, why is one Productive and the other Unproductive? So that if the cook at an hotel takes a place in a gentleman's family, she at once is turned from a Productive into an Unproductive Labourer! If a cook in a gentleman's family takes a place in an hotel, from being an Unproductive she becomes at once a Productive Labourer! It is obvious that such a distinction is mischievous, futile, and contrary to common sense.

Again, Smith allows all the various persons engaged in extracting the coal from the mine, transporting it to distant places, and placing it in a gentleman's cellar, to be Productive Labourers: but the footman who carries it from the cellar to the drawing-room is a menial, and therefore an Unproductive Labourer. By Smith's own doctrine, the Labour of each of the series of persons who extract and transport the coal to the cellar adds to its Value: but the cellar is the domestic mine: and for the same reason the Labour of the footman who extracts the coal from the domestic mine and carries it to the drawing-room adds to its Value. The terminus *à quo* the coal starts is the mine: the terminus *ad quem* it is to arrive is the drawing-room grate. If the coal gets no further than the cellar, it may as well remain in the mine, as far as the drawing-room grate is concerned. When the footman is one of the series of persons necessary to bring the coal from the mine to the drawing-room grate, why is the line of ignominious demarcation drawn at the cellar? Why is the Labour of the persons who bring it from the mine to the cellar Productive, and the Labour of the person who brings it from the cellar to the drawing-room grate Unproductive? The Labour of each is equally necessary and equally paid for. It is obvious that such a distinction is mischievous, futile, and contrary to common sense.

Why does a gentleman pay for a cook in an hotel or in his own house to dress his dinner? Simply to save himself the trouble of doing it for himself. Why does he pay the price for miners obtaining the coals, and dealers transporting it from place to place: and why does he pay a footman to carry coals from the cellar to the drawing-room? Simply to save himself the trouble of doing so himself. The same argument applies to everything else which is wanted and paid for: and yet some are called Productive and some Unproductive Labourers. Is not this contrary to all scientific classification?

Smith then classes the Labour of the Army and Navy as Unproductive, because the protection, security, and defence of the State which is the effect of their Labour one year will not purchase its protection, security and defence for the year to come.

But the food which a man eats one year and the fuel which keeps him warm one year will not maintain him and keep him warm the next year. Yet Smith classes those who produce food and coals as Productive Labourers, and those who produce security and defence as Unproductive Labourers. Can anything be more futile?

Smith then lumps together the Sovereign, the clergy, lawyers, physicians, men of letters, players, buffoons, musicians, opera singers, opera dancers, &c., and terms them all Unproductive Labourers.

Smith is here contradictory to himself, because he expressly classes the acquired and useful abilities of persons as Fixed Capital. And he says that a man is rich according to the degree in which he can enjoy the necessaries, conveniences, and amusements of life.

Surely, then, those men who can produce these sciences, knowledge, and amusements, which Smith acknowledges to be Wealth, are Productive Labourers.

10. Accordingly, Say protested against Smith's doctrine of Productive and Unproductive Labour: and extended the meaning of Productive Labour to include all Labour which is required and paid for.

'Labour,' he says, 'is Productive when it results in a service which has exchangeable Value, although this service is consumed at the same time that it is rendered. It is Unproductive when it results in no Value. Productive Labour is of three kinds: that of the man of science [and all mental Labour]: of the managers of Labourers: and of that of the workman.

He also combats Smith's doctrine of Unproductive Labour.

'A house, a piece of plate, or massive furniture are very durable products; clothes are less so; vegetables, fruits, still less so. But yet this difference of durability does not in any way affect their quality of products; all of them are wealth in proportion to their value. A farmer in the valley of Montmorency draws annually by the sale of his cherries a sum as real as the proprietor of a portion of the forest of Montmorency draws from cutting wood. It is only the amount of the whole which makes the difference, and if the cherries produced are of more value than the wood, the cherries represent the greater Production of Wealth. Nevertheless between the instant when these cherries are ripe, and when they must be eaten, there is no great interval; while the wood which serves to form solid buildings, is Wealth which lasts a long time. In reference to production, the amount of utility produced can only be determined by the price which men set on it. It is the price which measures the profit which the producer draws from it.

'Since, in regard to production, the durability of a product is of no consequence provided it has value; let us come from products to products, from those which are necessarily consumed a few instants after they are completely created, to those which are necessarily consumed at the very instant of their creation, and we see that a theatrical performance, for instance, is a product which may differ from some fruit of the earth by its duration, because its value cannot last beyond the instant of representation, but which do not differ in the conditions which make them each a product: I mean the property of satisfying one of our wants, of gratifying a taste, of capacity of being valued and sold. The actors meet to offer you the result of their Labours and talents: the spectators, on their side, meet to give in exchange for this agreeable product a sum which comes itself from the productions in which you or your parents have taken part. It is an exchange like any other.

'Adam Smith and other Economists have denied to immaterial products, the name of products, and to the Labour of which they are the fruit the name of Productive Labour, upon the ground that these products are consumed at once and have no durability, that they are not susceptible of accumulation and therefore can never increase the capital of the nation.

'The last reason is founded upon an error. Do we accumulate the products which are not preserved, such as the fruits of the earth; which they do not deny to be products?

'In short, is a value the less a product because it is consumed? Are not the greater part of the products of the year destroyed within the year? Are we to say of a man who has lived upon his revenue, that he has no revenue because nothing remains to him?

'Smith's doctrine upon this point does not comprehend the whole doctrine of production. He places in the class of Unproductive Labourers, and regards as burdens on society, a crowd of men who, in truth, furnish a real utility in exchange for their pay. The soldier who holds himself in readiness to repel an invasion of the foreigner, and who repels it at the peril of his life; the administrator who devotes his time and his knowledge to the preservation of the rights of society: the upright judge, the protector of innocence and justice: the professor, who diffuses the sciences painfully acquired: a hundred other professions which comprise persons the most eminent in dignity, the most eligible by their talents and personal character, are not less useful to society, and satisfy the wants which the nation as imperatively requires, as persons do clothing and shelter.

'If any of these services so rendered are not offered to sufficiently extensive competition, if they are paid for above their value, it is an abuse, with which we have no concern here. Undoubtedly there is Unproductive Labour, but that to which a price is freely given, and which is worth the price put upon it, when it may be refused, is Productive Labour, however short is the duration of the product.

'According to the writers who refuse to recognise immaterial products, the artificers who produce the fireworks which are to be let off next day in a public garden are productive labourers, while the actors who prepare the performance of a grand tragedy are unproductive labourers. Certainly if we could judge by the wealth produced and consumed on these two occasions, otherwise than by the price agreed to be paid for them, we should think that the actors who prepared the theatrical performance, from the talent required, from the duration of the performance, from the long remembrance one preserves of it, from the delicacy and the elevation of the sentiments it gives rise to, we should say that these actors are more productive labourers than the artificers who prepare the squibs, and crackers, and wheels, which vanish in smoke.'

11. These arguments are so perfectly obvious and conclusive, that it might have been expected that Mill, who was Say's disciple, would have seen their force and adopted them. More especially as he himself begins with the Definition that Wealth is *anything* which has Purchasing Power. Now, by Mill's own Definition, services which are paid for are Wealth. Hence, to produce a service which is paid for is by his own definition Productive Labour. Nevertheless, Mill has gone back very much to Smith's ideas, though he has somewhat enlarged them. Smith only admitted those to be Productive Labourers whose Labour was directly fixed and realised in some material vendible commodity. Mill includes those Labourers whose Labour results indirectly in a material commodity as Productive. Thus he includes the Labour of officers of Government, because it tends indirectly to the production and protection of material Wealth.

'All labour is in the language of Political Economy [? Mill] unproductive which ends in immediate enjoyment, without any increase of the accumulated stock of permanent means of enjoyment. And all Labour, according to our present definition, must be classed as Unproductive which terminates in a permanent benefit, however important, provided that an increase of material products forms no part of that benefit. The Labour of saving a friend's life is not Productive, unless the friend is a Productive Labourer, and produces more than he consumes. To a religious person the saving of a soul must appear a far more important service than the saving of a life; but he will not, therefore, call a missionary, or a clergyman, productive labourers, unless they teach, as the South Sea Missionaries have in some cases done, the arts of civilisation in addition to the doctrines of their religion. It is, on the contrary, evident that the greater number of missionaries or clergymen a nation maintains, the less it has to expend on other things : while the more it expends judiciously in keeping agriculturists and manufacturers at work, the more it will have for every other purpose. By the former it diminishes, *cæteris paribus*, its stock of material products ; by the latter it increases them.

'Unproductive may be as useful as Productive Labour ; it may be more useful even in point of permanent advantage ; or its use may consist only in pleasurable sensation, which, when gone, leaves no trace : or it may not afford even this, but may be absolute waste. In any case society or mankind grow no richer by it, but poorer. All material products consumed by anyone while he produces nothing are so much subtracted, for the time, from the material products which society would otherwise have possessed. But though society grows no richer by Unproductive Labour, the individual may. An Unproductive Labourer may receive for his labour, from those who derive pleasure or benefit from it, remuneration which may be to him a considerable source of wealth ; but his gain is balanced by their loss ; they may have received a full equivalent for their expenditure, but they are so much poorer for it. When a tailor makes a coat and sells it, there is a transfer of the price from the customer to the tailor, and a coat besides which did not previously exist ; but what is gained by an actor is a mere transfer from the spectator's funds to his, leaving no article of wealth for the spectator's indemnification. Thus the community collectively gain nothing from the actor's labour : and it loses, of his receipts, all that portion which he consumes, retaining only that which he lays by. A community, however, may add to its wealth by unproductive labour, at the expense of other communities, as an individual may at the expense of other individuals. The gain of Italian opera singers, German governesses, French ballet dancers, &c., are a source of wealth, as far as they go, to their respective countries, if they return thither. The petty states of Greece, especially the ruder and more backward of those states, were nurseries of soldiers, who hired themselves to the princes and satraps of the East to carry on useless and destructive wars, and returned with their savings to pass their declining years in their own country: these were unproductive labourers, and the pay they received, together with the plunder they took, was an outlay without return to the countries which furnished it ; but though no gain to the world, it was a gain to Greece. At a later period the same country and its colonies supplied the Roman Empire with another class of adventurers, who, under the name of philosophers or rhetoricians, taught the youth of the higher classes what were esteemed the most valuable accomplishments ; these were mainly unproductive labourers, but their ample recompense was a source of wealth to their own country. In none of these cases was there any accession of wealth to the world. The services of the labourers, if useful, were obtained at a sacrifice to the world of a portion of material wealth ; if useless, all that these labourers consumed was, to the world, waste.'

12. We have given this long extract in order to place before our readers fairly Mill's views on this important subject, which Malthus justly says goes to the root of the whole science, and as Mill says, brings us back to the discussion of what wealth is. For Productive Labour is Labour productive of Wealth. We see that Mill has somewhat extended the term beyond Smith's view of it : for while Smith only allows those to be productive labourers who are directly employed in the production of material products, Mill includes also those who are indirectly employed in that way ; and this, of course, is a considerably wider circle of persons. He admits ' officers of government' to be productive labourers. Hence managers of manufactories, foremen, the army, navy, and police, are gathered within the fold of Productive Labourers : but we are not sure whether the judicial *corps* rank as 'officers of Government.' We are inclined to think they do ; and in that case a barrister who earns an income by serving private parties would be an Unproductive Labourer, but a judge who earns an income by serving the State is a productive labourer. Authors and editors of newspapers take rank as Productive Labourers ; while actors, singers, opera dancers, clergymen, and others still remain out in the cold as Unproductive Labourers. Bankers may rank as Productive Labourers, because the operations of banking do undoubtedly cause a very great increase of material products. The Labour of railway and other *employés* engaged in transporting merchandise would be Productive, but in transporting passengers would be Unproductive. According to the distinction made by Mill, the labour of instructors teaching artisans and other Productive Labourers is Productive, the Labour of those engaged in educating gentlemen, or persons not engaged in business, is Unproductive. So the labour of a surgeon, or physician, healing a productive labourer is productive; healing a gentleman is unproductive. According to Mill, the delight the audience receives from witnessing the performance of a Garrick, a Kemble, a Siddons, a Talma, a Macready, a Wigan, a Taglioni, a Fanny Elsler, a Lablache, a Catalani, a Malibran, a Jenny Lind, a Grisi, a Mario, an Alboni, a Titiens, a Patti, and a Nilsson, is the result of Unproductive Labour, and the word is poorer by their maintenance, while the opulence of the world would be augmented by the Labour of as many pastry-cooks.

13. To show the extraordinary consequences of Mill's doctrine, we may take this case. Suppose the head-master of a great public school has a class of twenty pupils. Suppose that ten of these are noblemen and gentlemen of large estate, who will not be bound to work for their living: suppose the other ten to be boys of a poorer class, who are intended for industrial occupations, such as lawyers, doctors, men of business. The head-master bestows equal care and Labour in teaching each set of boys: and is paid exactly at the same rate for each set. According to Mill, his Labour in teaching the rich boys is Unproductive: and his Labour in teaching the poorer boys is Productive.

We do not think that such distinctions as these accord with general usage, or with sound practical philosophy: and on this point we entirely agree with Say, that Productive Labour is Labour which is Productive of Profit. When a person bestows his Labour in preparing some material substance, or in rendering some service, which he hopes will be required or demanded by others, what does he expect, and what is his object? It is to *draw forth* some reward in exchange for it. Everyone considers his Labour as Productive, not according to what he offers but according to what he obtains in return for it. A theatrical company may *produce* several pieces during the season, but whether their labour is *Productive* or not entirely depends upon the returns to their treasury. If they play to empty benches their Labour is Unproductive; if the house is crowded, and their treasury well filled, their Labour is Productive.

And it can be easily shown from Mill's own words that this is the true meaning, because he says that Productive Labour is Labour Productive of Wealth. And what is Wealth by his own definition? It is *anything* which has Power of Purchasing: whether, therefore, a thing is Wealth or not purely depends whether anything can be obtained in exchange for it. And of course the more that can be obtained in exchange for it the greater Wealth it is, and the more Productive. Hence, by Mill's own definition, whether anything is Productive or not does not depend upon the nature of the thing, but upon the quantity of other things it can draw forth in exchange, or the amount of the returns.

J. H. Burton says truly—'Whatever society pays for, and ought to pay for, may fairly be considered as Productive Labour for our present purpose.'

Hence, in accordance with general usage, and these extracts from Say and Burton, we shall always use Productive Labour to mean Labour which earns a Profit or reward. A Productive Labourer is any Labourer who earns an Income; no matter whether that Labour terminates in a material product or not. That is, a person who performs a service in exchange for a Profit. An Unproductive Labourer is one who Labours without a reward or Profit. And anything whatever which earns a Profit is, as Senior says all Economists are agreed, **Capital**.

On the **Division** of **Labour**.

14. We now come to the principle of the DIVISION OF LABOUR, which has acquired great celebrity from Smith having made it the commencement of the *Wealth of Nations*. Several writers, certainly, had observed it before him; but no one had brought it into that prominence which it really deserves as the most powerful method of increasing the quantity of produce, before the use of machinery. And its consequences and applications reach a great deal further than even Smith himself ever perceived.

An eminent Economist, Wakefield, has taken exception to the expression *Division of Labour*, as involving a fundamental misconception. He says that, notwithstanding the popularity of Smith's first chapter, it is not only very deficient, but also full of error.

'The use of the same term in different senses, or of different terms in the same sense, is *primâ facie* evidence that a writer is not thoroughly acquainted with his subject. Both kinds of oversight occur frequently in this chapter. To explain them would be more easy than it is, if, as I have ventured to say in the preface, the meaning of the commonest terms used in treating of Political Economy were not still unsettled.

' No one will deny, however, that there is a wide difference between an operation, work, or business which is performed by labour, and the labour which performs it. The muscular exertion by which a house is built is not the same thing as the operation of building a house; the operation of making a pin is something entirely distinct from the muscular exertion by which the pin is made. These different things are over and over again confounded by Adam Smith. To establish this position, it will be sufficient to mark a number of instances in which he expresses by some other term than " division of labour" what he generally employs that term to express :—

' " The important *business* of making a pin is, in this manner, divided into about eighteen *distinct operations*."

' " The separation of different *trades* and *employments* from one another."

' " How many different *trades* are employed [pursued] in each branch of the linen and woollen manufactures."

' " So complete a separation of one *business* from another."

' " It is impossible to separate so entirely the *business* of the grazier from that of the corn farmer as the *trade* of the carpenter is commonly separated from that of the smith."

' " Philosophy or speculation becomes, like every other *employment*, the principal or sole *trade* or *occupation* of a particular class of citizens. Like every other *employment*, too, it is subdivided into a great number of different branches."

'" The subdivision of *employment* in philosophy, as well as in every other *business*, improves dexterity and saves time."

' In all these instances, and not a few more, division is said to take place, not, as the writer says elsewhere, in the labour which performs operations, but in the operations which are performed by labour. The impropriety of using terms so dissimilar to express the same meaning is obvious enough; but this is not a dispute about terms merely, as will be seen by the following curious remarks; curious, that is, as appearing in a treatise on the *division* of labour :—

'" Observe the accommodation of the most common artificer or day-labourer in a civilised and thriving country, and you will perceive that the *number of people* of whose industry a part, though but a small part, has been employed in procuring him accommodation, *exceeds all computation*. The woollen coat, for example, which covers the day-labourer, as coarse and rough as it may appear, is the produce of the *joint labour* of a great multitude of workmen. . . . Without the assistance and *co-operation of many thousands*, the very meanest person in a civilised country could not be provided, even according to, what we very falsely imagine, the easy and simple manner in which he is commonly accommodated."

' Here then labour is said to be united, as in fact it is whenever employments are divided. Nature has divided labour into single pairs of hands. The greatest division of labour takes place among those exceedingly barbarous savages who never help each other, who work separately from each other; and division of employments, with all its great results, depend altogether on combination of labour, or co-operation. Such important consequences spring from this principle, that it deserves the most ample illustration.

'" Suppose," says Whately, "a number of travellers proceeding through some nearly desert country, such as many parts of America, and journeying together in a kind of cafila, or caravan, for the sake of mutual security: when they came to a halting place for the night, they would not fail to make some kind of extemporaneous arrangement, that some should unlade and fodder the cattle, while others should fetch firewood from the nearest thicket, and others water from the spring : some, in the meantime, would be occupied in pitching tents, or erecting sheds of boughs ; others in preparing food for the whole party ; while some, again, with their arms in readiness, would be posted as sentinels, in suitable spots, to watch that the rest might not be surprised by bands of robbers. It would be evident to them that but for such an arrangement each man would, have to go to the spring for water, and to the wood for fuel ; would have to prepare his own meal with almost as much trouble as it costs to dress food for the whole, and would have to perform all these tasks encumbered by his arms, and on the watch for a hostile attack."

'All this would be evident to them ; they would perceive, in short, the great utility of separating the different occupations required for their ease and safety. But in order that the traveller should thus apportion these different occupations among their own body, it would be necessary that they should first combine their labour by agreeing to travel together, and to help each other on the way. If each of them had travelled alone, each man's labour would have been separated or divided, not only from that of all the others, but again amongst the several occupations of going to the wood for fire, and to the spring for water, &c. : if the labour of the traveller had been so divided, there could not have been any, the slightest division of their employments. In like manner, the division of employments which takes place in a pin manufactory, results from, and is wholly dependent on, the union, generally under one roof, of all the labour by which the pins are made. Though no entire pin be made by any one person's united labour ; many persons whose labour is united, in order that the whole operation in which it is to perform, may be separated into distinct parts, and easily apportioned among the workmen. It appears, therefore, not only that " division of labour " is a most improper term as commonly used ; not only that this is the proper term for expressing a state of things under which what is commonly expressed by it—namely a division of employments—cannot possibly take place ; but that all writers on political economy, from Adam Smith downwards, while treating of the " causes of improvement in the productive powers of labour," have overlooked a principle of first-rate importance.

'This principle is, that all improvement in the productive powers of labour, including division of employments, depends upon co-operation.'

Wakefield, therefore, in his edition of Smith, universally substitutes division of employments for division of labour, and Mill heads his chapter, with treats of this subject, 'The Combination of Labour.'

It must be admitted that Wakefield's criticism on the incorrectness of the expression division of labour is correct. But, nevertheless, when a term has once got a firm and general hold of the public mind, it is very rarely possible to change it; the only thing that can be done is to point out the misconception involved in it, and to fix and define it in its true meaning. Numerous examples of this will occur to every one versed in the history of science. Thus, in Mechanics the terms Centripetal and Centrifugal Force are used to mean exactly the opposite to what they were when they were first invented, owing to the erroneous mechanical conceptions of their originators. The term Division of Labour has acquired such a firm position in Economics, that we shall, in the same way, retain it; but we shall use it in the sense which Wakefield has so clearly pointed out.

15. Smith has, moreover, erred in describing the origin of this principle. He says—'It is the necessary, though very slow and gradual, consequence of a certain propensity in human nature which has in view no such extensive utility, the propensity to truck, barter, and exchange one thing for another.'—'As it is by treaty, by barter, and by purchase that we obtain from one another the greater part of those mutual good offices which we stand in need of, so it is this same trucking disposition which originally gives occasion to the division of labour.'—'As it is the power of exchanging that gives occasion to the division of labour.'

Now this doctrine, that the principle of the division of labour arises out of the principle of exchange, and therefore cannot exist without it, is fundamentally erroneous. In the Socialistic and Communistic states of society in which all exchanges are peremptorily forbidden, and which are organised for the express purpose of abolishing all exchanges, the principle of the division of labour is as thoroughly well understood and acted upon as in Economic societies, where private property and free exchanges exist. For this principle conduces immensely to the increase of the quantity of the produce, no matter whether this produce belongs to the community in general or to each member separately. Whether this produce is to be ultimately distributed by public authority as in Socialist and Communist societies, or by the method of free exchange as in Economic societies, makes no difference: the division of labour only affects the *Quantity* of produce obtained, not the method of its Distribution.

When Smith also asserts that the principle of the division of labour originates in the trucking, bartering, and exchanging propensity of men, which he says is common to all men, and to no other race of animals, which seem to know neither this nor any other species of contract, he had clearly forgotten both his 'humanities' and his Natural History. Several writers had not only observed the principle of division of labour among animals, but even originated the name from observing the habits of animals.

Thus Aristotle long ago noticed that in a hive of bees different parties devote themselves to different parts of the common work, and was the first to use the very term division of labour with reference to them.—'And they have each of them their proper work allotted to them: some bring flowers, others bring water; others, again, smooth and perfect the honeycomb.'—'And they *divide the work* among themselves; and some work at the honey, some at the young bees, others at the bee bread: and some, again, mould the comb; others bring water to the cells, and mix it with the honey; and others go to work.' He also speaks of their public and private life.

So Pliny says—' Thus when in favourable weather the crowd has set forth to labour, some collect the flowers with their feet, some bring water with their mouths, and drops with the tender down of their bodies. The young bees go forth to their work, and bring back their stores in obedience to orders, the older ones work within the hive. For their *duties* within are *divided* (*officia divisa*), some build the comb, some polish it, others fill it, others extract the food from what is brought.'

And Virgil, too, as if to confute by anticipation Smith's assertion that no animals but man can enter into a contract, says—' Now come, I will discuss the natural qualities which Jove himself has bestowed upon bees, I will tell for what wages they, following the Curetes' ringing noise and rattling brass, fed the King of heaven within a Cretan cave. They alone have a community of children and jointly own the houses of their city, and pass their life beneath majestic laws. They alone acknowledge a fatherland and settled home, and mindful in summer of the winter that must come, practise hard toil and for the common use store up their gains. For some look to the supply of provisions, and by *settled covenants* (*fœdere pacto*) labour in the fields; part within the confines of their homes lay the tear of the narcissus, and the gluey gum from the bark of trees, to be the first foundation of the hive, next hang along the binding wax; others guide forth the grown offspring, the nation's hope: others pack close a wealth of purest honey, and with clean nectar swell wide the cells. Some there are whose lot has fallen to stand sentinels at the gates, and by turn they watch the watery clouds of heaven, or receive the loads of those that come to the hive, or in close array drive from the homestead the drones, a lazy herd. Hotly the work proceeds, and the stores of odorous honey are sweet with the smell of thyme.'

It is said that the details given by the above writers are not absolutely correct, as might naturally be expected, but modern observation has shown that bees carry their polity and division of labour much further than had been ascertained in ancient times.—' When bees begin to build the hive, they divide themselves into bands, one of which produces materials for the structure; another works upon these and forms them into a rough sketch of the dimensions and partitions of the cells. All this is completed by the second band, who examine and adjust the angles, remove the superfluous wax, and give the work its necessary perfection, and a third band brings provisions to the labourers who cannot leave their work. But no distribution of food is made to those whose charge in collecting propolis and pollen calls them to the field, because it is supposed they will hardly forget themselves; neither is any allowance made to those who begin the architecture of the cells. Their province is very troublesome, because they are obliged to level and extend, as well as cut and adjust the wax to the dimensions required; but then they soon obtain a dismission from this labour and retire to the fields to regale themselves with food, and wear off their fatigue with a more agreeable employment. Those who succeed them draw their mouth, their feet, and the extremity of their body several times over all the work, and never desist until all is polished and completed: and as they frequently need refreshments, and yet are not permitted to retire, there are waiters always attending, who serve them with provisions when they require them. The labourer who has an appetite bends down his trunk before the caterer to intimate that he has an inclination to eat, upon which the other opens his bag of honey, and pours out a few drops: these may be distinctly seen rolling through the hole of his trunk, which insensibly swells in every part the liquid flows through. When this little repast is over, the labourer returns to his work, and his body and feet repeat the same motions as before.' And, indeed, to describe fully the various instances in which the division of labour is carried out in the apiarian commonwealth would require a large treatise.

The same may be observed of ants, and, indeed, some naturalists go so far as to say that the brain of the ant is the most surprising thing in creation next to the human brain. Rennie says: 'In no department of natural history is it more necessary to be aware of the proper import of the term instinct than in studying the phenomena presented by the bee; for nowhere is it more difficult to discriminate between the regular operation of implanted motives, and the result of acquired knowledge and habits. The most striking feature of their history, and the one which apparently lays the foundation for those extraordinary qualities which raise them above the level of other insects, is the disposition to social union. It may in general indeed be remarked that animals which associate together, so as to form large communities, display a higher degree of sagacity than those which lead a solitary life. This is especially observable among insects. The spider and *formica leonis* may exhibit particular talents, or practise particular stratagems in the pursuit and capture of their prey; but their history is limited to a single generation, and embraces none of these interesting relations which obtain between individuals composing the gregarious tribes, such as the ant, the wasp, and the bee. Among these we trace a community of wants and desires, and a mutual intelligence and sympathy, which lead to the constant interchange of good offices, and which, by introducing a *systematic division of labour*, amidst a unity of design, lead to the execution of public works on a scale of astonishing magnitude.'

Among Mammalia the beaver is pre-eminently distinguished for the skill with which it constructs great engineering works for the defence and maintenance of its home. Nothing can better exemplify the advantage of co-operation of labour than the huge dams constructed by these animals to maintain the water at an uniform height. Having fixed upon the best situation, they begin to gnaw down one of the largest trees they can find, taking care that if on the bank of a river it shall fall directly across the stream. As many as can conveniently sit around the chosen tree, continue to gnaw it about eighteen inches from the ground, until it begins to give way. While one party is thus employed another is employed in cutting down smaller trees, and a third in making mortar and soft clay, and drawing it to the edge of the river where the bridge or dam is to be. Many of these dams are of great size, being 200 or 300 yards in length, and 12 feet thick. They are made of the trunks of the trees which the beavers have felled, cut into lengths of about a yard, and they are constructed in such a form as is best adapted to meet the force of the stream, being straight when the stream is not strong, and convex when it is powerful.

The examples in which the principle of the division of labour is carried out among animals might be greatly extended, but they would be far beyond the limits of this work. It may probably be said with safety, that it exists more or less among all animals which live in society, and certainly where they carry on works of construction. Therefore, either Smith's doctrine that the division of labour is the result of reason and speech, is incorrect, or else reason and speech must be conceded to a considerable portion of the lower animals. The latter alternative would probably now be adopted by naturalists; speech, of course, including other methods of communicating ideas and purposes besides articulate words.

16. This principle of the Division of Labour was long ago observed and acted upon. In Egypt Herodotus says that every medical man was compelled to confine himself strictly to one branch of the profession and no more.

Blanqui says that at Venice, in 1172, a tribunal was erected to superintend all manufactures, and a law was made which enacted that every workman should confine himself to a single employment in order to secure a better performance of the work: and the same law was enacted by Philip le Bel in France.

Beccaria also announces very clearly the doctrine of the Division of Labour:—'From these families spring necessarily the arts, and the different occupations of men. Each one learns by experience by applying the hand and the mind always to the same kind of work and production he finds the results more easy, more abundant, and better, than those which each one would make if each one by himself made everything necessary for himself alone; whence some tend the flocks, some card the wool, some weave it; one cultivates the corn, another makes it into bread; another makes clothes; another builds for the husbandmen and workmen; the arts thus increasing and linking themselves together, and men in this manner dividing themselves into various classes and conditions to their public and private advantage.'

Though the principle was recognised, certainly no one brought it into such prominent notice as Smith, and showed its application so strikingly, in a particular case. His description may be quoted—'The effect of the division of labour in the general business of society will be more easily understood by considering in what manner it operates in some particular manufactures. It is commonly supposed to be carried furthest in some very trifling ones; not, perhaps, that it really is carried further in them than in others of more importance : but in these trifling manufactures which are destined to supply the small wants of but a small number of people, the whole number of workmen must necessarily be small ; and these employed in every different branch of the work can often be collected into the same work-house, and placed at once under the view of the spectator. In these great manufactures, on the contrary, which are destined to supply the great wants of the body of the people, every different branch of the work employs so great a number of workmen that it is impossible to collect them all into the same work-house. We can seldom see more, at one time, than those employed in one single branch. Though in such manufactures, therefore, the work may really be divided into a much greater number of parts than in those of a more trifling nature, the division is not near so obvious, and has accordingly been much less observed.

'To take an example, therefore, from a very trifling manufacture—but one in which the division of labour has been very often taken notice of—the trade of the pin-maker, a workman not educated to this business (which the division of labour has rendered a distinct trade), nor acquainted with the use of the machinery employed in it (to the invention of which the same division of labour has probably given occasion), could scarce perhaps, with his utmost industry, make one pin in a day, and certainly could not make twenty. But in the way in which this business is now carried on, not only the whole work is a peculiar trade, but it is divided into a number of branches, of which the greater part are likewise peculiar trades. One man draws out the wire, another straights it, a third cuts it, a fourth points it, a fifth grinds it at the top for receiving the head ; to make the head requires two or three distinct operations ; to put it on is a peculiar business, to whiten the pin is another ; it is even a trade by itself to put them into the paper ; and the important business of making a pin is, in this manner, divided into almost eighteen distinct operations, which, in some manufactories, are all performed by distinct hands, though in the others the same man will sometimes perform two or three of them. I have seen a small manufactory of this kind where ten men only were employed, and where some of them consequently performed two or three distinct operations. But, though they were very poor, and therefore but indifferently accommodated with the necessary machinery, they could, when they exerted themselves, make among them about twelve pounds of pins in a day. There are in a pound of pins upwards of four thousand pins of a middling size. These ten persons, therefore, could make among them upwards of forty-eight thousand pins in a day. Each person, therefore, making a tenth part of forty-eight thousand pins, might be considered as making four thousand eight hundred pins a day. But if they had all wrought separately and independently, and without any of them having been educated to this peculiar business, they certainly could not each of them have made twenty, perhaps not one pin, in a day; that is certainly not the two hundred and fortieth, perhaps not the four thousand eight hundredth part of what they are at present capable of performing, in consequence of a proper division and combination of their different operations.

'In every other art and manufacture, the effects of the division of labour are similar to what they are in this very trifling one, though in many of them the labour can neither be so much sub-divided, nor reduced to so great a simplicity of operation. The division of labour, however, so far as it can be introduced, occasions in every art a proportionate increase of the productive powers of labour. The separation of different trades and employments from one another, seems to have taken place in consequence of this advantage. This separation, too, is generally carried furthest in those countries which enjoy the highest degree of industry and improvement; what is the work of one man in a rude state of society being generally that of several in an improved one. In every improved society the farmer is generally nothing but a farmer; the manufacturer, nothing but a manufacturer. The labour, too, which is necessary to produce any one complete manufacture is almost always divided among a great number of hands. How many different trades are employed in each branch of the linen and woollen manufactures, from the growers of the flax and the wool, to the bleachers and smoothers of the linen, or to the dyers and dressers of the cloth. The nature of agriculture, indeed, does not admit of so many subdivisions of labour, nor of so complete a separation of one business from another, as manufactures. It is impossible to separate so entirely the business of the grazier from that of the corn-farmer, as the trade of the carpenter is commonly separated from that of the smith. The spinner is almost always a distinct person from the weaver : but the ploughman, the harrower, the sower of the seed, and the reaper of the corn, are often the same. The occasions for these different sorts of labour returning with the different seasons of the year, it is impossible that one man should be constantly employed in any one of them.'

We may also quote from Say an instance equally striking, in which the division of labour is carried almost to a greater extent still, namely, that of playing cards—' It is not the same workmen who prepare the paper of which the cards are made, nor the colours printed on them : and in giving attention to only one employment in this matter we shall find that a pack of cards is the result of several operations of which each one occupies a distinct series of workmen, or workwomen, who are always employed in the same operation. It is always different persons, but always the same set, who sift the packets and the swellings of the paper which injure the quality of its thickness : the same set of persons paste together the three leaves of which each card is formed, and put them in the press : the same set of persons colour the backs of the cards : the same set always print the outlines of the figures : another set print the colours of the same figures : another set dry over the heater the cards when printed : another set polish them on both sides. It is a separate trade to cut them equally : it is another to collect them and form them into packs : another to print the cover of the packs ; and yet another to cover them : without counting the duties of the persons employed in buying and selling them, in paying the workmen, and keeping their accounts. In short, those in the trade say that each card, that is, that each little piece of cardboard of the size of the hand, before being fit to be sold, goes through not less than seventy different operations, which are each the subject of a distinct trade. And if there are not seventy kinds of workmen in each manufactory of cards, it is because the division of labour is not carried so far as it might be, and because the same workman performs two, three, or four distinct operations.

'The effect of this separation of employments is immense. I have seen a manufactory of cards in which thirty workmen produced every day 15,550 cards, that is, more than 500 cards per man. And it may be presumed that if each workman was obliged to perform each operation by himself, and supposing him skilful in his art, he would not complete more than two cards á day: and consequently the thirty workmen, instead of making 15,500, would only make 60.'

To give similar details of other trades would fill a volume. We will only give one. In watchmaking there are no less than 112 distinct trades, to each of which a boy may be apprenticed; and of which he knows none but that one. Now we should like to see some similar calculation made, as Say has given of cards, how many watches could these 112 men make in combination, and how many could they make, if each separate man made the whole watch: and not only the number but the quality of the watches!

Babbage has called attention to a result of the principle of the division of labour which has been overlooked by other writers. He says—' Now, although these are important causes, and each has its influence on the result, yet it appears to me that any explanation of the cheapness of manufactured articles, as consequent upon the division of labour, would be incomplete if the following principle were omitted to be stated :—

' That the master manufacturer, by dividing the work to be executed into different processes, each requiring different degrees of skill, or of force, can purchase exactly that precise quantity of both which is necessary for each process, whereas if the whole work were executed by one workman that person must possess sufficient skill to perform the most difficult, and sufficient strength to execute the most laborious, of the operations into which the art is divided.

'As the clear apprehension of this principle upon which a great part of the economy arising from the division of labour depends, is of considerable importance, it may be desirable to point out its precise and numerical application in some specific manufacture. The art of making needles is perhaps that which

I should have selected for the illustration, as comprehending a very large number of processes remarkably different in their nature ; but the less difficult art of pin-making has some claim to attention from its having been used by Adam Smith, and I am confirmed in the choice of it by the circumstance of our possessing a very accurate and minute description of that art as practised in France above half a century ago.'

Babbage then describes the process of pin-making, and shows the different classes of persons employed in the manufacture, from children at 6d. a day to women at 1s. 6d., and men at 5s. 6d Ten persons, he says, namely, four men, four women, and two children, can make one pound of metal into 5,546 pins in seven hours and a half at a cost of little more than a shilling, whereas if all the persons employed were of the necessary skill to make the most difficult part, it would cost nearly four times as much.

'The higher the skill required of the workman in any one process of a manufacture, and the smaller the time during which it is employed, so much greater will be the advantage of separating that process from the rest, and devoting one person's attention entirely to it. Had we selected the art of needle-making as our illustration, the economy arising from division of labour would have been still more striking ; for the process of tempering the needles requires great skill, attention, and experience, and, although from three to four thousand are tempered at once, the workman is paid a very high rate of wages. In another process of the same manufacture, dry pointing, which also is executed with great rapidity, the wages earned by the workman reach from 7s. to 12s., 15s., and even in some cases to 20s. a day, whilst other processes are carried on by children paid at the rate of 6d. a day.'

As a further illustration of this principle we may quote another example of a different sort given in the same work, p. 191—'We have already mentioned what may, perhaps, appear paradoxical to some of our readers—that the division of labour can be applied with equal success to mental as to mechanical operations, and that it ensures in both the same economy of time. A short account of its practical application in the most extensive series of calculations ever executed will afford an interesting illustration of this fact, whilst at the same time it will afford an occasion for showing that the arrangements which ought to regulate the interior of a manufactory are founded on principles of deeper root than may have been supposed, and are capable of being usefully employed in preparing the road to some of the sublimest investigations of the human mind.

'In the midst of that excitement which accompanied the Revolution of France and the succeeding wars, the ambition of the nation, exhausted by its fatal passion for military renown, was at the same time directed to some of the noblest and more permanent triumphs which mark the era of a people's greatness, and which receive the applause of posterity long after their conquests have been wrested from them, or even when their existence as a nation may be told only by the pages of history. Amongst their enterprise of science, the French Government was desirous of producing a series of mathematical tables to facilitate the application of the decimal system which they had so recently adopted. They directed, therefore, their mathematicians to construct such tables on the most extensive scale. Their most distinguished philosophers, responding fully to the calls of their country, invented new methods for this laborious task; and a work completely answering the large demands of the Government was produced in a remarkably short space of time.' M. Prony, to whom the superintendence of this great undertaking was confided, in speaking of its commencement, observes—' I devoted myself to it with all the ardour of which I was capable, and I first turned my attention to a general plan to execute it. All the conditions which I had to fulfil demanded the employment of a great number of calculators, and it soon occurred to me to apply to the accomplishment of these tables the *division of labour*, which the arts of commerce employ so usefully to unite perfection in the manufacture along with economy in expense and time.' The circumstance which gave rise to this singular application of the principle of the division of labour, is so interesting that no apology is necessary for introducing it from a small pamphlet printed at Paris a few years since, when a proposition was made by the English to the French Government that the two countries should print these tables at their joint expense. The origin of the idea is related in the following extract :—

'It is to the chapter of a justly celebrated English work that is probably due the existence of a work which the British Government wishes to present to the learned world. Here is the anecdote. M. Prony had engaged to the Committees of the Government to prepare for the centesimal division of the circle logarithmic and trigonometrical tables, which should not only leave nothing to desire as regards exactitude, but which should form the vastest and most important monument of calculation which had ever been executed, or even conceived. The logarithms of the numbers from 1 to 200,000 formed a necessary supplement to this work. It was easy for M. Prony to satisfy himself that, even by associating with himself three or four able assistants, the greater part of the life he might expect would not suffice for his engagement. He was filled with this melancholy thought, when, happening to be in a bookseller's shop, he saw the handsome English edition of Smith, published in London in 1776: he opened the work by chance, and hit upon the first chapter which treats of the *division of labour*, and where the manufacture of pins is quoted as an example. He had scarcely read the first pages, when by a kind of inspiration he conceived the idea of putting out his logarithms to *manufacture*, like pins: he was then giving at the Polytechnic School a course of lectures on a part of analysis similar to this kind of work, namely, the method of differences, and its application to interpolation. He went to spend some days in the country, and returned to Paris with the plan of *construction*, which was followed in the execution of it. It resembled two workshops which made separately the same calculations, and served for reciprocal verification.

'The ancient methods of computing tables were altogether inapplicable to such a proceeding. M. Prony, therefore, wishing to avail himself of all the talent of his country in devising new methods, formed the first section of those who were to take part in this enterprise out of five or six of the most eminent mathematicians of France.

'*First Section.*—The duty of this first section was to investigate, amongst the various analytical expressions which could be found for the same function, that which was most readily adapted to simple numerical calculation by many individuals employed at the same time. This section had little or nothing to do with the actual numerical work. When its labours were concluded, the formulæ on the use of which it had decided were delivered to the second section.

'*Second Section.*—This section consisted of seven or eight persons of considerable acquaintance with mathematics, and their duty was to convert into numbers the formulæ put into their hands by the first section, an operation of great labour; and then to deliver out these formulæ to the members of the third section, and receive from them the finished calculations. The members of this second section had certain means of verifying the calculations without the necessity of repeating, or even examining, the whole of the work done by the third section.

'*Third Section.*—The members of this section, whose numbers varied from sixty to eighty, received certain numbers from the second section, and using nothing more than simple addition and subtraction, they returned to that section the tables in a finished state. It is remarkable that nine-tenths of this class had no knowledge of arithmetic beyond the two first rules which they were then called upon to exercise, and that these persons were usually found more correct in their calculations than those who possessed a more extensive knowledge of the subject.

'When it is stated that the tables thus computed occupy seventeen large folio volumes, some idea, perhaps, may be formed of the labour. From that part executed by the third class, which may almost be termed mechanical, requiring the least knowledge, and by far the greater exertions, the first class were entirely exempt. Such labour can always be purchased at an easy rate. The duties of the second class, although requiring considerable skill in arithmetical operation, were yet in some measure relieved by the higher interest naturally felt in these more difficult operations. The exertions of the first class are not likely to require upon another occasion so much skill and labour as they did upon the first attempt to introduce such a method; but when the completion of a calculating engine shall have produced a substitute for the whole of the third section of computers, the attention of analysts will naturally be directed to simplifying its application by a new discussion of the methods of converting analytical formulæ into numbers.'

We may observe that the same method of a division of labour is eminently applicable to effect a work which is one of the most crying wants of the present day, namely, a great Digest of the existing Law of England, as a preparation for a great national Code. The present state of the Law of England, scattered through many hundreds of volumes of Statutes and Cases, filled with the most extraordinary contradictions and absurdities, is a scandal to a civilised Empire, and calls loudly for redress. A Royal Commission was, indeed, appointed some years ago for the purpose, and it made a commencement of the work, which it suddenly abandoned, for reasons which were never explained, but which may be readily imagined. Should the work, however, ever be resumed, it can only be done effectually, economically, and within a reasonable time, by an organisation thoroughly well planned on the principle of the Division of Labour. And if this were undertaken this great national work might be successfully accomplished.

Smith says that the great increase of the quantity of work which, in consequence of the division of labour, the same number of people are capable of performing is owing to three different circumstances: 1st, to the increase of dexterity in every particular workman; 2ndly, to the saving of the time which is commonly lost in passing from one species of work to another; and lastly to the invention of a great number of machines which facilitate and abridge labour, and enable one man to do the work of many.

'*First*, the improvement of the dexterity of the workman necessarily increases the quantity of work he can perform; and the division of labour, by reducing every man s business to some one simple operation, and by making this operation the sole employment of his life, necessarily increases very much the dexterity of the workman. A common smith who, though accustomed to handle the hammer, has never been used to make nails, if, upon some particular occasion, he is obliged to attempt it, will scarce, I am assured, be able to make above two or three hundred nails in a day, and these, too, very bad ones. A smith who has been accustomed to make nails, but whose sole or principal business has not been that of a nailer, can seldom, with his utmost diligence, make more than eight hundred or a thousand nails in a day. I have seen several boys, under twenty years of age, who had never exercised any other trade, and who, when they exerted themselves, could make each of them, upwards of two thousand three hundred nails in a day. The making of a nail, however, is by no means one of the simplest operations. The same person blows the bellows, stirs or mends the fire as there is occasion, heats the iron, and forges part of the nail : in forging the head, too, he is obliged to change his tools. The different operations into which the making of a pin, or of a metal button, is subdivided, are all of them much more simple ; and the dexterity of the person, of whose life it has been the sole business to perform them, is usually much greater. The rapidity with which some of the operations of those manufactures are performed exceeds what the human hand could, by those who had never seen them, be supposed capable of acquiring.

'*Secondly*, the advantage which is gained by saving the time commonly lost in passing from one sort of work to another is much greater than we should at first view be apt to imagine it. It is impossible to pass very quickly from one kind of work to another, that is carried on in a different place and quite different tools. A country weaver who cultivates a small farm, must lose a deal of time in passing from his loom to the field, and from the field to his loom. When the two trades can be carried on in the same work-house, the loss of time is no doubt much less. It is even in this case something considerable. A man commonly saunters a little in turning his hand from one sort of employment to another. When he first begins the new work, he is seldom very keen and hearty ; his mind, as they say, does not go to it, and for some time he rather trifles than applies to good purpose. The habit of sauntering, and of indolent, careless application, which is naturally, or rather necessarily, acquired by every country workman who is obliged to change his work and his tools every half hour, and apply his hand in twenty different ways almost every day of his life, renders him almost always slowful and lazy, and incapable of any vigorous application, even on the most pressing occasions. Independent, therefore, of his deficiency in point of dexterity, this cause must always reduce considerably the quantity of work which he is capable of performing.

Of these two causes, of which Smith attributes the enormous effects of the principle of the Division of Labour, the first is infinitely the more important. In almost every particular trade it takes an apprentice many years of industry to acquire a perfect mastery; and it seems almost impossible for the same person to acquire the ideas and habits necessary to give perfection in more than one trade. Perfection in one trade often disqualifies the bodily organs for another. The rough work of a carpenter, or a mason, would injure the hand for the delicate operations of the watchmaker, the painter, or the musician. The rapidity of manual execution which can be attained by long habit and devotion to one occupation is marvellous. The same is true, as Mill observes, of mental as of bodily operations. If a man were to learn several trades he would spend the greater part of his life in going through the necessary apprenticeship in each, and then the work in each would be very imperfectly done, from want of time for the necessary practice. How long would a person require to go through the 112 apprenticeships in watchmaking alone? And when 112 men had done that, how many complete watches could they make all working separately, compared to the same number each confined to his own separate department?

When we consider this principle carried out in all the ramifications of trade, we see how the actual quantity of produce obtained is infinitely augmented by the division of labour: and it also explains the doctrine that in an exchange *both* sides gain, which was long so mysterious a puzzle to the former schools of Economists.

Even supposing that the Quantity of Labour in each product is equal, as the Physiocrates and Ricardo maintain, each side gains, because the simple fact of each exchanging something he does not want for something he does want, is a gain. And even supposing the quantity of labour in each product equal, each obtains what he wants by a far less amount of labour than if he had to go through the trouble, labour, and expense of learning to make it for himself. He therefore obtains the result with a far less amount of labour than he otherwise would : and that itself is a gain. Each one by learning one trade thoroughly is as well off as if he had learnt every other, and that is an enormous gain to each member of the society. Hence we see the fallacy of the reasoning of the Physiocrates, who maintained that in an exchange neither side gains, because the quantity of labour in each product is equal ; whereas the truth is that both sides gain, because each obtains the result he wishes, by infinitely less labour than he otherwise would.

17. But however excellent Smith's account of the effect of the division of labour may be in increasing the quantity of produce, his doctrines as to its effects on the intelligence and minds of the workers are most inaccurate. He says—' Not only the art of the farmer, the general direction of the operations of husbandry, but many inferior branches of country labour, require much more skill and experience than the greater part of mechanic trades. The man who works upon brass and iron, works with instruments and upon materials of which the temper is always the same, or very nearly the same. But the man who ploughs the ground with a team of horses or oxen works with instruments of which the health, strength, and temper are very different upon different occasions. The condition of the materials he works upon, too, is as variable as that of the instruments which he works with, and both require to be managed with much judgment and discretion. The common ploughman, though generally regarded as the pattern of stupidity and ignorance, is seldom defective in judgment or discretion. He is less accustomed, indeed, to social intercourse than the mechanic who lives in a town. His voice and language are more uncouth and more difficult to understand by those who are not used to them. His understanding, however, being accustomed to consider a greater variety of objects, is generally much superior to that of the other, whose whole attention from morning till night is commonly occupied in performing one or two very simple operations. How much the lower ranks of people in the country are really superior to those of the town is well known to every man whom business or curiosity has led to converse much with both.'

And again—' In the progress of the division of labour the employment of the far greater part of those who live by labour, that is of the great body of the people, comes to be confined to a few very simple operations; frequently to one or two. But the understanding of the greater part of men are necessarily formed by their ordinary employments. The man whose whole life is spent in performing a few simple operations, of which the effects, too, are always the same, or very nearly the same, has no occasion to exert his understanding or to exercise his invention in finding out expedients for removing difficulties which never occur. He naturally loses, therefore, the habit of such exertion, and generally becomes as stupid and ignorant as it is possible for a human being to become. The torpor of his mind renders him not only incapable of relishing or taking a part in any rational conversation, but of conceiving any generous, noble, or tender sentiment, and, consequently, of forming any just judgment concerning many even of the ordinary duties of private life. Of the great and extensive interests of his country he is altogether incapable of judging; and unless very particular pains have been taken to render him otherwise, he is equally incapable of defending his country in war. The uniformity of his stationary life naturally corrupts the courage of his mind, and makes him regard with abhorrence the irregular, uncertain, and adventurous life of a soldier. It corrupts even the activity of his body, and renders him incapable of exerting his strength with vigour and perseverance in any other employment than that to which he has been bred. His dexterity at his own particular trade seems in this manner to be acquired at the expense of his intellectual, social, and martial virtues. But in every improved and civilised society this is the state into which the labouring poor, that is, the great body of the people, must necessarily fall, unless Government takes some pains to prevent it.'

Other writers have repeated these lugubrious doctrines, but Say has pointed out that they are to be received with great qualifications: and McCulloch has very severely and justly controverted these assertions of Smith's as contrary to the plainest experience—'There is no ground whatever for the notion that agricultural labourers are more intelligent than those employed in manufactures and commerce, or that the faculties of the latter are impaired in consequence of their being generally confined to particular callings. The fact is, indeed, completely and distinctly the reverse; the manufacturing population being uniformly better informed than the agricultural, and their intelligence having improved according to the increase of their numbers, and the greater subdivision of their employments. The notion that manufactures are hostile to the social and martial virtues of the workpeople engaged in carrying them on is, if possible, still more erroneous. The cities and countries both in ancient and modern times that have been more distinguished by their proficiency in the arts and in commerce, have at the same time been the most distinguished by their patriotism and courage. But it is unnecessary to travel out of Great Britain for conclusive proofs of the entire fallacy of every assertion of Dr. Smith in this paragraph. Our manufactures have increased to an unprecedented extent during the last half century, and the division of employments is carried further in England than in any other country; but though Government has done nothing in the way of education, or otherwise, for their improvement, who will presume to say that the people employed in workshops have become "stupid and ignorant"?—that they are less capable than the agriculturists of judging of "the great and extensive interests of their country"?—or that they are incapable of defending it in war"? There is not, and there never was, so much as the shadow of a foundation for such imputations. His giving them credit is one of the few instances in which Dr. Smith has suffered his judgment to be swayed by ancient prejudices. He might have known that General Elliot's regiment of light horse, which so highly distinguished itself during the seven years' war, was principally recruited from among the tailors of the metropolis. But as respects the statement that manufactures weaken the corporeal and martial powers, it is necessary only to call to mind that the great manufacturing and trading towns furnished by far the greater portion of recruits to the army during the late war: for everyone will allow that the events of that contest proved, beyond dispute, that whatever other changes may have taken place in the habits of our people, our troops are as much distinguished as ever for capacity to bear fatigue and invincible courage and resolution.'

The slightest experience of facts quite reverses Smith's notions of the superiority of agricultural labourers in intellect over artisans; and the reason is obvious. Agricultural labourers are engaged in the same perpetual round of labour, and they mix with but few persons out of their own class, whose ideas and occupations are precisely the same. Artisans work together, and in much greater numbers, and with a much greater variety of employment. They thus are brought into contact with a much greater variety of knowledge and interests, and their intellects are sharpened by the conflict of opinion. They have much greater access to newspapers. As a matter of fact, labourers engaged in subdivision of labour consisting of semi-automatical operations, manifest a higher degree of mental cultivation than others whose occupations are more varied. Hand-loom weavers study geometry; shoemakers are proficient in polemics; tailors especially affect politics, while engaged in labour consisting of simple movements, chiefly repetitions of motions, all of which are being superseded by machinery. The machinery itself requires a higher degree of responsible attention by the person directing it, but not all his attention, as assumed by Smith, who has overlooked the psychological fact, which would have become manifest to wider and closer observation, that distinct mental operations may often go on better together than separately. Such labourers in semi-automatical processes, and superintendents, and workers of machinery, often hire persons to read to them during the work, and employers commonly find the work go on the better for the accompaniment of the second train of ideas raised by the reading, as the march of the soldier is improved by the excitement of the imagination created by music. Subdivision of such labour, instead of confining the mind to the process, liberates it: instead of depressing the mind, gives room for its expansion, and opens it to the reception of agreeable impressions. With the educated workpeople singing and poetry attach themselves peculiarly to semi-automatical processes. If a man, being compelled to earn his own livelihood, would study, or indulge the imagination, he would seek for the purpose a peculiarly simple subdivision of labour.

On the Rate of Wages and the Cost of Labour

18. Ricardo affirms in his dogmatic way that Profits depend exclusively on Wages: that as Wages rise Profits must fall, and *vice versâ*: we have already shown that this is a plain arithmetical error, and that Wages and Profits may both rise and fall together.

The term Wages, however, is very apt to deceive. Ricardo, indeed, noticed incidentally that there are different qualities of labour; but he alludes to different kinds of labour, such as that of a working jeweller and a common labourer, which adjust themselves in the market. In speaking of the same kind of labour, his doctrine certainly is, that if wages rise, profits must fall; and if wages fall, profits must rise.

This, however, is a most grievous error: and nothing can be more fallacious than to consider daily wages as the measure of the cost of executing work, or as governing Profits; and, as Mr. Brassey says, it is quite possible that work may be more cheaply executed by the same workmen, notwithstanding that their wages have been largely increased.

He gives as instances—'At the commencement of the construction of the North Devon Railway the wages of the labourers were 2s. a day. During the progress of the work their wages were increased to 2s. 6d. and 3s. a day. Nevertheless, it was found that the work was executed more cheaply when the men were earning the higher rate of wages than when they were paid the lower rate. Again, in London, in carrying out a part of the Metropolitan Drainage Works in Oxford Street, the wages of the bricklayers were gradually raised from 6s. to 10s. per day: yet it was found that the brickwork was constructed at a cheaper rate per cubic yard after the wages of the workmen had been raised to 10s. than when they were paid at the rate of 6s. a day.'

In making the Paris and Rouen Railway ten thousand men were employed, of which four thousand were English. The

English navvies were paid 5*s*. a day, while the French were paid 2*s*. 6*d*. a day; yet it was found, on comparing the cost of two adjacent cuttings in precisely similar circumstances, that the excavation was made at a lower cost per cubic yard by the English navvies than by the French.

In the same quarry at Bonnières in which Frenchmen, Irishmen, and Englishmen were employed side by side, the Frenchmen received 3 francs, the Irishmen 4, and the Englishmen 6 francs a day. At these different rates the Englishman was found to be the most advantageous workman of the three.

'Both English and French masons were employed in large numbers on the Alderney breakwater in 1852. The Englishmen earned 5*s*. 6*d*. to 6*s*., and as a general rule they made 1*s*. a day more than the Frenchmen, whose average earnings did not exceed 4*s*. a day.

'It has been many times stated in the course of this work that, from superior skill or greater energy, the more highly paid workman will in many, perhaps in most, cases turn out a greater amount of work in proportion to the wages he receives. An opportunity occurred some years ago, during the construction of the refreshment room at Basingstoke, for testing this problem with great accuracy. On one side of the station a London bricklayer was employed at 5*s*. 6*d*. a day, and on the other two country bricklayers at 3*s*. 6*d*. a day. It was found, by measuring the amount of work performed, without the knowledge of the men employed, that the one London bricklayer laid, without undue exertion, more bricks in a day than his two less skilful country fellow-labourers.

'On the Grand Trunk Railway a number of French-Canadian labourers were employed. Their wages were 3*s*. 6*d*. a day, while the Englishmen received from 5*s*. to 6*s*. a day; but it was found that the English did the greatest amount of work for the money.'

The same results are observed in other branches of industry. The shipbuilders of Bordeaux, Marseilles, and Nantes described the collapse of their trade in France, and the impossibility of competing in point of price with the English shipbuilders; and yet the wages of the English workmen were in most cases nearly double that of the French.

'Mr. Redgrave, one of Her Majesty's Inspectors of Factories, says that, while the foreigner is under the same conditions, as to the raw material, as the English manufacturer, and his fuel is more expensive, his workpeople do not work with the same vigour and steadiness as Englishmen. Consequently, the same number of operatives, employed upon the same machinery, do not produce the same quantity of yarn as in this country. "All the evidence that has come before me," he says, " has gone to prove that there is a great preponderance in favour of this country. Comparing the work of a British with a foreign spinner, the average number of persons employed to spindles is —in France, one person to fourteen spindles : in Russia, one to twenty-eight spindles : in Prussia, one to thirty-seven : in Great Britain, one to seventy-four. But I could find many cotton spinning factories in my district, in which mules containing 2,200 spindles are managed by one minder and two assistants." "I have been recently told," he continues, "by one who had been an English manager in a factory at Oldenburgh, that though the hours of work were from 5.30 A.M. to 8 P.M. every day, only about the same weight of work was turned off under English overlookers as would be produced in a working day from 6 A.M. to 6 P.M. in this country. Under German overlookers the produce was much less. The wages were 50 per cent. less in many cases than in England; but the number of hands, in proportion to machinery, was much larger. In some departments it was in the proportion of five to three. In Russia the inefficiency of the foreign, as compared with the labour of the English operatives, is even more strikingly manifested, for, on a comparison of the wages, supposing the Russian operatives to work only sixty hours a week as they do in England, instead of seventy-five hours a week as they do in Russia, their wages would not be one-fourth the amount earned in England."'

Mr. Wells says—'Whereas female labour in the cotton manufacture is paid at from 12s. to 15s. a week in Great Britain; at from 7s. 3d. to 9s. 7d. in France, Belgium, and Germany; at from 2s. 4d. to 2s. 11d. in Russia; the one thing which is most dreaded by the continental manufacturers everywhere is British competition. The demand for protection is loudest in France, Austria, and Russia, where the average wages reach their minimum.'

So it is said by Jones—'Two Middlesex mowers will mow in a day as much grass as six Russian serfs, and in spite of the dearness of provisions in England and their cheapness in Russia, the mowing of a quantity of hay, which would cost the English farmer half a copeck, will cost the Russian proprietor three or four copecks.' The Prussian Councillor of State, Jacobi, is considered to have proved that in Russia, where everything is cheap, the labour of the serf is doubly as expensive as that of the labourer in England. In Austria the labour of a serf is one-third of that of a free hired labourer.

Precisely the same impossibility of determining the actual cost of labour by the nominal rate of wages is as fully shown by the experience of the shipowner as by that of the manufacturer.

'The wages of shipwrights and the pay of seamen are much more moderate in France than with us. Yet the cost of building ships is ten per cent. greater in France than in England; and the wages of a French crew, in consequence of their greater number, involve an expenditure for manning twenty-five per cent. greater than the corresponding expense in an English ship.

'If, on the other hand, we compare the cost of manning an American ship with the cost of manning an English ship, we shall see how our comparatively cheaper labour makes us more prodigal in the use of it. The average proportion of seamen in an English ship is one man to every fifteen tons; in an American ship it is one man to every twenty-five tons.'

We have merely taken these few examples from Mr. Brassey's interesting little work 'Work and Wages,' which contains much which may be useful to all persons who consider these questions.

Error *of Mill's* Four Fundamental Propositions *regarding* Capital

19. Mill has laid down what he terms Four Fundamental propositions regarding Capital, which have been very extensively quoted: these are—

1. '*That Industry is limited by Capital.*'

CH. X.   *Errors of Mill*   181

2. '*That all Capital is the result of saving.*'

3. '*That although saved and the result of saving all Capital is nevertheless consumed,* i.e. *destroyed.*'

4. '*That what supports Productive Labour is the Capital expended in setting it to work, and not the Demand of purchasers for the Produce of the Labour when completed. Demand for Commodities is not Demand for Labour.*'

We have already shown in § 6 that the first of these propositions is entirely erroneous unless Credit is admitted to be Capital : and that the second is entirely erroneous : that only *some* Capital is the result of saving.

The third proposition that although saved and the result of saving all Capital is consumed is also equally erroneous.

We have seen that Senior says that all Economists are agreed that *Whatever* brings in a Profit is justly termed **Capital.**

The Duke of Bedford and the Duke of Westminster are proprietors of vast districts of ground on which London is built : this ground yields them enormous revenues : it is, therefore, **Capital** to them : how is it **Consumed**?

Every great Joint-Stock Bank and every Banker trades with his Credit : every writer in the world who knew what he was writing about, has fully understood and said that the Credit of a Bank is **Capital** to it : because it trades with and makes a Profit of its Credit. How is its Credit **Consumed**?

A great author writes a successful work. The Copyright of it is **Capital** to him. If he sells the copyright to a publisher it becomes Fixed Capital to the publisher. How is it **Consumed**?

A person by his skill discovers some valuable trade secret which brings him in great Profits. This trade secret is partnership assets and **Capital.** How is it **Consumed**?

A professional man or a trader buys the Practice or the Goodwill of a business. Each of them is **Capital** to him. How are they **Consumed**?

The street crossings in London are valuable property, or estates in land : they are bought and sold : they are bequeathed : they form the subject of marriage portions, just like other estates in land: they are **Capital** to their owners. How are they **Consumed**?

The proprietor of land discovers a mineral spring on his land. The spring is found, or imagined, to be beneficial in many diseases. People crowd to it, a great demand for houses springs up: and the land produces a great revenue to the owner. The spring also brings him a revenue: it is therefore **Capital** to him: the spring flows on for ever: how is it the result of saving? how is it **Consumed**?

A Dock, a Canal, or a Railway Company collect subscriptions from their Shareholders: this is their Capital: they then expend this Money Capital in excavating the Dock or the Canal, or in'forming the Railway. The Dock, the Canal, or the Railway then produce a revenue: they are the fixed **Capital** of the Company: they may perhaps require a certain sum to keep them in repair: but how are they **Consumed**?

We might give many more instances if necessary to show that it is entirely erroneous to say that it is a Fundamental Proposition regarding Capital to say that **all** Capital is consumed: it is only true that *some* Capital is consumed.

20. Mill's fourth proposition regarding Capital originated with Ricardo, and has been adopted by his idolaters McCulloch and Mill.

Upon looking at the words of the fourth proposition above stated, they may be said to be a simple truism. Of course if we buy a commodity in a shop, we demand the commodity, we do not demand the Labour. But of what practical consequence this can be it would be difficult to conceive. Mr. Longe says it is like saying that a demand for beef is not a demand for oxen. When a purchaser buys something in a shop, of course he does not employ the Labour himself directly: but he puts into the shopkeeper's hands the price of it, which the shopkeeper may employ as wages in paying the workmen to produce a similar article to replace the one that is sold: and so on in succession: every succeeding purchaser puts the price of every successive product into the shopkeeper's hands to be employed in buying labour as long as the demand for the article continues. This is eminently a case where the maxim *qui facit per alium facit per se* applies. And what practical consequence to the labouring classes it can be whether the purchaser employs them directly himself, by paying them to produce the article, or pays them through the medium of the shopkeeper, it would be difficult to discover.

Nevertheless, as Mill and his followers attribute extraordinary importance to this doctrine, we shall lay before our readers what he says, and leave them to judge for themselves—

' The demand for commodities determines in what particular branch of production the labour and capital shall be employed ; it determines the *direction* of the labour ; but not the more or less of the labour itself, or of the maintenance or payment of the labour. These depend on the amount of the capital, or other funds [what funds ?] directly devoted to the sustenance and remuneration of labour.

' Suppose, for instance, that there is a demand for velvet ; a fund ready to be laid out in buying velvet, but no capital to establish the manufacture. It is of no consequence how great the demand may be, unless capital be attracted into the occupation there will be no velvet made, and, consequently, none bought ; unless indeed the desire of the intending purchaser for it is so strong that he employs part of the price he would have paid for it in making advances to workpeople, that they may employ themselves in making velvet : that is, unless he converts part of his income into capital, and invests that capital in the manufacture.'

We may observe that in such a case he would not convert his income into capital, unless he intended to sell the velvet with a profit. If he intended to use the velvet himself, what he paid would be income. If a purchaser buys goods from a shopkeeper the shopkeeper converts the money into capital by buying a fresh stock of goods to sell with a profit.

Mill proceeds—' Let us now reverse the hypothesis, and suppose that there is plenty of capital ready for making velvet, but no demand. Velvet will not be made ; but there is no particular preference on the part of capital for making velvet. Manufacturers and labourers do not produce for the pleasure of their customers, but for the supply of their own wants, and having still the capital and the labour, which are the essentials of production, they can either produce something else which is in demand, or, if there be no other demand, they themselves have one, and can produce the things which they want for their own consumption. So that the employment afforded to labour does not depend on the purchasers, but upon the capital. I am, of course, not taking into consideration the effects of a sudden change. If the demand ceases unexpectedly, after the commodity to supply it is already produced, this introduces a different element into the question; the capital has actually been consumed in producing something which nobody wants or uses, and it has, therefore, perished, and the employment which it gave to labour is at an end, not because there is no longer a demand, but because there is no longer a capital.'

Now, in the last passage what does 'Capital' mean? Is it the wages paid to the workmen, or is it the product, for which there is no demand? If the wages be the capital, they do exist: they exist in the hands of the persons to whom they were paid; and these persons may use them as Income or Capital exactly as they please. If the product be the capital, it, of course, ceases to be capital when no one will buy it. But of what consequence is that to the labourers? Mill himself says that a demand for products is not a demand for labour: therefore, according to his own doctrine, whether there be a demand for the product or not, it can in no way affect the labourers. If the workmen are paid for their labour, what does it matter to them what becomes of its produce? The fund which paid them is not destroyed; it remains in existence to effect endless exchanges in succession. How this case helps on Mill's argument it is impossible to perceive.

He proceeds—'This case, therefore, does not test the principle. The proper test is to suppose that the change is gradual and foreseen, and is attended with no waste of capital, the manufacture being discontinued by merely not replacing the machinery as it wears out, and not reinvesting the money as it comes in from the sale of the produce. The capital is thus ready for a new employment in which it will maintain as much labour as before. . . .

'This theorem, that to purchase produce is not to employ labour; *that the demand for labour is constituted by the wages which precede the production*, and not by the demand which may exist for the commodities resulting from the production, is a proposition which greatly needs all the illustration it can receive. It is to common apprehension a paradox; and even among political economists of reputation, I can hardly point to any except Mr. Ricardo and M. Say, who have kept it constantly and steadily in view. Almost all others occasionally express themselves as if a person who buys commodities, the produce of labour, was an employer of labour, and created a demand for it as really and in the same sense as if he bought the labour itself directly, by the payment of wages. It is no wonder that political economy advances slowly, when such a question as this remains open at its very threshold.'

We think, but we are by no means sure, that we have now some glimmer of Mill's meaning in the preceding paragraphs. He says that if there be a fund ready to buy velvet, but no Capital to establish a manufacture, no velvet can be bought because there is none made. To take a more familiar instance which we have already considered. Scotland, before the introduction of Credit, had abundance of fertile land, and of unemployed people, but no Capital to serve as wages in paying them to till and sow the land. Now, of course, there was always a demand for corn; but the Scotch proprietors could grow no corn because they had no Capital to pay as wages before the corn was produced, and they could get no Capital because they had no corn to sell. They were, therefore, in a deadlock: if they could once get a crop sown, that crop would produce the Capital to continue the crop for ever. The real difficulty was to start the operation, which, as Mill truly says, could not be set agoing without Capital spent as Wages previous to obtaining the produce. *Ce n'est que le premier pas qui coûte.* In fact, the corn was waiting for the wages, and the wages were waiting for the corn. It was an Economic position just like that of the two heroes—

> The Earl of Chatham, with his sabre drawn,
> Was waiting for Sir Richard Strachan;
> Sir Richard, eager to be at 'em,
> Was waiting for the Earl of Chatham.

No doubt there is the difficulty, as Mill says: but we have

already pointed out how this difficulty is obviated, and the hiatus bridged over. It is done by means of Bank Notes: a Scotch Bank, seeing this state of matters, establishes a branch in the district, and advances the **Present Value** of the future crops in the form of its own Notes, or Credit, and by this means the grand result is obtained of starting the operation. By this creation of Credit, used as wages, the land is reclaimed, the seed is sown, and the sale of the crop provides the funds partly to redeem the advances, and partly to renew the operation, which being once started may be carried on for ever. Hence the whole difficulty vanishes into air: and, virtually speaking, the person who buys the produce is the employer of labour, and creates the demand in all respects as effectually as if he himself had bought the labour directly, by the payment of wages.

Having thus shown how this imaginary difficulty is obviated, we now come to more tangible doctrine—

'I apprehend that, if by demand for labour be meant *the demand by which wages are raised, or the number of labourers in employment increased, demand for commodities does not constitute demand for labour.*'

Such an assertion is so contrary to the plainest experience that it is amazing that Mill could have made it: and, as is almost invariably the case, we have only to quote Mill to confute Mill. Elsewhere he says—' It is a common saying that wages are high when trade is good. The demand for labour in any particular employment is more pressing, *and higher wages are paid, when there is a brisk demand for the commodity produced:* and the contrary when there is what is called a stagnation: then workpeople are dismissed, and those who are retained must submit to a reduction of wages: though in these cases there is neither more nor less capital than before. This is true. . . .

'A manufacturer finding a slack demand for his commodity, forbears to employ labourers to increase a stock which he finds it difficult to dispose of: or if he goes on until all his capital is locked up in unsold goods, then, at least, he must of necessity pause until he can get paid for some of them. But no one expects either of these states to be permanent; if he did, he would at the first opportunity remove his capital to some other occupation, in which it would still continue to employ labour. The capital remains unemployed for a time, during which the labour market is overstocked, and wages fall. Afterwards the demand revives, and perhaps becomes unusually brisk, enabling the manufacturer to sell his commodity even faster than he can produce it: his whole capital is then brought into complete efficiency, and if he is able, he borrows capital in addition, which would otherwise have gone into some other employment [not necessarily so]. At such time wages in his particular occupation rise. If we supppose, what in strictness is not absolutely impossible, that one of these fits of briskness or stagnation should affect all occupations at the same time, wages altogether might undergo a rise or a fall.'

Now what can be more contradictory to the doctrine that 'demand for commodities is not a demand for labour, and does not affect wages,' than these two last passages? What need have we to refute Mill when he has done so effectually himself?

This doctrine of Mill's is so contrary to common sense that it would seem waste of time to refute it. But if it wanted refutation, what more excellent example of it can be had than the evidence and report of the Coal Committee? It was there distinctly proved that the price of iron rose immensely from the enormous demand for it; the immense demand for iron caused an immense demand for coal, and accordingly its price rose immensely: the increased demand for coal, and its increased price, caused an immense demand for labourers, and their wages, too, rose very greatly, though not in proportion to the rise of coal. Who after this can say that a demand for commodities is not a demand for labour? Who can say that an increased demand for the commodity does not lead to a rise of wages? We have already shown that it is now well understood by the workmen that the 'wages fund' is not existing capital, but the Price of the commodity produced; and their wages must rise and fall according to that price. We have shown that agreements are regularly made that wages shall rise and fall with the price of iron and coal.

Mill's doctrine is founded on the exploded fallacy of Ricardo that it is 'cost of production' or 'quantity of labour' which regulates Value : sometimes, it is true, it appears to do so, but we have irrefragably proved that it is as often just the reverse : and that it is the increased price of the product which provides an increased fund to be divided between masters and workmen : and of this the report of the Coal Committee is a preggant and decisive instance.

21. We have thus shown that Mill's fourth fundamental proposition regarding Capital is as baseless and untrue as the preceding three : and therefore it is wholly unnecessary to consider any more illustrations he may give. But there is one doctrine of his so extraordinary that we cannot pass it over.

'The consumer has been accustomed to buy velvet, but resolves to discontinue that expense, and to employ the same annual sum in hiring bricklayers. If the common opinion be correct this change in the mode of his expenditure gives no additional employment to labour, but only transfers employment from velvet makers to bricklayers. On closer inspection, however, it will be seen that there is an *increase* of the total sum applied to the remuneration of labour. The velvet manufacturer, supposing him aware of the diminished demand for his commodity, diminishes the production and sets at liberty a corresponding portion of the capital employed in the manufacture. This capital thus withdrawn from the maintenance of velvet makers, is not the same fund with that which the customer employs in maintaining bricklayers : it is a second fund. *There are therefore two funds to be employed in the maintenance and remuneration of labour, where before there was only one.* There is not a transfer of employment from velvet makers to bricklayers (?) : there is a new employment created for bricklayers, and a transfer of employment from velvet makers to some other labourers, most probably those who produce the food and other things which the bricklayers consume.'

We pause for our readers to examine this astounding doctrine. According to Mill, if all the buyers of commodities were suddenly to discontinue buying them, and employ those very funds which were previously used in buying commodities in hiring labour, it would double the labour fund ! ! Is it necessary to point out the obvious arithmetical blunder on which it rests? The reader will perceive that by Mill's own supposition the velvet makers are left unemployed. The labourers who are called upon to provide the food and necessaries for the bricklayers, previously provided that food for the velvet makers. Of course, if the velvet makers are left without wages they must starve, and cannot buy food : but the bricklayers can, because the very fund which formerly bought the velvet makers' food is now given to the bricklayers, and buys their food. To the producers of food it makes no difference whether they sell it to bricklayers or velvet makers. But by Mill's arrangement he has simply taken away the funds from the velvet makers, whom he has left to starve, and given them to the bricklayers, and by doing this he says the labour fund is doubled ! ! It is plain that so far as regards the food-producers it is only substituting bricklayers for velvet makers, and there is therefore no increased demand for food. Thus, according to Mill, to take away a fund from one set of persons, and to give the very same fund to another set, is to *double* the fund ! ! Most wonderful logic ! This is truly the discovery of the Philosopher's Stone.

22. We have now found the grand secret to multiply a fund any number of times. According to this doctrine, robbing Peter to pay Paul doubles the fund. If taking away the fund from velvet makers and giving it to bricklayers *doubles* the fund, then taking it away from bricklayers and giving it to carpenters, triples it : taking it away from the carpenters and giving it to ploughmen, quadruples it, and so on to any extent. Why should there ever be any want of funds to employ labour when they can be found so easily, simply by taking them away from some one else ?

Experience suggests to us a case where the application of this doctrine would be highly satisfactory. When *Paterfamilias* has a lot of boys clamouring for pocket money, he has only to take half-a-crown out of his pocket and give it to Roderick : Roderick is paid. *Paterfamilias* then takes away the half-crown from Roderick and gives it to Crichton : Crichton is paid. *Paterfamilias* then takes away the half-crown from Crichton and gives it to Keith : Keith is paid. *Paterfamilias* then takes away the half-crown from Keith and replaces it in his own pocket. By this means each of the boys has been paid his pocket money, and *Paterfamilias* has got it in his own pocket as well. It is possible that Roderick, Crichton, and Keith may not fully comprehend the nature of this operation: at all events, *Paterfamilias* is quite satisfied with it. If the boys feel any difficulty about it, if they have an imaginary vacancy in their pockets, where the half-crown is not, *Paterfamilias* simply refers them to Mill, the logical Pope of the British people, who will explain to them quite satisfactorily that by this operation the fund has been quadrupled, and that they have each had their pocket money, and leaves them to digest this elementary lesson in Logic and Economics as best they may. And this is a principle of very extensive application; which shows that Economics is well worth the study of all *Patrum-familiarum*.

23. We may, therefore, dismiss Mill's fourth fundamental proposition regarding Capital to the same limbo as the other three. And we cannot help observing that this is a striking example of the folly of literary men writing on subjects of which they have no knowledge. Here is a whole chapter of Mill, containing 30 pages, which is a complete mass of errors in itself, and on each separate part of it we have shown that Mill has contradicted himself. And thus the young student's mind is filled with erroneous notions on the fundamental principles of the subject, which he must utterly exterminate if he would understand modern commerce.

On Rate *of* Wages

24. Having thus shown that Money and Credit are the fund out of which Wages are paid, we have next to consider what circumstances determine the amount of Wages.

It was long stoutly maintained that Wages are governed by the price of food; and this, indeed, was one of the assertions on which the Protectionist system which formerly prevailed in this country was based. Burke said—'The squires of Norfolk had dined when they gave it as their opinion that it (Labour) might or ought to rise or fall with the market of provisions. The rate of wages, in truth, has no *direct* relation to that price. Labour is a commodity like every other, and rises or falls according to the demand. This is in the nature of things.'

Nevertheless, Smith says—'The money price of corn regulates that of all other home-made commodities.

'It regulates the money price of labour, which must always be such as to enable the labourer to purchase a quantity of corn sufficient to maintain him and his family. . . .

'By regulating the money price of all the other parts of the rude produce of land, it regulates that of the materials of almost all manufactures. By regulating the money price of labour it regulates that of manufacturing art and industry; and by regulating both, it regulates that of the complete manufacture. The money price of labour, and of everything that is the produce either of land or labour, must necessarily either rise or fall in proportion to the money price of corn.'

Thus it will be seen that Smith explicitly asserts that the price of corn regulates the value of Labour and of all other commodities.

And yet the same Smith also says—'The wages of labour do not in Great Britain fluctuate with the price of provisions (!) These vary everywhere from year to year, frequently from month to month. But in many places the money price of labour remains uniformly the same sometimes for half a century together. . . . The high price of provisions during these ten years past (1766–1776) has not in many parts of the kingdom been accompanied with any sensible rise in the money price of labour. . . .

'As the price of provisions varies more from year to year than the wages of labour, so, on the other hand, the wages of labour vary more from place to place. The prices of bread and butcher's meat are generally the same, or very nearly the same, through the greater part of the United Kingdom. These and most other things which are sold by retail, the way in which the labouring poor buy all things, are generally full as cheap or cheaper in great towns than in the remoter parts of the country, for reasons which I shall have to explain hereafter. But the wages of labour in a great town and its neighbourhood are frequently a fourth or a fifth part, twenty or twenty-five per cent., higher than at a few miles' distance. Eighteenpence a day may be reckoned the common price of labour in London and its neighbourhood. At a few miles' distance it falls to fourteen and fifteenpence. Tenpence may be reckoned its price in Edinburgh and its neighbourhood. At a few miles' distance it falls to eightpence, the usual price of common labour through the greater part of the low country of Scotland, where it varies a good deal less than in England. . . .

'The variations in the price of labour not only do not correspond either in place or time with those in the price of provisions, *but they are frequently quite opposite ! !*

'Grain, the food of the common people, is dearer in Scotland than in England, whence Scotland receives almost every year very large supplies. But English corn must be sold dearer in Scotland, the country to which it is brought, than in England, the country from which it comes; and in proportion to its quality it cannot be sold dearer in Scotland than the Scotch corn that comes to the same market in competition with it. The quality of grain depends chiefly upon the quality of flour or meal which it yields at the mill, and in this respect English grain is so much superior to the Scotch, that though often dearer in appearance, or in proportion to the measure of its bulk, it is generally cheaper in reality, or in proportion to its quality, or even to the measure of its weight. The price of labour, on the contrary, is dearer in England than in Scotland. If the labouring poor, therefore, can maintain their families in the one part of the United Kingdom, they must be in affluence in the other. Oatmeal, indeed, supplies the common people of Scotland with the greatest and the best part of their food, which is in general much inferior to that of their neighbours of the same rank in England. *This difference however in the mode of their subsistence is not the cause but the effect of the difference in their wages;* though, by a strange misapprehension, I have frequently heard it represented as the cause. It is not because one man keeps a coach while his neighbour walks a-foot, that the one is rich and the other poor; but because the one is rich he keeps a coach, and because the other is poor he walks a-foot.'

[Now, who has more clearly exhibited this misapprehension

than Smith himself, as we have shown in the preceding extracts?]

'During the course of the last century, taking one year with another, grain was dearer in both parts of the United Kingdom than during that of the present. . . . But though it is certain that in both parts of the United Kingdom grain was somewhat dearer in the last century than in the present, it is equally certain that labour was much cheaper,' &c.

Now is it possible to have a more flagrant contradiction than Smith's doctrine in these different parts of his work? And as we have shown that a similar contradiction pervades the whole of his work on almost every point in Economics, we can only leave the reader to judge of the worth of such a book as a scientific authority.

25. Ricardo follows in exactly the same strain—'Labour, like all things which are purchased and sold, and which may be increased or diminished in quantity, has its natural and its market price. The natural price of labour is that price which is necessary to enable the labourers one with another to subsist and perpetuate their race, without either increase or diminution.' 'The natural price of labour depends on the price of food, necessaries, and conveniences required for the support of the labourer and his family. With a rise in the price of food and necessaries, the natural price of labour will rise; with a fall in their price the natural price of labour will fall.'—'The market price of labour is the price which is really paid for it, from the natural operation of the proportion of the supply to the demand; labour is dear when it is scarce, and cheap when it is plentiful. However much the market price of labour may deviate from its natural standard, it has, like commodities, a tendency to conform to it.' A little examination will show how vague and inaccurate the ideas in these sentences are. What are the *natural* food, necessaries, and conveniences of a labourer? The standard varies in every country. Are we to take the wheaten standard of England, the oaten standard of Scotland, or the potato standard of Ireland? or the black rye bread standard of Poland? Which of these is the *natural* standard? Wages in the West Riding of Yorkshire used to be 14s., in Dorsetshire 7s. a week—

which of these was the *natural* standard? A little reflection will show that the idea of a natural standard is a mere chimera. The same principle determines the rate of wages in each of these cases; it is the proportion existing between capital, employment, and labourers in each locality. What made wages so low in Ireland and Dorsetshire? The abundance of labourers and the scarcity of capital and employment. What made wages so high in Yorkshire? The abundance of capital and employment and the scarcity of labourers. If any cause produces a change in the relative proportion of these three elements, a change in the rate of wages necessarily results. Since the famine and emigration have relieved Ireland of the superabundance of labourers, wages have risen greatly. Emigration has produced the same effects in Dorsetshire, and if the same proportions as now exist between these three elements be preserved, the ordinary rate of wages will continue as at present. We see, then, the extreme inaccuracy of speaking of the natural price of labour. What Ricardo means by the natural price is nothing more than the usual market price, which has been produced by a long-continued steadiness in the proportions between the elements of wages, but if any causes change that proportion, the ordinary market price changes with it. Hence, we see that the relation of supply and demand is the sole rule that governs wages.

26. It will be seen that Ricardo's views on the subject of labour are influenced by exactly the same error, which is the fundamental defect of his doctrine of Value, namely, an inversion of cause and effect. It is perfectly manifest that it is not the price of food which regulates wages, but the wages received which indicate the most expensive food which the labourer can afford to buy. Wages in England have not risen because the labourers eat wheaten bread instead of rye bread as formerly, but they eat wheaten bread because their wages enable them to do so. The wages in Ireland were not so low because the people eat potatoes, but the miserable peasantry were driven to feed upon potatoes because their wages were so low; because there were so many labourers and so little employment. So the people in Scotland eat oatmeal porridge and oatcakes because their wages were not sufficient to allow them to eat wheaten bread. Just for the same reason in the northern districts they used to wear kilts because they were too poor to wear better clothes. But since they have become better off they dress like their southern brethren, and they eat wheaten bread to a very much greater extent than formerly. And so it is on the continent of Europe. The people in a great many of the continental countries live so badly because their wages are so low. There are so many people, and there is, comparatively speaking, so little employment. Nothing can show more clearly the error of the idea that the price of food regulates wages than, on the one hand, the case of the United States of America and Canada, where food is extremely cheap and wages extremely high. What is the reason of this? It is that food is very abundant and labour very scarce. It is nothing but the supply and demand of each article. On the other hand, we may take as a reverse case, the example of the unfortunate needlewomen of London and other cities of Western Europe. Garnier remarks exactly the same thing of the needlewomen of Paris. 'A Paris, par exemple, tout le travail d'aiguille est tombé à un taux insuffisant pour fair vivre celles qui n'ont pas d'autre ressource.' And Dr. Mayer says that at Lille, the workwomen who make the lace gain from $1d.$ to $1\frac{1}{2}d.$ a day, working 16 hours. And population has increased so much compared to employment, that those who could gain two or three francs a day 30 years ago, in 1845 could gain only one franc, and those the most favoured. At the other extremity of the world, we may take China as an example of the same truth. Travellers give us accounts of the disgusting garbage which the poorer Chinese will eat: now, the rate of wages there does not depend upon what they eat, but they are driven to eat that abomination because the remuneration for labour is low. And this is on account of the prodigious numbers of the people.

27. The law of supply and demand, then, holds universally with regard to wages. An excessive increase of the people forces down wages by an inevitable law of nature, and as their numbers increase faster than employment, their wages must progressively diminish, and their comfort and scale of living become rapidly deteriorated. Nothing could save the scale of living of the poorer classes of this country from descending to the level of the Irish, or the Chinese, if their numbers went on increasing without a corresponding increase of employment. It is not unusual to hear persons of benevolence, who see the shocking misery which even now prevails among so many in this country, exclaim that employers ought to pay higher wages. But all such ideas are visionary. There is only one effectual mode of relief, and that is to diminish their numbers, by providing outlets for the superabundant hands, until the diminution of their numbers may again raise their wages, so that they can find constant employment, at wages which will enable them to live in comfort.

28. It is no mere speculative opinion that a general and long-continued low price of corn is not only not necessarily accompanied by a low rate of wages, but most probably by the very reverse. The most remarkable continuance of generally fine seasons and abundance of corn ever known occurred in the last century. For the extraordinary period of sixty-five years, from 1701 to 1,765, there was, with a few exceptions, a continued series of plentiful harvests. The average price of corn for that period was 16 per cent. less than the average price for the preceding century; but, notwithstanding that, the price of labour rose greatly during the same period, and, what was least to be expected, *agricultural labour rose* 16 *per cent.* Tooke says— ' The fact, indeed, of a rise of money wages in this country, coincidently with a fall in the price of corn during the long interval in question, rests on unquestionable authorities;' and, says Smith—' In Great Britain the real recompense of labour, it has already been shown, the real quantities of the necessaries and conveniences of life which are given to the labourer, has increased considerably during the course of the present century (i.e. the 18th). The rise in its money price seems to have been the effect, not of any diminution in the value of silver in the general market of Europe, but of a rise in the *real price of labour* in the particular market of Great Britain, owing to the peculiarly happy circumstances of the country;' and 'The money price of labour in Great Britain has indeed risen during the course of the present century. This, however, seems to be the effect, not so much of any diminution in the value of silver in the European market, as of an *increase in the demand for labour in Great Britain arising from the great and almost universal prosperity of the country.*' In the latter part of the century, the price of wheat rose enormously in consequence of a long succession of bad harvests, but there was no corresponding rise in wages.

29. It is no doubt true that there is a limit below which the wages of labour cannot fall for any permanent time, and which is determined by the price of food, but this only relates to the very lowest, rudest, and most unskilled species of labour, and even that limit has happily never yet been reached in England, because it depends upon the lowest, cheapest, and worst kind of food capable of supporting man. The poorest labourer in England has now wheaten bread to eat, such as probably, in the Mediæval Ages, for which there has been lately such a ridiculous enthusiasm, a nobleman could not obtain. If such bread as is usually consumed in many a nobleman's house on the continent were given to the inmates of an English workhouse, it would infallibly cause a riot. The lowest class of labourers have fortunately never been reduced to such a point continuously, though it may sometimes happen that when work is scarce, they can earn very little, and then they may be driven to receive relief from public or private charity, which takes them out of the operation of the law of supply and demand. It is also universally observed that when the price of bread rises very high, the wages of the lowest class of labourers never rise in any like proportion. The way of raising the wages of labour, then, is not by raising the price of food, but by diminishing the number of competitors for it, for it is the number of competitors compared with the quantity of work to be done, that influences the price of labour, and not the variation in the price of food.

30. J. B. Say has also remarked the erroneousness of the doctrine that the price of food regulates wages—'Experience also contradicts another assertion of Ricardo's. He says that while the price of labour regulates the value of products, it is the price of provisions of first necessity (in Europe, for example, corn) which regulates the price of labour, and that a rise in the price of corn diminishes the rate of profit and raises wages. Well, I am informed by the principal manufacturers of England and France, especially MM. Ternaux and Sons, who have mills at Liège, Louviers, Sedan, Reims, and Paris, it is exactly the contrary which happens. When corn becomes dearer wages go down. This result is not accidental; the same cause is always followed by the same effect; and the effect lasts as long as the cause. The explanation is not difficult; when corn is very high, the labouring classes are obliged to devote to purchasing grain a part of their wages which they would have employed in superior clothing, or rent, or furniture, or more succulent and various food: in a word, they reduce all their consumption: and the want of consumption reduced the required quantity of nearly all other products. Hence the reduction of the demand lowers profits of all sorts as well of masters as workmen.'

In fact, the doctrine that the price of food regulates wages is so utterly scouted by every person of practical knowledge that we should not have said so much about it if Ricardo had not still some believers, and his works are still recommended by official sanction in the Universities and the Civil Service. We shall say something more on this point further on.

31. The greater part of Smith's chapter, on 'Wages and Profits in different employments,' is a curious example of the same inversion of cause and effect, and a consideration of the phenomena detailed in it, will afford a further indication of the truth of the preceding principles. He says that there are five principal circumstances which make up for a small pecuniary gain in some employments, and counterbalance a great one in others :—

1. The agreeableness or disagreeableness of the employments themselves.

2. The easiness and cheapness, or the difficulty and expense, of learning them.

3. The constancy or inconstancy of employment in them.

4. The small or great trust which must be reposed in those who exercise them.

5. The probability or improbability of success in them.

These considerations of Smith have been very generally approved of, and have acquired some celebrity; yet it is quite easy to show that they are reducible to the general law we have arrived at, and that in some of them Smith has most manifestly inverted cause and effect.

When he says that the wages of the most agreeable trades are lower than the disagreeable ones, the reason is very plain. Persons in general prefer the more agreeable trades, consequently there are more competitors for employment in them ; but there is also a necessity for disagreeable trades as well, and higher wages in them must be offered to tempt workmen to embark in them. These causes are manifestly to be referred to the law of supply and demand, the various degrees of desirability of the different trades being merely the circumstances which influence the relation of supply and demand.

32. In the second place Smith has most manifestly inverted cause and effect, and his ideas are pervaded with the radical error of his system. After enumerating several species of business, he says—' Education in the ingenious arts, and in the liberal professions, is still more tedious and expensive. The pecuniary recompense, therefore, of painters and sculptors, of lawyers and physicians, ought to be much more liberal, and it is so accordingly.' A very slight consideration will show that it is exactly the reverse of what Smith says. The rewards of lawyers, doctors, &c., are not high because their education is expensive, but they expend much on education because the rewards are high. There is no better example of the truth of the principle we are contending for, and of the fallacy of the one we are combating, than these cases. There is, probably, no difference whatever in the expense of the education of the most able, and the least able, doctor or lawyer; but there is a prodigious difference in the result owing chiefly to the differences in the innate capacities of men, and the success or the contrary will in general depend upon the qualifications of each man ; the quality of the result, and not upon the cost of its production. We shall, however, consider these more fully under the last case.

33. The third case is also manifestly reducible to the law of supply and demand, just as the first is, because men naturally seek for constant employment rather than precarious employment, consequently they will crowd into one more than in the other. And the employers in the trade in which work is less constant must necessarily give higher wages than those in which it is more constant, to attract persons to it. Exactly in the same way, in places of trust, the qualities which fit persons for such employments are comparatively rare, and unless a high price be offered, it is not likely that the employers will find a suitable person.

34. The last cause which, according to Smith, influences the wages of labour is the probability or improbability of success in the employment. In considering this case, this celebrated author has suffered himself to be led away by one of the most curious instances of misanalogy anywhere to be met with. People speak figuratively of life being a 'lottery,' and of the uncertainty of success in it. Smith, seizing upon the word *lottery*, has been led away into a most curious fancy, which has also deceived some later writers. 'The probability that any particular person shall ever be qualified for the employment to which he is educated, is very different in different occupations. In the greater part of the mechanic trades success is almost certain, but very uncertain in the liberal professions. Put your son apprentice to a shoemaker, there is little doubt of his learning to make a pair of shoes; but send him to study the law, it is at least twenty to one if he ever makes such proficiency as will enable him to live by the business. In a perfectly fair lottery, those who draw the prizes ought to gain all that is lost by those who draw the blanks. In a profession where twenty fail for one who succeeds, that one ought to gain all that should have been gained by the unsuccessful twenty. The counsellor-at-law, who perhaps at near forty years of age, begins to make something by his profession, ought to receive the retribution, not only of his own so tedious and expensive education, but that of more than twenty others who are never likely to make anything of it. How extravagant so ever the fees of counsellors-at-law may sometimes appear, their real retribution is never equal to this. Compute in any particular place what is likely to be annually gained, and what is likely to be annually spent by all the different workmen in any common trade, such as that of shoemakers or weavers, and you will find that the former sum will generally exceed the latter; but make the same computation with regard to all the counsellors and students of law in all the different inns of court, and you will find that their annual gains bear but a very small proportion to their annual expenses, even though you rate the former as high and the latter as low as can well be done. The lottery of the law is, therefore, very far from being a perfectly fair lottery, and that, as well as many other liberal and honourable professions, is, in point of pecuniary gain, evidently under-recompensed.'

35. No one who really examines the foregoing ideas can fail to see their utter incongruity. In a lottery the chances of each individual who ventures in it are absolutely equal; no personal qualification can influence his chance in any way whatever; the greatest simpleton may draw the greatest prize, the wisest man may draw a blank. In many cases it may certainly be predicted of an individual who adopts a profession, whether he will succeed or fail, and success in all cases is the result of personal qualifications. In a lottery it is perfectly well known that only a certain number can by any possibility succeed, and all the rest must necessarily fail. In a profession it is quite a matter of possibility that all may attain success, and it is also a matter of possibility that none may attain success sufficient to enable them to live. To carry out Smith's analogy, we might just as well say that poetry is a lottery, and that the sum paid to the good poets should recompense all the waste of time by the bad poets.

36. It is quite evident that the fees of counsel are simply examples of the law of supply and demand. Nothing can be more erroneous than the idea that the fees are high, because the education is high. The truth is, that people spend much money upon a professional education *because* the rewards are so high; and the rewards are so high because they are of so great importance to mankind, and because great skill in them is comparatively rare. The fees of a Follett, or a Dunning, or a Scott, were not so high because there were so many Mr. Brieflesses, but simply because the talents of a Follett, or a Dunning, or a Scott, were so rare and so important. If their talents had become more general, the rewards of their labour would have diminished. It is exactly the same law in the other professions alluded to. It is the high rewards that may be won in them, that attracts high talent into them, and it is for the sake of these high rewards that men undergo a long, tedious, and expensive education, and course of labour. Exactly as the Roman tribune said—' *Eo impendi laborem ac periculum . . . magna præmia proponantur.*'

On the Workman's Share of the Price

37. It has been shown that the rough coarse statement that the 'Wages' Fund' is simply existing capital, and that the average Rate of Wages is simply the ratio between this capital and population, is a simple absurdity. Smith long ago observed that the same piece of money pays the incomes of different persons in perpetual succession:—' The amount of the metal pieces which are annually paid to an individual is often precisely equal to his revenue, and is upon that account the shortest and best account of its value. But the amount of the metal pieces which circulate in society can never be equal to the revenue of all its members. As the same guinea which pays the weekly pension of one man to-day may pay that of another to-morrow, and that of a third the day thereafter, the amount of the metal pieces which annually circulate in any country must always be of much less value than the whole money pensions annually paid to them.' If writers had only thought of this obvious truth of Smith's, they never would have committed such an error as saying that the average Rate of Wages is simply the ratio between population and capital. At all events, even if it were nothing but specie it would be the amount of specie multiplied by the number of times it is paid away in the course of the year. However, even that is a very inadequate account of the Wages' Fund.

The true **Fund** which provides for Wages, Profits, Rent, Cost of Materials, or anything else, is the **Price** of the product : and in case of necessity this fund is anticipated by means of Banking Credits.

This is the fund, and, in ordinary times, this only is the fund, which Capitalists and Workmen have to divide between them : it can by no possibility be exceeded, and, of course, the higher the price, the greater is the fund for division.

But the whole of this fund is not available for division : first of all there must be deducted a sum sufficient to maintain all the fixed and circulating Capital in efficient repair and full working order. Then there must be also deducted a fair interest on the sum invested as fixed and circulating Capital. Every intelligent workman must admit that the Capital must be maintained in full efficiency, and also produce the average rate of interest, or else it would be removed from that species of occupation to something else. So the payment of rent must also come out of it, which is only another name for interest on Capital. After making these deductions from the price of the product, the remainder is the fund available for division between masters and workmen, as the reward of their labour—labour, of course, including skill as well as manual industry.

Masters and workmen, however, often take different views as to the principle on which this fund should be divided.

The masters' view often is, that Labour is simply a commodity, which has its market value like any other, governed by the general law of Demand and Supply : and that the workmen have no right to inquire into the profits which they make by their skill and foresight, or which may accrue to them by a favourable turn in the market.

Workmen, however, are often far from agreeing to this view of the matter. They, or at least the reasonable ones, admit that the Capitalist is entitled to fair profits on the Capital engaged, and also to a reasonable reward for skill, management, superintendence, &c. After that, however, they think that the remainder should be divided among themselves as wages.

To which the masters reply, that in many cases in certain

trades, the business is often carried on at a heavy loss, and that if the workmen are to appropriate all the profits to themselves, they must also be called upon to share the losses: which is, as a matter of fact, impracticable: and, therefore, they have no right to share all the profits.

In many cases where expensive machinery is employed, like in cotton mills, the machinery must be kept going at any cost, and in a period of depression masters work at a heavy daily loss, simply to prevent the machinery deteriorating, and the workpeople from starving, and the necessity of breaking up their establishment. Now if the workpeople devour all the profits in time of prosperity, where are the funds to come from to maintain them in a period of depression? If the bees devour all the honey in summer, what is to feed them in winter? Hence it is plainly to the real advantage of the workpeople themselves that they should not devour all the profits as soon as they are made. By allowing them to accumulate in the hands of the masters they are in reality laying up an insurance fund for themselves for a rainy day.

Now this portion of the price of the product is a superior limit which wages cannot permanently exceed. It is a cast iron limit—the result of the inexorable law of Demand and Supply which imposes a superior limit on wages.

38. Now we may observe that there are two kinds of labour in commerce, one of which is necessary to produce the profit, the other which is not.

In a merchant's office, or in a bank, the clerks, servants, messengers, porters, &c., contribute nothing to the success of the business. Such labour as theirs is subject to the simple rule of Demand and Supply. They have no shadow of a claim to demand a share of the profits; and if the heads of the establishment give them a *bonus* in a successful year, that is mere grace and favour. So the servants of a railway company, engine drivers, guards, porters, and clerks, contribute nothing to the success of the enterprise. Their labour is a mere commodity, which must be paid for whether the line pays any dividend or not. They have no more claim to have a share of the profits than if the company buys engines and carriages from another company, that company would have a claim to be paid for their engines and carriages according to the profits the railway company was earning. Such persons have no more claim to a share of the profits than domestic servants would have to higher wages if their master were successful in business.

But the labour of operatives, miners, and artisans stands on a different footing altogether. Their labour, their skill, is indispensably necessary, and conduces directly to obtain the product and the profit. Their labour may justly be styled co-operative with that of the master: they are in reality quasi-partners with the capitalist in obtaining the profits, and without them the profits could not be made, and the master obtains a distinct profit out of the labour of such workmen which he can estimate in a very different sense to that of the labour of the other class.

The claim of such workmen to a share of the profit which is distinctly due to their work, stands on a totally different footing from that of the other class. It is now pretty generally recognised that such workmen have an equitable claim to a certain share of the profit which is the result of the joint efforts of the master and workmen: though what that share should be, and how they are to obtain it, is a very different matter: moreover, it is far easier to determine in some kinds of business than in others.

39. Mr. Brassey says that 'there is a maximum limit above which wages cannot rise, and a minimum below which they cannot fall. The minimum is determined by the cost of living according to the standard adopted by the people. Wages cannot long continue below the amount necessary for the support of the labourer and his family. On the other hand, wages cannot long continue so high as to deprive the employer of a fair return upon his capital, and a reasonable reward for the application of his time and abilities to the conduct of his business. If wages exceed the maximum limit determined by the necessity of fulfilling the conditions enumerated, capital will no longer be embarked in undertakings from which no adequate return can be obtained.'

What Mr. Brassey says of the superior limit of wages is

true; but what he says of the inferior limit is subject to great qualifications. While no power on earth can raise wages above the superior limit, which is determined by the inexorable law of Demand and Supply, the inferior limit is, unfortunately, very elastic. If there is only a certain amount of work to be done, and workmen persist in crowding into it, nothing can prevent their outbidding one another and lowering wages: and as their wages go down under this competition, so must their scale of living deteriorate. Was it because potatoes were so cheap that Irish wages were so low? Certainly not: it was the excessive population of Ireland, whose numbers were multiplied by a vicious system of small holdings, created for political purposes, and the absence of an effective poor-law, and the deficiency of employment for them, that compelled them to resort to potatoes for sustenance, and we all know the consequences. So that, even if it were true, this law could not take effect until the very lowest and cheapest food that would support human life, were discovered. To say that scale of living regulates wages is only true when the law of Demand and Supply is called in to aid it, and means be taken to limit the numbers of workmen, so that they can enforce their demand for wages to afford them superior food. There must be found some method of removing the superfluous numbers. In China, as is well known, infanticide is practised to an enormous extent: babies are destroyed with no more compunction than young kittens and puppies. In many continental States the most rigorous legal restrictions are placed on marriages; while in other countries emigration is the sovereign remedy.

On the Droit-au-Travail

40. A passionate cry, however, has gone up from many working men that human flesh and blood should not be treated as dead and senseless commodities by the cold, inflexible Laws of Supply and Demand. They and their self-appointed advocates often maintain that they have an absolute right to have such wages as will sustain themselves and their families in comfort, or at least that the State is bound to provide work for them. They abuse the science of Economics because it simply explains certain great and immutable Laws of Nature under which they live, and whose influence they cannot escape from.

The science of Economics is not the **Cause** of these Laws or these evils; it simply explains them as they exist. To vituperate Economics on account of human misery is as irrational as to vituperate Mechanics because a badly constructed boiler will burst and kill all around it: or a badly constructed house may fall and crush all the inmates: or to vituperate Chemistry because if a man were to take a dose of arsenic or prussic acid it would kill him: or if he were to stand on a barrel of dynamite or gunpowder it might blow him to atoms: or to vituperate Medicine because a man may die of a fever.

Mechanics, Chemistry, and Medicine are not the **Causes** of these human calamities: they only investigate the Causes, and endeavour to discover the remedies applicable to them.

Economics, like Medicine, sprang directly out of the observation of human misery and calamities: and is not their **Cause** it only investigates their Causes: and points out the appropriate remedy by which they can be mitigated and alleviated, so far as is consistent with the nature of things.

But men treat Economics as they do Fortune—

> Quest' è colei che tanto è posta in croc
> Pur da color che le dovrian dar lode,
> Dandole biasmo a torto e mala voce:
> Ma ella s' e beata e ciò non ode.

This is she who is so execrated by those who ought rather to give her praise, wrongfully repaying her with curses and malediction: but she is blessed, and heeds not what they say.

If only a full and true picture of the evils which erroneous doctrines and practices in Economics have inflicted upon the human race could be presented, men would hail Economics as beneficent a science as Medicine.

41. The doctrine that human beings should not be subject to the usual Laws of Demand and Supply, and that every workman is entitled to have Work or Wages found for him sufficient to enable him to live and bring up a family in comfort, under the name of the **Droit-au-travail**, has been very widespread among our neighbours across the Channel. It has been tried many times, and always with the most disastrous results.

So far back as 1545 edicts had been issued directing the establishment of public workshops for unemployed workmen. In 1685, 1699, and 1709, ordinances were issued for the regulation of these workshops. Louis XVI. exerted himself to extend this mode of relief throughout the kingdom, and endeavoured to encourage the establishment of public works in each province during the dead season by privileges.

The Constitution of 1791 decreed that there should be created and organised a general establishment of public assistance, to bring up foundlings, to relieve the infirm poor, and to furnish able-bodied poor with work who could not procure it for themselves. But this never could be carried out. Notwithstanding the assistance given, the misery of the poor went on increasing. and more and more workshops were closed every day.

The Constitution of 1793 was still more explicit. It declared that public relief was a sacred duty: that society owed subsistence to unfortunate citizens, either in procuring them work, or in assuring the means of existence to those who are not in a condition to work. This abortive Constitution maintained that the State is bound to find enough work for all its members, or should enable them to support themselves.

This doctrine was omitted in the succeeding Constitution: but the *Ateliers de Charité* survived, and the Law of the 24 Vendémiaire (year XII.) contains minute regulations for them: but it had no greater success than the former attempts. Babeuf drew from it his doctrine of the community of goods: and it sank deep in the minds of the people, and has formed one of the principal articles of the Socialist creed.

Fourier thus enumerates the doctrine of the *droit-au-travail*—' Scripture tells us that God condemned the first man and his posterity to work with the sweat of their brow: but he has not condemned us to be deprived of that work on which our subsistence depends. We can then, in accordance with the rights of man request philosophers and civilisation not to deprive us of that resource which God has left us at the worst and as a chastisement: and to guarantee us the right and the kind of labour to which we have been brought up. We have now passed the time to cavil at the rights of man without thinking of recognising the most important of all, without which the others are nothing. What a shame to the nations who think they understand social politics! Ought one not to dwell upon such a shameful error, to study the human mind and the mechanism of society which gives to man all his natural rights, of which society cannot guarantee or admit the principal one, the *droit-au-travail?*'

The principle of the *droit-au-travail* gradually worked its way in the public mind. Several persons whose names are more or less notorious—Considérant, Cabet, Proudhon, St. Simon, Louis Blanc—had been busying their brains with schemes to ameliorate the organisation of society, and when the catastrophe of 1848 took place—brought about in a great measure by the suffering from want of work of the population of Paris—the Socialist party had a grand opportunity of trying the practical effects of their ideas.

The revolution of 1848 proclaimed the *droit-au-travail.* On February 26 the Provisional Government issued a decree guaranteeing the existence of the labourer by work, and guaranteeing work to all citizens.

In accordance with this decree a Committee was appointed, with Louis Blanc at its head, and installed at the Luxembourg, to carry out the scheme of finding work for everybody. But one result could follow. It aggravated the distress and disorganisation of labour tenfold. The inflammatory proclamations which emanated from the Luxembourg destroyed all the remaining relations that existed between the private masters and their workmen. In a great number of establishments masters and workmen had come to a voluntary agreement as to the quantity and the hours of work and the rate of wages. But the proceedings of the Commission upset all these arrangements. They were forbidden by decree to enter into such engagements. Moreover, the Commission not only attempted to regulate the forms in which work was to be conducted and paid for, but also its hours. They decreed that a day's work should not exceed ten hours in all France. Having thus disordered all the relations between Capitalists and workmen, they threatened to appropriate all the manufactures to the State. The masters and contractors in despair requested the Government to take all the works off their hands. The Commission said they would, and pay them a large indemnity : but as they had no means of doing so at the time, it must be taken out of the resources of the future. The State would give them Obligations bearing interest secured on the value of the establishments given up, and payable in annuities by instalments.

By thus meddling with private contracts, the Government soon put all social order in danger. It wanted to appropriate to itself all Credit, all Insurance Companies, and all railroads. Instead of a remedy being provided for the existing distress, it was aggravated a thousandfold. Instead of the existing want of work being provided for, a universal stoppage took place. The Government were then driven to organise the *Ateliers Nationaux*, in which the State was to be universal employer, and all the ideas of Communism to be inaugurated. All employments were to be regulated on the same scale, and all wages were equal. Of course the whole mass of workmen and paupers rushed to them. The Right of Labour, if claimed as a Right, was nowhere considered as a duty. Every one was admitted indiscriminately. The numbers were never exactly ascertained, but in March they were about 6,000 : in June they were about 110,000 : when, the whole resources of society being fast devoured, they were obliged to be broken up, at the expense of the terrible insurrection of June.

With this experience before them, it might have been thought that the French Assembly would have been cured of the fatal doctrine of the *droit-au-travail*, and yet, during the time when one of the most sanguinary civil combats on record was going on, the new Constitution proposed, sanctioned, and confirmed in the most explicit terms this fatal doctrine. It said—'The *droit-au-travail* is that which every man has to live by his work. Society is bound by all the productive and general means it can dispose of to furnish work to able-bodied men who cannot get it for themselves otherwise.' 'The essential guarantees of the *droit-au-travail* are the freedom of labour, voluntary association, equality in the relations between masters and workmen, gratuitous instruction, professional education, provident institutions, and those of Credit, the undertaking by the

State of great works of public utility for the purpose of employing the persons thrown out of work during a stoppage.'

Public opinion, however, rebelled against this doctrine of the *droit-au-travail*: and some modification was made in its extreme terms: it was finally adopted on these terms—'The Republic is bound by a fraternal assistance to insure means of existence to necessitous citizens, either in procuring them work, within the limits of its resources, or in giving, during the inability of the family, relief to those who are not in a condition to work.'

In criticising the errors of our neighbours we must never fail to remember that the very same false principles infected our own legislation till within recent times. The old poor law, with its system of parish allowances making up the wages of labour to a certain arbitrary amount out of the property of the ratepayers, was the very same doctrine, and was fast devouring the property of the country. And if it did not produce the same appalling results in this country as it did in France, the reason was that it was chiefly applied in agricultural districts, where the population was scattered and there was more control over them: and they were not able to combine so readily as the French workmen. The poison was therefore more diffused. But in France the doctrine was applied to large masses or workmen concentrated in one body of inflammable materials without the possibility of exacting any work from them.

Moreover, the system of Protection which so long existed in this country was only another form of Socialism. The *droit-au-travail* is the right of the workman to have sufficient work and wages found for him by the State out of the means of society—it is the Socialism of workmen. The system of Protection is the right to have remunerative Profits provided for the producer by law out of the means of society—it is the Socialism of Capitalists. All these are parts of one vicious circle. In fact, Protection and Socialism are incompatible with the rights of property. If manufacturers or agriculturists can compel me to pay ten shillings extra for any commodities I may require beyond what I could get them elsewhere, in order to provide them with arbitrary profits, what difference in principle is there between that and the workman who maintains the *droit-au-travail*, when I must employ him and pay him wages, when I don't want anything he can produce? The two things are identical.

Experience and reason equally show that the *droit-au-travail* is erroneous. It is not **Men** who are purchased, but their **Labour**: and their Labour is a Commodity subject to exactly the same Laws of Value as all other Commodities. If a Shakespeare, a Macaulay, or a Scott were set to do the work of a copying clerk, they would not be paid as a Shakespeare, a Macaulay, or a Scott, but for the work of a copying clerk. If the rule of providing a certain Price for Labour can be enforced, it must also be enforced for Commodities. For how is Labour paid? Out of the Price of the Commodity. It is only the Demand for the Commodity which gives Value to the Labour. When a master pays wages to a workman to produce a Commodity, he only does so because he expects that there will be a Demand for the Commodity; and he can only pay wages in proportion to the Price he expects to obtain for the Commodity. To say, therefore, that a certain Price should be fixed for Labour is as much as to say that certain Prices should be fixed for Commodities: an error, indeed, which long prevailed, but which is now completely exploded. If, therefore, the Price of Commodities is left to be exclusively governed by the Law of Demand and Supply, it follows as a necessary and inevitable consequence that the Price of Labour must be so too: for it is the expected Price of the Product which is the sole inducement to pay wages, and regulates their amount.

In fact, if the *droit-au-travail* is an admissible principle at all, it cannot be restricted to handicraftsmen. If the shoemaker is entitled to call upon the State to provide him with shoes to make, when there are no feet to wear them: if the mason is to call upon the State to employ him to build houses when there is no one to live in them: if the tailor can call upon the State to pay him to make endless coats when there are no backs to be covered—why the same law is good for the lawyer, the doctor, the artist, the author, the editor. Every man who chooses to adopt the Law as a profession should have a certain number of ten-guinea briefs deposited by the State upon his breakfast-table every morning: every painter should be commissioned to paint endless Madonnas: every sculptor should be employed to produce perpetual Apollos: every author should have a certain number of copies of his work ordered by the State, which criminals perhaps might be sentenced to read: every editor should have a certain number of copies of his paper ordered by the State: though it might be somewhat difficult for the State to provide patients for medical men and surgeons at will.

The fallacy which pervades the French theory of the *droit-au-travail* is manifest. It demands that work shall be found for the workmen of the nature they are accustomed to. Now why is it that the workmen in any particular trade are in distress? Because there is not sufficient *Demand* for their Labour. Because that species of Labour is over-abundant. All commercial difficulties arise from *over-production* in one form or another, and never from *under-production*. And all commercial difficulties may be reduced to this general form of expression— that traders have provided, or got on hand, more of some commodity than is suitable for the circumstances of the times. And this is *over-production* no matter from what cause it arises. To provide more of any article, then, which is already over-abundant, can only aggravate the evil. What is really wanted is mere **Demand**. Now the State can, if it pleases, Produce, but it never can create Demand. Consequently the only result which those who produce by extraneous assistance more than is wanted can effect, is to aggravate and extend still further the area of suffering, and to reduce those who can maintain themselves to the same state as those who are already dependent on the public. Consequently if the Right to Labour be admitted at all, it must be of some nature wholly different from the workman's usual occupation. We must defer any further remarks on this subject till we come to speak of Poor Laws.

Working Men *do not* Create Wealth

42. We must now bring our remarks on this vast subject to an end; not because it is exhausted, but because it is so extensive and its application so various that it would rather require many volumes to do it justice. We may simply remark that Demand is the sole cause of the Value of Labour, as of its produce, and of everything else. It is Demand only which causes Labour and its produce to be Wealth. In recent times far too much attention has been given to the Producer and far too little to the Consumer. Working men, and those who flatter them for the purpose of gaining their votes, are constantly in the habit of proclaiming that they are the Creators of all Wealth. But working men are **not** the Creators of all Wealth. Did working men create corn, or make it grow? Did working men create cattle and all sorts of flocks? Did working men ever create any material substance whatever? Did they create the stone of which houses are built, or the marble of which sculpture is formed? Did they create the great sciences which have done so much for mankind, and by which so much of their labour is directed? Did they create the land? Did they create the skill, the foresight, and the Credit, by means of which modern commerce is carried on? They did none of these things. They bring nothing but their Labour to transport and transform the materials furnished by nature, to supply the wants of others. And whatever they may do, it is not *their* **Labour** which constitutes a thing Wealth, but the **Demand** of the *Consumer*. The Producer and the Consumer are both indispensably necessary to each other : and it is only by their joint action that anything is Wealth. Let all the skill and Labour possible be bestowed on any product, if there is no demand for it, it is not Wealth. As the whole body of ancient writers, all the first school of Economists, all the Italian Economists, show, it is Consumption or Demand which is the true essence of Wealth. Of what use would it be for working men to build miles of palaces if nobody wanted to live in them? Or to grow corn and bake bread if there were no Consumers to eat it? Or to make furniture, clothes, or watches, if there were no persons to buy them? At every turn in Economics this truth meets us, that it is not the Labour of the Producer which constitutes a thing Wealth, but the Demand of the Consumer.

Nothing can be more suicidal than the cry against rich men which so many wild Socialists and Communists have raised. Where would working men be without rich men? If a man has not Wealth of his own, but only his Labour to sell, does he go to a multitude of paupers like himself, who cannot buy it, or does he seek a concourse of rich men who will compete for it? What is most to his advantage? Of course that there should be as many rich men as possible to compete for it. Nothing can be more fatal than the cry against Capital so often unthinkingly uttered. How could working men exist without Capital? A Capitalist is a man whose business it is to rack his brains to provide work for working men : and to give them their reward before he gets any for himself : and often, indeed, he gives them their reward and gets none for himself. Working men can no more do without Capital than Capital can do without them : and it is for their interest that Capital should increase and multiply as much as possible to compete for their Labour. When working men complain of the tyranny of Capital and the low price of their Labour, *it is not the tyranny of Capital which is their enemy*, **but the tyranny of their own excessive numbers.** Their interest is to multiply their 'Tyrants,' and to diminish their own numbers. What they really want is more 'tyrants,' more Capitalists, more rich men, and fewer working men. And we are happy to think that working men are touched to a comparatively small extent with the insane phrensy of the Continental Socialists and Communists, whose object it is to destroy all Capital and all rich men. Their struggle in the main is only to obtain what they consider a fair division of the Fund which provides both Wages and Profits ; and it would be impossible to conceive a greater benefactor to his country than the one who could permanently reconcile the interests of Masters and Workmen, and put an end to the internecine wars of Capital and Labour.

CHAPTER XI

ON RIGHTS, OR INCORPOREAL WEALTH

1. WE have now to consider that gigantic mass of Property which consists only in the form of mere abstract Rights, wholly severed from any material substance, which is called Incorporeal Property or Incorporeal Wealth, which is the third order of Economic Quantities. This species of Property has increased in a much faster ratio in this country during the last century than Material Property, and now exceeds it many times.

This kind of Property consists in mere Rights to something which will only come into possession at a future time. But as these Rights may be bought and sold and exchanged, their *Value may be measured in money*, like that of any material chattel: they are included under the terms *Pecunia, Res, Bona, Merx* in Roman Law; χρήματα, πράγματα, ἀγαθὰ, οἶκος, περιουσία, ἀφορμὴ, in Greek Law; under Goods and Chattels, or vendible commodities, in English Law; and under **Wealth** in Economics.

The explanation of the Theory of the Value of Land already given will make the nature of these Rights readily intelligible. The Land is an Economic Quantity, producing a series of Profits in future time for ever: and each of these future Profits has a **Present** Value: and the Right to the future products is Incorporeal Property, and may be bought and sold like any material chattel.

It has also been seen that a trader exercising any profitable business is an Economic Quantity analogous to the land, producing a series of Profits: and he has the Right to these future profits to be earned by his industry, and he can trade with and sell these Rights to his future profits: which is his **Credit**. We have already exhibited the mechanism of the great system of Credit: which consists in the commerce of these Rights.

2. We have now to investigate the remaining forms of Incorporeal Property.

This commodity, Incorporeal Property, has exactly the same varieties as Corporeal Property. Some of it is immovable: some of it is movable: or, as it might be called by analogy, Real and Personal. Moreover, some kinds of Incorporeal Property are as truly the produce of Labour as any Corporeal Property: other large masses of Incorporeal Property are not the result of labour; just as there are masses of Corporeal Property which are not the result of Labour: also vast masses of Incorporeal Property are exported and imported, and affect the exchanges exactly in the same way as any other merchandise. But as these masses of Property pass through the Post Office and not through the Custom House, it is not possible to have any record of the quantities which are exported or imported: and consequently the subject of the Foreign Exchanges is a hopeless puzzle to those who look only at the official returns of the Board of Trade.

Incorporeal Property *is of* **Two** *kinds,* **Personal** *or* **Nominate,** *and* **Impersonal** *or* **Innominate**

3. Incorporeal Property, or Abstract Rights, is of two kinds, each of them containing many varieties and vast masses of Property.

(1) Where the Right of one person to demand a future payment is connected with the Duty of some other person to make that payment. The Right and the Duty constitute an Obligation, or *nexus*. This species of rights may therefore be called Rights of Obligation: or, as they are always Rights against some specific person, they may be called **Personal** or **Nominate** Rights.

This species of Property includes Annuities of all sorts, commencing with Credit, which is the lowest form of an Annuity, being usually the Right to demand a single future payment: Rents of houses, farms, copyrights, patents, pews, telegraph wires, mines, farms, &c. which are usually a limited series of payments: up to Property in Land, the Funds, Tithes, &c., which are the Rights to receive a series of payments for ever.

(2) Where the Right exists to receive some *expected* but uncertain profit—a payment which no person is bound to make, but which it is only **expected** that some one will. This is called the *emptio spei*, or the *emptio rei speratæ* of Roman Law. This species of Property may therefore be called **Rights of Expectation**: or, as they are mere abstract Rights without any corresponding Personal Duty, they may be called **Impersonal** or **Innominate** Rights.

To this class of Incorporeal Property belong Shares in Commercial Companies: Copyrights: Patents: the Goodwill of a Business: the Practice of a professional man: Tolls: Ferries: Fisheries: Shootings: Street crossings, &c.

On Rights of Obligation: *or* Personal or Nominate Rights

4. The Doctrine of Annuities is a curious commentary upon the arguments of Aristotle, Dante, and the mediæval theologians that interest for money is unnatural and abominable. The Theory of Annuities entirely depends on the principle that Money naturally produces interest: and that Interest also produces Interest, a doctrine which drove Plutarch wild.

An Annuity is the Right to demand a series of payments from some person: and the doctrine of Annuities rests entirely on the principle that each of these future payments has a **Present Value**: and that the Right to all or any number of them may be bought and sold like any material chattel.

The Present Value of an Annuity is therefore the sum of the series of the Present Values of all the future payments. Let us now consider the case of a Perpetual Annuity, or the Right to receive a series of payments at definite intervals for ever. If money bore no interest it is clear that the value of each such future payment would be exactly equal to the payment itself. Consequently, the Present Value of such an Annuity would be the aggregate of the sums to be paid for ever. That is, to purchase such an Annuity it would be necessary to pay down an infinite sum of money; which is manifestly absurd. Hence such a method of calculating the value of an annuity is manifestly erroneous.

Again, suppose that simple interest is charged: then each future payment is diminished by a certain definite sum of uniform amount. And it is evident that to buy an annuity on such a principle would involve exactly the same absurdity as in the former case. That is, to secure the annual payment of a finite sum it would be necessary to pay down an infinite sum: which shows that this method of calculation also is erroneous.

But if compound interest be charged it will be seen that each term of the series will progressively and rapidly diminish. A larger quantity will have to be subtracted from each term in succession, according as the payment is more distant. We shall then obtain a series of quantities in geometrical progression, the common ratio being a fraction, and by the laws of Algebra we know that such a series, even though infinite, has a finite limit. Each term to be added is smaller than the preceding one: until at last they diminish to 0: and that Finite Limit is the Present Value of the Infinite Annuity.

Hence it is seen that the Present Value of an Annuity must always be calculated at Compound Interest to obtain a rational result. The Present Value of each term is such a sum as improved at Compound Interest at a given rate would amount to the sum in a given time. And the Present Value of the whole annuity is the sum of the series of the Present Values of each term.

It is clear that Compound Interest is natural and proper: because, if a sum of money produces interest, it makes no difference whether it is called Principal or Capital or Interest: and as soon as Interest has accrued from the Capital, that Interest as naturally produces Interest as the Capital did.

If the doctrines of so many philosophers and divines had been followed in practice it would have been impossible to have bought landed property: but nature herself proves their error: because if seed-corn be sown in the ground it naturally multiplies in a geometrical ratio: and that produce also multiplies in an equal ratio: consequently all Capital naturally increases in a geometrical progression: and consequently, if money is lent to purchase the Capital, the Profit of the money naturally increases in the same ratio as the produce of the Capital.

5. We have already seen that a sum of money is always equal to a perpetual annuity. Thus we have

£100 = a Perpetual Annuity of £3, or

£100 = an Annuity of £10 for a certain number of years.

And as these Quantities are equal to each other, a person may pay down a capital sum to buy an Annuity: or he may pay an Annuity to buy a capital sum payable at a definite time or at a certain event, or only at an infinite distance of time as a perpetual loan.

We also observe that the symbol o denotes the Present Value of a sum of money that will only be paid at an infinite distance of time : and as the Present Value of any sum whatever, however large or however small, that will only be paid at an infinite distance of time, is exactly the same, *i.e.* = o, it shows that in Economics, as in every other branch of Physical Science, one o may be any number of times greater than another o, which sometimes puzzles juvenile mathematicians.

6. The subject of Annuities is of vast practical importance : and for a full account of them we must refer to the technical treatises on the subject. We can only give a general outline of their various kinds.

An Annuity is the Right to Demand a series of Payments from some person.

I. *The lowest form of an Annuity is the Right to demand a single future payment*

This comprehends the whole of Mercantile and Banking Credit : which is the Right to a single future payment. These Rights of action, under the form of Bank Credits, Bank Notes, Bills of Exchange, &c., form an enormous mass of Exchangeable Property, much larger than any other single species of Property except only the Land. We have already seen reason to believe that this species of Property cannot be much less than £6,000,000,000 in this country.

II. *An Annuity for a limited series of terms, but exceeding one and less than infinity*

This variety is much the most complicated : and includes a great number of sub-varieties, the calculation of whose value involves a considerable portion of the Theory of Probabilities. It includes the theory of the value of Leases : fines on the renewal of leases : estates in remainder and in reversion, vested and contingent : and life and survivorship annuities of all sorts. To enter into a full detail of the methods requisite to find the value of all these several annuities would require an immense amount of mathematical detail, which is wholly beyond the purpose of this work: and for which we must refer to the standard treatises on these subjects. All we can do here is to sketch very briefly the different classes which may be formed : and the species of property which is included in them.

We may have then—

1. *A series to commence immediately, and to terminate at a given time.*

(a) *And of this the termination may be certain.*

Under this form are included all leases for a certain number of years, as usually of farms and houses : and all annuities for a fixed number of years : a form in which public debts are sometimes contracted. In either of these cases the Capital is advanced, and in exchange for it the Right of receiving a series of payments is created, which is the annuity. In the case of the house and the farm, the use of them is granted for a certain number of years : and an annuity is received for their use, and at the end of the term the house or the farm is restored to its owner. In the case of terminable annuities, the interest is paid every year, together with a certain sum to replace the Capital by instalments, so that at the end of the term the whole Capital is restored.

(b) *Or the termination may be uncertain.*

Under this form are all life annuities commencing immediately.

(b 1) *And this termination may depend upon a single uncertain event.*

(b 2) *Or upon several uncertain events.*

Thus an annuity may be granted to continue during the life of a single person : or during the life of the survivor of several persons.

2. *A series to begin at a future time, and to continue during a limited number of years.*

(a) *Of this form the commencement and termination may both be certain and definite.*

Of this the fine paid for the renewal of an unexpired lease is an example.

(a 1) *Or the commencement may be certain and definite, and the end certain but indefinite.*

Thus an estate may be granted to A and his heirs for ten years: and then to B for life.

Or A may purchase an annuity for life, to commence at the end of a given term.

(a 2) *Or the commencement may be certain and definite: but the end uncertain and indefinite.*

Thus an estate may be granted to A for ten years, and then to B until some contingent event happens, as, for instance, till he marries, and then to C.

Or a husband may bequeath an estate to his widow so long as she remains unmarried.

(a 3) *Or the commencement may be certain but indefinite, and the end certain and definite.*

Thus an annuity for fifty years may be granted to B and his heirs, to commence at the death of A.

(a 4) *Or the commencement may be uncertain and indefinite, and the termination certain and definite.*

Thus an estate or an annuity for a term of years may be settled on B, contingent on his marrying and having a son.

(a 5) *Or the commencement may be uncertain and indefinite, and the termination certain but indefinite.*

Thus an annuity may be granted to twenty different living persons in succession separately for their lives.

Or a survivorship annuity may be effected by a husband in favour of his wife.

(a 6) *Or the commencement and the termination may both be uncertain and indefinite.*

Thus an estate may be granted to A until some contingency, such as marriage, bankruptcy, birth of a son, succeeding to another estate: then to B on similar contingencies: then to C: and so on.

3. *An annuity to commence at a future time, and to continue for ever.*

(a) *And of this the commencement may be certain and definite.*

Thus an estate may be sold to B, subject to a lease to A.

(b) *Or the commencement may be certain but indefinite.*

Thus an estate may be settled on A for life, with remainder to B in fee.

(c) *Or the commencement may be uncertain and indefinite.*

Thus an estate may be settled on A and his heirs; when failing on B and his heirs.

Or an estate may be granted to A until he becomes bankrupt, or innumerable other contingencies, and then to B and his heirs.

To this form belongs the whole theory of estates in remainder in reversion, vested or contingent: executory interests: springing and shifting uses: and executory devises, a subject of immense importance.

III. *The largest form of an Annuity,* i.e. *a series of future payments for ever*

This comprehends the whole theory of the value of estates in fee simple, and that portion of the Public Debts which consists of perpetual annuities. To purchase an estate in fee simple is merely to discount a series of future payments for ever, as already explained: and the same is obviously true of buying the Funds.

On the **Funds**

7. We must now explain the nature of the Funds, which has been the subject of much misconception.

It has been said in Chapter I. that the State is a *persona* quite separate from any individual citizens: and it can buy and sell and exchange like any private individual, and it can trade with or exchange with its own citizens as well as with anyone else.

It can also trade with its Credit like any private individual: this Purchasing Power of the State is termed Public Credit: and as we have seen that any Purchasing Power is Wealth, Public Credit is Public Wealth.

Thus the State may be in want of Money to carry on some object of public importance, such as a war, or a public work, or to find relief for some great public calamity, such as a famine; and it may 'borrow' Money like any private individual. This Money, of course, like any sum 'lent' to an individual, is a **Mutuum**, i.e. the absolute Property in it passes to the State, and in exchange for it the State gives the lender an annuity, or Right to demand a series of payments, either for ever or for a limited time.

When the annuity is for a limited time it is called a Terminable Annuity.

When the loan is perpetual, and the State pays nothing but the annual interest for ever, the annuity is what is in popular language called the Funds: because the capital sum is fixed or founded, and cannot be re-demanded from the State: but the legal name is 'Bank Annuities,' because, like the original Italian *Banchi*, they are the contribution of a number of persons.

These annuities were also formerly called Rent in English: but it has been discontinued in this country: it is retained in French, and the French Funds are termed *Rentes*: and a Fundholder is termed a *Rentier*: Turgot calls the moneyed interest *l'intérêt rentier*.

Though the Government does not bind itself to repay the principal, it reserves to itself the right to do so : if the annuitant wishes to get back his principal he can offer the annuity for sale to some one else.

On Tithes

8. Tithes in ecclesiastical law are the Right to demand the tenth part of the yearly produce or increase from the land: the stock upon the land: and the personal industry of the inhabitants.

Tithes of the produce of the land itself, such as corn, hay, hops, fruits of all sorts, are called **Prædial Tithes** : tithes from the increase of the stock upon land, such as calves, lambs, pigs, poultry, eggs, butter, cheese, &c., are called **Mixed Tithes** : and tithes from the produce of personal industry of all sorts, handicrafts, arts, professions, are called **Personal Tithes**.

All nations of antiquity, the Pelasgi, Jews, Syrians, Phœnicians, Arabians, Æthiopians, Carthaginians, Romans, and Greeks, seem to have considered the tenth part of the produce from any source as the portion due from the reverence of mankind to the Deity.

9. For four hundred years after the foundation of Christianity no such right as Tithes was claimed or allowed in the Christian Church. The bounty of the early converts far exceeded a tithe. At Jerusalem and many other places the infant community practised for some time a community of goods: but it was by no means universally adopted. St. Paul directed the converts at Corinth and in Galatia to make weekly collections, to which everyone should contribute according to his ability.

Afterwards the collections were made monthly: Tertullian, speaking about 200 A.D. of the flourishing condition of the African churches, says that all their wealth was raised by voluntary offerings, and not by taxes as the price of religion. These offerings were employed in supporting and burying the poor and destitute orphans, the old and the sick, and other charitable purposes.

Origen seems to have been the first who began to assert that Tithes are due by divine law, as part of the Mosaic law of perpetual right: but no other writer of the church seems for a long time to have repeated that doctrine. Cyprian, about half a century later, blames the general coldness of devotion in his day, and the neglect of giving offerings compared with the liberality of former times, and says that they did not even give tithes of their substance. Until the end of the fifth century there are no authentic documents to show that tithes were claimed as a right in the Christian Church: and for 600 years none of the councils of the Church make any mention of Tithes even in those canons relating to the lands, goods, offerings, and other revenues of the Church.

But about the end of the fifth century a custom gradually sprang up of endowing churches with Tithes for the payment of the abbots, the poor, and the clergy: and as voluntary liberality waxed colder, the duty of paying them began to be asserted more strongly and distinctly.

That intrepid prelate St. Ambrose, Bishop of Milan, was the first to assert that Tithes are due by divine right. He says: 'It is not sufficient for us to bear the name of Christians if we do not do Christian works : God orders that Tithes are to be demanded of us every year of all fruits, cattle, &c.' 'Whosoever is conscious that he has not faithfully paid his Tithes, let him immediately amend his fault, and faithfully pay his Tithes, and not offer less to God at any time of his corn or his wine, of the fruits of his trees, of his cattle, or his garden, or his business, or his hunting. God has reserved to himself the tenth part of all the substance he has given to men : and therefore it is not lawful for man to keep to himself what God has reserved to himself.' St. Augustine, Bishop of Hippo, is equally emphatic in enforcing this duty, and says that if they have no fruits of the earth to offer they should pay a tithe of whatever they live by—'Whatever mode of living supports you is of God : and hence he exacts a tenth part of your income : render a tithe of the spoils of war ; of the profits of trading, and manual labour—'Tithes are demanded of right : and he who refuses to pay them robs the property of another.'

A provincial council of Macon, in 586 A.D., seems to have been the first at which the payment of tithes is spoken of as of considerable antiquity : but it was not yet received as a part of ecclesiastical law. St. Jerome and St. Chrysostom, without affirming it to be a legal duty to pay tithes, exhort Christians to be not less liberal than the Jews in their offerings : and say that they should not give less than a tenth of all profits gained either from the earth, or by trade, or by any other just employment of person or estate. Agobard, Bishop of Lyons, says that no synod or general doctrine of the Church had determined what portion should be given either for the maintenance of priests or the building of churches.

Nevertheless, the clergy began more zealously to enforce the doctrine that Tithes are due by divine right : and consecration of them to various churches became more frequent. Pepin endowed the church of Utrecht with all tithes of slaves, lands, taxes, and other property.

At this time the quadripartite division of these offerings was made, one part for the maintenance of the ministers, a second for the relief of the poor, sick, and strangers : the third for the repair of the church : and the fourth for the bishop. This appropriation of tithe was confirmed by a law of Charlemagne in 778 A.D., in a general assembly of his Estates, both spiritual and temporal.

The doctrine that tithes are due by divine right was now asserted by several Councils and Popes: and at last the General Council of the Lateran, in 1215, confirmed this doctrine: thus making it a general law of the Church as well as of the Empire. The tenth of all the produce acquired by anyone, prædial or personal, was held to be due: and non-payment punished with a penalty fourfold in amount.

10. In England, as elsewhere, the clergy asserted that tithes are due by divine right: and several of the Anglo-Saxon kings passed laws to this effect. Offa, king of Mercia, and Ælfwald, king of Northumberland, in a synod in 786 A.D.: Athelstan in 930 A.D.: Edmund in 940 A.D.: Edgar in 970 A.D.: and Ethelred in 1010 A.D., enacted that everyone should pay tithes of all his possessions. Edward the Confessor, as might be expected, was very minute in his directions as to tithes, and after enumerating every species of the produce of land and cattle, he expressly orders them to be paid for business and everything which God has given.

After the Conquest, the injunction to pay Tithes was repeated in many synods: and the frequency of these enactments seems to show that their payment was much neglected or evaded. A very stringent canon was made in a Council held in London, 23 Edward I., in which, after making many minute regulations as to the payment of prædial and mixed tithes, it was ordained that all artisans and merchants should pay personal tithes from the profits of trade, as well as carpenters, smiths, masons, weavers, innkeepers, and all workmen for hire: severe penalties were enacted for non-payment.

Before the Reformation personal tithes were certainly paid. In 5 Henry VI. a certain William Russell had maintained that personal tithes were not payable by the law of God: and that everyone might dispose of them in such charitable purposes as he pleased. The University of Oxford issued a solemn letter under its seal to contradict this doctrine, declaring that personal tithes are payable equally by the law of God, the tradition of the Christian fathers, and the authority of the Church; and that whoever held that personal tithes are not payable by Divine law was to be considered as an heretic and excommunicated as a rotten member. Archbishop Chicheley ordered all parsons to preach that personal tithes are due by the Law of God and the Church. These Canons were confirmed by statute, 27 Henry VIII. c. 20, enacting that everyone should pay his tithes both prædial and personal, after the manner of the parish in which he lived.

By the Statute 31 Henry VIII. c. 13, and 32 Henry VIII. c. 7, for the dissolution of the monasteries, the possession of the dissolved monasteries was transferred to the Crown : and it was allowed to make grants of tithes to laymen in the same manner as any other estates in land : ecclesiastical persons were to pursue their remedy before the ordinary, and laymen who claimed under a grant from the Crown before the secular courts, in the same way as in the case of any other lay property. This was the first occasion on which tithes were allowed to become the property of laymen in England, though they had long done so on the Continent.

By Acts 27 Henry VIII. c. 21 and 37 Henry VIII. c. 12 the citizens of London were ordered to pay personal tithes on the profits of trading, as well as 2s. 9d. in the pound on the rent of their houses : and besides this, every Sunday and feast day one farthing in every ten shillings of rent was to be paid as ecclesiastical dues.

The last Act on the subject of tithes is 2 & 3 Edw. VI. c. 13, which enacts that all tithes, both prædial and personal, should be paid in the manner they had been during the last forty years.

11. The preceding extracts are sufficient to give an idea of the origin, nature, and law of tithes in this country. Stripped of all ecclesiastical dogmas, they were, in fact, a ten per cent. rate on the income of everyone in the country, from whatever source arising, whether land, cattle, trading, arts, or professions, and manual industry of all sorts.

The 2 & 3 Edw. VI. c. 13, s. 7, exempts servants in husbandry from tithes, which shows that they had been liable to pay them. Spelman says that in his day in many parts of England servants paid tithes on their wages. He says that those who have annuities and fees must pay a tithe out of every accession of wealth that God sendeth in any course whatever : so gains of buying and selling, and the great improvement arising by merchandise is under this title commanded, precisely in the same manner as these profits are taxed for the civil service of the Crown. In fact, by all laws, ecclesiastical and civil, everyone was placed exactly on the same footing as regarded his heavenly and his earthly sovereigns : he must pay a rate of ten per cent. on all his income, from whatever source arising, for the service of religion and charity : and he must in addition pay his taxes to his king.

12. We have shown most clearly that by the opinion of the doctors of the Church, by all the ecclesiastical canons and the statutes of the realm, personal tithes are due to the clergy exactly in the same way as prædial and mixed tithes. The tenth guinea earned by every lawyer, by every medical man, by every architect, by every engineer, by every merchant, by every artist, by every banker, by every trading concern, by the Bank of England, by all the Joint Stock Banks, by the 'Times,' the 'Standard,' the 'Daily Telegraph,' is as rightfully and legally the property of the clergy as the tenth sheaf, the tenth calf, the tenth lamb, the tenth pig, the tenth egg, or the tenth cheese : but, as a matter of fact, all classes of the community, with the single exception of those patient beasts of burden the agriculturists, have emancipated themselves from the burden of paying tithes, and kept them to themselves. Thus the clergy have been deprived of enormous revenues which are legally theirs : and the rates which the agriculturists have paid have been exclusively appropriated by the clergy, when by the original constitution of tithes they were intended to support the poor and the Churches as well.

13. Tithes, from the necessity of the case, were originally payable in kind : and so they continued to be for more than a thousand years. At last the general desire for agricultural improvement showed the necessity for abolishing the barbarous and antiquated system, as all other species of rent had been commuted into money. In most cases, indeed, the practical good sense of the people had commuted payment in kind into a payment in money. But liability to tithe was a serious, and in many cases an insuperable, bar to agricultural improvement.

During the commonwealth, when so many other reforms were attempted which have only been permanently realised in our own day, it had been proposed to commute the payment of tithes into a rent-charge : but it did not succeed. At length in 1836 this great reform was effected by the 5 & 6 Will. IV. c. 71. Tithes were commuted into a rentcharge at their then value. The average of seven years preceding 1835 was taken. The value of one third of the amount was estimated in wheat : one third in barley : and the remaining third in oats. The controller of the corn returns is ordered to publish in January every year the average prices of wheat, barley, and oats during the preceding year : and the tithe-payer has to pay an amount every year calculated on the average prices during the preceding seven years. On an average of 37 years since 1836 the tithe-owner has received £110 10s. for every £100 of tithe rent-charge. Other enactments are made regarding hops, market gardens, and other crops which need not be enumerated here.

Of Benefices *and* Advowsons

14. A Right to ecclesiastical dues is termed a **Benefice** : and the Right to present to a Benefice is termed an **Advowson** (*Advocatio*). The owner of the advowson is termed the patron of the benefice : but as such he has no property or interest in the tithes, or the glebe, which belongs to the incumbent. An advowson is simply the Right to present to a Right. It is computed that about three-fifths of the advowsons in England are in the hands of the Bishops of the respective dioceses, and the remaining two-fifths in the hands of private persons.

The advowson, or the Right of nominating a clergyman to the Benefice, was originally granted to the Lord of the manor in consideration of the tithes he was bound to pay : thus they became private property : and, like all private property, they have become saleable commodities. The value of an advowson is usually about eight years' value of the benefice.

On Policies of Insurance

15. Another large class of Incorporeal Property of this nature is **Policies** *of* **Insurance.**

Any sum of money being, as we have seen, equivalent to an annuity, an exchange may always be made between a sum of money and an annuity. A sum of money may be given to buy an annuity: and also an annuity may be given to buy a sum of money at some definite future time or some definite event.

In the case of the Funds or Debenture Stock, a person pays a sum of money to the State, or a Railroad Company, and in return receives an annuity, or a Right to a series of payments: in the case of a Policy of Insurance a person agrees to pay an annuity to a company, or in some cases to the State, and in return buys the Right to receive a sum of money on the happening of some contingency, either death, or arriving at a certain age: or some loss by fire, shipwreck, or other accident.

In this case we have an example how an Obligation may be Capital: a Policy is an obligation of the Company: but these Obligations produce them a revenue: and hence they are Capital to them.

All the Rights we have hitherto been considering are *Choses-in-action*: because they are always Rights against some particular person whose duty it is to discharge them: and if he fails to do so an action will lie against him: and for this reason they may be called **Personal** or **Nominate Rights.**

On **Rights** *of* **Expectation**; *or* **Impersonal** *or* **Innominate Rights**

16. There still remains another very large class of Incorporeal Property, which differs from the preceding class in this respect, that it is not a Right against any particular person. It is therefore not a Right of Obligation. It is a Right to receive an expected profit; but there is no particular person who is bound to make the payment or render the profit. Hence this class of Rights cannot be classed under the title *Choses-in-action*, though they are sometimes erroneously so. It is only hoped or expected that some person will do so. It is termed in Roman Law *emptio spei*, or *emptio rei speratæ*. Being merely the

Rights to some hoped for or expected Profits, they may be called **Rights** of **Expectation**: and as they are not Rights against any particular persons, they may be termed **Impersonal** or **Innominate Rights**.

To this class of Incorporeal Property belong Shares in Commercial Companies of all sorts : Copyrights : Patents : the Practice of a Professional man : the Goodwill of a business : Trade Secrets : Tolls : Ferries : Shootings : Fisheries : Street Crossings, &c.

Shares *in* Commercial Companies

17. In comparatively recent times a gigantic species of Property has come into existence. Commercial enterprises are now conducted on such a colossal scale that no single person possesses sufficient capital for them. They require the contributions of a large number of persons. When such companies are formed, the Company itself is a distinct **Persona** quite separate from its individual members. Each subscriber pays over his money to the company, and then he loses all right to it : and, in exchange for the money, he receives a certificate entitling him to share in the profits made by the company in the proportion in which he has subscribed to the Capital. These certificates are called **Shares**. The members of a Joint Stock Company are like the Fundholders : they have no right to demand back their subscriptions from the company : but they can sell their shares in the open market. Thus the Shares are a Property quite separate and distinct from the capital paid in : they are a mere abstract Right to share in the profits to be made by the future trading of the Company.

The Value of the Shares in no way depends upon the sum originally paid for them : but upon the income or profits made by the trading of the company : and of course on the usual rate of interest. If the profits made by the company fall short of the averate rate of interest, the Shares fall to a discount : if the profits exceed the usual rate of interest, the Shares may rise to an enormous premium. The most striking instance that we are aware of between the cost of production, or the sum paid as Capital and the value of the Shares as the Right to the future profits of the Company, is the value of the Shares of the New River Water Company. When Sir Hugh Myddelton and his co-adventurers constructed this canal, in the reign of James I., so little were the blessings of pure water understood by the citizens of London, that the patriotic projector was ruined, and obliged to sell his shares. However, the demand for water gradually grew, and with it the value of the shares rose, until an original share of £100 was at one time worth £20,000, and was considered a good dowry for the daughter of a wealthy city merchant. In 1878 parts of these shares were sold at the rate of £93,000 per share.

On Copyrights

18. Another species of Incorporeal Property of the nature of Rights of Expectation which has acquired an immense development in modern times, owing to the increasing intelligence and intellectual wants of the people, are **Copyrights**.

In former ruder ages, land, which was solid and immovable, was considered almost the only kind of Wealth: afterwards movable goods were admitted to take rank as Property: but still Property was considered essentially to consist in what was visible to the eye and tangible to the touch. But in process of time refinement increased, and men began to reflect that they had minds, and that their minds might be improved. Accordingly, services rendered to the mind began to have Value, and to be estimated in money. Services are rendered to the mind by communicating Ideas: and when men wanted to enrich their minds by acquiring new Ideas, they became willing to pay for them just in the same manner as they paid for things which satisfied their material wants. Hence Ideas acquired the character of **Wealth**: and the right of men was recognised to have property in Ideas. The law which gives men property in their own Ideas is called the Law of **Copyright** and of **Patents**.

The author of the dialogue termed the 'Eryxias' was the first to observe that if men can gain a living by giving instruction in the various sciences, then these sciences are Wealth, for the very same reason that gold and silver are Wealth—because they are exchangeable. That men have mental wants as well as bodily ones, and that the things they want and demand and pay for to satisfy their mental wants are Wealth, just as much as the things they want and demand and pay for to satisfy their animal wants—αἱ ἐπίστημαι χρήματα οὖσαι, as Socrates says in the 'Eryxias.'

19. Copyright is the exclusive Right to multiply and sell copies of books, prints, engravings, music, songs, and dramatic performances. These Rights cannot be seen nor handled: but their *Value may be measured in money*: they may be bought and sold, and transferred or exchanged : and consequently they are **Wealth**.

The only trace of Copyright which seems to have existed in ancient times was the remuneration paid by the managers of the theatres to dramatic authors for the right to represent their plays. There does not seem to have been any Copyright in literary works. In modern times the question of Copyright did not acquire any importance till the invention of printing. The expense of copying works was so great, and the demand for them so small, that the Right of copying them was valueless. But when copies were multiplied at an infinitely reduced price, and a greater demand for them arose, the Right began to acquire a Value. However, it could not be infringed, because no one was allowed to print without a licence : and such licence was only granted to the author or the printer or bookseller to whom he sold the Right of Copy.

When these Rights began to have Value in consequence of the increased demand for books, it was supposed that the author had a perpetual Right of Copy in the fruits of his own labour, as well as in any other property he might possess, which he could bequeath to his children, or as legacies, or to their widows for maintenance.

However, the licensing laws expired in 1694, and frequent invasions of copyright took place, to the great loss and damage of those whose Rights were infringed ; and their remedy at Common Law was quite inadequate, because they could only recover damages for the losses they could prove, and the pirates might sell innumerable copies without the knowledge of the injured parties.

In consequence of these repeated complaints, the first Act of Copyright was passed, the 8 Anne, c. 19, which enacted that the authors of books already printed who had not sold their Rights, and the booksellers who had purchased them, should have the sole right of printing them for 21 years from the 10th April, 1710, and no longer: and the authors of books not yet printed should have the sole right of printing them for 14 years from the day of publication; and if the authors should be alive at the end of that term, then for a further term of 14 years.

The author and his transferee having thus a distinct legal right, could move a Court of Equity for an injunction to restrain an infringement of it by an unauthorised person. But a curious question arose on the expiry of the term granted by the Act, whether Copyright existed at Common Law independently of the statute; and whether the assumed possessor of Copyright could have an injunction to restrain the infringement of his Right.

The Court of Equity held in several cases that the statute of Anne did not take away an author's perpetual Right of Copy at Common Law; and granted injunctions to restrain the infringement of Copyrights which had been transferred long previously to the Act of Anne.

At length, however, the question was formally raised in the great case of *Millar* v. *Taylor* (4 *Burr.* 2,308), where it was held by a majority of the King's Bench (Yates, J., dissenting), that perpetual Copyright existed at Common Law independently of the Act, and that it was not taken away by the Act.

But an injunction granted in accordance with the judgment of the King's Bench was taken by appeal to the House of Lords; and in a case of such importance the opinions of all the Judges were taken. A very large majority held that perpetual Copyright existed at Common Law, and that it was not taken away by the statute of Anne. But the Law Lords overruled this doctrine, and held that no Copyright existed at Common Law, and that it was created solely by the Statute of Anne.

The Universities, alarmed at this decision, which struck at a valuable Right which they had acquired, obtained an Act of Parliament, 15 George III., c. 53, which gave them perpetual

Copyright in any works which had already been acquired by them, or might be acquired at any future time.

The term of an author's Copyright was extended by 54 Geo. III., c. 156, s. 4, which enacted that an author might have Copyright for 28 years, or for the term of his natural life.

These Acts were repealed by the 5 & 6 Vict., c. 45 (July 1, 1842), by which Copyright is now regulated. It was enacted that Copyright in any work to be published in future should exist during the author's natural life and for seven years after: or if the said time expired before 42 years, then the Copyright should exist for 42 years: and that Copyright in every book published after the author's death should last for 42 years from the publication of it.

20. There is scarcely any department of human industry in which the truth is more conspicuous that value arises solely from **Demand**, and not from Labour. When men directed their attention to the primary objects of sale, such as corn, food of all sorts, &c., and which are all associated with Labour, many persons too hastily concluded that their value was due to Labour: whereas it was quite clear that the Demand for them was the sole cause of their value.

But what gives value to a Copyright? Most manifestly the **Demand** of the public for the work. By the very force of nature men feel a necessity for food, and therefore they labour to produce it. But they do not always feel the want of mental food by the force of nature: it requires cultivation and education to make them feel a craving for instruction. Now whether a Copyright has any value or not does not Depend on the Labour of the producer, or author, but purely on the **Demand** of the public for the work; on the appreciation of the public for his labours and their demand for them. And unless the demand for the work exists the Copyright has no value at all. Without enumerating the great works of the ancients, was there a less quantity of Labour in Chaucer or Spenser than in many modern works? Shakespeare, it is true, earned a modest competency by his share in a theatre: but it is certain that he never would have earned bread and cheese by the sale of his dramas. Without making invidious comparisons, is the fortune earned by a Tennyson, for example, compared to that earned by a Shakespeare or a Spenser, proportional to the quantity of Labour in their respective works? In no department of human industry is the fallacy of the doctrine that value is governed by Quantity of Labour more conspicuous than in Literary and Scientific work. Where would Newton have been without his fellowship? The writers of the most learned works do not earn the wages of a day labourer, whereas the writers of trashy and ephemeral novels may earn a fortune. And is this from Utility, or the Quantity of Labour in their works? It manifestly arises solely from the taste or the demand of the public for them.

21. It is strange, however, how chary the public are in acknowledging the Rights of authors in the products of their own labour. Macaulay, whose views as to the proper duration of Copyright are embodied in the present Act, argued vehemently against Copyright as an odious monopoly, as bad as those which her Parliament compelled Elizabeth to abolish—'Why not revive all those old monopolies which in Elizabeth's reign galled our fathers so severely that, maddened by intolerable wrong, they opposed to their sovereign a resistance before which her haughty spirit quailed for the first and the last time? Was it the cheapness and excellence of commodities that so violently stirred the indignation of the English people? I believe, sir, that I may safely take it for granted that the effect of monopoly generally is to make articles scarce, to make them dear, and to make them bad. And I may with equal safety challenge my honourable friend to find any distinction between Copyright and other privileges of the same kind: any reason why a monopoly of books should produce an effect directly the reverse of that which was produced by the East India's monopoly of tea, or Lord Essex's monopoly of sweet wines.' This surely is mere extravagance. It is strange that so distinguished a writer as Macaulay did not perceive the fallacy of such an argument. To make the cases parallel, it would be necessary to give a person a general monopoly of writing a History of England, for example—as one of the old monopolies was to write a Latin grammar. Then no doubt the consequences described by

Macaulay would follow; we should have very bad Histories of England and very bad Latin grammars. But no one proposes such an absurdity : only if a person bestows great labour and time in composing a particular History of England, or a poem, that he should have property in the fruits of his own Labour. Nothing would prevent any other person from writing a better history if he could, and winning the preference of the public. Because Thirlwall had copyright in his History of Greece, that did not prevent Grote also writing his History of Greece : and each had Copyright in his own work. Nothing can be more transparent than the fallacy of comparing the Property in the products of a person's own labour to the odious monopolies of Elizabeth and James. Indeed if it were such an odious monopoly, why should an author be allowed to have one for 14, 28, or 42 years? why should he have a monopoly for a single hour?

22. Smith says—'The property which every man has in his own Labour, as it is the original foundation of all other Property, so it is the most sacred and inviolable'—a sentiment in which everyone must agree. And what is literary and scientific work? It is pure **Thought**—pure **Labour**. And seeing that the productions of a man's mind are now recognised to be as truly his own Property, and the fruits of his Labour, as the products of material wealth, it is hard to see on what grounds he can be deprived of the same tenure in the one as in the other. It cannot be denied that a great work in literature is as great a service done to a country as a chair, or a table, or a ship : and yet the producer of the one is not allowed to derive the same benefit from the one service as from the other. In the latter case his right is acknowledged to be perpetual : and he may dispose of it as he pleases and transmit it to his descendants : as long as the thing continues in being ; but the Rights of the other are only transient, and after a brief period, by the existing law, cease for ever. The merchant who labours for commodities may found a family, and his descendants may enjoy for ever the wealth accumulated by their ancestor ; but the descendants of the author who may spend his life in producing a work which may adorn the literature, and be an everlasting possession to his country, may starve in the streets while all the world may appropriate to themselves the profits made by publishing the works of their ancestors. The Universities have taken excellent care to have their Rights secured to them in perpetuity by Law; and why should the Universities be allowed to have perpetual Copyright rather than the author himself?

These things should not be. There can be no just ground pointed out for the distinction. If an author's right in his own work exists at all, it exists for ever and cannot be limited to 7, 14, or 42 years, or any finite number of years : and just as the works of a Shakespeare, a Milton, or a Bacon, are a nobler possession for a country to inherit than the noblest ship that ever floated on the ocean, so ought the Rights of such a benefactor to his country to be preserved and guarded with a jealous care as those of the other in any country where the Rights of Property are held sacred. The progress of public opinion evidently tends in this direction : something was done by the last Act, but the advancing voice of refinement and the increasing perception of moral right will probably demand more. A Royal Commission was recently appointed on the subject, and the result will probably be that the Rights of authors will be still further extended. Why should a man who devotes his life to carve out an estate in fame be denied equal rights with one who seeks to agglomerate material wealth? Let us hope that the day is coming when the owners of the ideal ships that sail down the seas of time, freighted with the hoarded treasures of the wisdom and learning and worth of successive generations, to illumine the understanding and gladden the hearts of the latest posterity, may enjoy and transmit to their descendants the same Rights as the owners of the wooden and iron ships which bring corn and cotton and whatever else ministers to the material requirements of mankind.

On Patents

23. Another form of Property in Ideas is a **Patent**; which is the Right granted by letters patent from the Crown for the exclusive making, using, and selling some commodity : restricted in modern times by Statute to a new invention.

Formerly the Crown claimed the prerogative of granting and selling to private individuals the exclusive Right of importing, manufacturing, and selling commodities.

This abuse proceeded to great lengths under Elizabeth. The revenues granted to her by her Spiritual and Temporal Parliaments together amounted only to £65,000 a year. To eke out these scanty resources, in the 17th year of her reign she revived the old system of granting patents for trade monopolies. Almost every conceivable ware—even the writing of Latin grammars—was made a monopoly. These became so oppressive that strong remonstrances were made in the Parliament of 1597. These produced very little effect: and monopolies continued to increase. At last in the Parliament of 1601 a stern and fierce onslaught on them was organized. Bacon, Fleming and Cecil vapoured about the prerogative of the Crown as something so divine that it was to be neither examined, canvassed, nor discussed. But the House was not terrified: and Cecil acknowledged that in all his experience he had never seen such a commotion in the House. The Queen, discerning the true temper of the people, with her usual tact, thanked the House for its care of the public weal, and promised that these abuses should be put a stop to. But they were revived under James I.: at last the Statute 21, James I. c. 3, was passed that all monopolies of trade were contrary to the fundamental laws of the realm, and they were prohibited in future : except only that the Crown was empowered to grant letters patent for a period not exceeding 14 years to the first and true inventor of any new manufactures within the realm, which were not used by any one else at the time of granting the letters. And the principle, with some modifications, still remains good.

24. This kind of Right, though usually classed along with Copyright, as being a Right or Property in ideas, is surrounded with far greater difficulties : and its expediency is more disputable than that of Copyright.

It might be said that, as each is the fruit of a man's own Labour, he should be entitled to equal Property in them. This argument, though somewhat specious, is not conclusive. No two persons working independently on the same literary work ever produce the same Ideas. It would be a very remarkable circumstance if two independent persons should ever hit upon the same line of poetry, or construct a sentence of moderate length exactly the same word for word. It would be absolutely incredible that two persons writing independently should ever compose ten consecutive lines of poetry, or write half a page of prose word for word the same. Even, therefore, if they chose the same subject for a poem, a drama, or a history, the work of each would be absolutely independent. But when many persons' minds are bent on Science or Inventions, the case is different. Different persons thinking independently, constantly hit upon the same ideas in Science and Inventions. It has often been remarked that, if the greatest names in Science had never lived, some one else would have hit upon their discoveries.

A literary work is therefore more peculiarly a man's own Property than a work of Science. If Shakespeare had never lived there is no reason to suppose that we should ever have had *Macbeth*, *Hamlet*, or *Othello*. But if Newton had never lived there is every reason to suppose that by this time we should have had the Law of Gravity. In Science one man's discoveries are based upon the labours of his predecessors, and in turn his labours are the basis of the labours of his successors. He therefore adopts and uses the common property of mankind, and in return his discoveries become the common property of mankind. And thus there is constant progress: but there is no such constant progress in literature.

It is with Invention as with Science. In this inventive age when so many men's minds are turned towards the same subjects, they constantly hit upon the same invention. Inventions grow out of one another, and in the construction of some complicated machine, an inventor walks among traps and pitfalls at every step; and must carefully beware lest some one else has not already hit upon the same idea, and got a patent for it. The practical evils of this are so great that many able persons, including many distinguished inventors, have strenuously argued in favour of the total abolition of patents. This however opens a very wide question, which this is not the place to discuss. We have only to explain the nature of Patents as Incorporeal Property, and not to argue about their expediency.

25. There is one peculiarity about the Law of Copyrights and Patents which is worth noticing. No man can have a Property in a general truth or principle, but only in some application of it. Thus no one can have a Patent for a **Discovery**, but only for an **Invention**. As soon as a general principle is discovered it becomes universal property, and everyone can appropriate to himself any new demonstration or application of it he can devise. No one can appropriate to himself a general scientific truth : nor can he have a Patent for a principle. Thus no one can monopolise the general principle that steam, air, or electricity may be used as motive powers ; all he can do is to have Property in some particular form of machine in which the general principle is applied.

On **Trade Secrets**

26. Another form of Property in Ideas is a **Trade Secret**. Persons may devise methods of combining material things in a certain way which please the popular taste, and keep such methods secret. Such secrets may produce large revenues, and are capable of being bought and sold : and therefore their *Value may be measured in money* ; and consequently they are Wealth, and are partnership assets. Such Trade Secrets are evidently the produce of pure Thought or Labour ; as much as any material chattels : and are a very valuable form of Wealth.

A very curious question has been raised whether, if a person becomes bankrupt, he can be compelled to give up Trade Secrets to his Creditors like other property : but we are not aware whether it has been decided.

On the **Goodwill** of a **Business**

27. Another species of Incorporeal Property of this nature is the **Goodwill** of a business. When a person has established a successful commercial business of any sort, he has of course the right to receive the future profits to be made by the business. And this right to receive the future profits is a Property which is quite separate from and additional to the house or shop, and actual goods existing in them. This Property can neither be seen nor handled, but it can *be measured in money* and sold. It is the product of Labour, and care, and thought, as much as any material chattel, and is part of the assets of the trader. But as it is always fixed to some particular place, it may be called Incorporeal Real Property

An instance of this may be interesting. Boswell says that Thrale, the great brewer, appointed Johnson as one of his executors. In that capacity it became his duty to sell the business. When the sale was going on, 'Johnson appeared, bustling about, with an inkhorn and pen in his buttonhole like an exciseman: and on being asked what he really considered the value of the property to be which was to be disposed of, answered: "We are not here to sell a parcel of boilers and vats, but the **Potentiality** of growing rich beyond the dreams of avarice."' This latter phrase was merely Johnsonese for the Goodwill of the business.

If anyone were to conceive the audacious idea of buying up the 'Times' newspaper, what would its price comprehend? Would it be merely the brick buildings, the steam-engines, the presses, the types—which may be seen and handled? The price of these things would be utterly insignificant. The fact is, that by the energy and skill with which the 'Times' has been conducted it has established an enormous demand for it: and when an innumerable people require to make their wants known they go to the 'Times' to advertise in it. These advertisements produce an enormous annual revenue whose approximate value can be estimated: and the value of the 'Times' is the value of that Expectation or Potentiality of future profits.

When the great banking-house of Jones, Loyd, and Co., sold their business to the London and Westminster Bank, it was said in the papers that the sum paid for the Goodwill was £500,000.

In a similar way, every place of business in the country has a valuable asset in the Goodwill of the business, which is analogous to the Right to receive the future profits of the land: and it will be at once seen that this species of property is of immense magnitude.

The **Practice** *of a* **Professional Man**

28. In a similar way, when Professional men, such as doctors, surgeons, or solicitors, have established a reputation, they are entitled to reap the profits to be made by their exertions, and they can sell this Right, just as a trader can sell the Goodwill of his business. This Right is termed a **Practice**; in French a *clientelle*.

If a young doctor, surgeon, or solicitor wishes to enter business, it is usual for him to buy an established Practice : and of course such a purchase is an investment of Capital.

Tolls *and* Ferries

29. Tolls and **Ferries** are the Rights to receive the duties payable for the use of roads, ferries, docks, &c. : and are Incorporeal Property of the species of Rights of Expectation.

Shootings *and* Fishings

30. Other Rights of this species, which have acquired greatly increased value in recent times, are **Shootings** and **Fishings**. These are not the Rights to any particular birds or fish, but the Right of shooting at birds and killing them if the sportsman can ; and also the Right to try to catch fish.

Street Crossings

31. Another class of Incorporeal Property of this species are **Street Crossings**. These are made the subject of regular Property by the poorer classes, just as much as landed estates ; and they are the subject of marriage portions and bequests. There cannot be a more striking example of the *emptio spei* than these Street Crossings, as no one is bound to pay toll for them : their receipts depend purely upon the charitable feelings of the passengers : and yet they are Capital to their occupiers.

There are also other kinds of valuable Rights, but what we have enumerated will be sufficient to show the enormous magnitude of this species of property.

General Conclusion

32. We have now enumerated the different species of Incorporeal Property, both Rights of Obligation and Rights of Expectation. This species of Property has increased in a very much more rapid ratio in modern times than material property, and has now attained colossal dimensions. In all its various forms it amounts to certainly hundreds of thousands of millions of money in this country.

It is one of the fundamental defects of the usual Economical works that they entirely pass over and ignore this species of Property : and most of their definitions and doctrines are framed exclusively with regard to material chattels.

This shows the supreme importance of the doctrine of Roman Law that Rights are included under the term Wealth. All this mass of Property consists in mere abstract Rights, which are invisible to the eye and intangible to the hand : but yet they can all be bought and sold, or exchanged : their *Value can all be measured in money*; and therefore they are all to be included under the title of **Wealth**, according to the definition which all modern Economists are now agreed upon. In fact, in this great commercial country the amount of Wealth which consists exclusively in abstract Rights many times exceeds the amount of material wealth.

This shows the absolute necessity of exterminating from the science the doctrines which have too long infected it, that all Wealth is formed out of the materials of the globe, and is the produce of Land and Labour.

A person might be the wealthiest in the whole universe at the present day, and have not one particle of Wealth which could be seen by the eye or touched by the hand : but which might all be bought and sold. The most colossal branches of modern commerce consist exclusively in the exchanges of abstract Rights : and the values of these Rights and their changes of Value are determined by exactly the same causes and the same laws which determine the value of material chattels. And consequently the nomenclature, which was expressly devised and restricted to material products, becomes obviously inadequate, and must be enlarged so as to comprehend the commerce in Immaterial and Incorporeal objects as Wealth.

CHAPTER XII

ON THE FOREIGN EXCHANGES

Definition of an **Exchange**

1. An '**Exchange**' in commerce is when a person pays his Creditor by transferring to him a Debt due to him from some one else.

Thus, where a person pays a Debt by means of a Bank Note, or a Cheque on his banker, it is an 'Exchange.' It is an example of *Novatio* or *Delegatio* in Roman Law.

Two passengers are travelling in an omnibus. The fare is sixpence. One passenger pays the conductor a shilling. The conductor is then indebted to that passenger in sixpence. Another passenger has a sixpence in his hand ready to pay his fare. The conductor by a nod tells him to give the sixpence to the first passenger. Thus both Debts are paid. The Debt of the second passenger to the conductor, and also the Debt of the conductor to the first passenger, are both paid by the second passenger paying the sixpence to the first passenger. The whole transaction is an 'Exchange.'

Three parties and two Debts are thus necessary to an 'Exchange.'

The 'Exchanges' is that branch of commerce which treats of the remission and settlement of Debts between parties living in different places by means of Paper Documents, and the Exchange of the Money of one country for that of another.

The State of the Exchanges between any two places or countries depends upon two distinct things:—

1. The state of the Moneys of the two places.
2. The state of Commercial dealings between the two places.

The state of the Exchanges which depends upon the state of the Moneys of the two places is termed the **Nominal Exchange**.

The state of the Exchanges which depends upon the Commercial dealings between the two countries is termed the **Real** or the **Commercial Exchange**.

On the **Nominal Exchange**

2. Suppose that the Coinages of two countries are of the same metal, and the Coinage of one country is taken as the standard: then the Quantity of the Coin of the other which contains exactly the same quantity of pure metal is called the **Par** of **Exchange** between the two countries.

Suppose that the Exchanges between England and France were estimated in Gold. There is as near as possible one-fourth more pure Gold in an English sovereign than in a Napoleon or the French 20 franc piece.

If the English sovereign were taken as the standard, it would be equal to 1·25 Napoleon: and 1·25 would be termed the **Par** of **Exchange** between England and France.

The Exchanges between England and France are, however, estimated in francs, which are a silver coin. Moreover, the English sovereign is not exactly 1·25 Napoleon: accordingly 25·21 (francs) is usually considered as the Par of Exchange between England and France.

Effect of a **Depreciated Coinage**

3. We have observed in a former chapter that Coins may circulate at par in their own country at their full nominal value after they have lost a considerable amount of their weight by wear and tear, because persons in general are not very rigorous in weighing every Coin they receive.

But when they are exchanged for Bullion, or for the Coins of a foreign country, they are always weighed and exchanged weight for weight. If, therefore, from any reason whatever, the English coins have become degraded, worn, or clipped, and so lost their proper weight for any reason, they will evidently not buy so much bullion or full-weighted francs as if they were of their full legal weight. If English sovereigns were in this Depreciated state they might perhaps only purchase 24 francs instead of 25·21. This would be called a **Fall** in the Foreign Exchanges.

Or if an English merchant were obliged to pay a Debt of 2,521 francs in Paris, he would have to give *more* than £100 to purchase them. This would be called a **Rise** in the Foreign Exchanges: and the Exchange would be said to be so much *against* England by the amount of the difference.

When English Coin is used to buy French Coins, it may be looked at in two points of view—

1. A Fixed amount of English Coin may buy a certain amount of Foreign Coin.

2. A certain amount of English Coin may be required to buy a Fixed amount of French Coin.

In the first point of view, a Fixed amount of Depreciated English Coin will buy a **Less** amount of French Coin.

In the second point of view, it will require a **Greater** amount of Depreciated English Coins to buy a Fixed amount of French Coins.

Hence, when a Depreciated Coinage is said to produce a **Fall** *in the Foreign Exchanges, it means that a Given Amount of Home Coinage will purchase a* **Less** *Amount of Foreign Coin.*

When a Depreciated Coinage is said to produce a **Rise** *in the Foreign Exchanges, it means that it requires a* **Greater** *Amount of Home Coinage to purchase a Fixed Amount of Foreign Coin.*

A clear understanding of these expressions will prevent any confusion arising when they are used indiscriminately, as they often are, in discussions on the Exchanges: they are not contradictory, as they might appear to be: they only refer to two different methods of estimating the Coinage.

It is evident that this adverse state of the Exchanges will continue as long as the Depreciation of the Home Coinage exists: and that a restoration of the Home Coinage to its proper state will at once rectify the Exchanges.

It is evident that a Depreciation of the Coinage by a Debasement of its Purity will produce exactly the same effects.

There can be no **Par of Exchange** between Countries which use **Different** Metals as their Legal Standard

4. There can only be a Par of Exchange between two countries when they both use the *same* Metal as their Legal Standard.

There can be no true Par of Exchange between countries which use *different* Metals, such as Gold and Silver, as their Legal standard. The relative Market Value of the two Metals is always varying, from causes entirely beyond the control of any law. It is no more possible to have a fixed price of one in terms of the other than it is to have a fixed legal price for corn or for any other commodity.

In the year 1797, when the Bank of England stopped payment, the House of Lords appointed a Committee to investigate the subject. The Committee among other things wished to ascertain the Par of Exchange between London and Hamburg, and they examined several merchants on the subject. But they were quite unable to agree among themselves what the true Par of Exchange between the two places was : and the Committee reported that they were unable to come to a satisfactory conclusion on the subject. There cannot in the nature of things be any fixed or true Par of Exchange between England and any country which uses a silver standard. It is only possible to say that such is the *usual Rate of Exchange* between them. Hence, when it is said that 25·21 francs is the Par of Exchange between England and France, it means that it is usually reckoned the Rate of Exchange, at the present market values of Gold and Silver : and even the best authorities differ by several centimes in their estimate. And between such countries it is sometimes impossible to decide certainly which way the Exchange is, unless the difference exceeds a certain amount.

If the **Coinage** *is in a* **Depreciated** *State, to Determine whether the* **Exchange** *is* **Favourable,** *at* **Par,** *or* **Adverse**

5. Suppose that at any time when the English Coinage is at its full legal weight, £100 in sovereigns will purchase 2,521 French silver francs.

Suppose that the Coinage becomes Depreciated so that the Market Price of Bullion rises to £4 3s.

Then the Market Price of £100 in full weighted Coin is £106 11s. 7½d.

Suppose the Exchange on Paris is at 23·80 : or that £100 will purchase 2,380 francs : then £106 11s. 7½d. will purchase 2536·63 francs

But as the Par at the Mint Price is 2,521 francs, it is evident that the Difference between 2,521 francs and 2536·63 francs is the extent to which the Real Exchange is in favour of England. Therefore the Real Exchange is 15·63 francs in favour of England.

It is also easy to see how much the Exchange is depressed : because £100 ought to purchase 2536·63 francs : but they will only purchase 2,380 francs : consequently the Exchange is depressed by 206·63 francs : or the 100 sovereigns are deficient in that amount of their legal weight, and this will be found to tally with the rise of their Market Price above their Mint Price.

Hence a Depreciated Coinage necessarily produces a **Rise** *of the Market Price of Bullion above the Mint Price, and a* **Fall** *in the Foreign Exchanges below Par.*

Because it will require a *Greater* amount of the Current Coin to buy a *Fixed* amount of Bullion : and a *Fixed* amount of the Current Coin will buy a *less* amount of Foreign Coin.

And evidently a **Rise** *of the Market Price of Bullion above the Mint Price: and a* **Fall** *of the Foreign Exchanges below Par,* **Proves** *and* **Measures** *the* **Depreciation** *of the English Coinage.*

Hence we have the following rule—

Find the Market Price in London compared to the Mint Price:

Multiply the Market Price so found by the Rate of Exchange:

Then the Exchange is Favourable, at Par, or Adverse, according as the Result is Above, At, or Below Par.

And the Depression of the Exchange caused by the Depreciation of the Coinage is the Difference between the Sum so expressed in the Mint and Market Prices, multiplied by the Rate of Exchange.

In the excellent state in which our Coinage now is, the question of the Nominal Exchange is of little importance : but it is impossible to understand the history of the Currency without it. And it is essential as regards all Foreign countries which use an Inconvertible and Depreciated Paper Money.

On **Inconvertible Paper Money**

6. The above considerations affect Coinages of Gold and Silver: but in modern times a new species of Money has come into use, and nearly every country has had recourse to it in times of public difficulty—and that is **Paper Money**.

While Paper is convertible—i.e. while the holder of it can compel the issuer to give specie on demand in exchange for it—it is evident that it cannot circulate at a discount ; because if it fell to a discount the holders of it would at once go and demand Gold for it.

In quiet and ordinary times a Bank can keep in circulation a very much larger amount of Credit either in the form of Notes, or simple Bank Credits, than the Bullion they are obliged to retain. In fact, as has been seen in a former chapter, Banking profits can only be made by creating and issuing Credit in excess of Bullion. And so long as there is confidence in the issuers, this Credit circulates and produces in all respects identically the same effects as so much Gold.

But suppose some great public calamity happens such as war, or an invasion, this confidence vanishes and numerous persons would demand Gold for their Credit.

Under these circumstances, and with the enormous quantity of Paper in circulation in modern times, every country in Europe has been compelled to suspend payments in cash ; and to give an artificial value to the Paper by receiving it in payment for taxes, &c., at its nominal value in specie : and by making it Legal Tender. When this is done the Paper Money becomes in all respects equivalent to a **new** standard, just as much as Gold and Silver; and its value is affected by exactly the same principles as affect the value of Gold and Silver.

Under the old system of attempting to fix the price of Gold relatively to Silver, there was no power of convertibility of one into the other, similar to the convertibility of the Bank Note. If Silver fell to a discount as compared with Gold, no one could demand as a right to have his Silver exchanged for Gold. Consequently the inevitable result of a considerable change in the Quantity of either metal was a change in their relative values. In 1794, Gold rose to 84s. if purchased with *Silver* Bullion : but if the Silver Coin had been convertible into Gold like a Bank Note, this difference never could have arisen : any more than a Bank Note convertible into Coin can circulate at a discount as compared with Coin.

Now Paper Money when issued as a substantive Coinage follows exactly the same rules. If only the usual Quantity of it be issued, i.e. *no greater quantity than would have been issued if it had been convertible into Coin*, it will continue to circulate at its Par value. But if these issues be increased in Quantity, and if the natural correction of excessive issues be taken away, viz. payment in coin on demand, exactly the same result follows as attends a greatly increased Quantity of Silver—it falls to a Discount.

Lord King's Law of Paper Money

7. When either of two metals used as Coinage becomes greatly increased in quantity, it Diminishes in Value as compared with the other : and Gold and Silver Money not being convertible, if they are compelled to circulate at a fixed ratio, in accordance with Gresham's Law, the one which is underrated invariably disappears from circulation and is exported to foreign countries, where it may exchange for its true value.

When one metal diminishes in Value with respect to the other, it is not *Depreciation*, because it has a value of its own in the market of the world. But when Paper Money is used in a country which has no Value of its own, but merely an artificial Value, and it becomes excessive in quantity, it cannot be exported ; because it has only a Local Value and not a General Value in the Market of the world. It falls to a discount as compared with Coin : and in this case it is **Depreciation** :

because it professes to be equal in Value to Coin, and it is not so.

If it is attempted to maintain a fixed ratio between Paper Money and Coin after the Paper has fallen to a Discount, exactly the same result follows as took place when Coin of inferior value circulates at par with Coin of superior value. The Coin is all hoarded or exported: it entirely disappears from circulation: and nothing but Paper remains. As the quantity of Paper is increased it falls in Value: all Prices rise: the Foreign Exchanges fall: and all the Foreign Trade of the country is deranged.

A few years after the Bank of England suspended payments in 1797, the Price of Bullion rose and the Foreign Exchanges fell: deranging the whole course of the Foreign trade. Some able writers, the most conspicuous of whom was Lord King, maintained that this was due to the Depreciation of the Bank Note. Strong interests, however, contested this doctrine. The Bank contested it because they found it profitable to issue as much Paper as possible: merchants contested it because they were afraid that their accommodation would be restricted. After a short time the value of the Bank Note improved, and the question slumbered.

In 1809 the same phenomena recurred in a much more aggravated form, and gave rise to the appointment of the celebrated Bullion Committee. All the witnesses before this Committee except one maintained that it was not the Bank Note which had fallen, but that Gold had risen.

The Report, however, drawn up by Huskisson, Horner and Thornton, entirely disproved this assertion, and showed that the Rise of the Market Price of Bullion and the Fall of the Foreign Exchanges was due entirely to the Depreciation of the Bank Note from excessive quantity: and they recommended a Diminution of its issues so as to restore the Value of the Bank Note.

Resolutions in accordance with the report were moved by Horner: it was proved that there two prices in common use; a Paper Price and a Money Price; and that a £1 Bank Note and 7s. were commonly given for a guinea. Nevertheless, under the influence of party passion, the House of Commons voted that a guinea was equal to a Bank Note and 1*s.* in public estimation : or that 27 = 21. Freed by this vote from all control, the Bank made more extravagant issues than ever, so that in 1815 the Bank Note was only equal to 14*s.* 6*d.*

Howevers, the doctrine of the Bullion Report gradually convinced the Mercantile world : and in 1819 they were almost unanimously in its favour.

Lord King's law is this—

A Rise of the Paper or Market Price of Bullion above the Mint Price, and a Fall of the Foreign Exchanges below the Limits of the Real Exchange, is the Proof and the Measure of the Depreciation of the Paper Money.

This principle is so universally admitted now, and so perfectly evident, that there is no use in wasting more words to prove it.

It shows that Paper Money must always be restrained within certain Limits to maintain a Par Value with Gold. But if this be duly done, Inconvertible Paper Money may circulate along with Bullion.

If the Bank of England had duly limited its issues, its Notes might have circulated at par with gold. In 1874 the Inconvertible Notes of the Bank of France circulated at Par with Coin because they were carefully limited.

This doctrine contains the principle by which all Credit and Paper Currency, whether Convertible or Inconvertible, must be regulated—namely, a strict attention to the Price of Bullion and the state of the Foreign Exchanges.

The demonstration of the Bullion Committee was in course of time universally accepted by the Banking and Mercantile world; the only difficulty left unsolved was the Practical Measures to be adopted to carry it into effect.

However, after several unsuccessful attempts to discover the true method of giving effect to this doctrine, this problem has now been successfully solved : and thus the Theory of the Paper Currency is now complete.

On the Real or Commercial Exchange

8. We have now to explain the mechanism of the Real or Commercial Exchange.

Suppose A in London is Creditor to B and Debtor to B', both in Edinburgh, in equal amounts.

Then to settle these Debts it would be necessary for B in Edinburgh to send the money to A in London : and A in London would have to send an equal amount to B' in Edinburgh. This would require two transmissions of specie between London and Edinburgh, at some expense.

The business may be settled much more easily and cheaply if A sends B', his Creditor in Edinburgh, an order upon B, his Debtor : by this means both Debts are discharged by B paying over the money to B : that is, by the simple transfer of the money from B to B' in the same place, instead of by two transfers between London and Edinburgh. This order is termed a Bill of Exchange : and the operation is exactly similar to a person paying a Debt by a Cheque on his banker.

Thus an ' Exchange ' requires at least *three* parties and *two* Debts.

On Exchange with Four Parties

9. But the course of trade between two places gives rise to more complicated transactions.

In the above case we have supposed A to fulfil two characters : to be Debtor to one party and to be Creditor to another in Edinburgh.

But in the Exchanges it more usually happens that there are *four* parties.

Suppose A in London is Creditor to B in Edinburgh : and B' in Edinburgh is Creditor to A' in London.

Then to settle these Debts two transmissions of specie are necessary between London and Edinburgh.

But suppose that A' in London goes to A and pays him the money he owes to B' in Edinburgh, and buys from him his Debt against B in Edinburgh. He then sends this order to his own Creditor B' : and B' presents the order to B, and B pays him the money : hence both these Debts are settled by two local transfers, instead of by two transmissions of specie between the two places.

When the Debts between London and Edinburgh are exactly equal they may all be discharged by means of these '**Exchanges**' without sending any specie. The Exchanges are then said to be at **Par**.

The **Time Par** of **Exchange**

10. Suppose, however, that the Debts between London and Edinburgh are not equal : and that Edinburgh wishes to send more money to London than it has to receive from London. Then the Demand for Bills is greater than the Supply.

But as it is cheaper to send a Bill than the Cash, those who are bound to send Money will bid against each other for the Bills in the market as for any other merchandise : and the Price of Bills will rise : or a **Premium** will have to be paid for a Bill on London.

London is the great centre of commerce. It is the seat of Government, to which the revenue is remitted from all parts of the country. The great families from all parts of the country go to reside there, and their revenues must be remitted to them there. Hence there is always a much greater quantity of money seeking to flow to London from the country than the contrary. Consequently the Demand for Bills on London in the country is always greater than the Supply : and therefore Inland Bills upon London are always at a Premium.

This Premium is computed by **Time**. It is an essential part of the business of a banker to give these Bills. If a person in Edinburgh wants a Bill at sight on London, he has to pay 1s. per cent., or four days' interest. This is termed the **Time Par** of **Exchange** between Edinburgh and London. There is a similar Premium on Bills on Time Par of Exchange between all other towns in the country and London. This is termed **Inland Exchange**.

It appears from this that when in any place the Demand for Bills on any other place is greater than the Supply, and therefore when *Bills rise to a Premium*, the Exchanges are **adverse** to the first place, because it has more money to pay than to receive.

But when the Supply is greater than the Demand, *Bills fall to a* **Discount**, and the Exchanges are **favourable** to the first place, because it has more money to receive than to pay.

It must be observed, however, that the interests of Buyers and Sellers are opposite : if the Exchange is unfavourable to the Buyers of Bills, or those who wish to send money, it is equally favourable to the Sellers of Bills, or those who have to receive money.

Buyers of Bills are also termed *Remitters* : and Sellers are also termed *Drawers*.

On **Foreign Exchange**

11. The principle of Foreign Exchange is exactly the same as that of Inland Exchange. But there is considerably more complication, in consequence of different countries using different Metals as legal standards and different Coinages.

In Exchange between two foreign places, and of different Moneys, the Money of one place is always taken as **Fixed** : and the Exchange is always reckoned in the **Variable** Quantities of the Money of the other place which is given for it.

The former is termed the **Fixed** or **Certain** Price : and the latter the **Variable** or **Uncertain** Price.

Between London and Paris the £ is the *Fixed* Price, and the Exchange is reckoned in the variable sum of francs and cents given for it.

On the contrary, between London and Spain the Dollar is the Fixed Price, and the Exchange is reckoned in the Variable number of Pence given for it.

When any place is taken as a centre, if the Money of the Place is the **Fixed** Price, it is said to **Receive** the Variable Price.

But when the Money of the place is the **Variable** Price, it is said to **Give** the Variable Price.

Thus London *Receives* from Paris so many Francs and Cents for the £ : on the contrary, London *Gives* Spain so many Pence for the Dollar.

In the quotations of the Rates of Exchange it is usual to

omit the Fixed Price and name only the Variable Price : and then that sum is termed the **Rate** or **Course** *of* **Exchange**.

According to *Tate's* Modern Cambist the following are the present Rates of Exchange between London and the principal foreign cities :—

London **Receives** *from*

Amsterdam .	11·19 Florins and silver for £1.
Germany . .	20·43 Imperial Marks and Pfennigs for £1.
France . .	⎫
Italy . .	⎬ 25·30 Francs or Lire and Cents for £1.
Belgium . .	
Switzerland .	⎭
Austria . .	10·35 Florins and Kreuzers for £1.

London **Gives** *to*

Lisbon	53¼	Pence for	1 Milreis.
Spain	50¼	,,	1 Hard Dollar.
Gibraltar . . .	40½	,,	,,
St. Petersburg . .	37½	,,	1 Silver Rouble.
Rio Janeiro . . .	26¼	,,	1 Milreis.
New York . . .	49	,,	1 U.S. Dollar.
Calcutta . . .	23	,,	1 Govt. Rupee.

The above are the Mint Par Rates : but in some countries they are deranged by Paper Money being the circulating Medium of the country instead of specie.

Effects of the Exchanges being Favourable or Adverse to London

12. As a General Rule, when the Exchanges at any place, such as London, are *Against* the place, or Adverse, Bills on foreign places are at a **Premium**, because London has more money to send than to receive.

On the contrary, when the Exchanges are *favourable* to London, foreign Bills fall to a **Discount**, because London has more money to receive than she has to pay.

But in consequence of the *Opposite* modes of reckoning the Exchanges in London on different foreign countries, the very same effects will require to be expressed in **Opposite** terms, according as London Receives or Gives the Variable Price.

Exchange between London and Places **from** which it **Receives** the Variable Price

13. If the Exchange of London and Paris is *against* London: that is, if the Demand for Bills in London on Paris is greater than the Supply, and therefore Bills rise to a Premium, it is clear that they will purchase *Fewer* francs.

Hence, between London and Paris, when the Exchange is **against** London, the Rate of Exchange will **fall Below Par**.

On the contrary, when the Exchange is favourable to London: and the Supply of Bills is greater than the Demand: and therefore Bills fall to a Discount: the Rate of Exchange will **Rise Above Par**.

And the same is manifestly true with respect to all other places from which London Receives the Variable Price.

Exchanges between London and Places **to** which it **Gives** the Variable Price

14. But of course the contrary takes place between London and all places *to which* it *Gives* the Variable Price.

If the Exchange between London and Spain is against London: and Bills on Spain rise to a Premium; London must **Give more** Pence to buy a Spanish Dollar.

Hence between London and Spain, when Exchange is *Against* London; the Rate of Exchange **Rises Above Par**.

On the contrary, when the Exchange is *Favourable* to London, she will **Give Fewer** Pence to buy the Dollar.

Hence between London and Spain when the Exchange is *favourable* to London, the Rate of Exchange **Falls Below Par**.

And the same is manifestly true with respect to all other places *to which* London *gives* the Variable Price.

Hence, when the Rate of Exchange between London and any other place varies from Par, in order to determine whether the Exchange is favourable or adverse, it is always necessary to consider whether London *gives* the Variable Price *to*, or *Receives* the Variable Price *from*, that place.

One reason of the complication of the subject of Exchanges is that London *Gives* the Variable Price to some places and

Receives it from others: consequently the same Real State of the Exchange requires opposite expressions in these opposite cases. But it is exactly the same with all the other great centres of Exchange: they each *give* the Variable Prices *to* some places and *Receive* it *from* others.

On the Limits of the Variations of the Exchanges

15. When the Debts to be exchanged between any two places are exactly equal, the Demand and Supply of Bills at each place is exactly equal: and the Exchanges are at Par: because there is no money to be remitted from either side.

But if one place has to send more money than it has to receive, the Demand for Bills will cause them to rise to a premium.

It is the duty of the Debtor to place the money on the spot for the Creditor at his own risk and expense: consequently as it is cheaper to send a Bill by post than to send the cash with all the expenses of freight and insurance to pay, he would rather give a little more than the nominal value of the bill in order to save the expense of sending the cash.

But he will not give more than the Cost of sending the Bullion; because if the Price of Bills was higher than that, it would be cheaper to send the money itself.

Hence the Cost of sending the money is a **Superior Limit** to the Variations of the Real Exchange.

But the reverse case may also happen. The Supply of Bills in London or Paris may exceed the Demand. In that case London has more Money to receive than to pay. The Price of Bills will consequently fall. But for the same reason the Cost of transmitting Bullion will be an **Inferior Limit** below which the Price will not fall.

Hence the Limits of the Variations of the Exchanges are confined to **Twice** the cost of sending Bullion between the two places.

The **Limits** of the Variations of the Exchanges between two places are termed **Specie Points**: because when the Rates of Exchanges reach them, Bullion may be expected to flow in or out as the case may be.

It must be observed, however, that these Limits of the

Variations of the Exchange only apply to Bills payable at once and to considerable periods. During short periods and for Bills which have some time to run, fluctuations in the Exchanges may greatly exceed these Limits.

At the present time, the following are considered to be the Gold Specie Points between London and various centres of Exchange.

FRENCH	AMERICAN
Francs	Dollars
25·32½—4 per mille for us	4·86 —5 per mille for us
25·22½—Par	4·867—Par
25·12½—4 per mille against us	4·827—8 per mille against us
GERMAN	
Marks	AUSTRALIAN
20·52—5 per mille for us	
20·53—Par	£102 always for us
20·33—5 per mille against us	

Effects *of the* Restoration *of the* Coinage *on the* Exchanges

16. In the preceding remarks on the Nominal Exchange, it has been seen that the depreciation or degradation of the Coin in which the Exchanges are reckoned, must necessarily derange all the Exchanges of the country : and that the simple Restoration of the Coinage to its due state will be sufficient to Rectify the Exchange.

But the state of any other portion of the Currency or Circulating Medium than the one in which the Exchanges are reckoned, will not affect them.

In the early part of the reign of William III. the Silver Coinage in which the Exchanges were then reckoned had fallen into a most disgraceful state from clipping and other causes. On collecting bags of coin in different parts of the country, it was found that their weight scarcely exceeded one-half of what it ought to have been. In the beginning of 1696 the great work of re-coinage began, and by the middle of July the new coin began to be issued in considerable quantities. The state of the London Exchange will exemplify our remarks—

Statement of the Rates on the London Exchange during 1695–1696

	Amsterdam	Rotterdam	Genoa	Antwerp	Hamburg	Cadiz	Madrid	Venice
April 23, 1695 .	31·2	31·4	56·29	30·11	29·11	56·2	56·1	59·
Jan. 24, 1696 .	31·0	31·2	60·	31·	29·9	60·0	60·	63·
May 2 ,, .	30·1	30·2	64·	30·	28·8	60·	61·	61·2
July 19 ,, .	29·3	30·6	65·	29·	—	60·	—	—
July 28 ,, .	38·7	33·9	58·	33·	32·4	53·	58·	54·
Sept. 29 ,, .	36·5	36·7	54·	36·	35·	48·	49·	51·
Oct. 6 ,, .	36·8	36·10	53·2	35·7	35·8	48·	49·	—
Nov. 6 ,, .	37·4	37·6	52·1	37·2	36·4	47·	48·	49·
Dec. 16 ,, .	37·8	37·10	51·	37·8	36·8	46·2	47·	49·

On examining this table we see that a great change in the figures took place in July, 1696. Some *rise* very much and others *fall*. It was at this period that the new Coinage came out in great abundance. This rectified the Exchanges: the Exchanges on those places *from* which London *received* the Variable Price *rose*, because the good English Coinage would purchase more Foreign Coin. Those *to* which London *gave* the Variable Price *fell*, because it required a less amount of good English Coinage to purchase a fixed amount of Foreign Coin.

Bank of England Notes at this period were at a heavy discount because the Bank had suspended cash payments: but that produced no effect on the Exchanges, because they were not reckoned in Bank Notes, but exclusively in Silver Coin.

On **Exchange Operations**

17. Exchange operations consist in buying, selling, importing and exporting **Bullion**, called '**Bullion** operations,' and buying and selling **Bills**, called '**Banking** operations.'

The calculations necessary to ascertain the profit and loss on such operations are given at length in various technical works on the subject. Our object only is to examine the general causes which produce those movements of Bullion, which so sorely vex the banking and commercial world.

Exchange operations of both sorts may be either direct or

indirect; that is, they may take place directly between the two countries, or the final operations may be effected through the medium of one or more intermediate countries.

We have observed that for Bills payable at sight the limits of the variations of the Exchange cannot exceed the cost of the transmission of Bullion, which are called the specie points: because, when they are reached, Bullion may be expected to flow in or out.

When the Bills, however, have a considerable time, such as three months, or more, to run, before they are payable, causes may operate which may produce *temporary* fluctuations of the Exchange considerably beyond these limits. These are, chiefly—

1. The necessity that the holders of these long-dated Bills may have to realise them, even at a considerable sacrifice, to maintain their own position.

2. The doubtful position of the acceptors, or the general discredit of the place they are drawn upon.

3. The differing relative Values of the precious metals which are the standards of payment at each place.

4. The respective Rates of Discount at each place.

Now, it may very often happen that from these combined causes, it may be considerably more profitable to possess Bullion at one place than another. Whenever this is the case, exchange operators export Bullion from one place to another, for the sake of this profit. They create Bills upon such a place; they draw upon their correspondents, discount their Bills, and remit the proceeds to meet their drafts when due.

It used to be the dogma of many commercial writers, that Bullion is only exported to discharge a previous state of indebtedness: and that, consequently, a drain of Bullion comes to a natural end, when the indebtedness is discharged. But this is a most grievous error. The sufficient difference of profit in possessing Bullion at two places, will cause a fabrication of Bills for the purpose of exporting Bullion, without any previous indebtedness: and, of course, this will continue so long as this possibility of profit exists. Consequently, unless this profit is destroyed, the drain of Bullion will not cease. The effectual way of annihilating this profit is by raising the Rate of Discount.

It is manifest that, in such operations, the difference of profit between the two places must exceed twice the cost of transmitting Bullion, because, in such cases, the cost of transmitting the Bullion both ways will fall on those who originate them.

Between countries in which there are no restraints upon trade, the Exchanges will never vary much, except on some sudden emergency: but there are countries with which, owing to the prohibitive laws which still infest their commercial codes, the Exchanges are permanently unfavourable, because they will take nothing but Bullion for their commodities. Russia is one of these countries, and hence, if not modified by other circumstances, Bills upon Russia would always be at a premium; but here, again, the effect of trafficking steps in, which always has a tendency to equalise prices. The merchant (if we may call him so) who deals in Bills, acts upon the same principles as the dealer in any other commodities: he buys them where they are cheapest, and sells them where they are dearest. Hence he will try to buy up Russian Bills cheaper in other Exchanges, or Debt Markets, and sell them in the London Debt Market. On the other hand, from the course of trade between England and Italy, the debt which Italy owes to England is usually greater than the contrary; hence, Italian Bills will usually be at a discount, or cheap, in the London Debt Market. So the Bill merchant buys them up cheap here, and sends them to some other market—Paris, for instance—where they may be at a premium. By these means the price of Bills is raised where they are cheapest, and depressed where they are dearest; and the general result will be, to melt all the differences between separate countries into one general result, so that the Exchanges will not be favourable with one country and adverse with another; but they will be generally adverse or favourable with all the rest of the world.

Supposing, however, a merchant has to remit money to Paris, while the Exchange with Paris is unfavourable to England, he may possibly discover a more advantageous way of remitting it than by buying a Bill on Paris directly. Thus, for instance, while Bills on Paris are at a premium in London, those on Hamburg may be at a discount: and Bills on Paris may be at a discount in Hamburg. So if the merchant buys a Bill on Hamburg, and sends it to his agent there, and directs him to purchase a Bill on Paris with the proceeds, he may be able to discharge his debt in Paris at a less sum than he would have to pay for a Paris Bill in London. This circuitous way of settling his debt involves additional charge for brokerage, commission, postage, &c., but the effect of it is still further to equalise the exchanges between London and all other countries. This circuitous method is called the *Arbitration of Exchanges*, and the sum which is given in London for the ultimate price it realises in Paris is called its Arbitrated Price. When only three places are used in the operations above, it is called *Simple Arbitration*. When more than three are employed, it is called *Compound Arbitration*. The practical rules for working out these results are very simple, and will be found in any technical book on the subject. But it is very evident that the quicker, safer, and cheaper the communication between countries becomes, the less room will there be for such operations, because the limits of the variations of the real Exchanges, which are the margin which renders such transactions possible, will constantly diminish.

The scale on which these indirect operations of Exchange is carried on is immense, and peculiarly affects the London Exchange. There is no Exchange between places to and from which remittances have not constantly to be made. Consequently, when such places trade, their accounts must be settled by means of drafts upon some third recognised centre. Now, London is the banking centre of the world. From the enormous exports of England to all quarters of the globe, remittances have to be made to London from every part of the world. There is, therefore, a constant demand for Bills upon London to discharge the debts incurred for these commodities. Hence, although the exporters may send their goods to different countries, yet, if they can draw upon London, their bills will be sure to find some purchasers somewhere, to be remitted to England. Hence, Bills upon London bear a higher price, and meet with a readier sale, than those upon other places.

One country, A, may import from another, B, less than she exports, and, consequently, a debt is due from A to B. Also, B exports to another country, C, more than she imports; and, consequently, a debt is due from C to B, and A may discharge its debt to B, by transferring to it its claim against C.

As many countries trade with one another, between which there is no exchange, their claims are mutually adjusted by drafts upon London, the commercial centre. Hence, the London Exchange is the most important in the world, and requires the greatest attention to be paid to it.

In the same way that there are arbitrated rates of Exchange, there are arbitrated prices of Bullion, but we need not enter into them here.

On the Real or Commercial Exchange

18. We must now consider the causes that affect the Real Exchange, or the true Commercial one, which arises out of the transactions between this and other countries. As the British Islands do not produce the precious metals to any extent worth considering, they are only to be obtained in this country by importation, and we must now consider the various sources from which they come, and the different causes that produce an influx or efflux of them. They are to be treated in every other respect like any other foreign commodity, and are obtained by the same means as any other one that we require for domestic consumption which is not a native product.

The trade in Bullion may be divided into two distinct branches: the one where it is carried on directly with the countries in which gold and silver are native products: and the other with those countries which do not produce it; but which, like our own, have no means of supplying themselves with it except by foreign commerce.

I. *With Bullion-producing countries.*—Before the late discoveries in California and Australia, the chief Bullion-producing countries were Mexico and Peru. We need not specify others, because the same principle applies to them all, and to describe them all would rather belong to a work on commerce generally. British merchants have establishments, or correspondents, in those countries, to whom they consign their goods, and their agents exchange them for the Bullion brought down by the natives, and which is collected in large quantities, and usually brought home by men-of-war, for the sake of security. Most of the men-of-war on the Pacific and West India stations used to make a voyage along the coast, before they returned home, to collect Bullion from the merchants, and the captain received a commission on the freight. In those countries Bullion is treated exactly like any other commodity, such as tea, or wool, or wine, and the British goods, of all kinds, are exported to them for the express purpose of being exchanged for Bullion to be remitted home. The limits of this exportation are precisely similar to the limits of the exportation to any other country. It is clear, that by the time the Bullion reaches this country, it ought to be sufficient to cover the original price of the goods, and all the charges on them on their way out: as well as the agent's commission there, the charges for freight, insurance, and commission for bringing it home, and a fair mercantile profit over and above all these expenses. Unless it does that, the commerce is not profitable. If too many goods are exported to those Bullion-producing countries, their exchangeable value with Bullion falls, and they will not purchase a sufficient quantity of Bullion to afford this profit, and the further exportation of such goods to those markets must be discontinued until the goods first sent out are consumed, and fresh ones required. The purchase of Bullion, then, in those countries, is a very simple affair, and requires no further notice.

II. *With countries which do not produce Bullion.*— The causes which produce an inflow or outflow of Bullion, between this and other countries like it, which do not produce Bullion, are much more intricate, and have excited long and keen controversies. Taking this country as the centre, we may consider that the transmission of Bullion, to or from it, is influenced by the **Seven** following causes—

1. The Balance of Payments to be made to or by it.
2. By the state of the Foreign Exchanges.
3. By the state of the Currency.
4. By Remittances made to this country, as the commercial centre of Europe, to meet payments due to other countries.
5. By the Political Security of this and neighbouring countries.

6. By the state of the Money Market, or the comparative Rates of Interest in this and neighbouring countries.

7. By the free or prohibitive Commercial Tariffs of this and foreign countries, as they permit or forbid our manufactures to be imported into them.

There are, then, **seven** different causes which act upon the movements of Bullion; and, in any case, it is necessary to ascertain to which of these causes it is due. The inveterate error of mercantile opinion for a long time was, that there is only one cause which causes an export of Bullion, namely, a balance of payments to be made.

We have already shown that a degraded state of the Currency has the inevitable effect of driving away Bullion from here. As we may fairly hope that our Currency will never again be allowed to fall into such a disgraceful condition as it was till 1816, we may consider that this cause is not likely to operate again on the Bullion Market; but we may now proceed to develope the system of the **Foreign Exchanges**.

19. According to the crude ideas that were generally received about two centuries ago, gold and silver were almost universally considered to be nearly the only species of wealth, and it was considered to be the true policy of every country to encourage, by every means in its power, the influx of Bullion, and to discourage its export; and most, if not all, of the European nations have gone so far, at one time or another, as to prohibit its export. The profit of foreign commerce was estimated solely by the quantity of gold and silver it brought into the country; and the Theory of Commerce seemed to be reduced to a general scramble among all nations to see which could draw to itself most gold and silver from the others. According to this theory, the gain of one party was the loss of the other; every article produced in another country, and imported into this one, was considered to be a direct loss to the country. This was what was called the mercantile or commercial system. According to this theory, the leading maxim which governed the Legislature was, to make the exports to exceed the imports; and the conclusion drawn was, that the difference, or balance, must be paid for in cash by the debtor nation. When two

nations traded with one another, the difference of debts between them was called the 'Balance of Trade': and, when this was in favour of England, the exchange was said to be favourable, because Bullion had to be paid to her; on the contrary, when, on the result of trade, payments had to be made by her, the balance of trade was said to be against her, and the exchange unfavourable, and then gold was sent out of the country. According to this theory, the prosperity, or the contrary, of the country, and the profit or loss, of foreign commerce was exactly measured, according as gold had to be received or paid, or as the exchange was favourable, or the reverse.

The admirable chapter of Adam Smith on the Principle of the Mercantile System, is a masterly exposition of the fallacy of this theory, and is certainly one of the soundest and best written in his whole work, from the more than usual consistency of its ideas, and the lucidity of its style. There are, however, some things relating to the subject which require further enforcement and illustration.

So far from the principle of the mercantile theory being true that gold and silver are the most profitable and desirable objects of imports, the direct reverse is unquestionably true, that gold and silver are, of all objects of commerce, the most unprofitable; and it is a certain axiom of commerce in a state of freedom, *that Bullion will not be imported until it has become unprofitable to import any other article.* There are no class of traders who derive so little profit, in proportion to the capital invested in their business, as dealers in Bullion and Money of all sorts, whether they be Bullion merchants or Bankers. Although the opinions we have alluded to above were the prevalent ideas of the age, there were not wanting a few sagacious thinkers, who discovered the truth of what we last said, and maintained the unprofitable nature of gold and silver; but, like others who are before their age, their voice was unheeded, and the general object of commercial ambition and legislation was to accumulate treasures of gold and silver.

20. There is no expression in commerce of more frequent occurrence than the 'Balance of Trade,' and it may be as well to give the interpretation of it generally received during the last century, and which is not yet wholly extinguished. Mr. Irving, Inspector-General of Imports and Exports in 1797, defined it thus :—' The common mode of considering that question has been to set off the value of the imports, as stated in the public accounts, against the value of the exports, and the difference between the one and the other has been considered the measure of the increase or decrease of the national profit.' And Mr. Hoare, a banker of eminence for twenty-two years, said— ' I consider the only proper means of bringing gold and silver into this country to arise from the surplus of our exports over our imports, and that ratio or proportion which is not imported in goods, must be paid for in Bullion. In the year 1796, the imports of this country appeared to be £19,788,923, and the exports appear to be £33,454,583, which ought to have brought to this country Bullion to the amount of that difference, or £10,665,660.'

We have made these extracts because they convey, in the fewest words possible, the whole ideas on the subject, and they are made by persons of great commercial eminence before the Committee of the House of Commons. It is true that Mr. Irving, who was Inspector-General of the Exports and Imports of Great Britain and the British Colonies, expressly states that the application of this principle to the whole of the British trade would, in his judgment, be extremely erroneous. We, therefore, do not bring him forward as *approving* of the theory, but only as stating distinctly and authoritatively what it was. But Mr. Hoare, a banker of eminence and long experience, adopted it ; and we believe that this theory of the balance of trade still retains a hold on the minds of great numbers of persons who do not give themselves the trouble to sift it thoroughly. Nevertheless, there never existed a more complete chimera and pernicious delusion than this said doctrine of the balance of trade, nor one which has exercised so disastrous an influence on commercial legislation.

21. It appears that the simplest way of arriving at an accurate conclusion on the subject, is to consider that the dealings between nation and nation are only made up of the aggregate of dealings between individuals of the nations, and we have only to consider the variety of methods in which an individual merchant may trade, to have an accurate and comprehensive idea of the commerce of the nation. Instead of dealing with figures of vast amount, which make no definite impression on the mind, and which are produced by a number of complex causes, we shall now proceed to consider in how many different ways an individual merchant may trade with foreign countries, and we shall show, by considering the dealings of an individual, how utterly erroneous it is to suppose that an influx of Bullion is, *ipso facto*, a proof that commerce is flourishing and profitable to the country, and that, whether it is so or not, depends very much as to where it comes from, as well as a number of other circumstances.

With respect to those countries in which Bullion is a native product, and to which we trade for the express purpose of obtaining it, we have already shown that unless the quantity obtained in exchange for our goods exceeds a certain amount, the commerce is not a profitable one, and that the simple fact of Bullion being remitted from them, and, therefore, though the Exchanges with them must always be in our favour, it is no proof whatever of prosperity or profit.

Next, with respect to countries which do not produce Bullion, it is easy to show the extreme fallacy of the opinion that our exports should exceed our imports, and that the *difference* will be the *profit* of the country; in many cases the precise reverse is true, that our imports should exceed our exports, and the profits are measured by the exact sum by which the imports exceed the exports, or the excess of what we receive over what we give.

To prove this, let us take a simple case. Suppose a merchant in London sends out £1,000 of goods to Bordeaux, by the time they arrive there, the mere addition of freight, insurance and other charges, will probably have increased their cost of production, or the expense of placing them where they are, to £1,050, supposing them to be sold without any profit at all. But, as the merchant would never have sent them to that market unless he expected to realise a good profit, we may assume that the market is favourable, and that they sell for £1,500, and he would probably draw against his agent for £1,200. His correspondent at Bordeaux, instead of remitting the money to England, would find it far more profitable to invest the proceeds of the goods in some native product, which would fetch a good price in England. The chief native product of that country is *wine*, so the agent would invest the proceeds of the goods, after deducting all charges for freight, commission, &c., in Bordeaux wine, and send it to England. This wine would probably be sold at a considerable profit in the English market; say it would fetch £2,000; and, after deducting all the charges of every description on the cargoes both ways, the difference would be the merchant's profit In this case it is quite clear that no Bullion would pass between the countries: and the merchant would apparently import more than he exported: and it is also clear that his profits are exactly estimated by the **Excess** *of the* **Value** *of the inward cargo above that of the outward one*, after deducting all charges both ways: and just as this difference is the greater so is his gain greater. In this case, as no bullion would pass from either country to the other, there would be no question of exchanges.

It is clear that the London merchant's agent at Bordeaux would be governed by several considerations as to whether he would remit specie or wine to London, and he would be chiefly governed by the state of the wine markets, both at Bordeaux and London. For, supposing the goods to be sold at a good profit at Bordeaux, he must next consider the price of the wine at Bordeaux, and also what it might be expected to fetch in London. If some great disaster had happened to the vines so that there was a failure of the crops, the price of wine at Bordeaux might rule excessively high, but at the same time there might be a large stock of wine in London, and the price might not be unusually high; so that if he were to purchase wine at Bordeaux, and send it to London, it might be a loss. In such a case as this, if there were no other native product to send, he would find it more advantageous to remit specie, whatever he could sell the goods for, and then the exchange would be in favour of London; but, before the London merchant could reckon his profits, he would have to deduct the freight, insurance, &c., on the specie.

Whether the transaction was profitable or not to the London

merchant would entirely depend on the amount of specie he received after deducting all charges; and if he had purchased the goods he sent out from England cheap, and there was a scarcity of them at Bordeaux, he might realise high prices there, which might leave him a good profit. It would be very improbable that he could realise so much profit on that single operation as in the double one of exporting goods and importing wine. So that the import of the specie would be less profitable to him, and the nation at large, than the import of the wine.

The reasons which caused the export of specie from Bordeaux, and the import of it into England, in this case, are very plain; they were the scarcity and dearness of the native products at Bordeaux, and the abundant supply of them already in the London market. Hence, we gather that *the scarcity and dearness of native products are an infallible cause of the export of specie from a country*: on the contrary, an abundant supply of cheap products of all sorts, both foreign and native, will cause an importation of Bullion: and when products, both native and foreign, are scarce and dear, it will cause an export of Bullion.

We have before observed that the exchange being in favour of a country means nothing more than that Bullion has to be remitted to it. In the case above described, the exchange at Bordeaux would be in favour of London; but this simple case is as good as a thousand to show the extreme and dangerous fallacy of drawing any conclusion as to the advantage of the trade to England, from the simple fact of the exchange being favourable to her, and an inflow of Bullion taking place.

22. The example given above is of the simplest description, and a merchant of eminence, who has correspondents in several different parts of the world, might easily multiply these operations, so as to visit many markets before the returns of his cargo were brought home. Thus, instead of having the wine sent home from Bordeaux, his correspondent might find it more profitable to send it to Buenos Ayres, and dispose of it there. The chief native product of that place is hides, and we may suppose that his correspondent there might invest the proceeds of the cargo of wine in hides, which there might be a favourable opportunity of selling in the West Indies. When the cargo arrived in the West Indies, instead of remitting the proceeds directly home, it might very well happen that, owing to a scarcity of corn at home, it might be very high there, and cheap in Canada, so he would invest the proceeds of the hides in sugar, and dispatch that to Canada, where the merchant's correspondent there would dispose of it, and purchase corn, which he would send to England.

In the case just described, we observe that there are five distinct operations; and, as we may suppose, that there is a profit upon each of them, by the time the returns for the goods, which originally cost £1,000, are brought to England, it may very well be, that the corn, which forms the ultimate payment of them, may be several times as valuable as the original cargo; and, as we have supposed the charges on each operation to be deducted before investing the proceeds in other articles, it is clear that the merchant's profit upon the whole is exactly the difference in value in England between the articles last purchased and sent home, and the original cargo, after deducting all the expenses of sending home the last cargo; and we also observe that no specie has been sent from one country to the other in the whole course of the extended operation.

This example is sufficient to demonstrate the utter fallacy of the old idea, which is even yet not extinguished, of the Balance of Trade. Nothing can be more clear, that unless the value of the cargo which comes into England, in payment of the cargo that was sent out, is sufficient, not only to defray the cost of the original cargo, as well as all charges upon it and the return cargo, and leave a profit besides, the commerce could not be carried on. No English merchant could export goods unless he receives in return others of much greater value; and the obvious consideration, that the more he gets for what he sends out, the more profitable it is to himself and the nation, is sufficient by itself to explode the old fallacy of the balance of trade. One obvious source of error is that the value of the exports from this country is estimated at the time of their leaving the country, and before the charges for freight, &c., are incurred, which must necessarily raise their selling price in the foreign market, if they are not sold at a loss, and their value in that market is expected to be considerably higher than that. On the other hand, the value of the imports is estimated, not according to their value when they left the foreign country, but what it is upon their arrival here, including all their charges upon them.

23. If we suppose that Bordeaux had but one native product—wine—the chances of finding the market, both at Bordeaux and London, in a favourable state for importing produce instead of specie, would be limited to that single article. But if it had other products, such as olive oil, the chances would be increased of finding articles to suit the market, and the chances would evidently be multiplied according to the number and variety of its products.

24. Let us take another example and let New York be the starting place. The staple products of America are breadstuffs and provisions. A merchant of New York sends a cargo of corn to Liverpool, and his correspondent there will endeavour to invest the proceeds of that in British goods, if he finds the state of the markets in England and New York will make such an operation profitable. Suppose that the price of corn is very high here, and British goods are also very high here, and very low in America, it is clear that nothing but specie will be sent. In cases where a great and unexpected dearth of corn occurs in England, and its price rises enormously high, the infallible result is to cause a great drain of specie for the time being, because our necessity for food is much more pressing and immediate than their necessity or capability of consuming our cotton or woollen goods. And the only way to arrest such drain is to effect such a reduction in the prices of British goods as shall make it more profitable to export goods than specie.

25. In the cases we have hitherto been considering, we have described the operations as if merchants were left perfectly free to carry their goods whither they pleased, and were not met and obstructed by artificial obstacles purposely devised for interfering with their business, by the laws of different nations. But there are few nations, and our own among the rest, which have not habitually discouraged the importation of foreign goods, and imposed heavy duties for the specific purpose of excluding them, as they conceived the extraordinary idea that all foreign goods brought into the country were so much loss to it. Thus, the statute of William III. (1688, c. 24) says :—' It hath been found by long experience that the importing of French commodities of all sorts' (enumerating them) .'hath much exhausted the treasure of this nation, lessened the value of the native commodities and manufactures thereof, and greatly *impoverished* the English artificers and handicrafts, and caused great *detriment* to the kingdom in general.' If we consider the effect of these laws in one place, it will equally apply to every other ; thus, in the first instance, suppose that there are very high protecting duties at Bordeaux against British goods, as the customer must ultimately pay all the expenses and charges on the goods, it will have the effect of greatly raising the market price there, and diminishing the number of persons who can afford to buy them : and hence, as the market is so limited, a smaller quantity of goods will overstock it than if it were more extended. This will cause a much less quantity of goods to be sent from London, and it will cause a much larger proportion of specie to be remitted to pay for the productions of Bordeaux. This example shows that the inevitable effect of high protecting duties between country and country is to cause a much more frequent transmission of Bullion from one to the other than would be the case in an unfettered state of commerce ; unless, indeed, the smuggler steps in, who is the corrector provided by nature against this commercial insanity. The effect, then, of prohibitive duties is to cause an inflow of Bullion ; but we must carefully guard against supposing that this inflow is a favourable sign, as it is certainly the least profitable import a merchant can receive for his goods ; and there is this very marked difference between an inflow of Bullion under the Protectionist system and under a Free Trade system, that the former is accompanied with a great dearth of foreign commodities, but the latter is an infallible sign of great abundance of them, as Bullion is never imported when men are allowed to follow their own interests, until our markets are already so overstocked that every other article has ceased to be profitable.

26. The foregoing cases comprehend the different varieties of commercial transactions between this and any other country, and we gather from them the following results respecting the inflow or outflow of Bullion—

I. The cause of Bullion being imported is either when the price of goods is so **low** in England, and so **high** in the foreign market, as to tempt foreigners to send here to buy goods; or the price of goods is so high in the foreign market, and so low in England, that nothing but specie can be sent in payment of goods exported from England.

II. The cause of Bullion being exported from England is that there is some great and pressing demand for some article in this country, and other commodities are so scarce and dear that they cannot be exported with a profit, or that the article is required in such great quantities that the foreigner cannot consume our goods which we should prefer to send in payment fast enough, and so specie must be sent, and the greater the difference in price the greater will be the drain of Bullion: or that other markets are already overstocked with our productions, which are depressed below their usual market value there. This is what is meant by overtrading; and from this circumstance, we see that *overtrading is a sure precursor of a drain of Bullion from the country.* When there has been a great failure of the crops in this country, so as to cause a famine price, the demand for corn is so immediate and urgent that it necessarily causes a great drain of specie: and it is then of the greatest possible consequence that the prices of other commodities should be as low as possible, to enable them to be sent in payment of the necessary supplies of food, and prevent such a drain of Bullion as may disturb the whole monetary system of the country.

27. Overtrading, and a **failure** of the **cereal crops** of this country, are each of them sure **causes** of a **drain** of **Bullion.** The most disastrous event for the commerce of this country is when both these circumstances happen concurrently. It is like a spring tide of disaster. The most terribly disastrous commercial crisis this country ever experienced was preceded by some years of overtrading, followed by successive failures in the staple support of the people of England and Ireland. These two adverse events together produced the calamities of 1847. We shall see that the intended effect of the Bank Act of 1844 is to provide a remedy for such a state of things by causing such a reduction in the price of home commodities, in the event of a drain of specie taking place, as to render it more profitable to export them than Bullion, and so stop the drain. Whether the Act is effective for this purpose is another question, which it is not the proper place to discuss here.

28. There are some countries from which we draw articles of great necessity, but to which, from different circumstances, we do not expect to remit goods in payment. Russia was the great source of our supply of hemp, tallow, and flax, and we used to import these products to the value of £12,000,000 yearly, but, owing to the prohibitive character of her tariff, we were unable to send our own products in payment of these goods to anything like a similar amount in value. To such a country the difference must be remitted in cash, to the mutual loss of both parties; and, unless there were other means of equalising the exchanges with different countries, the exchange with Russia would always be unfavourable to England. The chief export trade from Ireland to England was in articles of food—pigs, cattle, oats, butter. Great quantities of these came from Ireland, but the inhabitants of that country were much too poor to be able to consume an equivalent amount of English goods; in consequence of which the difference had to be remitted in specie, and so the exchanges between England and Ireland were almost uniformly favourable to Ireland. Now, if Ireland had been sufficiently wealthy to have consumed English goods instead of specie, it is evident that it would have been far more advantageous for both countries; for English industry would have been promoted, and Ireland would have gained a more valuable import. These two examples offer a further illustration of what we said before, that the frequent transmission of Bullion between countries which do not produce it, is a system of a less profitable trade than it would be if goods were transmitted.

29. In the operation first described above, we have supposed it to originate with the English merchant who remits his goods to his correspondent abroad, and who reaps the profits, and the proceeds must be remitted to him after deducting the freight charges, and commission of the agent there. But it is also probable that there will be native merchants at Bordeaux, who will send wine to England on their own account to their correspondents here, and then the whole transaction will be reversed. The English correspondent will endeavour to purchase English goods as low as he can, and if he can get them low enough to realise a profit in the Bordeaux market, he will send goods out; but if the English goods are too high for that purpose, he must send specie. It is also evident that, even if the goods be at no unusual height in England, still, if the market at Bordeaux be already overstocked with them, or, as it is called, 'glutted,' it would be useless to send more goods to force the price down still further, and the consequence will be that nothing but specie will go.

From this we see, that if specie be coming in from a country it is proof that we have already got so many of their goods, that it will not pay to import any more, and if specie be going out to a country, it shows that we have already sent out so many of our goods to that market that it is already overstocked. The different barbarous laws which every country has enacted under the erroneous appellation of protection, by aggravating the price, limit the markets in every country for the products of other countries, and cause much fewer commodities to pass between nations than otherwise would, and cause the markets of any country to be much sooner overstocked than they would otherwise be. By preventing this interchange of commodities which every nation would naturally prefer, it necessitates payments in specie to a much larger extent than would be the case if commerce were free, to the common impoverishment of all parties.

30. The foregoing considerations show that it is possible to carry on any amount of foreign trade without the necessity of any remittances being made in specie. In the instance above taken, the English merchant purchases goods and sends them to his correspondent abroad, who realises them, and invests the proceeds in that market, and sends them to England, and the English merchant disposes of them in England, and gains the profits there, and no specie is sent from one country to the other. Similarly, the foreign merchant sends his goods to his correspondent in England, who disposes of them there, and invests the proceeds of them in England, in English commodities, and sends them to his foreign correspondent, who gains his profit, either by selling them in his own country, or by sending them to some other market, where he may make a higher return; and, as in the former case, no specie passes between the two. Nor is the result in any way different if the trade be conducted by the more circuitous method of three or more transactions. Hence, in a healthy state of the markets of different countries, scarcely any specie will pass between them: and the very fact of there being a necessity for making frequent and large remittances of specie from one country to another, is in itself a proof of there being something irregular and unhealthy in the state of commerce in general: and in the state of the markets in one country or the other: either that they are overstocked or understocked: or that there is some legislative interference with the natural course of trade between nation and nation. Nothing can be more certain than that Bullion is the least profitable of any article of commerce, except from Bullion-producing countries: and that when merchants have recourse to it, it is because some disturbance has taken place in the profitable relations between supply and demand of other commodities.

31. Now, supposing commerce to be in that desirable and healthy state in which no specie passes between non-bullion-producing countries, who could tell how what is called the Balance of Trade is inclined? Who can tell what the Balance of Trade is? Each country would show a favourable balance, taking the values of the exports and the imports at their market prices in each country. Each country would show that their imports exceeded their exports in value: that is, each would show that they had gained by their commerce: for the very simple reason, that the value of the article they received would be greater in their own market than the value of the one they gave; and, unless it was so, it is manifest that trade could not be carried on: because all the expenses and profits of trade are provided for, by the difference in value between what they give and what they receive. Hence, unless both parties gain by the transaction, commerce cannot be carried on. But this shows that the expression 'Balance of Trade' is a gigantic delusion, and it is greatly to be wished that it should be for ever exploded and laid aside, as the fountain and origin of incalculable mischief to the world, in the suicidal effort every nation has made to secure to itself that great chimera—a favourable balance.

The mistake of unreflecting writers, who think that the price of foreign goods sold in this country goes into the pocket of the foreigner, consists in this, that the probability is, that the English merchant who imports these goods has already purchased them with English goods, so that their money price goes into the pocket of the English merchant, and not that of the foreign one, and is, probably, re-invested in English goods, if there is a prospect of a favourable opening for them.

The fundamental fallacy about the balance of trade, which seems to have taken possession of the Legislature, was, that the interests of the State were different and opposite to the interests of individuals. They seemed to have entertained the idea that every merchant had entered into a conspiracy to ruin the country, which he tried to carry into effect by becoming as prosperous himself as he could. It seems most unaccountable how long they missed the obvious truism, that the prosperity of the State is made up of the prosperity of the individuals composing it, and that every one is far keener in discerning what conduces to his own prosperity than the State can be: and that if private merchants found it to be to their individual advantage to import commodities rather than Bullion, it could not be beneficial to the State to force trade into a contrary direction.

Notwithstanding the prevalent idea that foreign trade was profitable just in proportion to the money it brought into the kingdom, and that this was indicated by the so-called balance of trade, there were a few enlightened persons who saw through the fallacy and combated it. In reference to a certain 'balance' which occurred in the trade between Holland and England, and which was a subject of much gratulation, Craik well observes that it would be irrational to suppose that the English must necessarily be the chief gainers by this trade, as it would be to maintain that the productive labourer must always be a greater gainer on the article he produces than the capitalist who employs him. That the Dutch were in the position of the capitalist, and the English of the labourer, and that while the Dutch had the goods, the English had the money; just as, while the master had the goods, the workman had his wages. But that the excess of profit, or real advantage, should rather be with the labourer than with the capitalist, may fairly be presumed to be as unusual, and as little likely in the nature of things, in the case of nations as of individuals.

An attentive consideration of these various methods of trading will show what a complete phantasy the old, and still too common, idea of the 'Balance of Trade' is; and, as nothing more conduces to error and confusion in any science than a nomenclature and technical phrases which are founded upon misconceptions of the principles of that science, so nothing has exercised a more malignant influence upon legislation, and popular ideas generally, than this phrase; and it would be very desirable if some means could be taken to discontinue its use altogether. But, as it does occur in the course of trade that transactions between nations have to be settled in specie, we must now consider the operations of the foreign exchanges.

The course of the foreign exchanges, then, entirely depends upon the fact of persons in one country having to make payments to persons in another country, from whatever causes these payments have to be made. And there are but two causes which influence their rates: first, the depreciation of one or both of the currencies which have to be exchanged, secondly, the relative amounts of money that have to be remitted from one country to the other.

On the **Rate of Discount** *as influencing the* **Exchanges**

32. We have now to treat of a cause of the movement of bullion which has acquired an importance in modern times far exceeding what it ever did before; in fact, it is now probably more important than any other, namely, a difference in the rate of **Interest** or **Discount** between two countries. In former times when the communication between different places was slow and expensive, before the days of railroads and steamers, a considerable difference might exist in the rates of interest in two places, without causing a movement of bullion from one place to the other. But that is not possible now. The communication between places is so rapid now that directly the difference between the rates of interest in any two places is more than sufficient to pay for the expense of sending the bullion, an immediate flow of bullion commences from one place to the other. And this is in exact accordance with the usual mercantile principle that operates in every other case, that if the difference of price of the same article in any two markets is more than sufficient to repay the cost of sending it from one to the other, it will be sent; and this movement will continue as long as the difference in price continues. Now, if the rate of discount in London is 3 per cent., and that in Paris is 6 per cent., the simple meaning of that is that gold may be bought for 3 per cent. in London, and sold at 6 per cent. in Paris. But the expense of sending it from one to the other does not exceed $\frac{1}{2}$ per cent., consequently, it leaves $2\frac{1}{4}$ or $2\frac{1}{2}$ per cent. profit on the operation. The natural consequence immediately follows, gold flies from London to Paris, and the drain will not cease until the rates of discount are brought within a certain degree of equality. It used to be the common delusion of mercantile men that gold was only sent to pay a balance arising from the sale of goods, and that, therefore, it must cease of itself whenever these payments were made. But this is a profound delusion. When the Rates of Discount differ so much as is supposed above between London and Paris, *persons in London fabricate bills upon their correspondents in Paris* for the express purpose of selling them in London for cash, which they then remit to Paris, and which they can sell again for 6 per cent. And it is quite evident that this drain will not cease so long as the difference in the rates of discount is maintained. Moreover, merchants in Paris immediately send over their bills to be discounted in London, and, of course, have the cash remitted them. Now, the only way of arresting such a drain is to equalise the Rates of Discount at the two places. These simple facts are a perfectly conclusive answer to those writers, and they are many, who complain of the variations of the rate of Discount by the Bank of England, and suppose that it is possible to maintain a uniform rate. Consequently, at the present day it is the imperative duty of the Bank of England to keep a steady watch upon the rates of discount of neighbouring countries, and to follow these variations so as to prevent its being profitable to export bullion from this country.

On **Foreign Loans, Securities,** and **Remittances,** as affecting the Exchanges

33. Besides the state of national indebtedness arising out of Commercial operations, other causes may affect the Exchanges.

Formerly, during foreign wars, England, being more abundant in money and material resources than in men, used to subsidise foreign powers to a considerable extent : and the method of transmitting such a loan to the best advantage to the remitting country is an operation of considerable nicety and delicacy. To withdraw a very large amount of actual coin at any given time from a commercial country might produce the most disastrous consequences when so many fixed engagements have to be met at a fixed time.

The method of operating was simply an example of what we have so fully illustrated in the preceding chapters, that the *Release of a Debt* is in all cases equivalent to a *Payment in Money*; or that $- \times - = + \times +$

Instead of transmitting vast amounts of Coin, the method always adopted in such cases is by purchasing Bills of Exchange on the place of Payment : and by operating on a number of different centres to prevent the disturbances which would arise from withdrawing too large an amount of Circulating Medium from any one place.

In 1794 the English Government agreed to lend the Emperor of Germany £4,000,000, and the problem was to send the money from London to Vienna with as little disturbance as possible to the London money market.

Mr. Boyd, who conducted the operation, says—' The remittance of so large a sum as £4,000,000 I considered a matter of infinite difficulty and delicacy, so as to prevent its producing any remarkable effects upon the course of Exchange. It was necessary to vary the modes of remitting, and to make use of the various means for that purpose presented by all the different Exchanges of Europe. It was not necessary to remit Bills upon Hamburg only, because it frequently happened that it answered better to remit to Hamburg upon other places, such as Madrid, Cadiz, Leghorn, Lisbon, Genoa, &c., than to remit direct upon Hamburg: and having constantly orders from Vienna with regard to the rates of the different remittances to be made, our attention was directed to the accomplishment of these orders on the best possible terms. In fine, it was necessary to take Bullion, Bills direct upon Hamburg, and Bills upon other places all into our means of remittance, and to make the most of these modes of remittance without giving the decided preference to that mode which was the most favourable, because any one mode invariably adhered to would soon have exhausted and destroyed that mode: whereas by turning occasionally to all the modes, and not sticking too long to any one particular mode, we had the good fortune to make upon the whole very favourable remittances.'

McCulloch gives another example of a similar operation. 'In 1804 Spain was bound to pay France a large subsidy, and, in order to do this, three distinct methods presented themselves. First, to send dollars to Paris by land: second, to remit Bills of Exchange direct upon Paris: thirdly, to authorise Paris to draw directly upon Spain. The first of these methods was tried, but found too slow and expensive: and the second and third plans were considered likely to turn the exchange against Spain. The following method, by the indirect or circular exchange, was therefore adopted:—

'A merchant or *banquier* at Paris was appointed to manage the operation which was thus conducted. He chose London, Amsterdam, Hamburg, Cadiz, Madrid, and Paris as the principal hinges on which the operation was to turn: and he engaged correspondents in each of these cities to support the circulation. Madrid and Cadiz were the places in Spain from whence remittances were to be made, and dollars were, of course, to be sent, when they bore the highest price, for which bills were to be procured on Paris, or any other place that might be deemed more advantageous. The principle being thus established, it only remained to regulate the extent of the operation, so as not to issue too much paper on Spain, and to give the circulation as much support as possible from real business. With this view London was chosen as a place to which the operation might be chiefly directed, as the price of dollars was then high in England, a circumstance which rendered the proportional exchange advantageous to Spain.

'The business commenced at Paris, where the negotiation of drafts issued on Hamburg and Amsterdam served to answer the immediate demands of the State: and orders were transmitted to these places, to draw for the reimbursement on London, Madrid, or Cadiz, according as the course of exchange was most favourable. The proceedings were all conducted with judgment and attended with complete success.

34. The most gigantic operation, however, of this nature, which ever took place, was the payment of the indemnity which France was obliged to pay to Germany, in consequence of the unfortunate result to her of the war. A most minute account of this operation was presented to the National Assembly by M. Léon Say, from which we take the following details, sufficient, we hope, to make a general outline of the operation intelligible.

By the definitive treaty of peace between Germany and France, signed at Frankfort, May 10, 1871, France became bound to pay to Germany the sum of 5 milliards of francs, equal very nearly to 200 millions sterling, at the following dates—500 millions thirty days after the restoration of order in Paris; 1,000 millions in the course of 1871; 500 millions on May 1, 1872; and 3,000 millions on March 2, 1874, together with 5 per cent. interest on the last three milliards.

Payment might be made in gold or silver, Notes of the Banks of England, Prussia, Holland, Belgium, or first-class Bills of Exchange.

The thaler was valued at 3·75 francs, and the German florin at 2·15 francs.

All bills not domiciled (i.e. made payable) in Germany, were to be valued at their net proceeds, after deducting all costs of collection.

It was subsequently agreed that the portion of the Eastern Railway of France, situated in Alsace, should be accepted in compensation, or set off, to the debt to the amount of 325 millions; also that 125 millions should be received in notes of the Bank of France; and the sum of 98,400 francs, which remained due to the city of Paris after the payment of the indemnity, should be received as a set-off against the debt of France.

Besides the indemnity payable by France, the city of Paris had to pay an indemnity of 200 millions of francs; 50 millions in specie; 50 millions in notes of the Bank of France; $37\frac{1}{2}$ millions in two month bills on Berlin, at the exchange of 3·75 francs for the thaler; and 63 millions in bills upon London, at six and fifteen days' sight, at the exchange of 25·20 francs for the pound sterling.

The bills upon London were bought at the exchange of 25·3488; and those on Berlin at an exchange of 3·7325; Paris, therefore, lost 14·88 cents on each pound sterling, and gained 1·75 cent. on each thaler. The total cost of the indemnity was 1,965,240·30 francs, and, after it was all settled, there remained a balance of 98,400 francs in favour of Paris, which, as above said, was taken as a set-off in favour of France.

The total operation was divided into two parts; the payment of the first two milliards, and that of the last three.

. The first thing to be done was to put the Government in funds to effect the payment. To do this they negotiated a loan with the Bank of France of 1,530 millions, and created two public debts of 2,225,994,045 and of 3,498.744,639 francs.

The first loan was authorised by a law of June 21, 1871; it was opened to public subscription on the 27th, and made payable in 17 monthly instalments.

The second loan was authorised by a law of July 15, 1872; the subscription was opened on the 28th, and made payable in 21 monthly instalments.

On July 31, 1874, the first loan was fully paid up, and of the second only 7,136,000 francs remained due.

The Government being thus in funds commenced its exchange operations, and the debt was finally liquidated in the following way :—

By Compensations	325,098,400 francs
By Bank Notes and German Money .	742,334,079 francs
By Bills of Exchange	4,248,326,374·26 francs

To effect this stupendous operation all the great bankers in Europe were invited to assist, and in June, 1871, a London agency was opened to assist and to receive subscriptions and bills. Other agencies were opened at Brussels, Amsterdam, Berlin, Frankfort, and Hamburg. The Treasury gave its correspondents $\frac{1}{4}$ to $\frac{1}{2}$ per cent. commission on its first loan, and on the second 1 per cent. at first, which was reduced to $\frac{1}{2}$ and $\frac{1}{4}$. In the first loan the pound sterling was received at 25·30 ; the thaler at 3·75 ; the Frankfort florin at 7 florins for 4 thalers ; the marc banco at 2 marcs for one thaler ; and Belgian paper at par. In the second loan the pound sterling was received at 25·43 ; the thaler at 3·76 ; the Frankfort florin at 2·14$\frac{7}{8}$; the marc banco at 1·87$\frac{1}{2}$ for 1 thaler ; and Belgian paper at par.

The exchange operations in London began in June, 1871, and lasted till September, 1873. The exchange was at 25·21$\frac{1}{4}$ in June, but, in consequence of acting somewhat too precipitately, it rose to 26·18$\frac{3}{4}$ in October. In 1872 the lowest was 25·26$\frac{1}{4}$ in April, and the highest 25·68$\frac{1}{2}$ in November. In 1873 the lowest was 25·33 in March, and the highest 25·57$\frac{1}{2}$ in June. The mean average of the whole was 25·4943.

In the course of the operation, the Treasury purchased 120,000 foreign bills, amounting in the whole to rather more than 4$\frac{1}{2}$ milliards. It opened subscriptions in foreign countries, and received foreign bills in payment of the loan opened in Paris. The subscriptions to the first loan comprised 213 millions of francs, and the subscriptions to the second 389 millions, in foreign bills.

M. Léon Say then gives some details respecting the three classes of payments above named as compensations ; bank notes and German money ; and Bills of Exchange.

The details respecting the compensations need not detain us; but with regard to the second, it comprised the following items :—

Notes of the Bank of France	125,000,000
German Bank Notes and Money	105,039,145.1
French Gold Money	273,003,058.10
French Silver Money	239,291,875.75

The German bank notes and money were collected from the sums which the German armies had brought with them in the invasion.

The third class, viz. Bills of Exchange, included German bills taken at their full value, 2,799,514,183·72 francs, and other foreign bills taken at their net proceeds, after deducting all charges, 1,448,812,190·54.

M. Léon Say then gives some details of the commercial operations undertaken to support these gigantic payments, but he at once acknowledges that it is impossible to explain their complete theory, on account of a new article of merchandise which has only recently been introduced into commerce.

'It is not possible to explain the operations of a portfolio which contains 120,000 bills of a value exceeding 4 milliards.

'There were all sorts of bills, from less than a thousand francs to more than five millions; some mentioned the purchase of merchandise; others appeared only to be fabricated for the purpose, and destined themselves to be covered at maturity by bills which were to be created to pay real transactions.

'Bank Credits, the paper circulating between head offices and branches, circular exchanges, payments for invoices, the remission of funds for the ultimate purchase of merchandise, the settlement of debts abroad to France under the form of coupons, shares, and commercial obligations, were all in these effects, making up the most gigantic portfolio which was ever brought together.

'After all this, to give a detailed classification is an absolutely impossible task. One can do no more than determine the classes of the operation, and make some general remarks on these classes, and on the importance and meaning of the business effected on each of them.

'Fifty years ago there were no other international operations than merchandise and money; merchandise, gold, and silver, were the only subjects of export and import; the balance of commerce was settled in gold and silver. Everything which was bought from the foreigner was paid for in gold or silver, if not in merchandise.

'One might find, then, in the statistics of the Custom House *data* more or less exact, but at least real *data*, of the course of business between two countries; but things have greatly changed within fifty years.

'There has appeared, especially within the last twenty-five years, in international commerce, what may be called a *new article of export*, an article which in every country has acquired a greater importance than any other, and which has had the result of completely distorting the meaning of Custom House returns. *This new article is Securities*; it is transmitting across the frontiers of different States the property of Capital by representation, which is easy to transport, viz. these Capitals of the form of bills of exchange, public funds, shares and obligations of railways and other companies.

'To understand the real course of international business, it is necessary to know not only the imports and exports of merchandise, the imports and exports of specie, *but also the imports and exports of Securities*; and this last class, which is the most important, and which is the key to the two others, escapes all kinds of returns.'

This is exactly the doctrine we have been enforcing for so many years, and shows the profound error of those Economists who exclude Incorporeal Property from the Title of Wealth, and of those who write books on Economics, and who are either ignorant of, or who ignore, its existence; for, as we have said, in such a country as this it is the largest class of property of any. M. Léon Say then gives some notices of the imports and exports of merchandise, specie, and securities, which we need not enter on.

We will give, however, the final result of the operations, showing the pieces in which the debt was liquidated :—

	Payment of Two Milliards	Payment of Three Milliards
Notes of Bank of France	125,000,000	—
French Gold	109,001,502·85	164,000,555·25
French Silver	63,016,695·	176,275,180·75
German Money and Bank Notes	62,554,115·93	42,485,029·25
Thalers	312,650,509·01	2,172,663,212·03
Frankfort Florins	25,816,752·37	209,311,400·42
Marcs Banco	116,575,592·13	148,641,398·27
Reichs Marcs	—	79,072,309·89
Dutch Florins	250,540,821·46	—
Belgian Francs	147,004,546·40	148,700,000
Pounds sterling	624,699,832·28	12,650,000
	1,836,860,367·43	3,153,800,085·86

Now, we observe that the whole of the above sum that was paid in French specie was 273 millions in gold, and 239 millions in silver, being somewhat over 20 millions sterling, wh· reas $4\frac{1}{4}$ milliards, or 160 millions sterling, were paid by Bills of Exchange. This fact is especially worthy of notice, because some financial writers maintained that if England had met with a similar misfortune, she could not have paid such a ransom, on account of the small quantity of specie in the country. These figures, however, show that this is a complete delusion, as England could pay by bills, if ever she were driven to such a dire extremity, to a far larger amount than France; and we see that in France herself, where specie is alleged to abound, the part that was paid in specie was less than an eighth part of the payment by bills.

M. Léon Say notices, as one of the results of the war, the liquidation of the famous Bank of Hamburg, founded in 1619, in imitation of those of Venice and Amsterdam, for the purpose of securing a uniform standard of mercantile payments, by means of credit in its books, which was called the marc banco.

After the establishment of the German Empire it was resolved to adopt a gold currency; and the marc banco of Hamburg (which was absorbed in the Empire) violated the new Imperial system in two ways; first, it was a local money, and all local moneys were to disappear before the Imperial currency; and it was silver, whereas the Imperial standard was gold.

The marc banco, which was worth a half thaler, or $1·87\frac{1}{2}$

franc, was abolished by law, and the reichs thaler imperial, of 1·25 franc, was substituted. The bank was ordered to liquidate all its accounts in fine silver by February 15, 1873; and after that, anyone who had claims against the bank was credited with a half thaler for the marc.

The preceding are examples of loans raised in this country with the consent of the Government, and, consequently, every care was taken to have them transmitted in such a way as to produce as little disturbance of the exchanges as possible. But it has become very common for foreign Governments to raise loans in England without any sanction of the Government at all. During the late unhappy war in America, both the belligerent Governments sent over enormous quantities of their securities, or stock, to be disposed of for specie in the European markets for what they would fetch, and the proceeds were remitted either in cash or bills. So also vast numbers of foreign companies of all sorts seek to raise capital in England.

There is, lastly, to be considered the sums required by residents abroad for their expenditure. The drafts of the great English and Russian families on their bankers at home affect the exchanges exactly in the same manner as any other drafts.

The India Council Bills

35. The most extensive operations of this sort are the India Council Bills : or the Bills which the Council of India in London draws upon the Governments of the different Presidencies.

India has enormous and continuous payments to make in London on the following accounts :—

1. The establishment of the India Office in London, and of the Engineering College at Cooper's Hill, is maintained by India.

2. The interest on the Public Debt is chiefly payable in London.

3. The Military and Civil Pension List.

4. The Military charges for the transport of British Troops to India and military stores of all sorts.

5. Civil Stores of all sorts : materials for Railways, telegraphs, &c.

In 1880-81 the sum total of Disbursements to be made in London exceeded 18 millions sterling. And these charges are all payable in fixed amounts in Gold.

To meet these charges the Council of India in London draws every Wednesday a certain amount of Bills on the Governments of the different Presidencies.

These sums are payable in Gold in London; but the Governments in India pay in Silver Rupees: it is therefore requisite to draw for such a sum in Rupees as shall produce the required amount in Gold in London.

It is for this reason that the relative *Value* of Gold and Silver is of such deep importance to the Government of India.

Every Wednesday the India Office sends tenders to the Bank of England—usually amounting at present to about 35 or 40 crores of rupees, or about £350,000, offering to sell that amount of Bills at the Current Market Price of Silver.

These tenders are open to all the world: just as the Mint is open to anyone to have his bullion coined: but practically speaking the tenders are confined to a certain number of Indian Banks: who buy these Bills either on their own account, or on account of their customers, who have payments to make in India. And as a matter of fact the balance of payments to be made by the merchants usually agrees pretty nearly with the amount of payments to be made by the Indian Government in London.

The great importance of these Bills, however, is the effect they have on the Market Price of Silver: and they have in fact been one of the most potent factors in recent years in causing the diminution in the Value of Silver as compared to Gold.

Selling Bills for Silver in the London Market is in reality exactly the same thing as selling so much Silver itself. Consequently, as Silver is nothing but a commodity in England, the more of it which is pressed for sale, the lower the price must go.

The Government Rupee, which since 1862 has replaced the old Company's Rupee, being however exactly of the same weight and fineness, is 180 grains troy Silver $\frac{11}{12}$ fine: or 165 grains fine silver to 15 grains alloy.

The British Shilling, coined at present at the rate of 66 to the lb. weight of Silver Bullion, contains $80\tfrac{8}{11}$ grains of fine silver: hence the Florin contains $161\tfrac{8}{11}$ grains of fine silver.

When the price of British standard Silver is 60d. per ounce the Rupee is worth 1s. 10·2973d., or nearly 1s. 10·3d. sterling.

In recent years several causes have combined to reduce greatly the Market Price of Silver : these are the greatly increased production of the metal : the demonetisation of Silver by Germany : the vast amount of Paper Money on the Continent : and the greatly increased amount of the India Council Bills.

The more India Council Bills are sold, the more the Diminution in the Value of Silver is increased : and as the Council must sell a sufficient quantity to produce the required amount in Gold : a still larger amount must be sold to make up for their diminished Value : and consequently the heavier is the taxation on the people of India to meet the deficiency.

To estimate truly this deficiency it is necessary to consider the relative Value of Gold and Silver at some fixed era.

In converting Indian accounts into sterling the Rupee is conventionally valued at 2s., or the 10th of a £ : and from 1850 to 1857 did really continue about that price : but since then there has been a rapid declension in its value, coincident with the increased production of the metal : the demonetisation of silver by Germany : and the great increase of the India Council Bills.

It is evident that no correct estimate of the Diminution of the Value of Silver as compared with Gold can be made unless the era of their Value at Par be agreed upon.

Statement showing the Disbursements in England made by the Government of India: the Bills of Exchange drawn on India: the average rate of the Rupee: and the Cash Balances of the Government of India in England: and the average price of standard Bar Silver per ounce: from 1834–35 *to* 1880–81.

Year	Disbursements during the Year	Bills of Exchange drawn on India	Average rate obtained for Bills on India	Cash Balance at the close of the Year	Average Price of Bar Silver per oz.
	£	£	s. d.	£	
1833–34 . .	—	—	—	3,772,901	—
1834–35 . .	5,559,723	732,804	1 10$\frac{3}{4}$	3,625,488	59$\frac{15}{16}$
1835–36 . .	3,367,982	2,045,254	1 10$\frac{5}{8}$	5,405,807	59$\frac{11}{16}$
1836–37 . .	8,475,317	2,042,232	1 10$\frac{1}{4}$	2,737,440	60
1837–38 . .	3,093,923	1,706,184	1 11	4,246,960	59$\frac{9}{16}$
1838–39 . .	5,905,984	2,346,592	1 11$\frac{5}{8}$	2,928,132	59$\frac{1}{2}$
1839–40 . .	3,315,450	1,439,525	1 11$\frac{1}{2}$	2,020,227	60$\frac{3}{8}$
1840–41 . .	3,356,741	1,174,450	1 11$\frac{1}{2}$	1,038,299	60$\frac{3}{8}$
1841–42 . .	3,757,787	2,589,283	1 10$\frac{5}{8}$	1,687,561	61$\frac{1}{16}$
1842–43 . .	3,382,996	1,197,438	1 11$\frac{1}{2}$	988,199	59$\frac{7}{16}$
1843–44 . .	4,023,327	2,801,731	1 11	1,407,791	59$\frac{3}{16}$
1844–45 . .	3,571,345	2,516,951	1 9$\frac{5}{8}$	1,290,787	59$\frac{1}{2}$
1845–46 . .	4,210,910	3,065,709	1 9$\frac{3}{4}$	1,348,494	59$\frac{1}{4}$
1846–47 . .	3,984,261	3,097,042	1 10$\frac{5}{8}$	1,069,499	59$\frac{5}{16}$
1847–48 . .	4,016,537	1,541,804	1 10	727,755	59$\frac{11}{16}$
1848–49 . .	4,231,535	1,889,195	1 9$\frac{7}{8}$	1,344,431	59$\frac{1}{2}$
1849–50 . .	4,167,705	2,935,118	1 10$\frac{1}{2}$	2,106,977	59$\frac{3}{4}$
1850–51 . .	3,862,558	3,236,458	2 0$\frac{1}{4}$	2,756,460	60$\frac{1}{16}$
1851–52 . .	3,510,829	2,777,523	2 0$\frac{1}{8}$	2,365,848	61
1852–53 . .	3,796,802	3,317,122	1 11$\frac{7}{8}$	2,210,357	60$\frac{1}{2}$
1853–54 . .	4,369,009	3,850,565	2 0$\frac{1}{8}$	2,410,280	61$\frac{1}{2}$
1854–55 . .	4,272,589	3,669,678	1 11$\frac{7}{8}$	4,767,582	61$\frac{1}{2}$
1855–56 . .	5,036,793	1,484,040	2 0$\frac{1}{8}$	3,431,553	6 $\frac{5}{16}$
1856–57 . .	4,983,849	2,819,711	2 0$\frac{1}{8}$	3,041,944	61$\frac{5}{16}$
1857–58 . .	9,354,728	628,499	2 0$\frac{5}{8}$	3,351,600	61$\frac{3}{4}$
1858–59 . .	13,470,617	25,901	— *	2,819,398	61$\frac{3}{16}$
1859–60 . .	15,253,578	4,694	— *	4,196,093	62$\frac{1}{16}$
1860–61 . .	10,646,185	797	— *	2,053,063	61$\frac{11}{16}$
1861–62 . .	11,242,685	1,193,729	1 11$\frac{7}{8}$	5,733,711	60$\frac{13}{16}$
1862–63 . .	10,863,137	6,641,576	1 11$\frac{5}{8}$	5,248,910	61$\frac{7}{16}$
1863–64 . .	16,818,982	8,979,521	1 11$\frac{7}{8}$	4,596,274	61$\frac{3}{8}$
1864–65 . .	9,480,062	6,789,473	1 11$\frac{7}{8}$	3,914,891	61$\frac{3}{8}$
1865–66 . .	10,419,741	6,998,899	1 11$\frac{3}{4}$	2,818,780	61$\frac{1}{16}$
1866–67 . .	10,924,952	5,613,746	1 11	4,098,779	61$\frac{1}{8}$
1867–68 . .	12,681,606	4,137,285	1 11$\frac{1}{8}$	2,833,009	60$\frac{9}{16}$
1868–69 . .	13,661,553	3,705,741	1 11$\frac{1}{8}$	3,025,981	60$\frac{1}{2}$
1869–70 . .	14,509,939	6,980,122	1 11$\frac{1}{4}$	2,892,483	60$\frac{7}{16}$
1870–71 . .	13,523,477	8,443,509	1 10$\frac{1}{2}$	3,305,972	60$\frac{9}{16}$
1871–72 . .	13,486,813	10,310,339	1 11$\frac{1}{8}$	2,8·1,091	60$\frac{1}{2}$
1872–73 . .	13,831,718	13,939,095	1 10$\frac{3}{4}$	2,998,444	60$\frac{5}{16}$
1873–74 . .	15,532,844	13,285,678	1 10$\frac{3}{8}$	2,013,637	59$\frac{1}{4}$
1874–75 . .	14,480,643	10,841,615	1 10$\frac{1}{8}$	2,796,370	58$\frac{5}{16}$
1875–76 . .	14,356,598	12,389,613	1 9$\frac{5}{8}$	919,899	56$\frac{7}{8}$
1876–77 . .	15,696,372	12,695,800	1 8$\frac{1}{2}$	2,713,967	52$\frac{3}{4}$
1877–78 . .	15,904,685	10,134,455	1 8$\frac{3}{4}$	1,075,657	54$\frac{13}{16}$
1878–79 . .	18,739,711	13,948,565	1 7$\frac{3}{4}$	1,117,925	52$\frac{9}{16}$
1879–80 . .	18,200,357	15,261,810	1 8	2,270,107	51$\frac{1}{2}$
1880–81 . .	18,118,800	15,239,677	1 8	4,128,187	52$\frac{1}{4}$
Total . .	429,453,735	242,466,548	—	—	—

* In consequence of the Mutiny it was necessary to refrain from drawing on India in these years.

On **Monetary** and **Political Convulsions** as *influencing* the **Exchanges**

36. As an immediate consequence of the preceding principles, it follows that a Political or Monetary Convulsion in any country will immediately turn the foreign exchanges in favour of that country, if such an event is not prevented by the issue of an inconvertible paper currency. The reason is plain; any political or monetary convulsion is attended by a great destruction of *Credit*. Now, that Credit, while it existed, performed the functions of money, but as soon as it is destroyed there is an intense demand for money to fill the void. Money rises enormously in value. Multitudes of persons are obliged to sell their goods at a sacrifice. The consequence is that money, having risen greatly in value, both with respect to goods and debts, an immense quantity will flow in from neighbouring countries. Thus, in 1800-2, there was a great commercial crisis at Hamburg. The rate of discount rose to 15 per cent. That immediately drained the bullion from the Bank of England. In 1825 there was a great commercial crisis in England. For a considerable period the Bank, by making extravagant issues at a low rate of discount, had turned the foreign exchanges against the country. But no sooner did the crisis occur in December than the foreign exchanges immediately turned in favour of it. Exactly the same thing happened in 1847. No sooner had the crisis in that year fairly set in than the exchanges turned in favour of the country. In the French revolution in 1793, and subsequent years, immense quantities of inconvertible paper were issued, which kept all the French exchanges in a very depressed state. In 1796 this Paper Currency was annihilated, and the exchanges immediately turned in favour of France. The same thing was observed in 1848. Things were to be had so cheap then that multitudes of persons went over to buy.

On the **Means** of **Correcting** an *Adverse* **Exchange**

37. The preceding paragraphs show upon what complicated causes these great movements of bullion depend which produce such important consequences. There are three great Economic

Quantities—PRODUCTS, BULLION, and DEBTS—all seeking to be exchanged, all flowing from where they are cheaper to where they are dearer.

But all this vast superstructure of Credit—this mighty mass of exchangeable property—is based upon GOLD BULLION. Different methods of doing business require different quantities of Bullion; but, however perfect and refined the system may be, we must come at last to the basis of Bullion as its moderator and regulator. If, therefore, the Bullion be suffered to ebb away too rapidly, the whole superstructure is endangered, and then ensues one of those dreadful calamities—a monetary crisis.

We have endeavoured to explain the different causes which produce an adverse exchange, so that if one takes place the proper corrective may be applied. If it be caused by a Depreciated Currency, there is no cure but a restoration of the currency to its proper state.

When, however, it arises from a balance of indebtedness from commercial transactions, there are but two methods of correcting it—an export of produce, and **a Rise in the Rate of Discount.**

It used to be a favourite doctrine that an adverse exchange is in itself an inducement to export on account of the premium at which the bills can be sold. What truth there is in this doctrine can only be known to those actually engaged in such operations. But a very much more certain means of producing an export of goods is *a lowering of their price.*

This was one of the fundamental objects of the framers of the Bank Act of 1844. They truly observed that the prices of goods had often been unduly inflated by the excessive creation of credit, while gold was rapidly flowing out of the country. Thus, when prices were kept too high here, nothing but gold would go. One object of the Act was, therefore, by causing a gradual and compulsory contraction of Credit as Bullion ebbed away, to lower the prices of goods and encourage an export of them.

The reasoning of the framers of the Act was undoubtedly correct in that respect. But the only thing is, whether the same object may not be attained another way. This is not the place to discuss fully the policy of that Act, because there are several other conflicting theories involved in it, which we cannot fully discuss until we come to the consideration of a commercial crisis.

It is sufficient to say here that all the objects of that Act are obtained by paying proper attention to raise the rate of discount as rapidly as bullion flows out. If the Directors of the Bank had understood and acted upon that principle, there never would have been any necessity for the Act. It is true we cannot blame them too much, as before 1833 they were prohibited by law from raising it above 5 per cent., a rate wholly inadequate to check a great outflow; and for many years there was a great prejudice against doing so.

We have observed that a difference in the rate of discount between any two countries more than sufficient to pay for the transmission of bullion causes a flow of bullion from one to the other. But it must be remembered that, as all the cost of the transmission both ways falls upon the operator, the difference will be more considerable than might appear at first sight. And, if they are three months' bills, of course the profit reaped will be only one-fourth of the apparent difference. Thus, Mr. Goschen says, there must be a difference of 2 per cent. between London and Paris before the operation of sending gold over from France for the sake only of the higher interest will pay. And between other continental cities, of course, the difference may be much greater.

But whatever the difference may be, the *method* is absolutely certain. Directly the rate of discount rises here, people cease to export bullion from here, and the continental bankers and brokers increase their demand for English bills. And as the rate rises the demand will increase, until at last the price reaches the specie point, and gold begins to flow in; and as the rate rises more, more powerful will be the attraction, until at last the necessary equilibrium is restored between bullion and credit.

CHAPTER XIII

On Law's Theory of Paper Money

1. It now becomes an essential and most important duty to investigate a Theory of Currency which has acquired great celebrity, not only from its historical interest as having led to some of the most extraordinary public calamities on record, but because it is still extensively believed in at the present day. It is necessary not only to lay the true foundations of monetary science, but also to point out the fundamental fallacy of a Theory which has brought the most disastrous consequences upon those nations which have adopted it, as will always be the case when the eternal laws of nature are systematically and perseveringly violated.

This Theory we shall designate as **Lawism**: not because John Law was the original inventor of it, but because he was the first to write a formal treatise on it, and he had the opportunity of carrying it out on the most extensive scale. His name, therefore, must always be most prominently associated with it: and it is one so specious, but so dangerous, and so widely prevalent at the present hour, that it requires to be branded with a distinctive name, and to be combated with all the power of argument that can be brought against it.

2. The question, shortly stated, is this. All persons except those who advocate an inconvertible paper money, agree that a paper currency must be convertible into some article of value, and bullion has been generally chosen for that purpose. Now the idea has occurred to a great many persons—If it is only necessary that Paper Currency should be convertible into some article of value, why should it not represent any or all articles of value, such as land, corn, silk, or any commodities, and

among others the public Funds. And this has actually been tried in several instances; yet they have universally failed, and in many cases have been attended with the most frightful calamities. Now this has uniformly happened; and, as we shall show further on, it must happen, it necessarily follows that there must be some radical error in the principle: and that it must violate some great law of nature. And this is one of the most momentous problems in Economics—Why is it improper. to issue a Paper Currency on any other basis than that of bullion? All the most eminent British Statesmen have instinctively resisted such proposals, although repeatedly pressed to do so. No doubt it has been a most fortunate instinct for the country; but all their reasonings on the subject, if only pursued to their legitimate consequences, tend to that result. The Bank Act of 1844 was the first occasion on which a small bit of this theory was introduced, which, if only followed out to its legitimate conclusion, would produce in this country the horrors of the Mississippi scheme in France. But though the British Parliament, by a blind unreasoning instinct, has always, with the exception just named, resisted such fatal advice, this will not satisfy the demands of science. Science imperatively demands a reason *why* such a plan is wrong: she will not be satisfied with a simple dogmatic assertion that it is wrong: even though that dogma may be right; but she must know the reason why: and until a true scientific reason is given why such plans are fatal, there will be a constant demand for them.

It is, moreover, this thing which has brought the name of Law into such unhappy notoriety. Law has in many respects very great merit as a writer. In many respects he had clearer and sounder views on Monetary Science: he had infinitely more practical insight and scientific knowledge of what he was writing about than the most eminent modern Economists. In his various writings is to be found the refutation of all the absurd follies of the Government and of the Bank of England in 1811. But all this was marred by a single defect. He was the great advocate of what many persons advocate now—basing a Paper Currency upon any article of value besides bullion. The only difference between him and our greatest statesmen is that he carried out their arguments to their legitimate conclusion. He had the opportunity of carrying this theory into effect, and the result has been to obscure all his other merits, and to brand him for ever as a charlatan. What, then, was his error?

Upon sifting his theory to discover his error, we shall obtain one of the most beautiful triumphs of pure reasoning to be found in any science. We shall find that the plausible scheme which we shall designate by his name is founded on a direct contravention of the fundamental conception of the nature of a Currency established in this work, and the proposition which directly flowed from it: viz. **that where there is no Debt there can be no Currency**. It is, in fact, creating a Currency where there is no Debt: and thus, as we have seen that the Quantity of Debt in a country is sometimes called the Channel of Circulation; it is, in fact, forcing a quantity of Stuff, or Material, into the Channel of Circulation, which is already full; and as the new material is of inferior natural value, Gresham's Law acts, and the original and more naturally valuable material is driven out of circulation, and the material of inferior natural value alone remains. We shall find that these awful monetary cataclysms, which have shaken nations to their foundations, producing calamities more fell than famine, tempest, or the sword, have been brought about by attempting to carry into practice a philosophical fallacy which involves a contradiction in terms.

3. It is impossible to say who first invented the theory we are going to notice: in fact, it must have sprung up indigenously among almost any people who began to form theories of Paper Currency. Several persons about the same time seem to have hit upon it. The most notorious precursors of Law were Dr. Hugh Chamberlain, who brought forward a rival scheme to the Bank of England in 1693, and Mr. Briscoe, one of the chief promoters of the Land Bank of 1696. Chamberlain's idea will be noticed a little further on. He strongly accused Law of having stolen his idea from him, which Law strenuously repudiates, and points out the distinction between them, and it must be allowed that Law's ideas were not so extravagant as Chamberlain's. Law first published his theory in a tract called 'Money and Trade Considered,' at Edinburgh, in 1705. He was the son of a goldsmith, and of dissipated

habits, but of an extremely acute intellect : and up to a certain length his views are sagacious and correct—much more so, indeed, than those of many writers of the present day. He observed the extreme poverty and barbarousness of Scotland, which he thought might be cured by bringing an additional quantity of money into the country : and, as silver was scarce, he attempted to devise a scheme for providing a substitute for it.

He begins by many very sound and acute remarks on the value of commodities, and the causes of their change of value. He describes the qualities which fit silver to be used as money above every other commodity. He attributes the very inconsiderable trade of Scotland to the small quantity of money she possessed. This is the first fundamental fallacy, because the fact was it was just the reverse. Scotland had little money *because* she had little trade. He, however, perceived the fallacy of lowering interest by law. He then goes on to consider the various means which have been employed to increase the quantity of money. He says that some countries have raised money in the denomination : some have debased it : some have prohibited its export under the severest penalties ; some have obliged traders to bring home bullion in proportion to the goods they imported. But he says that all these measures have been futile and vain, and none of them have been found to increase or preserve money. He then says that the only effectual method hitherto discovered for the increase of money was the erection of banks. He then describes various banks. Some made it a principle to issue no more notes than they had of actual bullion. He then mentions the Bank of England, and the superiority of its notes over those of the goldsmiths. He then describes the Bank of Scotland, and says that it issued notes to four or five times the value of the money in the Bank, which he very justly says were equivalent to so much additional money. He then points out the absurdity of supposing that raising the denomination of the money added to its value ; that if the shilling was raised to 18*d*. it paid debts by two-thirds of what was due, but did not add to the money : 'for it is not the sound of the denomination, but the value of the silver, is considered.' The wonderful philosophers of 1811, no doubt, looked down with prodigious disdain upon Law, but they might have studied him with advantage. He then points out, with much detail, the fraud and inutility of tampering with the Currency. He describes the additional effect which Credit may give to Money: but says that Credit which promises a payment of money cannot well be extended beyond a certain proportion it ought to have with the Money. Nothing can be more sound and judicious than his remarks upon Credit—that it must always vary in proportion to the metallic basis it is built upon: and, up to this point, his sagacity and penetration are in advance of the doctrines of a century later: but here is the boundary, after which he plunges into that fatal and delusive fallacy which is the distinctive feature of what we denominate **Lawism**.

4. Thinking that Money was so scarce in Scotland that any Credit that could be built upon it would be insignificant, he says—

'It remains to be considered whether any other goods than silver can be made Money, with the same safety and convenience.

'From what has been said about the nature of money, it is evident that **any other goods which have the qualities necessary in Money may be made money equal to their value with safety and convenience.** There was nothing of humour or fancy in making silver to be money: it was made because it was thought best qualified for that use.

'I shall endeavour to prove that another Money may be established, with all the qualities necessary in money in a greater degree than silver.'

5. He then proceeds to show at great length that silver had some peculiarities that disqualified it from being the best substance to form money of: that it varied in value: that it had increased much faster in quantity than the demand for it, and had therefore fallen in value. In fact, he tries to prove that silver had varied in value more than any other kind of goods within the last two hundred years: that goods would always maintain a uniformity of value, because they only increased in proportion to the demand: that land would always rise in value, because the quantity would always remain the same, but the demand would continually increase; but that silver would always fall in value, as the quantity increased faster than the demand.

6. Law then denies that he had taken his ideas from Chamberlain, of which the latter had accused him: and it must in candour be admitted that his ideas were many degrees less mad than those of Chamberlain. Law asserts that he had formed his schemes many years before he had seen any of Chamberlain's papers.—' Land indeed is the value upon which he founds his proposals, and 'tis upon land that I found mine : if for that reason I have encroached upon his proposal, the Bank of Scotland may be said to have done the same. There were banks in Europe long before the doctor's proposal, and books have been written on the subject before and since. The foundation I go upon has been known so long as money has been lent on land, and so long as a heritable bond has been equal to a quantity of land.'

7. The difference between Chamberlain's theory and Law's was this. Chamberlain maintained that if land was mortgaged for 100 years, it was a good security for 100 times its annual value : so that, if a man had landed property worth £1,000 and if he mortgaged it for 100 years to the State, the State might issue notes to him to the amount of £100,000, which were to be declared equal in value to silver, and made legal tender for their nominal value. Now, if this theory be true, there is no good reason why land should be pledged for only 100 years : why not for one million years? which would do the thing on a somewhat more magnificent scale. But what need of stopping there ? Why not pledge it to all eternity? and then every inch of property might be covered with paper notes, and they might be piled high enough to reach the moon, where the deviser of this scheme would probably find his lost wits. Law properly points out that the fallacy of this theory was, that Chamberlain assumed that the value of £100, to be paid 100 years hence, is still £100. He says—' No anticipation is equal to what already is : a year's rent now is worth fifteen years' rent fifty years hence, because that money lent out at interest by that time will produce so much.' But, says Lord Macaulay, 'On this subject Chamberlain was proof to ridicule, to argument, even to arithmetical demonstration. He was reminded that the fee simple of land would not sell for more than twenty years' purchase. To say, therefore, that a term of 100 years was worth five times as much as a term of twenty years, was to say that a term of 100 years was worth five times the fee simple : in other words, that a hundred was five times infinity. Those who reasoned thus were refuted by being told they were usurers : and it should seem that a large number of country gentlemen thought the refutation complete.'

8. Law's theory was to calculate the value of the fee simple of the land at twenty years' purchase, and to coin notes to the value of that amount, and advance them to the owner of the land. This plan, though absurd, had a limit. It was bounded, in the first instance, by the value of the land, expressed in silver money : but Chamberlain's had positively no limit at all to carry it out to its full length : the advance might be made to infinity : consequently, in mathematical language we should say that Chamberlain was *infinitely* more mad than Law.

9. Law showed that notes issued upon Chamberlain's plan would immediately fall to a heavy discount : but yet he says that though £500 of these notes were only equal to £100 in silver, yet the nation would have the same advantage by that £500 in notes as if an addition of £100 had been made to the silver money.

'*So far as these bills fall under the Value of silver money, so far would Exchange with other countries be raised.* And if goods did not keep their price, i.e. if they did not sell for a greater quantity of these bills, equal to the difference betwixt them and silver, goods exported would be undervalued, and goods imported would be overvalued.

'The landed man would have no advantage by this proposal, unless he owed debt, for though he received £50 of these bills for the same quantity of victuals he was in use to receive £10 silver money : yet that £50 would only be equal in value to £10

II.　　　　　　　　　　　X

of silver, and purchase only the same quantity of home or foreign goods.

'The landed man who had his rent paid him in money would be a great loser, for, by as much as these bills were under the value of silver, he would receive so much less than before.

'The landed man who owed debt would pay his debt with a less value than was contracted for, but the creditor would lose what the debtor gained.'

This passage is the first that we are aware of in which the great principle that a Depreciation of the Paper Currency would produce a Fall in the Foreign Exchanges, which was so ardently contested in 1811 and subsequent years, is asserted. And it has all the more merit that it is a *prediction* and not an *observation*.

10. Law then says—'Notwithstanding any Act of Parliament to force these bills, they would fall much under the value of silver: but allowing that they were at first equal to silver, it is next to impossible that two different species of money shall continue equal in value to one another.

'Everything receives a value from its use, and the value is rated according to its Quality, Quantity and Demand.

'And as he leaves it to the choice of the debtor to pay in silver money or bills, he confines the value of the bills to the value of the silver money, but cannot confine the value of the silver money to the value of the bills, so that these bills must fall in value as silver money falls, and may fall lower, may rise above the value of these bills, but these bills cannot rise above the value of silver.'

Law succeeds with great skill and acumen in exposing the wild insanity of Chamberlain's plan, and truly predicts the results which would follow from it, or at least some of them, for there are many important ones he has omitted. The exact consequences which he predicted were manifested in Ireland and England a century later: and the sentences we have quoted, if we did not know their origin, might have been supposed to have been written to rebuke the folly of the Directors of the Banks of Ireland and England, and the mercantile witnesses of 1804 and 1810. But, having demolished Chamberlain, he comes to his own proposal, which he says is '**to make money of land** equal to its value, and that money to be equal in value to silver money, and not liable to fall in value as silver money falls.'

He then says—'**Any Goods that have the Qualities necessary in money, may be made Money equal to their value.**' Five ounces of gold is equal in value to £20, and may be made money to that value: an acre of land rented at two bolls of victual, the victual at £8, and land at twenty years' purchase, is equal to £20, and may be made money equal to that value, for it has all the Qualities necessary in money.'

11. In this sentence is concentrated the whole essence of that eternal delusion, so specious and so plausible, and so fatal, which we designate **Lawism**. It is indeed nothing but the stupendous fallacy *that Money represents commodities, and that Paper Currency may be based upon commodities.* Now the great fundamental doctrine established by Turgot was that *money does not represent commodities at all.* **Money** *represents only* **Debt**, *or services due, which have not yet received their equivalent in commodities.* The least consideration will show that Law's theory of Paper Money involves this extraordinary doctrine, that *a person can have the commodity, and also its price in money as well.*

If a person has a quantity of money, it shows that he has done services for which he has received no equivalent: that the world, in fact, is in debt to him: but when he satisfies any desire, he has, by buying something with his money, received an equivalent: his debt is paid: the world no longer owes him anything. And it is quite clear that he cannot buy the commodity, receive the satisfaction, and have the price of it as well. This is, as we have observed before, to pour fresh Quantities of Stuff, or Material, into the Channel of Circulation, which is already full: all the portion of the existing currency composed of gold or silver will fly away abroad; and there will be nothing but Paper, which cannot be exported; and will be depreciated in proportion to the increased issues of it. The necessary and inevitable consequence, then, of issuing vast quantities of Paper Money on the assumed value of property, is simply to cause a total subversion of the foundation of all value, and of all property, and to plunge every creditor into irretrievable ruin. The only result of such an attempt carried out into practice must be the most tremendous convulsions, and destruction of Credit and all monetary contracts.

Law saw through and exposed the wild absurdity of Chamberlain's plan. His own was that the value of all the land in Scotland should be estimated at 20 years' purchase, and that a parliamentary commission should be appointed, with power to issue Paper Money to that amount. He says—'**The paper money proposed will be equal in value to silver,** *for it will have a value in land pledged equal to the same sum of silver money that it is given out for.* . . . **This Paper Money will not fall in value as silver money has fallen or may fall.**'

12. Law therefore did not advocate unlimited issue of Paper Money. Quite the reverse. But, seeing that convertible Paper Currency could only be based upon bullion to a certain limited extent, preserving its equality in value with bullion, his idea was to base a **Paper Money** upon some other article of value. And he thought it would preserve its equality in value with silver on an independent basis. He thought it was only necessary to make it represent some article of value. But this attempt was contrary to the very nature of things. His Paper Money, though avowedly based upon things of value, had exactly the same practical effect as if it had been based upon silver. It became redundant, and swamped everything; as may be clearly seen from the reasons we have given.

13. To give a full account of Law's banking career in France would far exceed our limits, and to give an imperfect one would be of no use. We must therefore content ourselves with referring those of our readers who want information on the subject to our *Dictionary of Political Economy*, Art. *Banking in France,* where a full account of Law's scheme is given. His career, like his writings, is divided into two parts. His writings are on Banking and **Paper Credit**: and his scheme of **Paper Money**; which are quite distinct from each other. Nothing can be sounder or more judicious than the first. He clearly saw that Paper Credit must be limited by specie—his scheme was to create a **Paper**

Money beyond the limits of Paper Credit, based upon specie, which he expected would maintain an equality of value with specie. Multitudes of people have thought the same, and multitudes of people believe in it to the present hour. In 1705, the Parliament of Scotland fortunately turned a deaf ear to Law's specious proposal of creating Paper Money based upon land : and this country learned wisdom at the expense of their neighbours.

Nothing could be more extraordinary than the restoration of prosperity caused by the foundation of Law's Bank in 1716. It is probably one of the most marvellous transitions from the depth of misery to the height of prosperity, in so short a space of time, in the annals of any nation. And if Law had confined himself to that, he would have been one of the greatest benefactors any nation ever had. It was only when, after three years, he had attained the very pinnacle of success, that he determined to carry out his scheme of **Paper Money**, which was the famous Mississippi scheme.

Examples of **Paper Money** *based upon* **Land**

14. The next example of Lawism was the Ayr Bank. The proprietors of this Bank were enormously wealthy, and, because they were so, they thought that their known wealth would sustain the credit of any amount of paper issues. But their experience too fully verified the sagacity of the directors of the Bank of Scotland, who, in 1727, in answer to a proposal for enlarging their Credit, said—'For the quota of Credit in a banking company must be proportionate to the stock of Specie in the nation, learnt and understood by long experience, and not extended to a capital stock subscribed for, which cannot in the least help to support the company's Credit, if the Specie of the nation decay.' This doctrine contains the refutation of many wild schemes, and the true plan of regulating a Paper Currency is simply to discover how a certain proportion shall be maintained between Specie and Credit.

15. The third great outburst of Lawism took place in the same country that witnessed his first exploits. In preparation for it, Law's 'Money and Trade Considered' was translated into French in 1789, as if all the memory of the great catastrophe sixty-nine years before had perished. The National Assembly had confiscated the property of the Church, valued at £80,000,000, but, instead of yielding a revenue, it cost the nation £2,000,000 a year more than it produced. At last it became necessary to sell it : but no purchasers could be found, for all persons in that terrible political earthquake wished to have their property in as portable a shape as possible, and few were willing to trust to a revolutionary title. In this dilemma, the municipalities agreed to purchase a considerable portion of it, in the first instance, and resell it in smaller portions to individuals. But, as there was not specie enough to complete the sale, they issued their promissory notes to the public creditor, to pass current until the time of payment came : but, when they became due, the municipalities had no means of discharging them. To meet them the Assembly, in the spring of 1790, authorised the issue of £16,000,000, and in September £32,000,000 of assignats on the security of land. Talleyrand opposed the new issues, and predicted their depreciation : but Mirabeau supported them, and denied the possibility of their depreciation.—'It is vain to assimilate assignats secured on the solid basis of these domains to an ordinary Paper Currency possessing a forced circulation. They represent real property, the most secure of all possessions, the land upon which we tread. Why is a metallic circulation solid? Because it is based upon subjects of real and durable value, as the land, which is directly or indirectly the source of all wealth. Paper Money, we are told, will become superabundant : it will drive the metallic coin out of circulation. Of what paper do you speak? If of a paper without a solid basis, undoubtedly : if of one based on the firm foundation of landed property, never. There may be a difference in the value of a circulation of different kinds : but that arises as frequently from the one which bears the higher value being run after as from the one which stands the lower being shunned—from gold being in demand—not paper at a discount. There cannot be a greater error than the terrors so generally prevalent as to the over-issue of assignats. It is thus alone you will pay your debts, pay your troops, advance the revolution. Re-absorbed progressively in the purchase of the national domains, this Paper Money can never become redundant; any more than the humidity of the atmosphere can become excessive, which descends in rills, finds the river, and is at length lost in the mighty ocean.'

16. The assignats bore 4 per cent. interest, but they speedily began to depreciate; and by June 1791 they had lost one-third of their value. In September 1792 further issues were decreed. Out of assignats to the value of £130,000,000 created, only about £12,000,000 remained unspent. In 1793 the Convention decreed six years' imprisonment in chains to anyone who bought or sold assignats for any sum in specie different to their nominal value, or made any difference between a Money price and a Paper price in payment of goods. But in vain: in June the assignats had lost two-thirds of their value, and in August five-sixths. The exchange with London fell exactly in a corresponding ratio with the depreciation of the assignat at home. In June 1791 it fell to 23: in January 1792 to 18: in March 1793 to 14: in June 1793 to 10: on the 2nd of August to $4\frac{1}{4}$: and soon after ceased to be quoted at all. Cambon, the Minister of Finance, proposed a further issue to the value of £33,000,000: the public domains he calculated at £350,000,000. Hence, upon the theory of Law and Mirabeau, there was an ample margin, and the assignats should not have depreciated below the value of silver, and in fact, according to them, it was impossible they should. Wonderful commentary upon the wisdom of the philosophers who maintain that if a Paper Currency only represents *value*, it cannot be depreciated.

We must refrain from detailing the terrible misery caused by the forcible issue of assignats which were legal tender at their nominal amount, the destruction of debts, the famine from the scarcity of provisions, the laws of the maximum, the penalty of death enacted against all who should keep back their produce from the market. All specie disappeared from the country, and from circulation: those who possessed any, not deeming it secure from revolutionary violence, exported it to London, Hamburg, Amsterdam, and Geneva. But many persons stoutly maintained in pamphlets that it was not the Paper which was depreciated, but the specie which had risen.

The intolerable misery caused by this state of things induced the Government which succeeded the reign of Terror to make an attempt to withdraw a portion of the assignats from circulation by *demonetising* them: that is, depriving them of their quality of money, and forcing their holders to receive payment in land for them. But when a man wanted to buy food to eat, what was the use of giving him land? The report that a portion of the assignats were going to be demonetised, sent down their value still lower: and a decree against it was obliged to be passed to appease their holders. All sorts of plans were devised to withdraw them from circulation: lotteries, tontines, a land bank, where they were to be lodged and bear 3 per cent. interest. But the constant issue of them, required for the necessary payments of the State, rendered all such attempts useless.

In January 1796 the assignats in circulation amounted to 45 milliards, or about £2,000,000,000, and the paper money had fallen to the one-thousandth part of its nominal value. The Government then determined to issue *territorial mandates*, at the rate of 30 assignats to one mandate, which were to be exchangeable directly for land at the will of the holder on demand. The certainty of obtaining land for them made them rise for a short time to 80 per cent. of their nominal value: but necessity compelled the Government to issue £100,000,000 of these mandates, secured upon land, supposed to be of that value. This prodigious issue sent the mandates down to nearly the same discount as the assignats were, and consequently, as one mandate was equal to 30 assignats, the latter had fallen to nearly the one thirty-thousandth part of their nominal value. At length, on the 16th July, 1796, the whole system was demolished at a blow. A decree was published that everyone might transact business in the money he chose, and that mandates should only be taken at their current value, which should be published every day at the Treasury. Two days afterwards it was decreed that the national property remaining undisposed of should be sold for mandates at their current value. The public creditors received payment of their debts in the same proportion.

No sooner, however, was the great blow struck at the Paper Currency of making it pass at its current value, than specie immediately re-appeared in circulation. Immense hoards came forth from their hiding places: goods and commodities of all sorts being very cheap from the anxiety of their owners to possess money, caused immense sums to be imported from foreign countries. The exchanges immediately turned in favour of France, and in a short time a metallic currency was permanently restored. And during all the terrific wars of Napoleon the metallic standard was always maintained at its full value.

Such is a plain statement, founded upon incontrovertible facts, of the results of the greatest experiment the world had yet seen, of issuing a Paper Currency secured upon land, and a practical result of **Lawism**. When the issues of assignats were at their height, they were certainly not anything equal to the value of the fee simple of the land they were based upon, expressed in silver money. And according to the predictions of Law and Mirabeau, it was impossible that they should ever become depreciated; and what was the result? Even though the experiment was not carried out to its fullest extent, the value of the paper assignat sank to one 30,000th part of its value in silver! There were 2,400 millions of promises of mandates issued against property valued at 3,785 millions, and yet in July 1796, the note for 100 livres was worth only 5 centimes! Such was the inevitable consequence of basing a Paper Money upon land, and such it ever must be, because, if such issues are once begun, there is no legitimate conclusion whatever until all the land in the country is coined into notes. Pass the legitimate limits of a circulating medium by one hair's-breadth, and there is no logical conclusion but in the French assignats.

17. The next example we shall cite is the Bank of Norway, which was founded in 1816 at Drontheim, with branches in the provinces. This Bank was especially founded to forward improvements in agriculture. Its principal business consisted in advancing its own inconvertible notes, upon first securities on land, to an amount not exceeding two-thirds of the value of the property according to a general valuation taken in the year 1812. The borrower paid half-yearly to the Bank the interest of the sum that was at his debit, at the rate of 4 per cent. per annum, and was bound also to pay off 5 per cent. yearly of the principal, which was thus liquidated in twenty years. Mr. Laing bestows great commendation on this institution, and describes it as well imagined and well managed, and there cannot be a better example to test the truth of Law's principles. We must bear in mind that Law especially maintains that on his principle *his Paper Money could not fall below the value of silver*. We shall now observe what took place with regard to this Bank, which was founded purely on his principle. By the fundamental law of this Bank it should, after a certain time, have begun to pay its notes in specie : but in 1822 they could only be exchanged at Hamburg for silver at the rate of 187½ paper dollars for 100 silver dollars ! That is, in six years, the notes had fallen to about 45 per cent. discount ! Was there ever a more striking and conclusive example of the entire fallacy of Law's predictions than this Bank ? In 1822 the Storthing passed a law that the Bank should only be compelled to give 100 silver dollars for every 190 paper dollars : but that the directors might at their own discretion reduce the rate to 175 without a new law. In 1824 the value of the notes at Hamburg rose to 145 : in 1827 it rose to 125 : and in 1835, when Mr. Laing wrote, it stood at 112 : which could only have been done by a contraction of its issues. It is clear that if the Bank had been called upon to pay its notes at par at any moment, it would have stopped payment. This happened at Paris, in 1803, when the Land Bank failed, and J. B. Say observes that all Banks founded upon this principle have uniformly failed.

Now, as we have seen in a former chapter that the Land Banks of Germany have produced the most wonderful effects in that country, and yet caused no derangement of the circulating medium, we must point out the difference between them. The Bank of Norway made all its advances in its Notes, which circulated as **Money** ; and therefore were at once thrown into the channel of circulation : the notes became redundant, and so fell to a discount : the German Land Banks made their advances in **Bonds**, which did not circulate generally as Money ; though no doubt they may have been used in particular instances to pay debts with, just as stock is here : the advances of the German Bank were advances of **Stock**, not of **Money** ; and hence they did not enter into the general channel of circulation : and did not come into general competition with Money. They were used as **Investments**, and not as **Money**.

On Issuing **Paper Money** on **Securities**.

18. We have given some examples of the failure of Law's theory of issuing Paper Money on the security of Land. There is one species of property, however, which, from its being more nearly confounded with money in the public ideas than any other, is supposed by many persons, who would repudiate any imputation of being disciples of Law, to be a sound basis for a Paper Currency. This property is Public Stock. A very prevalent idea is that all Banks of Issue should give security by purchasing the Public Funds, and then deposit this stock with a Government office. But what is this but the plainest, rankest, and most odious **Lawism**? The rule that is good for one is good for all. If the public funds are a proper basis for £1,000 of Paper Currency, they must be equally a good basis to their whole extent. If one bank or banker may issue Paper on the security of Stock, why should not every other bank and banker do the same, until the whole funded debt of Great Britain is coined into Paper? If £100 of public debt is coined into £100 of notes, we must by an irresistible conclusion have £800,000,000 of Stock coined into £800,000,000 of Notes. The principles of basing a Paper Currency upon Land and upon the Public Funds are absolutely identical, and equally vicious ; and if carried out to their legitimate lengths would produce equal monetary convulsions. To permit a man to spend his money in buying part of the Public Debt, and to have it also in the form of Notes, is as rank an absurdity as to permit him to spend it in Land, and to have it also as Notes, and would lead to exactly the same results.

As a practical example of the results of this plan, we may cite the case of America. That country was unhappily deeply bitten with the Currency mania of basing issues of Paper on Securities. In most of the States the Legislature passed Acts permitting any individual or bank to issue Notes to any amount upon depositing with a Public Comptroller Securities of equivalent value. These Securities might be public Stock, or mortgages upon improved, productive, and unencumbered lands. These Securities remained the property of the vendors, and they might appropriate the revenues from them, as long as payment of the Notes was not demanded from the Comptroller; and people saw that they might derive a profit from the security as well as from the Notes which represented its value. There was accordingly a prodigious rush to deposit securities—an enormous issue of Notes during 1834-5-6. The prices of everything rose enormously. The people of the Western States with their pockets full of these Notes, gave large orders for goods to the merchants of New York, Boston, and Philadelphia, who duly executed them. The bills given for the purchases were payable in these eastern cities, and when the western debtors went to their own bankers for bills on these places, in return for their local Notes, the bankers discovered that their home customers had bought more from the eastern cities than they had sold: that they had already drawn on the east for every dollar which the east was indebted to them, and could draw no more. The western merchants then sent their own local notes to the eastern cities in payment, but, unfortunately for them, the merchants there had already paid all they owed to the west, and nobody in New York or Philadelphia wanted western notes for any purpose of use ; and no one was disposed to travel 600 or 700 miles to request the cashiers of the western States to pay their notes: or in those States in which security had been given to require the Comptroller to sell the pledged securities and pay them the money produce. Moreover, everyone knew that it was physically impossible in either case to obtain the amount in money, for there was no money in which the pledged property when sold could have been paid, except Bank Notes resting on securities, or on the mere promise of the banker. During this time specie disappeared from circulation. The extended paper issues led the Americans to order immense quantities of goods from Europe, and, prices being very high from the bloated paper currency, they could send no goods in return to pay for them. For some time they sent over great quantities of their stock, but this became superabundant, and at last no one in Europe would buy it. It then became necessary for them to pay their debts in specie: but specie there was none. In 1837 all the Banks in America, without exception, stopped payment. The general suspension began at New York on the 11th May, and spread in every direction. In May

1838 the New York banks resumed payments in specie, which were followed by all the New England banks in August 1838. On the 1st January, 1839, all the banks in the Union professed to do so. No sooner, however, were they set up again than they resumed the same wild operations on Credit, and on the 9th October, 1839, out of 850 banks in the Union, 343 suspended payment entirely and 62 partially. The United States Bank, with a paid-up capital of £7,000,000, was found to be utterly insolvent. This was the result of the principles of Law applied to issuing Paper Notes based upon Securities.

19. What, then, is the only true foundation of a Paper Currency? Every consideration of sound reasoning and science proves that the only true foundation of a Paper Currency is that substance which is the legal or the universally accepted representative of **Debt**: i.e. of services due, whatever that substance may be. Now, among all civilised nations, gold or silver bullion is the acknowledged representative of **Debt**. Consequently, gold or silver bullion is the only true basis of a Paper Currency. Among all civilised nations the *weight of bullion is the acknowledged measure of value*: and consequently bullion is the only true basis of the 'promises to pay.' Many unthinking persons declaim against the absurdity of founding a Paper Currency upon the **Commodity** of gold bullion rather than upon any other commodity, such as wheat, or silk, or sugar. But it is not as a **Commodity** that bullion is the basis of a Paper Currency, but as the substance which is the acknowledged representative of **Debt**. It would be perfectly possible to make a yard of broadcloth, or a Dutch cheese, the symbol of Debt and the measure of value: then broadcloth or Dutch cheeses would be the only true basis of a Paper Currency: and to issue Paper upon the basis of bullion would in such a case be as improper as to issue Paper on the bases of broadcloth or Dutch cheeses, under existing circumstances. But all nations are agreed that Bullion is better fitted by nature for such a purpose than broadcloth or Dutch cheeses: and, consequently, as it seems to be the substance pointed out by nature itself for representing Debt, it is the substance which is the only true basis of a Paper Currency.

CHAPTER XIV

ON THE DEFINITION OF CURRENCY

1. HAVING completed a general survey of the mechanism of Exchanges, inland and foreign, we must now examine the peculiar system of Banking which is at present established in this country. But we must first explain more fully than we have done the meaning of the word **Currency** : because the whole system of Banking devised by Sir Robert Peel is based upon a peculiar Definition of the word Currency : and it is expressly intended to carry out a peculiar Theory of Currency.

We have already in Chapter I. given a short account of the meaning of the word Currency : but we must now repeat it a little more fully : and explain the meaning of the word as maintained by those who devised the Bank Act of 1844.

The word Currency originated in certain laws of our Saxon ancestors. They utterly discountenanced and prohibited the sale or exchange of any goods, merchandise, or cattle by private bargain. It was their fixed policy that no sales should take place except in the presence of witnesses. A series of laws were made by the Saxon kings, extending from 683 A.D. to the Conquest, that no sale was valid unless effected in ' Port,' that is, in Market overt.

These ancient dooms are the Common Law of England at the present hour. If any person finds or steals any chattel belonging to another person, and sells it privately to a third person, the true owner may recover it from that third person, even though he bought it honestly, and gave full value for it, and had no suspicion it was stolen. The Law holds in general that no one can sell anything to which he has no right : and it does not allow that the true owner has lost his Property in the chattel or goods, because he may have accidentally mislaid or lost them, or had them stolen from him : it is the *jus vindicandi*.

If, however, the thief or finder managed to sell the goods in market overt, the buyer is allowed in Common Law to retain them against the true owner.

Thus, in *Every Man in his Humour*, when Down-right claims his cloak, Stephen mendaciously says—

> Your cloak, Sir! I bought it even now in Open Market.

But by Stat. 24 & 25 Vict. (1861), c. 96, § 100, it is enacted that, if the true owner prosecutes the thief to conviction, the Court may grant a writ of summary restitution to the true owner, so that he may recover them, even though the purchaser bought them in market overt.

Such is the Law with regard to all kinds of goods, merchandise, and cattle. But with regard to **Money** the case was always different. If a person found or stole money belonging to anyone else, the true owner could compel him to give it up if he could prove the fact. But if the finder or thief paid away the money in the ordinary course of business, as if a shopkeeper sold goods to the thief and took the money in the usual way, and without knowing it had been stolen, he could retain it against the true owner, even though he could identify it. That is to say, *the Property in the money passed along with the honest possession* in every sale or exchange.

From this peculiarity money was said to be **Current**, i.e. the Property in it passed by delivery. This was necessary by the very nature of money : because no transaction could take place if the seller was bound in every sale to inquire into the right of the buyer to the money. And from this exceptional property the expression arose of the **Currency** of money : but no one for a very long time ever thought of such a barbarism as to call the Money itself Currency.

About the beginning of the last century, by a most extraordinary confusion of ideas, and as far as we have been able to discover, it arose in our American colonies, the Money itself began to be called Currency. This name occurs very rarely in Smith, but since then it has become very common.

To show the extreme absurdity of this name, we have only

to consider a few similar cases. It is quite usual to say that such an opinion or such a report is *Current*: and we speak of the *Currency* of such an opinion or such a report. As Tom Paine says—' I went into the coffee-houses to learn the **Currency** of opinion' But who ever dreamt of calling the report or the opinion itself **Currency**? It is usual to speak of the *Currency* of the session of Parliament: but who ever dreamt of calling the session itself *Currency*?

To call Money itself Currency, because it is current, is as absurd as to call a wheel a *rotation*, because it rotates: or to call a horse a *velocity*, because it gallops.

Such as it is, however, this Yankeeism is far too firmly fixed in common use to be abolished: and hence it must be accepted: and we must endeavour to fix its scientific sense.

Currency, therefore, is not the actual money itself, but a certain attribute appurtenant to money: and when in course of time Bills of Exchange and other securities for money came into use, the custom of merchants, or the *Lex Mercatoria*, applied the same principles of Currency to them as applied to money: that is to say, the *Property in them passed by delivery and honest possession*. Commerce could not have gone on if the vendor of goods had been obliged to inquire into the title of anyone who offered a Bank Note or Bill of Exchange in payment of goods. Consequently the principle of **Currency**, or **Negotiability** as it is called, was applied to all transferable securities for money.

And so important is this principle of the Currency of Securities for money, that in the Statute respecting the restitution of stolen property it is expressly provided that it shall not apply to Negotiable Instruments.

Thus the Law has taken the utmost precaution to preserve the **Negotiability** or **Currency** of all Securities for money, under all circumstances whatever. And if such a barbarism be accepted as to call Money **Currency**, all Securities for money must equally be called **Currency**: because they are all equally subject to the same rule of law from which money derives that name.

To this rule the law has recently made one exception: it is now allowed to write the word *non-negotiable* on cheques: which means that they follow the rule of goods : and that the transferee has no better title than the transferor.

2. This doctrine is so important that we may refer to a few cases. In the case of *Miller* v. *Race* (1 *Burr.* 452) a Bank Note had been stolen and came into the possession of Miller honestly, in the course of business. The true owner stopped the Note at the Bank, and Miller brought an action against Race, a clerk in the Bank, who detained the Note, and refused to pay it. Lord Mansfield ruled, with the concurrence of the Court, that Miller had the right to have the note given back to him as his property, 'because Bank Notes have the Credit and Currency of Money to all intents and purposes. An action would lie against the finder : that no one disputed : but *not after the note had been paid away in* **Currency**. An action did not lie against a person who took a Bank Note in the course of **Currency**. A Bank Note is constantly and universally, both at home and abroad, treated as Money or Cash : and it is necessary for the purpose of commerce that their **Currency** should be established and maintained.'

In the case of *Grant* v. *Vaughan* (3 *Burr.* 1516) it was held that the same rule applies to Cheques, which are the same as Bank Notes.

In *Peacock* v. *Rhodes* (2 *Doug.* 633) Lord Mansfield applied the same rule to Bills of Exchange : he said 'the holder of a Bill of Exchange or Promissory Note is not to be considered in the light of an assignee of the payee. An assignee must take the thing assigned subject to all the equity to which the original party was subject. If this rule applied to Bills and Promissory notes it would stop their **Currency**. The law is settled that a holder coming fairly by a Note or Bill has nothing to do with the transaction between the original parties : I see no difference between a Note indorsed blank and one payable to bearer. *They both go by delivery, and possession proves property in both cases.*'

So in *Collins* v. *Martin* (1 B. & P. 648), Eyre, C. J., said— 'for the purpose of rendering Bills of Exchange negotiable, the Right of Property in them passes with the bills. Every holder of the bills takes the property, and his title is stamped upon the bills themselves. The Property and the Possession are inseparable.'

In *Gorgier* v. *Mieville* (3 B. & C. 45), it was held that 'a foreign bond is in its nature precisely analogous to a Bank Note payable to bearer, or a bill of exchange indorsed in blank. Being an instrument therefore of the same description, it must be subject to the same rules of law, that whoever is the holder of it has power to give title to any person honestly acquiring it.'

In *Wokey* v. *Pole* (4 B. & *Ald.* 1), the same principle was held to apply to Exchequer Bills. Best, J., said—' The question which the Court is called to decide is whether Exchequer Bills are to be considered as **Goods**, or as the **Representatives of Money** : and as such subject to the same rules as to the transfer of the Property in them as are applicable to money. The delivery of goods by a person who is not the owner, except in a manner authorised by the owner, does not transfer the right to such goods : but it has long been settled that the right to money is inseparable from the possession of it . . . . It was given for a Debt due to Government, it is payable (the blank not being filled up) to bearer, and transferable by delivery, and is on its face made **Current**, and to pass in any of the public revenues or at the receipt of the Exchange.

Holroyd, J.—' It has long been fully settled that bank notes or bills, drafts on bankers, bills of exchange or promissory notes, either payable to order and indorsed in blank, or payable to bearer, when taken *bonâ fide* and for a valuable consideration, pass by delivery and vest a right thereto in the transferee without regard to the title, or want of title, in the person transferring them. . . . These cases have proceeded on the nature and effect of the instruments which have been considered as distinguishable from goods. In the case of goods, the property, except in market overt, can only be transferred by the owner, or by some person having either an express or implied authority from him : and no one can, by his contract or delivery, transfer more than his own right, or the right of him under whose authority he acts. But the Courts have considered these instruments, either promises or orders for the payment of money or instrument entitling the holder to a sum of money, as appendages to money, and following the nature of their principal.

.... These authorities show that not only money itself may pass and the right to it may arise by **Currency** alone ; but further that these mercantile instruments which entitle the bearer of them to money may also pass, and the right to them may arise, in the like manner, by **Currency** or **Delivery**. These decisions proceed upon the nature of the property (viz. money) to which such instruments give the right, and which is itself **Current** : and the effect of the instruments which either give to their holders merely as such, the right to receive the money, or specify them as the person entitled to receive it. The question then is, whether these principles apply to the present case, or whether this exchequer bill and the right thereto, follow the nature of goods, which, except in market overt, can only be transferred by the owner, or under his authority? In order to ascertain that, we must consider the nature and effect of the instrument, both as to the property which it concerns, and as to its **Negotiability** or **Currency** by law. . . . The instrument is created by the Statute, and is thereby made **Negotiable** and **Current** . ... in it are these words— "And for the better supporting the **Currency** of the said exchequer bills, and to the end that a sufficient provision may be made for circulating and exchanging the same for ready money, during such time as they or any of them are to be **Current**, the Commissioners of the Treasury are empowered to contract with persons who will undertake to circulate and exchange them for ready money." An exchequer bill is therefore an instrument for the repayment of money originally advanced to the public, purporting thereby to entitle the bearer to receive the money put into circulation, and made **Current** by Law. It is not, therefore, like goods saleable only in market overt, and not otherwise transferable, except by the owner or under his authority, but is in all those several respects similar to bills of exchange and promissory notes, and transferable in the same manner as they are. The case, therefore, stands thus. This Exchequer bill was a **Current** and **Negotiable** Instrument for the payment of money. Now, money passes from one person to another by reason of its **Currency**, and for that reason only, and not because it has no ear mark, it cannot be recovered from the person to whom it has been passed. The exchequer bill therefore seems to me upon the same principle to follow the nature of the money for which it is a security . . . . This, like the case of a bill indorsed in blank, is payable to bearer, where the right arises from the instrument itself, and it is not necessary to deduce the title through the intermediate holders.'

In *Ingham* v. *Primrose* (7 C. B. N. S. 85) Williams, J., said—' It is, we think, settled law that if the defendant had drawn a cheque, and before he had issued it, he had lost it, or had it stolen from him, and it had afterwards found its way into the hands of a holder for value without notice, who had sued the defendant upon it, he would have had no answer to the action. So if he had indorsed a bill in blank or a bill payable to his order, and it had been lost or stolen before he delivered it to anyone as indorsee. The reason is that such Negotiable Instruments have by the law merchant become part of the **Mercantile Currency** of the country : and in order that this may not be impeded, it is requisite that innocent holders for value should have a right to enforce payment of them against those who, by making them, have caused them to be a part *of the* **Currency**.'

In *Shute* v. *Robins* (1 M. & M. 133), Lord Tenterden spoke of banker's paper as being part of the **Circulating Medium** of the country.

3. We have thus laid before our readers an authoritative exposition of the true Legal meaning of the word **Currency**, and the subjects which are included in it. We see by a series of legal decisions, which are now the established Law of the country, that the word **Currency** simply means **Negotiability**, and nothing else : that the honest possession and the property of these things which possess this attribute are inseparable, contrary to the general principles of the common law regarding stolen goods, merchandise, and cattle. And this exceptional class includes Money and Securities for money of all sorts : and also Post Office Orders and Postage Stamps.

In strict legal phraseology the word **Currency** can only be applied to those Rights which are recorded on some material. An abstract Right cannot be lost or mislaid, stolen, and passed away in commerce. But if it is recorded on some material substance, it may be lost, stolen, and sold like any other material substance: and the word **Currency**, then, simply refers to some legal rules relating to the transfer of the property in it, in the case of its being stolen and passed away in commerce. For an Obligation to be **Currency** in law, it must be recorded on some material, so as to be capable of being carried in the hand, or put away in a drawer, and dropped in the street, and stolen from the drawer, or from a man's pocket, and carried off by the finder, or thief, and sold like a piece of goods. The word **Currency** has no reference whatever to any property it has of paying, discharging, and closing debts.

4. So far all is clear: but when we use the word Currency as a scientific term in Economics, synonymous with Circulating Medium, a difficulty arises: because there is a vast mass of Credit, or Rights, which are not embodied in any material instrument, and which therefore cannot be lost or stolen, or passed away in commerce, without the owner's consent: and consequently, though these cannot be subject to the legal rules of **Currency**, they perform a gigantic part in commerce, in every way as if they were recorded on paper.

Taking a banker and his customer as the standard case of Debtor and Creditor; If I have a Right of action against my banker for money, it makes not the slightest difference in the nature of the Right whether it is recorded on paper or not. If I wish to transfer the right to some one else, I may do it by means of a Bank Note or Cheque, or a verbal order to my banker to transfer a certain quantity of the Credit in my name to some one else's name. We have seen that in Roman and English Law the Creditor, the Debtor, and the Transferee might meet, and the Creditor transferred the Debt orally to the Transferee. Whether the Right is transferred orally or in writing can make no possible difference in the nature of the Right. Consequently, if I have a Right against my banker, and if I write a Cheque for the purpose of transferring this Right to some one else, this does not affect the nature of the existing Right: it is nothing more than a convenient way of transferring it to some one else. Writing a Cheque does not create a new Right: it merely records on paper an existing Right: and it equally exists whether it is recorded on paper or not. Payment, therefore, by means of a Bank Note, a Cheque, or a Bank Credit, is absolutely the same. Now Bank Notes and Cheques are Currency in strict legal phraseology : but Bank Credits are not legal Currency, because they cannot be lost, mislaid, stolen, and passed away in commerce, without the consent of the owner.

So also of a Book Credit or Book Debt in a tradesman's books. If I buy goods from a tradesman on Credit, that Credit has performed exactly the same part in **Circulating** the goods as money : because we have expressly defined Circulation to be the sale of goods for Money or Credit : and the Credit has been equally the medium of Circulation, or Sale, whether it is recorded on paper or not : but it is not legal **Currency**, because it cannot be dropped in the streets, stolen, and transferred to some one else by manual delivery.

So also with Verbal Credits between individuals : the Right exists exactly the same whether it exists merely as an abstract Right or is recorded in a book or on paper.

If, then, we are compelled to adopt this barbarism, and employ the word **Currency** as a scientific term, it must most manifestly be extended to include Bank Credits or Deposits, Book Credits, and Verbal Credits of all descriptions.

And this is exactly what Mercantile Law does. It treats any form of Credit payable by a banker on demand, as money or cash, whether it is a Bank Note, a Cheque, or Bank Credit. They are all Payment equally in law : none of them are legal money : that is, a Debtor cannot compel his Creditor to take them in payment of a Debt : but if he chooses to do so without objection, they all stand on exactly the same footing as Payment. A Cheque operates as payment until it has been presented and refused. So if a person agrees to have a sum placed to the Credit of his account, that is the same thing as if he had been paid in money. Thus, though in a *legal* sense only Bank Notes and Cheques can be **Currency** : yet in a scientific sense Bank Credits are equally **Currency**.

So in Law Bank Credits are always treated as 'ready money.' It has been held that Bank Credits pass under the terms 'moneys in hand,' 'ready money,' 'moneys' in a will, in several decisions.

The importance and the practical bearing of these decisions are evident. In modern times private bankers discontinued issuing notes, and merely created Credits or Deposits, to be circulated by Cheques. Now many persons, seeing a material Bank Note, which is only a Right recorded on paper, are willing to admit that a Bank Note is cash : but from a want of a little reflection, they feel a difficulty with regard to Deposits. They admit that a Bank Note is an **Issue** and **Currency** and **Circulation,** but they fail to see that a Bank Credit is exactly in the same sense equally an **Issue, Currency**, and **Circulation.**

When a banker, in exchange for money, or in exchange for a Bill of Exchange, gives his Notes to his customers, he creates and **Issues** a Right of action against himself which the customer may transfer to anyone else. But when a banker, in exchange for money and bills of exchange, creates a Credit in his books in his customer's favour, he equally creates and **Issues** a Right of action against himself : and by delivering a cheque-book to his customer, he thereby engages to pay the Credit to anyone else to whom his customer may transfer it. Either form of Credit, therefore, is equally the **Issue** of a Right of action to the customer. He has exactly the same right to demand payment of his Credit from the banker, and exactly the same right to transfer it to anyone else, whether it be by Note or Cheque.

Some persons see only so many figures in a book: they are startled at hearing them called Wealth : but, in fact, these figures are only the evidence of so many transferable Rights of action as the banker's Creditors. These Rights are as much **Issued** and in **Circulation** as if they were Notes. They are equally liabilities to pay on demand. It is doubtless usual in banking accounts to distinguish between Notes and Credits. But, if they are simply called Liabilities, cannot everyone see that they stand on exactly the same footing?

Thus these Bank Credits, or Deposits, are a mass of Property, just like so much corn or timber : they are *Pecunia, Bona, Res, Merx*; they are now, though of course legally only Debts, for all practical purposes the current coin of commerce : and the great medium of payment of the country : and specie is now only used occasionally, and as a supplement to payments in Credits of different forms. All these Credits are, in the ordinary language and practice of commerce, exactly equal to so much Cash or Currency.

Lord Overstone's Doctrines *of* **Currency**

5. After the authoritative exposition we have given of the real meaning of the word Currency, and the judicial decisions of what it includes, it is rather a work of supererogation to cite the opinions of lay writers. The controversies as to the meaning of Currency did not arise until Smith had been several years in his grave. However, Bills of Exchange are evidently included under his designation of Paper Money.

Some time afterwards, however, great differences of opinion arose as to what Currency is : whether it includes Bills of Exchange and Cheques and Deposits. However, we shall pass over all these controversies until we come to the opinions of Lord Overstone and his school, because it is their doctrines which were adopted by Sir Robert Peel, and his Bank Charter Act of 1844 was expressly designed to carry out their theories.

It will be better to let Lord Overstone speak for himself. He said to the Committee of the House of Commons in 1840—

2655. What is it that you include in the term Circulation ? —I include in the term Circulation metallic Coin, and Paper Notes promising to pay the metallic Coin to bearer on demand.

2661. In your definition, then, of the word Circulation, you do not include Deposits ?—No, I do not.

2662. Do you include Bills of Exchange ?—No, I do not.

2663. Why do you not include Deposits in your definition of Circulation ?

To answer that question, I believe I must be allowed to revert to first principles. The precious metals are distributed to the different countries of the world by the operation of particular laws which have been investigated and are now well recognised. These laws allot to each country a certain portion of the precious metals, which, while other things remain unchanged, remains itself unchanged. The precious metals, converted into Coin, constitute the Money of each country. That Coin circulates sometimes in kind : but in highly advanced countries, it is represented to a certain extent by paper notes, promising to pay the Coin to bearer on demand : these Notes being of such a nature in principle that the increase of them supplants coin to an equal amount. Where these Notes are in use, the metallic coin, together with these Notes, constitute the Money or Currency of that country. Now this money is marked by certain distinguishing characteristics: first of all, that its amount is determined by the laws which apportion the precious metals to the different countries of the world: secondly, that it is in every country the common measure of the value of all other commodities, the standard by reference to which the value of every other commodity is ascertained, and every contract fulfilled: and, thirdly, it becomes the common medium of exchange for the adjustment of all transactions *equally at all times, between all persons, and in all places*. Now, I conceive that neither Deposits nor Bills of Exchange, in any way whatever, possess these qualities. In the first place, the amount of them is not determined by the laws which determine the amount of the precious metals in each country: in the second place, they will in no respect serve as a common measure of value, or a standard by reference to which we can measure the relative value of all other commodities: and, in the next place, they do not possess that power of universal exchangeability which belongs to the money of the country.

2664. Why do you not include Bills of Exchange in Circulation?—I exclude Bills of Exchange for precisely the same reason that I have stated in my former answer for excluding deposits.

2667. What are the elements which constitute Money in the sense in which you use the expression 'Quantity of Money'— What is the exact meaning you attach to the words 'Quantity of Money'—'Quantity of Metallic Currency'?—When I use the words, Quantity of Money, I mean the Quantity of Metallic Coin and of Paper Notes promising to pay the Coin on demand, which are in circulation in this country.

2668. Paper Notes payable in Coin?—Yes.
2669. By whomsoever issued?—Yes.
2670. By country banks as well as other banks?—Yes.

At this period, and for a long time preceding, the greatest part of the Circulating Medium of Lancashire were Bills of Exchange, which sometimes had as many as 150 indorsements on them before they came to maturity. Lord Overstone was asked—

3026. Does not the principal Circulation of Lancashire consist of Bills of Exchange ?—As I contend that Bills of Exchange do not form a part of the Circulation, of course I am bound, in answer to that question, to say no.

6. Mr. Hume had a long fencing-match with Lord Overstone as to the distinction between Bank Notes and Deposits. Lord Overstone admitted that a debt might be discharged either by the transfer of a Bank Note or by the transfer of a Credit in the Books of the Bank : but he strongly contended that Bank Notes are Money, and that Bank Credits or Deposits are not.

3148. Do you consider any portion of the Deposits in the Bank of England as money ?—I do not.

3150. Could 20,000 sovereigns have more completely discharged the obligation to pay the £20,000 of bills than the Deposits did?

Where two parties have each an account with a deposit Bank, a transfer of the Credit from one party to the credit of another party may certainly discharge an obligation in the same manner, and to the same extent to which sovereigns would have discharged that Obligation.

3169. Will not the Debt between the two be discharged thereby ?—Yes.

3170. In the one case I have supposed that payment of £1,000 was made by means of notes in circulation : payment was made by the delivery of these notes from one hand to another, and they are transported from place to place : but in the case of a payment made by means of a transfer in the books of the Bank from one account to another, I ask you, are not those payments equally valid, and would not the debt be discharged equally in either case ?—In the one case the Debt has been discharged by the use of money : in the other case the debt has been discharged without the necessity of resorting to the use of money, in consequence of the economising process of deposit business in the Bank of England.

3171. Can the debt of £1,000 which one person owes to another be discharged without money being paid as its value ? —A debt of £1,000 cannot be discharged without, in some way or other, transferring the value of £1,000: but that transfer of value may certainly be effected without the use of money.

3172. Was not the deposit transfer in the Bank of England, to satisfy that debt of £1,000, of the same value as the £1,0co notes which passed in the other case?—A credit in the Bank of England I consider is of the same value as the same nominal amount of money: and if the Credit be transferred, the same value I consider to be transferred as if money of that nominal amount had been transferred.

3178. Have you not said that Deposits do not in any way whatever possess the qualities of money?—If I have said so, I shall be glad to have the statement laid before me.

3179. Have you not, in Q. 2663, enumerated certain distinguishing characteristics of money?—I have.

3180. Have you not in the same question stated that Deposits do not in any way whatever possess those characteristics? —Yes; I have.

3181. Have you not, in answer to previous questions, admitted that, for the discharge of debts, Deposits have the characteristics of money?—All that I have admitted is, I believe, that a deposit may, under certain supposed circumstances, be used to discharge a certain supposed debt.

Lord Overstone also said (3132)—'Will any man in his common senses pretend to say that the total amount of transactions adjusted at the Clearing House are part of the money, or circulating medium, of the country?

Now, of course no one says that a *transaction* is money: but the operations of the Clearing House consist exclusively of the transfers of Bank Credits from one bank to another : and most undoubtedly these Bank Credits are part of the Circulating Medium of the country.

Lastly, we may quote Colonel Torrens, because he was not only one of the most influential of this school, but it has been alleged that he was in reality the author of the scheme which Sir Robert Peel adopted in his Bank Charter Act of 1844. He says—' The terms Money and Currency have hitherto been employed to denote those instruments of exchange which possess intrinsic or derivative value, and by which, from law or custom, Debts are discharged and transactions finally closed. Bank

Notes payable in specie on demand have been included under these terms as well as coin, because, by law or custom, the acceptance of the notes of a solvent bank, no less than the acceptance of Coin, liquidates debts and closes transactions: while bills of exchange, bank credits, cheques, and other instruments by which the use of money is economised, have not been included under the terms Money and Currency, because the acceptance of such instruments does not liquidate debts and finally close transactions.'

Examination *of* Lord Overstone's Doctrine *of* Currency

7. We have now given sufficient extracts from these writers to exhibit their opinions. The definition of Currency which they adopt is that which '*finally closes debts and transactions,*' that which is '*received equally at all times, between all persons, and in all places,*' and they assert that Money and Bank Notes payable to bearer on demand alone satisfy these conditions, and therefore alone come under the title of **Currency**.

We have now to examine these assertions. It is not a little amusing to find the celebrated phrase of the Roman Catholic Church—*Quod semper, quod ubique, quod ab omnibus*—starting up and meeting us in a discussion on Currency. In Lord Overstone's opinion, Money and Currency are identical; and include the coined metallic money and the paper Notes promising to pay the bearer Coin on demand: and he says that the characteristic of their being money is, that they are received equally at '*all times, between all persons, and in all places.*' For the sake of shortness let us designate this phrase by 3 A, from the three alls in it. He excludes Bills of Exchange from the designation of Currency, because 'they do not possess that power of universal exchangeability which belongs to the money of the country.' This definition is fatal to Lord Overstone's own view. In fact, if it be true, there is no such thing as Money or Currency at all. In the first place, it at once excludes the whole of Bank Notes. The Notes of a bank in the remote district of Cumberland would not be current in Cornwall: therefore they are not 3 A: *therefore* they are not Currency. Again, the Notes of a bank in Cornwall would not be current in Cumberland:

therefore they are not Currency. Similarly, there are no country Bank Notes which have a general Currency throughout England : *therefore* no country Bank Notes are 3 A : *therefore* no country Bank Notes are Currency. Till within the last fifty years or so Bank of England notes had scarcely any Currency beyond London and Lancashire : in country districts a preference was universally given to local notes : *therefore* Bank of England Notes were not 3 A : they had not a power of 'universal exchangeability' : therefore they were not Currency. Bank of England notes would even now not pass throughout the greater part of Scotland. If, therefore, the test of 3 A and 'universal exchangeability' be applied, the claims of all Bank Notes to be considered as Currency are annihilated at once. The acceptance of a Baring or a Rothschild would be received in payment of a debt by a far larger circle of persons than the notes of an obscure and remote country bank.

But the universality of Lord Overstone's assertion is fatal to his argument in other ways. On the Continent, in some countries, silver is the legal measure of value : in England, silver, like copper, is merely coined into small tokens, called shillings, and which are made to pass current above their natural value, and are only legal tender for a very trifling amount, hence it cannot be used in the adjustment of *all* transactions : therefore it is not 3 A : therefore it is not Currency. There are some countries where Gold is not a legal tender : therefore it fails to satisfy Lord Overstone's test : therefore it is not Currency. If, then, the test proposed by Lord Overstone be considered as correct, it is easy to see that there is no substance or material whatever that will not fail under it : and, therefore, *there is no such thing as Currency.*

8. The fact is, that the only difference between a Bank Note and a Bill of Exchange is that the former is a promise to pay on demand, and the latter is a promise to pay at a given time : and therefore there is less risk in taking a bank note than a bill of exchange. For this reason a Bank Note possesses a greater *degree* of circulating power than a bill of exchange. Besides, there is not the same inducement to put a bill of exchange into circulation as a Bank Note : because the former increases in value every day, and it is unprofitable to keep a note idle. But it is to the last degree unphilosophical to maintain that these two obligations are of different *natures*, because they are adapted to circulate in different *degrees*. In the Midland Counties of England it used to be quite common for the banks to issue the bills of exchange they had discounted, with their own indorsements upon them : which rendered them actual Bank Notes. Moreover, a Bill of Exchange is payable on demand the day it is due : and therefore it is Currency on that day, by Lord Overstone's own definition : and if it is Currency on the day it matures, what is it before that?

9. But the *Law of Continuity* shows the fallacy of the doctrine that Bank Notes payable to bearer alone are Currency. Lord Overstone rigorously restricts the term to such Notes. But would not Notes payable one minute after demand be Currency? or one hour? or two or three hours? Would not Notes payable one day after demand be Currency? or two or three days? Lord Overstone denied that Bank Notes which are issued payable after seven days after sight, are Currency. According to this doctrine, if a man places money in a bank, and receives in exchange for it a bank note payable on demand—that is Currency : but if for his own convenience he takes a Note payable seven days after sight—that is not Currency! But the Note becomes payable on demand on the seventh day after sight ; and then by his own definition it is Currency. What was it before? It used formerly to be the custom for country banks to issue Notes payable 20 days after demand. These notes circulated and produced all the effects of money. If they were not Currency, what were they? Cheques are payable on demand : why are they not Currency as much as Notes? Bills of Exchange must be Currency on the day they mature : what are they before? It is quite plain there can be but one answer. They are all species of Currency, though differing in degree, and the distinction between them is untenable.

10. Nay, according to this doctrine a Bank Note itself is only Currency during about six hours out of the twenty-four : because it is only payable *on demand* during banking hours—say from

9 A.M. to 3 P.M. As soon as the clock strikes three the Note is not payable till next day : and, consequently, it is not Currency, and has ceased to affect the foreign exchanges. Therefore at 5 minutes before 3 it is Currency, and 5 minutes after three it is not Currency : so 5 minutes before nine A.M. it is not Currency : at five minutes after nine A.M. it is Currency. Our readers must judge whether such doctrines are sound philosophy.

11. But we must point out the further conclusions which the doctrines set forth by these witnesses lead to, which may somewhat surprise their advocates.

They say that the fundamental essence of Currency, or Money, is that it 'closes a debt.'

To this we may reply, as was the fashion in the glorious old days of special pleading—(1) there is no debt to close : and (2) it does *not* close the debt.

1. When Money is exchanged for goods no debt arises : and if it be said that the Money closes the Debt which would have arisen on the sale of the goods, it is perfectly obvious that it may equally be said that the goods close the Debt which would have arisen on the sale of the money. It is simply an exchange : and the Goods and the Money close the Debt equally on each side. Therefore, if it be the essence of Currency to 'close debt,' the Goods are Currency for precisely the same reason that the Money is.

It is quite common in the City to discharge a debt by stock : by this the 'debt is closed' : consequently, according to this doctrine, the Stock is Currency or Money.

It is quite usual to discharge a Debt by a payment of goods. A baker or a tea merchant becomes indebted to a wine merchant, and for the sake of convenience he may take payment in bread or tea. If he does so, the debt is closed : and by this doctrine the bread and the tea are Currency or Money.

In all cases of Barter or Exchange of goods, the goods on each side 'close the debt' which would have arisen without the exchange : consequently the goods exchanged on either side are equally Currency or Money.

We will also test the doctrine by other cases regarding paper documents.

A merchant, suppose, puts his acceptance into circulation:

another person happens to be indebted to him in an equal amount, and chances to come possessed of his acceptance. The merchant asks for payment of his debt, and the debtor hands over to the merchant his own acceptance. By this means the 'debt is closed': therefore, according to this doctrine, the merchant's acceptance is Currency or Money.

A banker issues notes and discounts a merchant's acceptance. When the acceptance falls due, the merchant collects an equal amount of the banker's Notes. Each is then equally indebted to the other : and in payment of their reciprocal claims, the merchant hands the Notes to the banker, and the banker hands the acceptance to the merchant. By this means the Debts are mutually closed : and if the Notes are Currency because they have closed the Debt, is it not equally manifest that the acceptance is equally Currency because it has equally closed the Debt.

So if two merchants issue their acceptances for the same amount, and they get into each other's hands, each will offer to the other his own acceptance in payment of the Debt due by him. By these means the Debts are mutually closed. And consequently each acceptance is Currency or Money.

Thus we see that the dogmas of these writers are transfixed by darts drawn from their own quiver !

The same doctrine may be extended to other cases. Suppose a person buys a Railway ticket ; the company owes him a journey : but when they have carried him to his journey's end, the 'debt is closed ': therefore, according to this doctrine, the carriage of the passenger is Currency or Money.

If a person buys an opera ticket, the manager is indebted to him : but when he has witnessed the play the 'debt is closed': therefore the performance of the play is Currency or Money.

If a person buys Postage Stamps, the Post Office owes him the carriage of a letter : but when the letter has been carried the 'debt is closed.' Therefore the carriage of the letter is Currency or Money.

And the same principle holds in many other cases.

2. In the next place, we affirm that a payment in Money does *not* 'close the debt': because all Economists have shown that the transaction is *not* closed until some product or satisfac-

tion has been obtained in exchange for the one originally given. The earliest Economists pointed out that on a sale for money the exchange is not consummated.

A baker wants shoes: he sells his bread for money: but can he wear his money as shoes? certainly not: he must exchange away his money for shoes. Therefore the Physiocrates said that the exchange was not consummated, or completed, until the baker had got his shoes. And J. B. Say called a sale a demi-exchange.

And it is precisely for this reason that all Economists, from Aristotle downwards, have perceived and declared that Money itself is only a species of Credit or general Bill of Exchange. Hence Money and Bills of Exchange are fundamentally analogous: they are each of them merely the evidence of a debt due to their possessor: and the payment of a bill of exchange in money is only the exchange of a particular and precarious instrument of Credit for a general and permanent one. But as Economists we have nothing to do with satisfaction and enjoyment: we have only to do with *exchanges*: and the exchange of goods for a bill or note is one exchange: the exchange of a bill or note for money is another exchange: and the exchange of money for goods is another exchange: they are all equally exchanges: and therefore Economic phenomena.

But, while we contend that Lord Overstone's criterion of a Currency is fatal to his own view, we are quite willing to accept it. For what is it that exists in all places, in all times, and among almost all persons—**Debt**, or **Services due**. And what is it that is universally required to measure, record, and transfer them? **Some Material**. All Currencies are more or less local, none are universal. The idea in the word alone is universal. The notes of a country banker, only circulating in his own neighbourhood, are like a country *patois*, each district has its own. A national Currency rises to the dignity of a language. But that is only local on a larger scale. The ideas alone expressed in the language are universal. We are therefore strengthened in our conviction that the only true idea of a Currency is that it is the **Representative of Transferable Debt**, and that *whatever represents* **Transferable Debt is Currency**.

CHAPTER XV

ON THE ORGANISATION OF THE BANK OF ENGLAND

1. WE are now at length in a position to take a comprehensive survey of the organisation of the Bank of England, and of the Bank Act of 1844. Few persons are aware of its complicated nature. We sometimes hear of the Principle of the Act of 1844 : as if there were but one principle involved in it : or as if the *object* of it were the same thing as the *principle* : the object it aims at the same thing as the Theory it adopts to attain that object. As a matter of fact the Bank Act of 1844 is founded on several theories : and moreover it devises a particular machinery for carrying them out. Now each of the theories it is based upon may be erroneous : and even if they were correct, the machinery devised for carrying them out may be erroneous and insufficient for its purposes. We are now however in a position to examine the Theories upon which it is founded : and to test them by the fundamental principles of monetary science established in the preceding chapters.

2. The doctrines of the school whose principles are expressly intended to be embodied in the Act are—

1. That the term Currency is to be exclusively restricted to Coin and Bank notes, payable at demand : to the exclusion of all other forms of Credit.

2. That when Bank notes are permitted to be issued they ought to be exactly equal in quantity to the Coin they displace.

Hence when any quantity of Coin leaves the country, an exactly equal quantity of Bank notes ought to be withdrawn from circulation.

Such are the Principles which the Bank Act of 1844 is intended to enforce.

With regard to these Principles we may observe that in the preceding chapter we have given the real explanation of the term **Currency**; and shown that it is quite erroneous to restrict the term Currency to Coin and Bank Notes payable on demand: and that as a matter of pure Mercantile Law, all forms of Paper Credit are included under the term Currency.

Also that no Bank constructed on the Currency Principle ever did so, or by any possibility could do, banking business for profit. Several Banks, such as those of Venice, Amsterdam, Hamburg, &c., have been constructed on this principle. They created Credit only in exchange for specie deposited in them. These Banks were the exact realisation of the Currency Principle: when the Money went in the Credit came out: when the Credit went in the Money came out: exactly in accordance with the sigh of the Chinese writer in 1309.

But no Bank of this nature ever existed in England: we have shown in a preceding chapter that *all Banking Profits are made by creating Credit in excess of Specie.*

Foundation *and* Constitution *of the* Bank *of* England

3. The Bank of England was founded by certain clauses in the Act, Statute 6, Will. & Mary (1694), c. 20, to provide means to carry on the war against France. It was formed of a Company of persons who advanced £1,200,000 to government, in exchange for which they received stock, bearing interest at 8 per cent. per annum, or an Annuity of £100,000 : and *besides* that they were authorised to create and issue Bank Notes to an equal amount: and to receive cash and do business as an ordinary banker.

We thus see the essential distinction between the Bank of England and the Banks founded on the Currency Principle, such as those of Venice and Amsterdam. These latter banks kept the bullion paid into them in their vaults: and so long as it was so, the Credit created by them was exactly equal to the bullion paid in. They simply exchanged Credit for Money, and Money for Credit; and they created no increase of the Currency.

But the Bank of England paid over to the government the

whole of its subscribed Capital, in exchange for which it received an Annuity at 8 per cent.: and it was *also* allowed to create Bank Notes to the amount of its Capital, which it could employ in commerce. Thus the Bank not only sold its Capital to the Government, but it was allowed to have it, too, in the form of Notes.

This proceeding manifestly augmented the Currency by the sum of £1,200,000. And the Bank made a *double* Profit: first, the Stock bearing 8 per cent. interest, for which they sold their Cash: and secondly, the commercial profits made by trading with their Notes.

Therefore, so far as this went it was clearly an example of **Lawism**: exactly similar to what was done by the American banks in 1837.

4. In 1697 the Bank was allowed to increase its Capital, in consequence of circumstances we have described elsewhere. The increase was £1,000,000: and of this sum £800,000 was received in Exchequer tallies, and £200,000 in its own Notes, then at a discount of 20 per cent. Both the Exchequer tallies and its own Notes were treated as specie at their full nominal value: and upon this augmented Capital of tallies and Bank Notes they were allowed to *create an equal amount of new Notes to trade with*!

In 1709 the Bank was allowed to double its Capital: and again to *create an equal amount of Notes to trade with*.

If the same Principle had been carried out to the present time it is clear that all the Public Funds would have been Bank Stock; and that the Bank Notes would have equalled the amount of the National Debt, or about £800,000,000!

Thus each loan to Government was attended with the creation of Property to twice its own amount: first, the Annuity, and secondly the Bank's Notes. To a certain amount this might be done with no evil consequences: but it is clear that as a general principle it is utterly vicious. *For it is creating Currency where there is no Debt:* it is simply pouring new quantities of Stuff into the existing Channel of Circulation. There is nothing so wild in Law's Theory of Paper Money as this. His scheme of basing a Paper Money on land is sober sense compared with it. For in Law's scheme there was a limit; but in this plan there is positively no limit whatever! Because if the principle is true, the Government may go on creating Debt for ever, and at the same time create an equal amount of Bank Notes! If this principle is true, what need is there of going to California and Australia for gold?

In 1711 the Bank was released from limiting their Notes to the amount of their Capital; and they were allowed to issue any amount of Notes they pleased, provided they were payable on demand in specie. But after this the insane plan of creating an equal amount of Notes, for every increase of Public Debt, was discontinued: and no limits were imposed on the Bank's power of issue till the Bank Act of 1844.

5. So the Bank went on till 1797, when it stopped payment again, and Parliament appointed a Committee to investigate its affairs. They reported it to be in the most solid and flourishing condition, and that it had a surplus of nearly four millions of assets above its liabilities, besides the Government Debt amounting to £11,686,800.

The reason of this was plain: the Notes issued were given in exchange for mercantile securities: and therefore the Bank had as security for its Notes *both* the Government Debt and the Mercantile Bills.

This, no doubt, amply secured the solvency of the Bank, and the payment of its Notes; but it played utter havoc with the Currency Principle.

6. In 1696 the Bank was obliged to suspend payments in cash in consequence of the great monetary disorder, caused by the bad state of the coinage. Bank Notes fell to a heavy discount, the lowest being 24 per cent. in February, 1697. After that they gradually rose till they reached par in October, 1697. In this crisis no one ever thought of saying anything else than that the Notes were at a discount. No one ever thought of saying that the Notes were the standard and that Gold had risen.

Soon after the suspension of cash payments in 1797 the price of gold began to rise. In May it was £3 17s. 6d: in

December it was £4: at which price it continued till September, 1799. In December 1800 it rose to £4 6s.: and the exchange on Hamburg, which had been considerably above par for several years, fell to 29·8, being upwards of 14 per cent. against England.

This state of matters gave rise to several publications. Lord King published a pamphlet to show that it was due to the **Depreciation** of the Paper Currency, and maintained that the value of the Paper was to be estimated by the Market Price of Bullion, and the state of the Foreign Exchanges.

In 1804 a great derangement took place in the Irish Currency. The Bank of Ireland had been compelled by law to suspend cash payments at the same time as the Bank of England, although there was no necessity for it, as the Exchanges were favourable to Ireland, and always were so, from the course of trade between England and Ireland. Released from the necessity of paying in cash, the Bank of Ireland enormously extended its issues: in 1804 they were fivefold what they had been in 1797. In consequence of this, Bank of Ireland Notes fell to a heavy discount. Guineas were commonly sold at a premium of 2s. 4d. or 2s. 6d. when paid in paper. The exchange fell to 20 per cent. against Dublin, where payments were made in Bank Notes: whereas the exchange was favourable to Belfast, where Irish notes did not circulate, but all payments were made in specie.

A Committee of the House of Commons was appointed to investigate the matter, and they declared that the depressed state of the exchange with Dublin was due to the excessive issues of the Bank of Ireland: and that it was their duty to limit their issues during an unfavourable exchange, just in the same manner as they had done before the Restriction Act. This was the first declaration by a Parliamentary Committee that the issues of Notes should be regulated by the state of the Exchanges.

7. A few years afterwards the same phenomena manifested themselves in England. In February, 1809, the price of gold rose to £4 10s., and the Exchange on Hamburg fell to 31·0: in January, 1810, it fell to 28·6. This state of matters caused such a derangement of commerce that the Bullion Committee was appointed, and came to precisely the same conclusion as the Irish Committee in 1806, that these effects were produced by the excessive issues of Bank Notes. They said that the true value of paper was to be estimated by the Market or Paper price of gold, and the state of the Foreign Exchanges. In former times a high price of Bullion, and an adverse state of the Exchanges, had compelled the directors to reduce their issues to counteract the drain of guineas, and to preserve their own safety. Since the restriction they had not followed the same principles, as they did not feel the inconvenience. Nevertheless they ought to observe the same rules as before the restriction, and continue to regulate their issues by the Market price of Bullion, and the state of the Foreign Exchanges.

Some proposals had been made of remedying the evil by a compulsory limitation of the Bank's power of issuing Notes. *But the Committee entirely discountenanced the plan of imposing a numerical limit on the Bank's issues :* because the necessary quantity could never be fixed : *and such a course might very much aggravate the severity of a temporary pressure.*

A very important distinction, however, was to be observed between a demand for gold for domestic purposes, sometimes great and sudden, and caused by a temporary failure of confidence, and a drain arising from the unfavourable state of the Foreign Exchanges: *that a judicious increase of accommodation was the proper remedy for the former phenomenon : but a diminution of its issues the correct course to adopt in the latter.*

The Report emphatically declared that the mere numerical amount of Notes in circulation at any time was no criterion whatever of their being excessive : *the only sure criterion was to be found in the Price of Gold and the state of the Foreign Exchanges.*

The doctrines of the Bullion Report were however, entirely rejected by Parliament : and while it was clearly proved that light guineas were selling at 27s., the House of Commons voted by a large majority that in public estimation guineas and Bank Notes were equal : that is, that $21 = 27$. This is probably the most extraordinary vote of any assembly in the world ; and can never be alluded to without feelings of the greatest shame :

but such was the force of party spirit that among the names of the majority was Robert Peel.

8. However, the Bank being freed from all restraints by this vote, increased its issues, which became still more depreciated, until in August, 1813, the price of Gold Bullion rose to £5 10*s.*, and the real value of the Bank Note was 14*s.* 2*d.* After the first abdication of Napoleon the price of gold rose to about £4 16*s.*, making the value of the Note 18*s.* 11*d.* During the hundred days Gold rose to £5 7*s.*, and the Note fell to 14*s.* 5*d.* After Waterloo the price of gold rapidly fell, and the value of the Note rose. In January, 1816, the price of gold was £4 2*s.*, and the value of the Note 19·03.

When the Bank was relieved from all fear of having to resume cash payments, country banks had multiplied greatly: in 1811 there were 728, in 1813 they had risen to 940: and the amount of their issues was supposed at the most moderate calculation to be £25,000,000.

In consequence of a long series of bad harvests, and the excessive issue of paper, wheat in August, 1812, stood at 155*s.* the quarter. It was supposed that these prices would be permanent, and vast quantities of land were brought into cultivation. Rents rose to treble what they were in 1792: all new agricultural engagements were contracted on the basis of these prices, and family settlements were calculated on the same scale.

In 1814 the ports of Russia and North Germany were thrown open to British Commerce, which gave rise to immense overtrading : prices of all commodities rose immensely: but the harvest of 1813 was very abundant, and in July, 1814, wheat had fallen to 68*s.* a quarter. A violent revulsion and depression of prices of all sorts of property began, which entailed universal losses and failures among the agricultural, commercial, manufacturing, mining, shipping, and building interests. The disasters began in the autumn of 1814, continued during 1815, and reached their climax in 1816–17. During these years eighty-nine country bankers became bankrupt : and about four times that number ceased business. By these means the issues of country notes were reduced to about one half in 1816 of what they were in 1814.

The numerous failures of country banks so greatly diminished the mass of the Paper Currency that the value of the whole rapidly rose. In May, 1815, the Market Price of Gold was £5 6s., the exchange on Hamburg, 28·2, and that on Paris 19·3 : in October, 1816, the Paper Price of gold was £3 18s. 6d., the exchange on Hamburg 38· : and that on Paris, 26·10 : and they remained with little variation at these prices till July 1817.

Here was manifested the most complete triumph of the principles of the Bullion Report. The great plethora of country paper being removed, the value of the whole Currency was raised nearly to par : and very slight attention and care would have brought it quite to par : and if means had been taken to prevent the increased issues of Country notes, cash payments might have been resumed as a matter of course.

In 1815, when peace was finally secured, the Bank made preparations to resume cash payments. In November, 1816, they gave notice that on January 1, 1817, they would pay off all notes dated before January 1, 1812 : and in April, 1817, all notes dated before January 1, 1816. But the nation had got so accustomed to paper that there was scarcely any demand for gold. In October, 1817, they offered to pay off all notes dated before January 1, 1817.

At this time, however, several Continental nations began to replace their depreciated paper by metal, and they negotiated large loans in England for this purpose. In consequence of these the Paper Price of Gold began to rise and the Exchange to fall. The Bank took no pains to reduce their issues ; and in January, 1819, the price of gold was £4 3s., the exchange on Hamburg 33·8, and that on Paris, 23·50. In July, 1817, the new coinage began to be issued from the Mint in large quantities, which was immediately bought up for exportation. The British Government reduced the interest on Exchequer Bills, and the much higher rate of interest abroad caused a great demand for gold for export. While this drain was going on, the Bank, in defiance of the principles of the Bullion Report, greatly increased their issues, and at the same time greatly increased issues of country paper took place.

The drain of gold became so severe that it was evident that the Bank would soon be exhausted : so in April, 1819, an Act was passed to prevent the Bank from making any payments in gold whatever.

Committees of both Houses were appointed : and nothing could be more remarkable than the change in Mercantile opinion since the Bullion Report of 1810. They had now, with scarcely an exception, adopted the principles of the Bullion Report, and among the converts was Peel, the chairman of the Commons Committee, who was entrusted by the Government with the conduct of the bill subsequently brought in. Peel now fully adopted the doctrine that a certain definite weight of gold bullion, of a certain fineness, was the only true standard of value : and that *the sole test of the excess of the Paper Currency was a comparison with the price of Gold.*

It had been proposed to prescribe such a limitation of the issues of Bank Notes as would secure the power of the Bank over the Foreign Exchanges. He for one thought this is a very unwise position : and for this reason that it depended so much on circumstances whether there was or there was not an excessive issue of Notes. *There were occasions when what was called a run upon the Bank might be arrested in its injurious effects by an increase of its issues.* There were other occasions when such a state of things demanded a curtailment. In the year 1797, when a run was made upon the Bank, while the exchanges were favourable, and the price of gold had not risen, it was proved that an extension of issues might, by restoring confidence, have rendered the original restriction unnecessary, and prevented the evils of the existing panic. On the other hand, if the run was the effect of unfavourable exchanges, and the consequent rise in the price of gold, the alarm must be met by a reduction of issues. *It was therefore impossible to prescribe any specific limitation of issues to be brought into operation at any period, however remote soever.* The quantity of notes which was demanded in a time of confidence varied so materially from the amount which a period of despondency required, that the House *must feel the absolute incapability of fixing on any circumscribed amount.*

9. An Act was passed by which the Bank was bound on and after February 1, 1820, on anyone presenting an amount of their notes of the value of not less than 60 ounces to pay them in standard gold bullion at £4 1s. the ounce: between October 1, 1820, and May 1, 1821, to pay them in a similar way at the rate of £3 19s. 6d. the ounce; and between May 1, 1821, and May 1, 1823, at £3 17s. 10½d. the ounce.

The trade in gold bullion and coin was declared entirely free and unrestrained.

The Bank was finally to resume payment in gold coin on May 1, 1823.

This is the Act which is usually called Peel's Act of 1819, and it is commonly supposed that it was the Act under which the Bank eventually resumed payments in cash. This, however, is a great error: it was nothing but a fantastic scheme of Ricardo's, which never came into operation at all. The Government, in 1820, repaid £10,000,000 of the debt it owed the Bank: and the Bank, having accumulated much treasure, in 1820 they felt themselves able to resume cash payments: and they obtained an Act, Statute 1821, c. 26, which enacted that the Bank might resume payments in gold coin on May 1, 1821.

This was the real Act under which payments in gold coin were actually resumed: and thus it is seen that all the praise and all the blame and vituperation which have been heaped on Peel's Act of 1819, as it has been called, are entirely thrown away: it was a complete dead letter: it neither advanced nor retarded cash payments by one hour.

The Monetary Crisis of 1825

10. During 1822–23–24 the interest of money was extremely low. For the first time in their history the Scotch Banks gave no interest on deposits. This gave rise to a great spirit of speculation. In the beginning of 1825 multitudes of schemes for foreign loans for various purposes were started. In January, 1824, the bullion in the Bank stood at £13,000,000; and a drain commenced then which continued steadily throughout the whole of 1824 and 1825. About the summer of 1825 a feeling of apprehension began, which increased as the autumn went on, and everyone foresaw that a monetary crisis was going to take place. The policy to be adopted by the Bank was much discussed, and it was anticipated that the Bank would rigidly restrict its issues, and leave commerce to take care of itself. By December, 1825, the bullion had been reduced to little over a million. At the end of November some great country banks failed. On Saturday, December 3, the troubles began in London; one of the leading City banks was in difficulties, and received large assistance from the Bank of England. During the following week the alarm increased, and on Monday, the 12th, fairly became a panic. During Monday and Tuesday the Bank pursued a policy of the most rigid restriction, and some great City banks with extensive country connections failed. The directors expected that the Bank would stop payment. But on Wednesday, when universal failure appeared imminent, the Bank completely changed its policy, and lent on every species of security with the utmost profuseness. This policy was crowned with the most complete success: the panic was stayed almost immediately. In three days the Bank issued £5,000,000 of notes. Demands, however, still came in from the country: the directors accidentally discovered a box of their £1 notes which had not been used, and they sent it down to the Gurneys at Norwich, and the run was immediately stopped. In this crisis 76 banks failed, and it was supposed that about four times that number stopped. Much of the evil having been supposed to have arisen from the £1 and £2 notes of the country banks and the Bank, the Government brought in a bill to suppress them; and it was enacted, Act, Statute 1826, c. 6, that they should not be permitted to circulate after April 5, 1829.

11. In 1827 the Bank was at last convinced of the truth of the principles of the Bullion Report, and the resolution of 1819 was expunged from its books. In 1832 Mr. Palmer, the Governor, explained to a Committee of the House how the Bank endeavoured to carry them into effect. The plan adopted was this. In a period of full currency, or when the Exchanges were at par, the Bank considered it desirable to invest two-thirds of their liabilities in interest-bearing securities, and one-third in bullion: the circulation of the country being thus regulated by the action of the Foreign Exchanges. The Bank was desirous to avoid using any active power of regulating its issues, but to leave that entirely to the public. The action of the public was fully sufficient to rectify the exchanges without any forced action on the part of the Bank in buying and selling securities. He thought it desirable to keep the securities very nearly at the same amount, because then the public could always act for themselves in returning notes for bullion for exportation when the exchanges were unfavourable : and if there was a great influx of gold the Bank could always resume its proportions by transferring part of its bullion into securities. He considered that the discount of private paper was one of the worst methods which the Bank could adopt for regulating its issues, as it tended to produce a very prejudicial extension of their issues.

12. In the debate on renewing the Bank Charter, in 1833, Peel gave it as his opinion that there should be but one Bank of Issue in the Metropolis, in order that it might exercise an undivided control over the issue of paper, and *give facilities in times of difficulty and alarm*, which it could not give with the same effect if it were subject to the rivalry of another establishment.

By the Bank Charter Act of 1833 Bank Notes were made legal tender by all persons except the Bank itself and any of its branches for all sums above £5, so long as the Bank paid its Notes in cash on demand.

Colonel Torrens strongly condemned the principle by which the Bank regulated its issues. He said that the Directors freely acknowledged that their predecessors in 1796, 1812, and 1819 were ignorant of the elementary principles of Money and Currency, and caused by their mismanagement ruinous fluctuations in the value of property.

One-fourth of the debt to the Bank by the public was paid off.

13. The Bank professed to have adopted the principles of the Bullion Report, i.e. to regulate their issues by the Foreign Exchanges, and in order to carry them out their plan was to keep their securities as nearly equal as possible, the cash and bullion at one-half the securities, and therefore equal to one-third of their liabilities. Having got the Bank into this position when the exchanges were at par, to throw any action of the increase or decrease of their Notes on the public, either by means of the Foreign Exchanges, or by an extra internal demand for gold. In October 1833 the Bank was got into this normal condition, and its liabilities, i.e. its Notes and Deposits, were £32,900,000, the Securities were £24,000,000, and the Bullion £10,900,000. But during 1834 and 1835 the Bank was in this position :—

1834	Liabilities	Securities	Bullion
March 11	£31,372,000	£24,777,000	£8,901,000
June 15	37,554,000	31,735,000	8,298,000
September 9	31,058,000	26,643,000	7,010,000
1835			
January 13	33,071,000	29,165,000	6,608,000
May 5	29,417,000	26,179,000	5,951,000

Thus in May 1835 the Specie was little more than one-fourth of the Securities, instead of one-half, and only one-fifth of the Liabilities instead of one-third.

In 1838 the Bank was got into its normal position : on March 30th its Liabilities were £31,573,000, the Securities £21,046,000, and the Specie £10,527,060. But at the end of 1838 another period of disorganisation began, as shown by the following figures :—

1838	Liabilities	Securities	Bullion
December 10	£28,120,000	£20,776,000	£9,794,000
1839			
January 15	30,305,000	24,529,000	8,336,000
February 12	26,939,000	22,628,000	7,047,000
March 12	26,088,000	22,173,000	6,580,000
April 30	26,475,000	24,536,000	4,445,000
May 14	25,711,000	24,098,000	4,117,000
July 16	28,860,000	26,846,000	2,987,000

The Bank then seemed suddenly to awake to the fact that

it was rapidly drifting into bankruptcy : and to save itself it negotiated some foreign loans at Paris and Hamburg.

These figures showed either that there was some natural impossibility in adhering to the rule the Directors had devised in 1832, or that they had not sufficient firmness to contract their securities in time of pressure to maintain it. The flagrant disproportion which these figures had assumed, which would have been most dangerous in an ordinary banking-house, but which were perilous to the last degree in the Bank of England, which was the last resource of every bank in the kingdom in time of difficulty, turned the attention of writers to devise some plan by which, if possible, the Bank should be compelled to maintain the proper proportion between Bullion and Liabilities. Colonel Torrens appears to have originated the idea which was eventually adopted of dividing the Bank into two distinct departments independent of each other, one for the purpose of issuing a regulated number of Notes : and the other for carrying on the business of banking.

In 1840 a Committee of the House of Commons was appointed in consequence of the flagrant mismanagement of the Bank.

1. The principle propounded in 1832 for the management of the Bank, for the purpose of conforming with the principles of the Bullion Report, was totally condemned.

2. The great modern heresy that Bills of Exchange form no part of the Currency or Circulating Medium, which was first asserted before the Committee of 1832, was now maintained by the great majority of the Mercantile and Banking witnesses.

3. This seems to have been the first occasion on which the 'Currency Principle' was first prominently brought forward by Mercantile men.

Lord Overstone observed in his evidence that it was the fundamental vice of the principle devised by the Directors in 1832 to carry out the doctrines of the Bullion Report that all the gold might leave the country without causing any diminution of the amount of Notes in the hands of the public : we have seen that this assertion was completely verified in 1839.

14. In 1844, Sir Robert Peel, being in power, determined to carry out the views of this school of Economists. In bringing in his bill he said—' I must state in the outset that in using the word Money I mean to designate by that word the Coin of the realm and Promissory Notes payable to bearer on demand. In using the words Paper Currency, I mean only such Promissory Notes. I do not include in these terms Bills of Exchange, or drafts on bankers, or other forms of Paper Credit. There is a natural distinction, in my opinion, between the character of a Promissory Note, payable to bearer on demand, and other forms of Paper Credit, and between the effects which they respectively produce upon the price of commodities, and upon the Exchanges. The one answers all the purposes of Money, passes from hand to hand without indorsement, without examination, if there be no suspicion of forgery: and it is in fact what its designation implies it to be—**Currency** or **Circulating Medium**. . . . I think experience shows that the Paper Currency, that is the Promissory Notes, payable to bearer on demand, stands in a certain relation to the gold Coin and the Foreign Exchanges, in which other forms of Paper Credit do not stand.' And after quoting from the Bullion Report some cases of the derangement of the Exchanges, he said—' In all these cases the action has been on that part of the Paper Credit of the country which has consisted of Promissory Notes payable to bearer on demand. There has been no interference with other forms of Paper Credit : nor was it contended then, as it is now contended by some, that Promissory Notes are identical in their nature with Bills of Exchange, and with Cheques on bankers, and with Deposits ; and that they cannot be dealt with on any separate principle.'

Sir Charles Wood, now Lord Halifax, followed Sir Robert Peel—' It is not enough, then, to enact that the Bank Notes shall be convertible. The Paper circulation must not only be convertible, but must vary in amount from time to time as a Metallic Circulation would vary. A system therefore of Paper Circulation is required which will attain this object, and insure a constant and steady regulation of the issues on this principle. This and this alone affords a permanent security for the practical convertibility of the Notes at all times, and for the consequent maintenance of the standard.'

Organisation of the Bank under the Bank Act of 1844

15. In order to carry out these principles the Bank was divided into two departments, the Issue Department and the Banking Department.

The Directors were to transfer to the Issue Department Securities to the value of £14,000,000, of which the Debt due by the public was to form a part: and also so much of the Gold and Silver Coin and Bullion as should not be required for the Banking Department. The Issue Department was then to deliver over to the Banking Department an amount of Notes exactly equal to the Securities, Coin and Bullion deposited with them. The Banking Department was forbidden to issue Notes to any person whatever, except in exchange for other Notes, or such as they received from the Issue Department in terms of the Act.

The proportion of Silver on which Notes might be issued was not to exceed one fourth part of the gold coin and bullion.

All persons whatever might demand Bank Notes in exchange for standard Gold Bullion at the rate of £3 17s. 9d. per ounce.

No person should issue Bank Notes in any part of the United Kingdom, except bankers lawfully issuing their Notes on May 6, 1844.

If any bankers who were lawfully issuing their own Notes on May 6, 1844, should cease to do so, the Crown in Council might authorise the Bank to increase its issues against securities to two-thirds the amount.

At the time this Act was passed the issue of Notes by private bankers was £18,350,864; at the present time these have been reduced to £14,962,985; and the Bank has been authorised to increase its issues against securities by the amount of £1,575,000.

Consequently at the present time the Bank's power of issuing Notes is limited to £15,575,000, plus the amount of Bullion held by the Issue Department.

It was supposed that these provisions insured that the quantity of Notes in circulation, i.e. in the hands of the public, would always be exactly equal to what a Metallic Currency would have been: and that the outflow of Bullion would by its own natural operation have the mechanical effect of withdrawing Notes from the public to an equal amount. Having made these provisions, the framers of the Act supposed that they had taken out of the hands of the Bank all power of mismanaging the Currency, and that they might manage the Banking Department at their own discretion.

Examination of the **Fact** *whether the Organisation of the Bank agrees with the* **Theory** *of its Framers*

16. It is a very intelligible proposition to say that the Notes should only equal the amount of specie they displace: and several Banks have been constructed on that principle. But no Bank constructed on this principle ever did, or by any possibility could do, banking business for profit. Every time a Bank discounts a bill it is a violation of the '**Currency Principle**'; because, as has been shown in a former chapter, all '**Banking**' advances are made in the first instance by creating Credit. The Banks constructed on the **Currency Principle** were pure Banks of Deposit: they never did any discount business: they did nothing but exchange Credit for Specie, and Specie for Credit. And if the Bank of England was forbidden to discount, there is no reason why it should not be reconstructed on this principle.

But it is a plain and manifest error to suppose that the Bank Act does really carry out this Theory into actual practice. In the first place, it is evident that the £15,575,000 of Notes issued against securities are a direct violation of the **Currency Principle**. The Bank obtained these securities by purchase. The purchase money of these securities is in circulation; and the Notes created on their security are in circulation as well. These £15,575,000 of Notes are therefore a distinct **augmentation** of the Currency to that amount. If these £15,575,000 of Notes are not an **increase** of Currency, it would on a similar principle be no increase of the Currency to coin the whole £800,000,000 of National Debt into Notes: and then there would be no more Notes in circulation than under a purely Metallic Currency!

It is quite clear that this is pure and simple **Lawism** : and if we may coin the Funds into Money, we may just as well coin the Land into Money.

Certainly it is an excellent plan for everyone to buy the Funds with their Cash, and then to be allowed to have it too in the form of Notes! This is certainly eating one's cake and having it too!

17. But even this does not show the full extent of the error of those who think that the Bank Act of 1844 does really carry into effect the **Currency Principle**. The Banking Department does business like any other Bank. It not only creates Credit in exchange for Specie : but it purchases or discounts Bills of Exchange : now it purchases these by creating a Credit in its books : *that is it creates Liabilities in the form of Deposits in excess of the specie it holds* : and every bill it discounts is a distinct violation of the **Currency Principle**. The reserve of Notes and Gold being the basis of the Bank's power of creating Credit, they of course must use their judgment as to how far they may safely extend their Credit, just as every other banker does.

It is quite clear that those who seriously maintain that the Bank Act of 1844 really carries into effect the 'Currency Principle' must maintain this proposition—

$$\text{Twice } £15{,}575{,}000 + \text{an indefinite number of millions} = £15{,}575{,}000$$

As a matter of pure Arithmetic, therefore, the Bank Act completely fails to carry out the Principle it was intended to do.

The very principle of Banks constructed on the Currency Principle is that the Credit created shall be exactly equal to the specie deposited.

But this is notoriously not the case with the Bank : the Bullion in it scarcely ever exceeds 40 per cent. of its Liabilities.

On October 15, 1884, the Liabilities of the Bank were £55,102,482, and the bullion was £20,489,479, or in the ratio of about $2\frac{1}{4}$ to 1.

Those who maintain that the Bank Act carries out the Currency Principle must maintain that $2\frac{1}{4} = 1$.

Examination whether the Mechanical Action of the Act conforms to the Intentions of its Framers

18. It has been seen that Lord Overstone, in his evidence before the Committee of 1840, showed that the fundamental defect of the plan devised by the Directors to carry out the principles of the Bullion Report was *that all the gold might leave the country without producing any diminution in the amount of the Notes in the hands of the public*, and this assertion was verified in 1839.

The Bank Act was expressly devised to remedy this evil, and to cause a withdrawal of Bank Notes from circulation, i.e. *from the hands of the public*, exactly equal in quantity to the gold withdrawn from the Bank in accordance with the Currency Principle. And it was supposed and intended that, if the Directors neglected this duty, the Mechanical Action of the Act would compel them to fulfil it: and cause an exactly equal amount of Notes to be withdrawn from the public, as gold was drawn out of the Bank. We have now to see how this expectation was fulfilled.

No occasion arose for testing its power till April, 1847. In consequence of the disasters of 1846, a steady drain began in September: but the Bank made no alteration in its rate of discount till January, 1847, when the Bullion being below 14 millions, it raised its discount to $3\frac{1}{2}$. Having lost another million, it raised its discount to 4. Having lost three millions more, it raised its rate to 5. Thus the Bank committed exactly the same error as on so many previous occasions: an immense drain of Bullion took place, and no sufficient measures were taken to stop it. But the pressure was an excellent example to test the alleged **Mechanical Action** of the Act. It will now be seen—

(1). How far the Bank was inclined to act on the principle.

(2). Supposing they were disinclined to do so, how far the Act, by its own self-acting principle, or its Mechanical Action, could compel them to do so.

The following figures speak for themselves.

	Bank Notes		Total Amount of Bullion	Minimum rate of Discount per Cent.
	Held by the public	Held in Reserve by the Bank of England.		
1846	£	£	£	
August 29	20,426,000	9,450,000	16,366,000	3
October 3	20,551,000	8,809,000	15,817,000	,,
November 7	20,971,000	7,265,000	14,760,000	,,
December 19	19,549,000	8,864,000	15,163,000	,,
1847				
January 9	20,837,000	6,715,000	14,308,000	,,
,, 16	20,679,000	6,546,000	13,949,000	3½
,, 30	20,469,000	5,704,000	12,902,000	4
February 20	19,482,000	5,917,000	12,215,000	,,
March 6	19,279,000	5,715,000	11,596,000	,,
,, 20	19,069,000	5,419,000	11,232,000	,,
April 3	19,855,000	3,700,000	10,246,000	,,
,, 10	20,243,000	2,558,000	9,867,000	5

These figures show the futility of the idea that as the Bullion diminishes the Act can compel a reduction of Notes in the hands of the public: for the Notes in Circulation when the Bullion was £9,867,000 were greater than when the Bullion was £15,163,000! Consequently nothing could be a more total and complete failure of the Act of 1844 on the very first occasion that its services were required. And it was manifestly proved that it provided no effectual check against mismanagement on the part of the Bank.

Cause of the Failure of the Mechanical Action of the Act

19. The complete failure of the Act to cause a necessary reduction of the Notes in circulation according as the Bullion was drained away caused the greatest surprise among many who had supported it, and we must now explain how this failure arose.

The framers of the Act supposed that there is only **one** way of extracting Gold from the Bank: namely, by means of its Notes: and that if people want Gold they must bring in Notes: and that as Gold comes out Notes must go in.

But as a simple matter of banking business there are **Two** methods of extracting Gold from the Bank—viz. by Notes and **Cheques**. Depositors, or those persons who have a Credit in its books, have only to present **Cheques**, and thus they may draw out every ounce of Gold from the Banking Department without a single Bank Note being withdrawn from the public!

Instead of withdrawing the Notes from the public, as was intended by the Act, the directors threw the whole effect of the drain of Gold on their own reserves. And this happened in this way. The public has **two** methods of drawing Gold out of the Banking Department—Notes and **Cheques**—but the Banking Department has only **one** method of drawing Gold out of the Issue Department—namely, its Notes in reserve. And when the Bank felt a drain on its Banking Department for Gold, it had to replenish it by obtaining a fresh supply from the Issue Department; at the same time giving up an exactly equal amount of Notes. And thus the whole drain fell on its own reserves.

No legislation can prevent this power of extracting Gold from the Bank by means of Cheques. And thus is explained the complete failure of the Mechanical Action of the Act to compel the directors to carry out the Currency Principle.

Thus it is clearly shown that the Bank Act of 1844 has exactly the same radical defect as the plan devised by the directors to carry out the principles of the Bullion Report, viz. *that every ounce of Gold may be drained out of the Banking Department without withdrawing a single Note from the public.*

The Monetary Panic of 1847

20. The monetary pressure passed away in May: but in the autumn a fresh series of calamities began. Many of the largest houses engaged in the corn trade failed. The Bank was called upon to give assistance in all quarters, and did so with the greatest liberality as long as it was able. But the monetary difficulties increased and the resources of the Bank constantly diminished. From Monday the 18th to Saturday the 23rd October was the height of the panic. Several large banks in the provinces failed: a complete cessation of private discounts followed: and commerce seemed likely to be brought to a standstill. At last, on Saturday the 23rd, when the reserve of the Bank was reduced to £1,547,000, the Government authorised the Bank to increase its issues upon securities beyond the limits allowed by the Act, at a rate of discount of not less than 8 per cent. If any infringement of the Act took place, they would bring in a bill of Indemnity. The Government letter was made public about one o'clock on Monday the 25th: and no sooner was it done so than the panic passed away like a dream. No infringement of the Act took place: and the whole issue of notes in consequence of the letter was only £400,000. No sooner was it known that Notes might be had than the demand for them ceased.

The Monetary Panic of 1857

21. The panic of 1847, and the necessity of authorising the Bank to exceed its legal issues, gave a great blow to the prestige of the Act of 1844; but it was determined to preserve it unaltered. In the meantime much more attention was paid to the Rate of Discount than formerly, and the Bank learnt the practice of meeting drains with more rapid rises of the rate of Discount with the best effect.

In the autumn of 1857 a general run took place on the New York banks: out of 63 banks only one maintained its payments. This immediately reacted on Liverpool and Glasgow. At the end of October the monetary trouble had reached London. On November 5 the Bank raised its rate to 9 per cent. On the 9th the Western Bank of Scotland stopped payment. The Bullion had sunk to £7,719,000, and the reserve to £2,834,000. The same day the Bank raised its rate to 10 per cent. Other banks stopped. On the 11th the bullion was reduced to £6,666,000, and the reserve to £1,462,000.

The stoppage of so many banks produced a banking panic. Private banks stopped discounting altogether: this of course produced a run upon them. On November 12 the total of Notes in London was £68,085, in the branches £62,545: of Gold coin in London, £274,953: in the branches, £83,255: of Silver coin in London, £41,106: in the branches, £50,807: that is, the total resources of the Bank of England on November 13 were

£580,751 to face Liabilities amounting to £39,391,068 payable on demand!

Of course it was well known that the Government must follow the precedent of 1847. Accordingly, on November 12 they sent a letter to the Bank authorising them to issue Notes beyond their legal limit, at a rate of not less than 10 per cent.: and as before the panic passed away like a dream on the morning of the 13th: but on this occasion the Bank was obliged to issue nearly £8,000,000 of Notes beyond its legal limits to alleviate the commercial pressure.

The Monetary Panic of 1866

22. In November 1865 a strong foreign drain began, the Exchanges fell, and in January 1866 the Bank raised its rate to 8 per cent. In February the monetary difficulties began. There were a number of Finance and Discount Companies which had advanced funds to promote railways and other schemes which would not repay their cost for a long time. Several great railway contractors suspended, involving the companies with which they had 'financed.'

In the beginning of May everyone knew that a monetary panic was impending. On the 9th the Bank raised its rate to 9 per cent. On the 10th, Overend, Gurney, and Co., with Liabilities of £10,000,000, stopped. On this day there was a general run upon all the London Banks: and the Chancellor of the Exchequer announced in the House that the Government had authorised the Bank to follow the precedents of 1847 and 1857, and of course the panic was completely allayed next morning. But the pressure was so severe that in five days the Bank advanced £12,225,000. Thus in the space of nineteen years the Bank Act had to be suspended three times in order to save, not only the Bank itself from stopping payment, but also the complete ruin of the banking and commercial worlds.

Cause of the Failure of the Bank Act of 1844

23. As the Bank Act has completely failed to produce the effects it was intended to do, it is an important matter to enquire why it so failed.

In former times it was a Mercantile dogma that the Exchanges could only be against this country because it was indebted to other countries. Nothing can be more remarkable than the vicious circle in which the Mercantile witnesses argued before the Bullion Committee in 1810. They maintained with unflinching perseverance that the Exchanges could only be against the country because it was indebted : and as the Exchanges were adverse, they maintained that the country must be indebted, without the slightest enquiry into the fact.

However, the Bullion Committee completely disproved this Mercantile dogma. They showed that the Depreciated Paper Currency was the cause of the Exchanges being apparently adverse : and that if the depreciated Paper was reduced to its true value in gold, the Exchanges were in reality in favour of the country.

The Mercantile witnesses alleged that when the indebtedness was paid off the drain of bullion would cease of itself. But the Bullion Committee proved that, with a Paper Currency so depreciated as Bank Notes then were, the drain would not cease until all the specie in circulation had left the country or disappeared : which was amply verified in England then : and has been verified in many countries since.

The Bullion Committee thus showed that there are two causes of a drain of bullion.

1. The Indebtedness of the country.
2. A Depreciated Paper Currency.

But in 1856 we showed in our *Theory and Practice of Banking* that there is a *third* cause of a drain of Bullion and an adverse Exchange, irrespective of any indebtedness of the country or of the state of the Paper Currency.

The principle is this—

'*When the Rate of Discount between any two places differs by more than sufficient to pay the cost of sending Bullion from the one place to the other, Bullion will flow from where Discount is lower to where it is higher.*'

When such a difference in the Rates of Discount between two places exists, Bullion dealers **fabricate Bills for the express purpose of exporting Bullion.** Without having had any dealings giving rise to debts, they simply draw bills upon their correspondents and sell them for specie, which they remit to their correspondents.

Now, when Bullion dealers fabricate these Bills for the purpose of buying Gold for exportation, this practice causes no increase of Bank Notes in circulation. Bank Notes are not wanted: it is **Gold** which is demanded and taken for export. As soon as the Bullion dealers get their bills discounted they draw out the Gold by means of Cheques, without any Bank Notes: and consequently the Gold is withdrawn and exported, without withdrawing a single Note from circulation.

Moreover, if bankers in this country perversely maintain the Rate of Discount lower here than in foreign countries, and therefore lower than the natural rate, persons in foreign countries send over their Debts and Securities here for sale, and the specie is also remitted abroad without any demand for Bank Notes; and thus gold is exported without diminishing the Notes in circulation. **Hence a depression in the Rate of Discount below that of neighbouring countries is a sure cause of a drain of Gold.**

This principle was certainly not sufficiently understood when the Bank Act of 1844 was passed, and indeed we do not remember any allusion to it in any of the discussions which took place.

But in our work on Banking (1856) we stated this as a fundamental principle of the Currency.

An improperly low Rate of Discount is in its practical effects a Depreciation of the Currency.

Hence, when such a state of things arises, the Bank must as an indispensable measure to preserve its own security, raise its Rate of Discount so as to destroy these profits and arrest the drain which is exclusively caused by the differences in the Rates of Discount in the two places. The only method of striking at this demand for gold is by raising the Rate of Discount: and consequently the supreme power of governing and controlling Credit and the Paper Currency is by carefully adjusting the Rate of Discount by the state of the Foreign Exchanges and the Bullion in the Bank.

Bullion dealers are the natural enemies of bankers: and they are constantly on the watch to take advantage of the weakness of bankers if they sell gold too cheaply : and they want this gold, not for the purpose of internal commerce, as other traders do, but for the express purpose of sending it to foreign countries where it has a higher value.

The weak point of the Act of 1844 is that it takes no notice of this grand principle : it takes no precaution that the Directors should recognise it and counteract it. It leaves them in full power to repeat their oft committed error of causing a depreciation of the Currency from an unnaturally low Rate of Discount. And the fundamental vice of the Bank Act of 1844 is exactly the same as Lord Overstone said was the fundamental vice of the Bank principle of 1832.—The whole of the Gold may be drawn out of the Banking department without withdrawing a single Note from circulation, i.e. from the hands of the public.

It is certainly true that, in consequence of the Act, it is provided that there is a store of Gold in the Issue Department : but there is no method by which this Gold can be extracted from the Issue Department unless the Bank goes into liquidation, or by a direct violation of the Law.

On the Causes which compelled the Suspension of the Bank Act in 1847, 1857, and 1866

24. We have now to explain the reasons which made the Suspension of the Bank Act necessary in the great monetary panics of 1847, 1857, and 1866, and why it was successful.

Ever since the enormous development of the System of Credit in modern times, great commercial failures have periodically recurred, producing the most widespread distress : and there have been two conflicting Theories as to what the action of the Bank should be in a Monetary Crisis.

1. One Theory maintains that in such a Crisis the Bank should liberally **Expand** its issues to support Commercial Credit : and this Theory may be called the **Expansive Theory**.

2. The other Theory maintains that in such a Crisis the Bank should rigorously **Restrict** its Issues to their usual amount, or even Contract them more than usual: this Theory may be called the **Restrictive Theory**.

Both these Thories have been tried in practice, and discussed by the most eminent writers: and we may succinctly examine the results. However, we may state that in a general elementary work on Economics like this we can only state general results: for more detailed information we must refer to our Theory and Practice of Banking.

The Monetary Crisis of 1763

25. The first great Monetary Crisis in modern times took place in 1763, after the termination of the Seven Years' War. This great crisis took place at Amsterdam, Hamburg, and other places where the 'Currency Principle' was fully enforced: and there was no Banking Credit except what represented specie. Immense failures took place at Amsterdam, Hamburg, and Northern Germany. The Crisis extended to England: and Smith says that the Bank advanced a million to merchants.

This instance of a Monetary Crisis shows that the 'Currency Principle' is no protection against one: and on this occasion the Bank acted on the **Expansive Theory**.

The Monetary Crisis of 1772

26. In 1772 the severest Monetary Crisis since the South Sea scheme took place. For the two preceding years there had been the most extravagant overtrading throughout Europe. Several London bankers stopped payment: but the Bank of England came forward to assist commercial credit, and the panic was at length stayed. On this occasion also the Bank acted on the **Expansive Theory**.

The Monetary Crisis of 1783

27. In 1782 the unhappy war with America was brought to an end, and an immense extension of commerce took place. The Bank extended its issues very incautiously, and a severe drain of bullion took place. The Directors considered that the returns in specie for the exports would bring in gold in a more rapid manner than it went out. They therefore determined to contract their issues until the Exchanges turned in their favour. They continued this policy till October 1783, when, the Exchanges having turned in their favour, they advanced freely to Government.

The Monetary Crisis of 1793

28. In 1793 the first of the really great modern Crises took place. After 1782 the commercial energies of the nation were greatly developed. In 1750 Burke says there were not 12 bankers out of London: in 1792 there 400 issuing Notes. The great majority were petty shopkeepers. In the autumn of 1792 great failures took place in Europe and America. In January 1793 the general alarm was greatly increased by the progress of the French Revolution. Some great failures took place in London in February, and the panic soon spread to the bankers in the country. Of these, 100 stopped payment, and 200 more were greatly shaken. The pressure in London was intense: and the Bank was strongly pressed to come forward and support commerce. But, being greatly alarmed, it refused, and resolved to contract its issues.

The pressure extended to Scotland. The public banks were quite unable, with a due regard to their own safety, to support the private bankers and commerce. Universal failure seemed imminent, when Sir John Sinclair remembered that the public distresses in 1697 had been allayed by an issue of Exchequer Bills. A Committee of the House of Commons reported that the sudden discredit of so large an amount of bankers' notes had produced a most inconvenient deficiency in the Circulating Medium: and that unless more was supplied a general stoppage must take place. They recommended that £5,000,000 of Exchequer Bills, in sums of £100, £50, and £20, should be issued under the direction of a Board of Commissioners.

An Act for this purpose was accordingly passed: and £70,000 was immediately sent down to Glasgow and Manchester. This unexpected supply, coming so much earlier than was expected, operated like magic, and had a greater effect in restoring credit than ten times the sum would have had at a later period.

When the whole business was completed a report was presented to the Treasury. It said that the knowledge that loans might be had, in many instances operated to prevent them being required. The whole number of applications was 338; the sum applied for was £3,855,624; of these, 238 applications were granted, amounting to £2,202,000 : 45, for sums to the amount of £1,215,000, were withdrawn, and 49 rejected. The whole sum advanced was repaid : two only of the parties assisted became bankrupt : all the rest were ultimately solvent, and in many instances possessed of great property. A large part of the loan was repaid before it was due, and the remainder with the utmost punctuality. After all the expenses were paid, the transaction left a clear profit to the Government of £4,348.

The restrictive policy of the Bank was expressly condemned by all the leading authorities of the time. The Bullion Report condemned it, and cited it as an example of the principle which they laid down, that an enlarged accommodation is the true remedy to be adopted in an internal commercial crisis.

This Crisis was a striking example of the efficacy of the **Expansive Theory** in staying a Monetary Crisis.

The Monetary Crisis of 1797

29. Towards the end of 1794 the Exchanges began to fall, and in May 1795 it became profitable to export bullion. While the Exchanges were thus adverse, the Bank immensely extended its issues, from various causes which are too long to detail here, but which we have narrated at full length elsewhere. The directors, being seriously alarmed, rigorously contracted their issues, and succeeded so far that the Exchanges became favourable in April 1796, and continued to be so until February 1797.

The stringent measures adopted by the Bank to contract its issues caused the greatest inconvenience to merchants, and plans were devised to afford some relief. The numerous failures in 1793 had caused a great diminution in the country issues, and Thornton says that Bank Notes were no higher in 1796 than they had been in 1782, though commerce had greatly increased. *As the public could not get Notes, they made a steady demand for guineas*; and although the Exchanges were favourable and gold coming in, there was a severe drain on the Bank for gold. In February 1797 great failures of country bankers took place. The panic reached London, and a general run began on the bankers. The Bank still used the most violent efforts to contract its issues : in the space of five weeks they had reduced these by two millions. The private bankers were of course obliged to follow the example of the Bank. Persons were obliged to sell their stocks of all descriptions at an enormous sacrifice to meet their payments. The Three per cents. fell to 51.

At length, on February 25, the drain of gold increasing every day, an order in Council was issued directing the Bank to suspend payments in cash : accordingly, on February 27, the Bank suspended payments in cash, and did not resume them till 1817.

The most eminent authorities afterwards censured the management of the Bank. Thornton said that *the excessive contraction of Notes had shaken public credit of all sorts, and had caused a severe drain for guineas* ; that the Bank should have extended its issues to supply the place of the country notes which were discredited. In 1810 the Governor of the Bank said that many of the directors repented of the policy of restriction : and the Bullion Committee explicitly condemned the policy of the Bank both in 1793 and 1797.

Nothing, in short, could be more unfortunate than the Bank's regulation of its issues. When the Exchanges were adverse, so that it was profitable to export gold, they enlarged them to an extravagant extent : when the Exchanges were favourable, and gold was flowing in, they contracted them with merciless severity. The issues, which were £14,000,000 when the Exchanges were adverse, were reduced to £8,640,250 when they were extremely favourable : and abundant evidence proved that *it was this excessive restriction of Credit which caused the severe demand for Gold.*

The practical results of the two policies were now seen : when all Banking and Mercantile Credit were on the verge of ruin in 1793, owing to the **Restrictive Theory** being persevered in, they were saved by the adoption of the **Expansive Theory**. In 1797 the **Restrictive Theory** was carried out to the bitter end, and the **Result was the Stoppage of the Bank**.

A consideration of these circumstances induced the Bullion Committee in 1810 to condemn the **Restrictive Theory** in the most emphatic terms. And all the greatest mercantile authorities of that period, including Peel himself in 1819 and up to 1832, entirely concurred in this doctrine.

The Monetary Crisis of 1825

30. The next great Crisis was in 1825. For two days the Bank followed the rigorously **Restrictive Theory**, and the result was that several banks were ruined which turned out afterwards to be perfectly solvent: universal ruin was imminent, when, on the third day, the Bank completely reversed its policy, and discounted with the utmost profusion, and the country was saved.

The circumstances of this Crisis are the most complete and triumphant vindication of the truth of the principles of the Bullion Report and of the **Expansive Theory**: and signally vindicate the wisdom of Peel in 1819, who followed the principles of Horner, Huskisson, and Thornton, and refused to impose a numerical limit on the Bank's power of issue.

The Monetary Crisis of 1837

31. The next Crisis was in 1837: but the Bank, foreseeing it, judiciously anticipated it, and made the most liberal issues to solvent houses which required it. By thus adopting the **Expansive Theory** in good time, nothing more occurred than a severe monetary pressure, which was prevented from deepening into a Crisis solely by the judicious conduct of the Bank.

The Monetary Crisis of 1847

32. However, the Bank having been unquestionably mismanaged, Peel, being under the influence of the school of Lord Overstone, Colonel Torrens, and others, determined to adopt the **Restrictive Theory**, and impose a legal limit upon the Bank's power of issue, which every eminent authority of former times, himself included, had solemnly condemned.

The Bank Act passed amid general applause, but on the very first occasion on which its powers were tested, in April, 1847, it completely failed to compel the directors to carry out its principles, and one-third of its bullion ebbed away without any of its Notes being withdrawn from circulation.

In October, 1847, a most severe Crisis took place. The Bank, being restricted by Law, was unable to adopt the **Expansive Theory**: and when the stoppage of the whole banking and commercial world was imminent, the Government suddenly authorised the Bank to issue at discretion: and the panic vanished in ten minutes.

Thus on this occasion the **Restrictive Theory** wholly failed: and the **Expansive Theory** saved the country, and was the only means of saving the Bank itself from stopping payment.

The Monetary Crisis of 1857

33. The next great Crisis was in 1857, which was far more severe as regards the Bank itself than the Crisis of 1847. On November 12 the Bank had exactly £580,751 to meet liabilities payable on demand amounting to £39,391,098. The Bank could not have kept its doors open for an hour on the 13th if the Government had not issued a letter authorising them to exceed the limits of the law. As soon as this was done the panic passed away. And, in accordance with this letter, the Bank issued nearly £8,000,000 of notes, and so saved commerce.

Thus on this occasion again the **Restrictive Theory** wholly failed; and the **Expansive Theory** was the only means saving the Bank itself and every bank in the country from stopping payment.

The Monetary Crisis of 1866

34. The next great Crisis took place in 1866, which was more severe than any preceding. On this occasion again the **Restrictive Theory** was obliged to be abandoned: and the **Expansive Theory** saved the Bank itself and every bank in the country from stopping payment.

Thus we see the entire failure of Peel's expectations. He imposed a rigorous numerical limit on the issues of the Bank, under the extraordinary delusion that he could thereby prevent the recurrence of commercial crises. But the crises recurred with the same regularity as before; and when they did occur, it was decisively proved that the Act was wholly incompetent to deal with them.

Not only does the Act not carry out the 'Currency Principle,' but where it was really in operation it did not in any way prevent panics. It has been seen that the great Crisis of 1764 prevailed with the greatest severity exactly in the country where the Currency Principle was in operation. In 1857 a similar Monetary panic took place at Hamburg, where the Bank was constructed on the Currency Principle, and had no power to aid commerce by issuing Notes in a crisis. But in that year the Magistrates were obliged to issue City Bonds to support the Credit of the merchants and prevent universal failure: exactly as the Government issued Exchequer Bills in 1793. Here also the **Restrictive Theory** wholly failed, and the **Expansive Theory** was obliged to be adopted to prevent general ruin.

The experience of other countries exactly confirms the experience of England. The Bank of Turin was constructed on some principle of limitation; but in 1857 it was found necessary to suspend its constitution, and allow it to issue Notes to support Credit.

The very same principle was conspicuously proved in 1873. In Austria, in North Germany, and in America the Banks were all constructed on principles of limiting their issues. But in the severe monetary panics in each of these countries, in that year, it was found necessary to suspend their constitution and authorise them to issue Notes at discretion to support Commercial Credit.

Thus it is proved universally throughout the world by abundant experience that the **Restrictive Theory** cannot be maintained in a Commercial Crisis after it has reached a certain degree of intensity; and that it is absolutely necessary to adopt the **Expansive Theory** to avert universal failure.

An **Excessive Restriction** *of* **Credit Causes** *and* **Produces** *a* **Run** *for* **Gold**

35. The unanswerable argument against the Restrictive Theory is that it is a fact perfectly well known to all bankers that **the Excessive Restriction of Credit Causes and Produces a Run for Gold.**

Sir William Forbes says of the Crisis of 1793—'These proceedings, which obviously foreboded a risk of hostilities, were the signal for a check of Mercantile Credit all over the kingdom ; and *that check led by consequence to a demand on bankers for the Money deposited with them in order to support the wants of mercantile men.'*

The Bullion Report expressly attributed the great demand for guineas, which caused the stoppage of the Bank in 1797, to the merciless restriction of Credit.

Henry Thornton, writing in 1802, says—' Two kinds of error of the affairs of the Bank of England have been prevalent. Some political persons have assumed it to be a principle that in proportion as the gold of the Bank lessens, its Paper, or, as is sometimes said, its loans (for the amount of the one has been confounded with that of the other) ought to be reduced. It has been already [shown that a **Maxim of this sort, if strictly followed up, would lead to Universal Failure.**

The Bank Act of 1844 is constructed on this very principle, and Thornton's prediction has been strictly verified.

In 1857 and 1866 discount had entirely ceased at all private banks : the consequence was a general run upon all the London Banks, and this run was undoubtedly caused and produced by the total denial of Credit : and it was only stopped by the suspension of the Act.

Indeed, the fact is so perfectly well known to all practical bankers, that it is quite superfluous to produce any more evidence on the point.

Under the present System of Commercial Credit there must be some **Source** *with the power of issuing* **Undoubted Credit** *to support* **solvent Commercial Houses** *in times of* **Monetary Panic.**

36. It has been conclusively shown that it is entirely futile to expect that Commercial Crises can be prevented : and that they occur with precisely the same violence in places where there is a purely Metallic Currency as anywhere else. Hence the illusions in this respect on which the Act was founded are now completely vanished.

In all cases houses which are clearly insolvent ought to be

compelled to stop without hesitation : to keep such houses going is a fraud upon their creditors. But under our complicated system of commerce the Credit of even the most solvent house is so intertwined and connected with others, that no one can tell how far any house, even of the highest name, is solvent. Everyone is affected by general discredit. Houses which are really solvent may have their assets locked up in forms not readily convertible in times of panic. Under such circumstances it is absolutely indispensable, to prevent universal ruin, that there should be some source which can issue undoubted Credit to houses which can prove their solvency at such periods. And there are only two sources which can issue such Credit—the Government and the Bank of England : and very convincing reasons show that it ought to be the Bank rather than the Government.

Such a duty is quite out of the usual business of the Government. They must issue a special Commission to investigate the solvency of those merchants who ask for assistance. Such a Commission will never be appointed until matters have become very severe : and much suffering is caused by the unnecessary delay.

But such is the ordinary and everyday business of the Bank. The merchants go in the ordinary way of business to the directors and satisfy them of their solvency : give them the necessary security, and receive assistance without delay.

These considerations, and others which might be adduced, show that the proper source to have this power is the Bank and not the Government.

Difference of Principle between the supporters of the Act of 1819 and those of the Act of 1844 .

37. The supporters of the Act of 1844 strenuously maintain that it is the complement of, and in strict accordance with, the principles of the Act of 1819. It may be conceded at once that the framers of both Acts had the same object in view—to preserve the convertibility of the Note : but the principles they held were entirely different : and the following are the differences between them :—

I. The Bullion Report declares that the mere numerical amount of Notes in circulation at any time is no criterion whether they are excessive or not.

The theory of the framers of the Act of 1844 is that the Notes in circulation ought to be exactly equal in quantity to what the gold coin would be if there were no Notes; and that any excess of Notes above that is a Depreciation of the Currency.

II. The Bullion Report declares, and the supporters of the Act of 1819 maintained, that the sole test of the Depreciation of the Paper Currency is to be found in the Price of Gold Bullion and the state of the Foreign Exchanges.

Ricardo says—'The issuers of Paper Money should regulate their issues **solely** by the Price of Bullion, and **never** by the Quantity of their Paper in circulation. The quantity can never be too great or too little while it preserves the same value as the standard.'

According to the supporters of the Act of 1844 the true criterion of an excess of Paper is whether it does or does not exceed in Quantity the Gold it displaces.

III. The Bullion Report explicitly condemns any numerical limitation of the issues of the Bank. Peel, in 1819, 1826, and 1833, fully concurred in this condemnation.

The Bank Act of 1844 expressly imposes a numerical limit on the issues of the Bank.

IV. The Bullion Report, after discussing the most important Monetary Crises which had occurred up to that time, expressly condemned the Restrictive Theory in a Monetary Panic: and said that it would lead to universal ruin, and recommends the Expansive Theory.

The Bank Act of 1844 expressly enacts the Restrictive Theory by Law, and prevents the Expansive Theory from being adopted.

On all these fundamental points the principles of the Bullion Report and of the supporters of the Act of 1819 are diametrically opposed to the principles of the supporters of the Act of 1844. And ample experience has shown that the Bullion Report was framed with far truer wisdom and scientific knowledge of the principles of Paper Currency than the Act of 1844. The only deficiency in the Bullion Report was that, having shown that the issues of Paper should be regulated by the Price of Bullion and the state of the Foreign Exchanges, it failed to point the practical method of carrying this principle into effect. But this method is now conclusively proved to be by adjusting the Rate of Discount by the state of the Foreign Exchanges and the Bullion in the Bank. Hence the Theory of the subject is now complete and perfect.

Examination of the Arguments alleged for maintaining the Bank Act

38. It has now been clearly shown that the Bank Act has completely failed both in Theory and Practice. It is based upon a definition of Currency which is entirely erroneous both in Mercantile Law and in Philosophy. It professes to adopt a Theory of Currency which it entirely fails to carry out. It has been seen that the Mechanical Action of the Act entirely fails to prevent the directors mismanaging the Bank exactly as they did before, if they choose to do so. The Act was expressly framed with the expectation that it would prevent Monetary Panics: whereas it has wholly failed in doing so: and hitherto Monetary Panics have occurred with exactly the same regularity as before. Furthermore, though the Act is in no sense whatever the original cause or source of Commercial Crises, yet when they do occur and have reached a certain degree of intensity, the operation of the Act is to deepen a severe Commercial Crisis into a Monetary Panic, which can only be allayed by its suspension and a violation of its principles.

In every one of these respects the Bank Act has completely failed: and in regard to these things its credit and reputation is utterly dead and gone. It is, therefore, necessary to examine fairly the arguments alleged in its favour: and the reasons urged why it should still be maintained.

The supporters of the Act, allowing that it has failed in some respects, yet maintain that, the directors having committed the same errors as they had done before, it arrested their mismanagement much sooner than would otherwise have been the case: and that in 1847 it was only through the Act that the Bank had six millions to meet the panic : and that by this means the convertibility of the note was maintained.

So far as regards the crisis of 1847, it must be admitted that there is much truth and force in this argument. At that period the directors showed that they had not acquired the true principles of banking. And it must be admitted that it was entirely owing to the Act that they were checked in their mistaken policy while there were still six millions of gold in the Bank.

But the same censure did not apply to 1857. In the interval between 1847 and 1857 the directors at last grasped the true method of controlling Credit and Paper Currency by means of the Rate of Discount. The truth and efficiency of this principle was probably more enforced upon their attention by the operation of the Act than it would otherwise have been. It was never alleged that the crisis of 1857 was in any way due to the Bank. Since that date the Bank has fully adopted and recognised the principle of controlling Credit and the Paper Currency by means of the Rate of Discount. The same rule has been adopted by the Bank of France : and it is now the recognised principle by which every Bank in the world is managed. Since 1857 there has been no reason to impeach the general management of the Bank. Granting every merit which can fairly be due to the Act—that it has compelled the recognition and adoption of this principle some years earlier than it otherwise would have been —it may be said that the Act has now fulfilled its purpose. It has done all the good that it can do. The directors now perfectly understand, and have for the last 24 years conducted the Bank with the greatest success on sound principles. Having, therefore, accomplished this great purpose, the Act has done its work, and has ceased to be necessary : and its operation in other most important respects being proved to be injurious by the most overwhelming evidence, it may now be safely and advantageously repealed, so far at least as regards the limitation of its power of issue.

Conclusion

39. The whole weight of practical considerations is in favour of restoring the Bank to its original condition, and abolishing the separation of the departments, which, as has been shown, was intended to carry out a particular Theory, but which it fails to do : and one, moreover, which is entirely unnecessary. For while times are quiet, or even during a moderately severe monetary pressure, the Act is wholly in abeyance : it is entirely inoperative. But when a real Commercial Crisis takes place—which it wholly fails to prevent, as it was expected to do—and when the crisis has deepened beyond a certain degree of intensity, then the Act springs into action with deadly effect. It prevents by Law the only course which the unvarying experience of one hundred years has shown to be indispensable to avert panic, namely, timely and liberal assistance to solvent houses : then come failures and wild panic : and if the Act were rigorously maintained, universal failure.

The true object of the Act is to ensure the convertibility of the Note. But the principle of the Act, or the machinery devised for that purpose, is merely a means to that end, and it has been proved to be defective. A better means of obtaining the object of the Act has been ascertained and demonstrated to be true by the strictest scientific reasoning, as well as by abundant experience since the passing of the Act; which is acknowledged to be efficacious : and therefore the Act is no longer necessary. The necessity for passing the Act was a deep discredit to the directors of the Bank: it was a declaration that they were not competent to manage their own business. But as they have now shown that they are perfectly able to do so, it is no longer necessary. It may sometimes be necessary to put a patient into a strait waistcoat : but when the patient is perfectly recovered and restored to his right mind, the strait waistcoat may be removed, especially as it is found that under certain circumstances the strait waistcoat not only strangles the patient, but scatters death and destruction all around.

www.ingramcontent.com/pod-product-compliance
Lightning Source LLC
Chambersburg PA
CBHW032027220426
43664CB00006B/393